THE
SOCIAL
FABRIC

Editor
James F. Short, Jr.

THE
SOCIAL
FABRIC

Dimensions and Issues

American Sociological Association Presidential Series

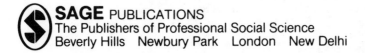
SAGE PUBLICATIONS
The Publishers of Professional Social Science
Beverly Hills   Newbury Park   London   New Delhi

For information address:

SAGE Publications, Inc.
275 South Beverly Drive
Beverly Hills, California 90212

SAGE Publications Inc.
2111 West Hillcrest Drive
Newbury Park
California 91320

SAGE Publications Ltd.
28 Banner Street
London EC1Y 8QE
England

SAGE PUBLICATIONS India Pvt. Ltd.
M-32 Market
Greater Kailash I
New Delhi 110 048 India

Printed in the United States of America

Library of Congress Cataloging-in-Publication Data

Main entry under title:

The Social Fabric.

(American Sociological Association presidential series)
    Based on papers presented at the 79th Annual Meeting of the American Sociological Association, held in San Antonio, Tex., Aug. 27-31, 1984.
    Includes bibliographies and index.
    1. Sociology—Congresses. 2. Social systems—Congresses. 3. Social institutions—Congresses.
I. Short, James F. II. American Sociological Association. Meeting (79th : 1984 : San Antonio, Tex.) III. Series.
HM13.S524   1986   301   86-1191
ISBN 0-8039-2788-6
ISBN 0-8039-2789-4 (pbk.)

FIRST PRINTING

Contents

Preface

THIS VOLUME IS BASED on papers prepared for plenary and thematic sessions at the 79th Annual Meeting of the American Sociological Association, held in San Antonio, Texas, August 27-31, 1984. This book's title was the theme of that meeting.

The announcement of this theme, published in the Association's newsletter, *Footnotes,* challenged ASA members and others to address such questions as the following: What have we to say about the nature of the social fabric, its strengths, and its weaknesses? What is it that holds societies together despite conflicts of interest? How do we account for the seeming paradox of the persistence of institutional forms in modern societies in the face of extreme vulnerability (to terrorism, for example) and rapid change? How, and with what consequences, is the balance struck between coercion and cooperation, between centralized control and local autonomy, between leaders (and would-be leaders) and constituencies, between experts (and would-be experts) and those whose lives depend on specialized knowledge?

The theme was also a charge to the 1984 Program Committee, which I had the privilege of serving as chair.[1] Together, we organized a program of plenary and thematic sessions, thus giving substance to the guiding metaphor of the social fabric. Organizers of "regular" and other sessions were asked to be mindful of the theme, also, as they reviewed papers submitted for inclusion in the program.

The centerpiece of the program was—and is in this book—a session titled "How Is Social Order Possible?" The three papers presented at this session (by Mary Douglas, William J. Goode, and Peter H. Rossi and Richard A. Berk) are published here—much revised—together with a commentary by Morris Zelditch, Jr., and an introduction by Neil Smelser. These five chapters constitute Part I of the book. In them is a veritable feast of metatheoretical and empirical approaches

7

to thinking about the nature of social order. Part I is preceded by my overview of the volume and its themes.

Part II includes three papers presented at the opening plenary session of the meetings, titled "The Orwellian Vision: Sociological Assessments." Regrettably, papers from a session on "Utopian Views of the Social Fabric" are not published here.[2] Of course, 1984 was the year symbolic of George Orwell's depiction of a future world dominated by totalitarian governments. There were three sociological assessments of that vision—by Morris Janowitz, Kai Erikson, and Gary T. Marx—presented at the ASA meeting and published here. Although Orwell's vision is found wanting in important respects, the papers point to important lessons to be learned from the writings of that extraordinary novelist and essayist.

If social order is *sui generis,* as sociologists argue, it is nevertheless constrained by the biophysical environment. Part III of the book, therefore, begins by directing attention to another question posed by the Program Committee: "To what degree is a social system dependent on its resource base?" This question was posed initially to William R. Catton, who was asked to organize a thematic session around it. Together with Gerhard Lenski and Fred H. Buttel, Catton summarizes the position of what has been called a "new environmental paradigm" with regard to constraints on social life that are linked to the biophysical environment.

Organizers of thematic sessions for the San Antonio meetings were asked to prepare chapters for this volume based upon papers presented at their sessions—summarizing, synthesizing, or assessing the state of knowledge reflected by those papers. Chapter 11 is a collaborative effort of this sort. The remaining chapters in Part III, seven in all, represent various adaptations to my request. Chapters by Irving Tallman, Robert Wuthnow, and Sandra Ball-Rokeach (treating the family, religion, and mass media, respectively) summarize, synthesize, and interpret recent theoretical and empirical work in these areas. Richard D. Schwartz (on sociology of law) and Thomas S. Moore and S. M. Miller (on government and social structure) prepared their papers initially for a session on "The Limits and Possibilities of Government," which was organized by the Program Committee.[3] Eric M. Leifer and Harrison White's chapter, "Control in Decentralized Federal and Multidimensional Systems," began as a paper for a session titled "Mediating Structures in the Social Fabric," organized and chaired by Gerald Suttles, to whom I am grateful for recommending the topic for inclusion in the volume. Charles

Moskos organized the session on "The Military and the Social Fabric," for which his paper ("Citizen Soldier Versus Economic Man") was the centerpiece.

Two chapters make up Part IV: Theodore Caplow's "The Role of Sociologists in the Nuclear Debate" and Harriet Zuckerman's "The Uses and Control of Knowledge." These chapters summarize and provide additional interpretations of these long-neglected topics, based on papers given at sessions organized by their authors. Both point to new opportunities and research, and to initiatives recently undertaken by sociologists in these important areas.

I must not end this preface without expressing my profound gratitude to the 1984 Program Committee and my coauthors, as well as to all who participated in the San Antonio meetings. It was not possible to include in this volume all of the papers presented at the plenary and thematic sessions. A few who were invited to do so chose not to prepare or submit papers. I am grateful nevertheless to all who participated, whether as organizers, presenters, or chairs.

Inevitable gaps occur in books such as this, only in part as a result of such omissions. I have tried to compensate for some of these omissions in the first chapter, but no single volume can encompass the topics of relevance to the variegated and ever-changing reality, which can only be suggested by the metaphor of the social fabric. At the very least, we have tried to address some of the important issues raised by consideration of the nature of that reality. I am happy to be a part of the enterprise, and proud to be associated with colleagues who continue to make it possible.

In addition to those already acknowledged, I have many others to thank: the membership of the ASA for allowing me to serve the discipline and the profession in a variety of capacities over the years; special thanks to the ASA Executive Office, without whom annual meetings and many other facets of professional activity would be impossible; to Washington State University colleagues, who have been so supportive and patient with me (including Susan Miller and Patti Mangelsdorf, bright and efficient secretary and research assistant, respectively, who compiled the index); and Jack P. Gibbs, colleague extraordinaire. Last, but certainly not least, I thank my parents, Ruth W. Short and the late J. Frank Short, whose inspiration, love, and support it has been my privilege to experience.

—James F. Short, Jr.

Notes

1. Members of the 1984 Program Committee were as follows: Andy B. Anderson, Sandra Ball-Rokeach, Edgar F. Borgatta, Theodore Caplow, Herbert L. Costner, James F. Short, Jr., Roberta G. Simmons, Neil J. Smelser, Franklin D. Wilson, and Morris Zelditch, Jr.

2. My effort to secure papers from this session collapsed when all but one of the papers presented at this session were unobtainable for original publication in this volume. I am grateful to the participants in this session: Immanuel Wallerstein, whose "Marxisms as Utopias: Evolving Ideologies," is forthcoming in the *American Journal of Sociology*; Edgar F. Borgatta, whose discussion of "Anarchy as Utopia" is part of ongoing work, soon to be published, and to Norman Birnbaum (discussant), Michael Novak (presenter), and Robert Boguslaw (organizer and chair).

3. This session was chaired by Albert K. Cohen.

Introduction and Overview

1

The Social Fabric as Metaphor and Reality

James F. Short, Jr.

I ONCE EDITED a book about the Chicago School of Urban Sociology for the Heritage of Sociology Series. At the suggestion of Series Editor Morris Janowitz, the book was called "The Social Fabric of the Metropolis" (Short, 1971). Although I thought the title felicitous, I scarcely referred to it in my lengthy introduction and made no attempt to specify the metaphor.

A dozen years later, when I was given the opportunity to set the theme for the 1984 meetings of the American Sociological Association, I chose "The Social Fabric," again without a great deal of thought as to precisely what was intended. Not surprisingly, the 1984 Program Committee found the theme vague and ambiguous. Forced to defend myself, I explained that I wished the 1984 meetings to focus on those things that are most fundamental to the discipline rather than on the special interests that divide sociology and sociologists. In this sense the metaphor includes all that is of general concern to the discipline—not a very helpful guideline, neither specific nor delimiting.

My chief concern was—and remains—two-fold: (1) specialization within the social sciences, and sociology in particular, has led to the neglect of phenomena that have not generated a body of specialized

13

knowledge, and (2) specialization has inhibited communication across specialties that, in fact, have much to learn from each other. I addressed the first of these issues in my ASA presidential address by focusing on risk and risk analysis (Short, 1984). It has been my hope that this volume might address both.

It is, of course, in the nature of science that knowledge becomes specialized. The more advanced the discipline, the more specialized is knowledge, within as well as between disciplines. Particularly when specializations develop around specific subject matter areas (e.g., crime or any other "social problem," religion, the family, science or the arts) rather than general processes or characteristics of social systems (e.g., social stratification, culture, group processes), neglect of subjects that have not become "traditional" and problems related to communication between specializations are likely to occur. For this reason, there are no "sociologies of" (including sociology of the social fabric) in this volume. The focus, instead, is on research and theory concerning the nature of social order and social processes, and of contexts in which social life takes place.

The Social Fabric at Risk

My concern with the pitfalls of specialization was heightened by the discovery that risk analysis has received relatively little sociological attention. Yet risks in enormous variety have become a matter of acute concern for governments, communities, and institutions, which are themselves often at risk. However, risk analysis as a profession, and governments, communities, and institutions, typically—and necessarily—focus on narrowly defined risks; for example, on toxic waste disposal or crime in the streets rather than on threats to democratic institutions, quality of life, civil liberties, or freedom of movement and association.

Most of my reading in risk analysis had been written by psychologists, anthropologists, economists, political scientists, and technical specialists. Although "disaster research" was a recognized sociological specialization, it had not been well integrated into the mainstream of sociological thought. Environmental sociology was a growing specialization within the discipline, as was "social impact assessment," but neither seemed to address the broad sociological issues with which I was concerned.

I soon learned that there are important exceptions to these impressions (e.g., Kreps, 1984a, 1984b; Perrow, 1984; Dunlap and

Catton, 1979; Catton, 1984) and healthy controversy and growth in sociological work concerning risk (see, e.g., Freudenberg, 1986). My ASA address, though focused on risk analysis, proposed that sociological concerns with the social fabric might serve as a bridge between various sociological specializations. The point is more general. Bridging concepts, methods, and substantive concerns are necessary if the limitations of specialization are to be overcome and its advantages fully realized.

Metaphors sometimes provide a bridging focus, as do concepts such as hazard and risk. That is the hope in this volume. Such concepts encourage thought beyond more narrowly defined concepts, topics, and methods. In the case of the 1984 ASA program, the social fabric theme generated a variety of suggestions by the Program Committee, converging on the question, "How is social order possible?" and on the sociological significance of utopian and dystopian thinking, the latter stimulated in part by the year symbolic of the Orwellian vision.

A series of thematic sessions also emerged. Some focused on major institutions: government and law, the family, religion, mass media of communication, the military. A few cut across institutional areas: mediating structures in the social fabric, the dependence of social systems on biophysical resources and demographic factors, institutional and interpersonal trust, the arts and the social fabric, the uses and control of knowledge. There were three sessions that focused as much on sociologists' and other social scientists' activities as on theory and research per se: the role of sociologists in the nuclear debate, the measurement of social well-being, and the diffusion of social science knowledge into the social fabric. Not all of these topics could be included in this volume, but the papers published here provide ample grist for the sociological mill.

My purpose is to introduce the chapters to follow, and to discuss a few of the many implications that these chapters have for pursuing the social fabric metaphor. I will draw occasionally on papers that were presented at the San Antonio meetings but that are not here published.

The Nature of Social Order

Part I is a book in itself, including a thoughtful introduction by Neil Smelser; three brilliant but very different papers by William J. Goode, Mary Douglas, and Peter H. Rossi and Richard A. Berk; and an equally thoughtful summary discussion, by Morris Zelditch, Jr. Guided initially by the question, "How is social order possible?" these chapters constitute a rich assembling of theoretical and empirical observations on the nature of social order, its structural forms and effects, and multiple agenda for research.

Douglas's chapter presents a special challenge to sociologists, who are accused of failing to develop "a precise tool for describing institutional structures . . . to match the precise psychological tools for assessing emotional and cognitive bias." Her discussion of institutionalized public memory ranges from "remembering" and "forgetting" in primitive societies to similar phenomena in scientific circles. What makes a "fact" memorable or part of a forgotten past? Why do some ideas flourish while others fail to achieve lasting impact? Douglas's analysis is a subtle and sophisticated structural and cultural theory of cognition, the first and most significant principle of which is that the survival of facts, ideas, and theories depends on how well they fit in with "the cognitive procedures that guarantee other kinds of facts." These procedures, Douglas suggests, are culturally and structurally valid in science much as in traditions among primitive peoples.

Doubtless other processes influence these matters; for example, whether a fact, condition, or claim attracts followers with the power to press a case (see Schneider, 1986; Goode, this volume). In most contemporary societies—Third World as well as postindustrial, informational societies—media attention assumes special importance (see Ball-Rokeach, this volume).

The Orwellian Vision: Sociological Interpretations

"The task before us," Immanuel Wallerstein (forthcoming) concludes in his essay on Marxisms as utopias: evolving ideologies, "is precisely to place the activities of the intelligentsia (that is, social science) and the activities of political organizations in a framework in which . . . they illuminate the historical choices rather than presume to make them."[1]

A few of the chapters in this volume are perhaps utopian in this sense rather than in the classic version of an end to history in an ideal form. This is hardly the case with the chapters in Part II, however. The year 1984 brought with it a flood of commentary and interpretation of the work of George Orwell, whose bleak portrayals of both contemporary society and the future were decidedly dystopian. There has been surprisingly little published sociological analysis of Orwell's work.

Part II includes assessments of the great writer's work by three sociologists. They bring both good and bad news. Both Morris Janowitz and Gary Marx note that Orwell was incorrect in his portrayal of a future dominated by oppressive totalitarian governments. Janowitz applauds Orwell's effort "to spread understanding of the vast human destruction that total control permits and generates," but he is critical of Orwell the novelist for his failure to probe more deeply into structural and institutional aspects of the totalitarian state and survival strategies of those who live in such states.

Janowitz has another concern of interest in the present context. He notes that neither Orwell nor the teachers in the nation's schools who assigned his books to their classes had an *agenda*. Orwell contributed to the political education of the new generation by posing questions, but "to pose questions without presenting social and political alternatives is indeed unsatisfactory and even dangerous."[2]

Marx agrees with Janowitz concerning the inadequacy of Orwell's portrayal of the future as prediction—a task in any event denied by Orwell—and the value of that portrayal in avoiding such a future. Marx's chief concern, however, is with "Totalitarian Potentials Within Democratic Structures," the subtitle of his chapter. Marx sees such potentials in modern technologies that increase the ability of governments and large-scale organizations alike to intrude into private lives. The documentation of technological possibilities is impressive, suggesting a multifaceted research agenda. A more hopeful note was sounded in S. M. Lipset's discussion of the papers presented at this session. Lipset noted that the human spirit has proved to be resilient even under the most repressive conditions, and that governments have not, in fact, been very effective in monitoring their citizens.

Issues of governmental and other large-scale organizational intrusion and control are not limited to personal surveillance. In the final chapter of the book ("Uses and Control of Knowledge") Harriet Zuckerman observes that although there is a "small but lively literature" concerning the effects on social science research of government support, study of the effects on different sciences of "varying conditions of external control and the effects of restraints on autonomy for varying periods of time" has been lacking. Issues thus raised extend beyond intrusive social and political effects of governments and organizations, important as those are. Political, economic, and social control of knowledge lies at the heart of the production of knowledge, as well as its uses (see, e.g., Etzkowitz, 1983a, 1983b).

Social Systems, Institutions, and Processes

On Problems of Survival

A third paper in the Orwell session, by Kai Erikson, discusses the meaning of war in *1984* and in sociological analysis. For purposes of the present discussion, I shall group Erikson's chapter with several chapters from Parts III and IV.

William R. Catton, Gerhard Lenski, and Fred H. Buttel lead off Part III by addressing the dependence of social systems on the biophysical environment. They argue that the realities of that environment, and its degradation, presage great problems for the social fabric of the future. Political and economic policies concerning consumption of nonrenewable resources are responsible for these problems. They characterize as "a great sociological irony of our time that lifestyles about which we can be so ethnocentric are so inexorably temporary" as a result of policies that deplete biophysical resources of the earth more rapidly than they can be replaced.

The challenge issued by Catton et al. is unmistakable. Yet, as the late great British historian Arnold Toynbee (1946) noted, challenges and responses to challenges have been of fundamental importance to the success and failure of world civilizations. The irony of the terrible risks associated with such hazards as exceeding the earth's carrying capacity, nuclear winter, or world starvation, which may result from release of even a fraction of the world's nuclear arsenals, is that they may force creative solutions to the (by comparison) petty conflicts that divide nations, peoples, and cultures over the earth. Solutions are certain to be suggested and tried. Their success may well depend as much on creative social responses as upon advances in the "hard" sciences and technology.

One basis for creative response to the consumption/carrying capacity problem, Catton et al. suggest, is to be found in comparative and historical study of societies that demonstrate and elaborate just how social systems and social life in general on planet earth are dependent on basic resources. A second lies in the study of disciplines that focus on the biophysical environment.

Although exceeding the carrying capacity of the earth may in the long run be equally serious and intractable, avoidance of nuclear war will seem to many both more immediate and dramatic. With notable exceptions, as documented by Theodore Caplow and his colleagues in Chapter 18, sociologists have paid little attention to nuclear war. Readers who are especially interested in sociological approaches to this issue may prefer to begin their reading by turning to that chapter and to others noted in this discussion. Caplow briefly reviews four papers on the role of sociologists in the nuclear debate: his own and papers by Elise Boulding, Kurt Finsterbush, and Louis Kreisberg. These papers present multiple agenda for research; for example, application to the problem of war of what is known about conflict, exploration of alternatives to the existing international system, and a variety of symbolic issues. In addition to Kai Erikson's reflections on Orwell, noted above, other chapters are relevant to the topic.

Erikson examines the functions of war among the totalitarian states constituting the world depicted by Orwell. In Oceania, war was perpetual, a mechanism for using up surpluses—of energy, materials, and of enthusiasms for ideas other than those prescribed by the state. The Orwellian future depicted a seemingly deliberate stalemate among superpowers that had neither expansionist, material, nor ideological goals.

The real history of wars is quite different, as many have remarked. Charles Tilly's (1985, p. 169) analysis of the European experience is apposite, and bears upon the nature of social order as well: War making was critical to state making, and in both "coercive exploitation played a large part." Indeed,

> A portrait of war makers and statemakers as coercive and self-seeking entrepreneurs bears a far greater resemblance to the facts than do its chief alternatives: the idea of a social contract, the idea of an open market in which operators of armies and states offer services to willing consumers, the idea of a society whose shared norms and expectations call forth a certain kind of government [see Goode, this volume].

The views of war held by our sociological forebears were different still. Erikson cites Herbert Spencer, William Graham Sumner, and Robert E. Park, and Caplow notes that Robert Cooley Angell's 1951 ASA presidential address dealt with "Sociology and the World Crisis." Sumner's treatise on the subject pictured war as arising from the competition of life that was a fundamental condition of human existence. In the process, war bound people together, and made possible the building of society. More recent sociological initiatives on war, Caplow suggests, have been "encapsulated by scholarly indifference."

Ironies abound. As war has become more threatening, sociologists have studied it less. Perhaps this is because it does not seem to fit our customary paradigms, or because "scenarios of nuclear danger fall outside our inherited symbolic repertory," as Caplow suggests. Scientific and technological "advances" in modern warfare have developed to the point that the entire world may be bound together in a community of fate (see Heimer, 1985), as never before in history. The precise nature of the threat is not clear, and its binding force even less so. Warfare, which once created cohesiveness and released energies necessary to build societies (albeit often by force), now threatens to destroy the possibility of society. Faced with the threat of nuclear destruction, societies may be faced with imperatives of organization and the structuring of trust that previously have been unimagined, and in any case not so necessary.[3]

The key to the development of a world community of fate may lie in reconstruction of the international order, the bases for which are examined by Caplow and Richard D. Schwartz, the latter in Chapter 11. Caplow's thesis is "that there is no conceivable way to prevent nuclear war in the existing international system," and he proposes that social research can be most useful by helping "to transform world government from a nearly vacuous concept to a set of thoroughly researched alternatives and practicalities."

As though in response to this call, Schwartz's historically based sociology of law essay examines three great world civilizations (China, India, and the West) with the object of extracting principles (in his terminology, *jural postulates*) that might serve as the basis for an emerging world civilization under the rule of law. The result is a profound and wide-ranging historically based inquiry, with suggestive applications to the present. Some of the jural postulates found in the great civilizations have been conducive to unity, for example, harmony, respect for the dignity and well-being of ordinary people, and toleration for diversity of beliefs (China), humility through asceticism (India), and openness to upward mobility (the West); whereas some have led to disunity (e.g., intolerance in the West, belief in innate inequality in India, and the fact that none of the three has succeeded in stemming seemingly limitless acquisitive appetites while tolerating the misery of the less privileged).

What shall we make of such a bold proposal? Is agreement on jural postulates a necessary condition for the emergence of a world order based on law? Is it possible to disagree on some postulates (which ones?) while maintaining governing structures and processes that are granted sufficient legitimacy to maintain such a legal order? What sorts of organizational structures and processes might serve this end? How shall peace be maintained in such an order?

Even the assumptions with which such problems are approached have consequences, as Charles Moskos demonstrates in Chapter 14 ("Citizen Soldier versus Economic Man"). Moskos examines assumptions underlying recruitment and maintenance of the armed forces in the United States, and their consequence for the nature of those forces and for keeping the peace. Moskos and Morris Janowitz, in particular, have argued that the "citizen soldier" concept of service in the armed forces of this country has played an important role in "education for civic consciousness" (see, especially, Janowitz, 1983).

Additional questions follow. How shall civic consciousness in a new world order be defined? What individual and collective rights and obligations will be entailed? Must they be universal? What are the limits and consequences of diversity of beliefs, norms, governing structures, and processes in such an order? These types of questions serve as reminders of the importance and the consequences of popular support for political regimes. In state-making, Tilly (1985, pp. 183-186) notes,

> When ordinary people resisted vigorously, authorities made concessions: guarantees of rights, representative institutions, courts of appeal. . . . European states built up their military apparatuses through sustained struggles with their subject populations and by means of selective extension of protection to different classes within those populations. The agreements on protection constrained the rulers themselves, making them vulnerable to courts, to assemblies, to withdrawals of credit, services, and expertise.

Such constraints and protections can hardly be expected to be any less important if and when a world order based on law is to emerge.[4]

What sorts of organizational arrangements and leadership skills might be appropriate for a reconstituted world order? While their chapter is not addressed to this question, Leifer and White's analysis (Chapter 13, "Wheeling and Annealing") is highly suggestive. Theories of large-scale organization, they note, find it difficult to deal with informal relations within formal structures, even when they regard them as important. Wheeling and dealing tends to be regarded as residual, as "friction" that impedes the proper functioning of formal organizations. Leifer and White turn such notions on their heads by suggesting that wheeling and dealing "is core, and not frictional, in the nature of control at the upper echelons of large-scale organizations." Examples are drawn from bureaucracies, multidivisional businesses, and political federalism. An ideal-type model is developed in which skill in the exercise of control is critical, skill that "is tied to the diffusion of control rather than its concentration."

The theory and practice of federalism under the U.S. constitution is exemplary. In theory, "dual" federalism

> provided a model for intergovernmental relations where the autonomy of established and heterogeneous state governments was not threatened by the newly established National government . . . the distinct functions assigned to state governments made them complementary rather than subordinate to the national government. . . . The intergovernmental relations of American Federalism were nonrelations, where complementarity of function performance is more of an issue than the power balances or imbalances that can grow from competitive relationships.

In practice, however, "the functions are shared" and the states and the federal government are interdependent. Noting that "interdependence is not a reliable situation for domination," Leifer and White conclude that "interdependence between formally autonomous units has produced a relationship where, when functioning ideally, nonauthoritative means are used and control is diffuse." Further, the effective handling of interdependence leads to decentralization or diffusion of power that, in turn, safeguards the autonomy of state and local governments.

The "annealing" part of the ideal type analysis proposed by Leifer and White draws upon a process that has been useful in the physical sciences. Annealing involves reversible processes whereby "bad starts" can be reversed and the process repeated. By analogy, management of "garbage can" decision making in organizations requires management skills akin to annealing. President Franklin Roosevelt, Leifer and White argue, "was a matter of the annealing process, hovering over an arena of coalitions of cartelists, central planners, and antitrusters that formed and dissolved as the Depression lingered on. . . . Working within the very flexible framework of the New Deal, Roosevelt's 'true' leanings toward these completely inconsistent groups was prudently almost impossible to discern. Roosevelt was annealing, not directing."

The ideal-type of organization and control developed by Leifer and White can only be suggestive with respect to the problem of world order. The focus on control, rather than authority, and on interdependence, rather than separation of functions, however, may be an important beginning. Coupled with other analyses, such as those discussed, above, it is possible to identify types of research and policy questions that must be addressed in order to specify more closely how such an ideal type might be applied to the problem of world order.

It may be useful, for example, to examine more closely the notion of a "community of fate," drawn from Carol A. Heimer's analysis of how insurance companies handle "reactive risks." Reactive risks are risks that are affected by the behavior of the insured. Faced with the possibility that policyholders may increase insured risks (by negligence or fraud, for example), insurance companies employ a variety of strategies to stabilize risks and to make them more predictable. One of these strategies is to create incentives for policyholders "so that they, as well as their insurers, benefit from . . . loss prevention efforts or suffer from their negligence" (Heimer, 1985, pp. 205-206). By such means, insured and insurer are cast together in a "community of fate."

Heimer notes that collective as well as individual strategies are employed by insurance companies, as when companies work toward more effective building codes and zoning laws. Collective standard setting has advantages for both policyholders and insurance companies. But insured and insurer alike must be alert to outdated bargains, as when property values fluctuate widely in relation to insured value. "The general lesson to be drawn," notes Heimer (1985, p. 214), "is that bargains need to be renegotiated in the light of changing circumstances." This sounds very like the annealing analogy.

Interdependence is also a feature of effective insurance bargains because "(t)hreats of market failure are due to excessive control by one of the parties." Heimer's (1985, p. 215) analysis suggests that "while the primary condition for a simple market is that the likelihood of an outcome not change as a result of decision making (that is, that the cost of providing some commodity not depend on the behavior of the purchaser), the primary condition for an effective if imperfect market is that *control not interfere with calculation*" (emphasis in original).

The market analogy should not be pressed too far, as noted in Chapter 3. A major value of Heimer's (1985, p. 218) analysis is that it proposes "universal strategies for the management of reactive risk." Toward this end she draws upon analyses of decision making concerning sexual relationships and the management of reactive risks in products liability. In neither is the market analogy sufficient to explain decision making. In both, development of a community of fate (e.g., as in marriages and in contracts) is a primary strategy employed by interested parties. The problem of reactivity is quite different here from that of insurance companies, however, for in these cases the goal is "to make organizations and people take into account the interests of others, rather than trying to *prevent* them from responding to the fact that their losses are covered by insurance" (Heimer, 1985, p. 229).

Creation of a new international order is likely to entail reactive risks of both types, for example, "free rider" problems with respect to financial and personnel contributions necessary to public health and security (Olson, 1965), similar to the insurance case. Securing the cooperation of local (national) governments and multinational commercial and industrial organizations with respect to agreed-upon jural postulates is akin to the problem of products liability, that is, making such entities take into account the interests of others.

Heimer (1985, p. 233) notes that collective or third-party loss prevention may be especially important "in those cases in which there is no community of fate." However, even the strongest community of fate may require collective loss prevention, for example, in order to circumvent the "free rider" problem. Analogously, international terrorism may pose problems for whatever international order is to evolve, under any type of community of fate, no matter how strong the bonds thus created.

This brief analysis is intended only to suggest the range of theories and research concerning social systems and institutions—some of them published in this volume—that might be relevant to problems posed by the threat of nuclear war. The soundness of the suggestions can only be demonstrated by theoretical development and empirical inquiry. In any case, the analysis is not meant to be restricted to the nuclear debate. It might as well be applied to problems posed by Catton et al., for example. Nor should the principles at issue be restricted to global problems. The object is to suggest general social science approaches to the understanding of problems, and possible ways of coping with them.

System Complexity and Mediating Institutions

So rapid is scientific and technological advance that one is tempted always to characterize it as revolutionary. For our purposes, that overused term obscures more than it enlightens, however, and frightens more than it informs. I mean neither to deny nor belittle the far-reaching consequences of rapid change, or for that matter the gravity and complexity of both change and consequences. Revolution as description, however, is no substitute for careful, comparative study of the past and present. Only recently, for example, has the reciprocal nature of relationships among science, technology, and social organization become clear, though much remains to be learned concerning the precise nature of these relationships (as discussed, for example, in Chapter 19).

A common theme of much work reported here and elsewhere (see, e.g., Perrow, 1984) concerns the enormous complexity of technological and organizational systems, and the fact that these often are mutually reinforcing. Technological and organizational complexity, in turn, creates the need for mediating mechanisms, roles, and processes within and between systems, and between systems and the citizenry. Several chapters in Part III analyze mediating processes within a variety of institutional contexts. Viewed from this perspective, for example, Leifer and White focus on mediating processes and skills associated with control in multi-divisional and federal systems. Chapters 12, 15, 16, and 17 focus on the roles of institutions as mediators between systems (e.g., economic and political systems) and between systems, constituencies, and individual citizens.

Thomas S. Moore and S. M. Miller (Chapter 12) analyze the multiple roles of government in the making of social structure. State and civil society emerge from this analysis as increasingly inter-dependent, with government as a major mediator of social services and economic well-being of citizens. An activist role for government is necessary, Moore and Miller argue and seek to demonstrate, because "prosperity inevitably and increasingly depends upon the equity of the social arrangements that are being created" (surely a jural postulate candidate, as per the discussion, above; emphasis added).

Irving Tallman notes that kinship is an important and universal basis for social structure, in all cultures and times, and that the family plays a mediating role between individuals and social structure. These are two of the themes developed in Chapter 15. Basing his analysis on the work of social historians who work within a life course perspective, Tallman also develops the rudiments of a theory of norm formation (see chapters in Part II).[5]

Robert Wuthnow's evaluation of recent comparative, evolutionary theories of religion (Chapter 16, "Religion and the Social Fabric") stresses the mediating roles of religion; for example, the church as "a symbol of wholeness in a broken world." Review of recent work of Bellah, Habermas, and Luhmann suggests that religion has become but one of a number of increasingly autonomous social systems, in the process of which religion has lost its integrative function and its capacity to legitimate political and economic systems and actions. Religion has thus become increasingly privatized, while continuing to play an important role in dealing with the contingent nature of life. These contingencies are extremely varied; many are related to advances in science and technology.

Sandra Ball-Rokeach examines recent trends in media research, concluding with her assessment of "Media Linkages of the Social Fabric" (Chapter 17). She notes that the media cut across all institutional areas. They do so with varying degrees of completeness, and the reality they portray has been the subject of much debate. For many individuals, however, media portrayals, coupled with inter-pretations that occur within a variety of social networks, are the most important linkages between institutional areas and between indi-viduals, their networks, and structures and processes of the larger social order. Media, in this sense, may compete with religion.

Paul Dimaggio (1984), writing on "Cultural Typographies as Systems of Classification," observes that the "demand for symbolic information" increases as the ratio of interactions with strangers increases relative to interactions with intimates. Media messages and symbols help to meet this demand, serving as symbolic linkages between strangers as well as among acquaintances and intimates. But so do other symbolic systems. DiMaggio's chief concern is with the ways people use art in the construction of their social worlds, thus introducing another major institutional area.

The consequences of the institutional processes discussed in this section extend to many areas of social life. As an example, mediating functions both accompany and are an important part of the process of culture building, as when people "invent culture" in the process of searching for solutions to common problems. Howard Becker (1982) describes how this occurs at the micro level: By sharing concerns and experiences, shared understandings as to appropriate behavior emerge. Similarly, Michal McCall (1984, p. 29) studies storytelling by "ordinary people" as "a major way people develop the shared understandings that make society possible. . . . Ordinary people telling stories are inventing culture."[6]

The book closes with two chapters that describe sociological attention, or its lack, to two very different yet related issues: the nuclear debate and the uses and control of knowledge. The issues differ in both public and scholarly attention, in the sense of immediacy that attends each and the energies and resources that are devoted to them. In fundamental ways, however, they are indeed related. The nuclear debate is political in nature. Its consequences are political, economic, and social in the broadest sense, including the production, use, and control of knowledge and of inquiry in the broadest sense.

Conclusion

It has not been possible within these brief pages to convey the full richness of the papers developed for and from the 1984 ASA meetings. The issues discussed and the research agenda suggested surely are enough to convince even the most hardened skeptic of the value of theory and research concerning the fundamental nature of the social processes, cultures, and social structures that constitute social life and of the forces that shape them.

The usefulness of metaphors varies by the purposes of their use. My purpose has been to encourage inquiry into the most fundamental characteristics of social life, and to explore implications of such inquiry for social life. The success of the enterprise lies not in what I make here of our collective efforts nor in any chapter or collection of chapters, but in continuing efforts within and between disciplines to expand the knowledge base.

Notes

1. See Wallerstein (forthcoming). Wallerstein's review is broader than Marxist thought, both preceding and following Marx in scope, focusing chiefly on Sir Thomas More's *Utopia*, Friedrich Engels's *Socialism: Scientific and Utopian*, and Karl Manheim's *Ideology and Utopia*, and on social science in general.

2. Janowitz's agenda is set forth in Janowitz (1983).

3. S. N. Eisenstadt and Luis Roniger posit the necessity of trust in building society, and analyze the manner in which trust, as found in intimate interpersonal relationships, is transformed and structured in the larger social order. Other recent discussions of the role of trust in society are found in Barber (1983) and Lewis and Weigart (1985).

4. Tilly (1985, p. 186) sounds a warning from recent history: States formed since World War II, through decolonization or by means of "reallocations of territory by dominant states," have tended to acquire their military organization and strength "from outside, without the same internal forging of mutual constraints between rulers and ruled."

5. "New norms," Tallman hypothesizes, "evolve out of discontinuities in the social structure that . . . (alter) the opportunities for families . . . to attain . . . personal, social, economic or political goals." Discontinuities develop "when historical time, social or family time, and individual time" are not synchronized. This puts in motion "efforts on the part of relevant parties to alter existing social relationships." Power and dependency relationships influence the character and the success of such efforts, as "through collective action, political activity, educational programs, individual negotiations, or simply by changing life styles." A similar, more psychologically based theme is developed by students of community organization who theorize that community as a form of collective action . . . (occurs) because mobilization has its roots in the private troubles of individuals" (Summers, 1986).

6. The papers by DiMaggio and McCall were presented at a thematic session on "The Arts and the Social Fabric," organized and chaired by Howard S. Becker. DiMaggio notes that his focus "begins to articulate the sociology of art with fundamental problems of social organization." At the microlevel, the technique described by McCall could be adapted to study more systematically the nature of linkages between people and institutions.

References

Barber, B. 1983. *The Logic and Limits of Trust.* New Brunswick, NJ: Rutgers University Press.

Becker, H. 1982. "Culture: A Sociological View." *Yale Review* (Summer): 513-527.

Catton, W. R., Jr. 1984. "Probable Collective Responses to Ecological Scarcity: How Violent?" *Sociological Perspectives*, 37, 3-20.

DiMaggio, P. 1984. *Cultural Typographies as Systems of Classification.* Paper presented at the annual meetings of the American Sociological Association.

Dunlap, R. E. and W. R. Catton, Jr. 1979. "Environmental Sociology." Pp. 243-273 in *Annual Review of Sociology*, 5. Edited by A. Inkeles, J. Coleman, and R. Turner. Palo Alto, CA: Annual Reviews.

Eisenstadt, S. N. and L. Roniger. 1984. *Patrons, Clients and Friends: Interpersonal Relations and the Structure of Trust in Society.* Cambridge: Cambridge University Press.

Etzkowitz, H. 1983a. "Solar Versus Nuclear Energy: Autonomous or Dependent Technology." *Social Problems* 31: 417-434.

Etzkowitz, H. 1983b. "Entrepreneurial Scientists and Entrepreneurial Universities in American Academic Science." *Minerva* XXI.

Freudenberg, W. 1986. "Social Impact Assessment." In *Annual Review of Sociology.* Edited by R. Turner and J. F. Short, Jr. Palo Alto, CA: Annual Reviews.

Heimer, C. A. 1985. *Reactive Risk and Rational Action: Managing Moral Hazard in Insurance Contracts.* Berkeley: University of California Press.

Janowitz, M. 1983. *The Reconstruction of Patriotism: Education for Civic Consciousness.* Chicago: University of Chicago Press.

Kreps, G. 1984a. *Classical Themes, Structural Sociology, and Disaster Research.* Paper prepared for the annual meetings of the American Sociological Association, San Antonio.

Kreps, G. 1984b. "Sociological Inquiry and Disaster Research." Pp. 309-330 in *Annual Review of Sociology*, 10. Edited by R. Turner and J. F. Short, Jr. Palo Alto, CA: Annual Reviews.

Lewis, J. D. and A. Weigert. 1985. "Trust as a Social Reality." *Social Forces* 63: 967-985.

McCall, M. 1984. *The Significance of Storytelling.* Paper presented at the annual meetings of the American Sociological Association.

Olson, M. 1965. *The Logic of Collective Action: Public Goods and the Theory of Groups.* Harvard Economic Studies. Cambridge, MA: Harvard University Press.

Perrow, C. 1984. *Normal Accidents: Living with High-Risk Technologies.* New York: Basic Books.

Schneider, J. W. 1986. "Social Problem Theory: The Constructionist View." In *Annual Review of Sociology.* Edited by R. Turner and J. F. Short, Jr. Palo Alto, CA: Annual Reviews.

Short, J. F., Jr. (Ed.) 1971. *The Social Fabric of the Metropolis: Contributions of the Chicago School of Urban Sociology.* Chicago: University of Chicago Press.

Short, J. F., Jr. 1984. "The Social Fabric at Risk: Toward a Social Transformation of Risk Analysis." *American Sociological Review* 49: 711-725.

Summers, E. 1986. "Rural Community Development." In *Annual Review of Sociology.* Edited by R. Turner and J. F. Short, Jr. Palo Alto, CA: Annual Reviews.

Tilly, C. 1985. "War Making and State Making as Organized Crime." Pp. 169-191 in *Bringing the State Back In.* Edited by P. B. Evans, D. Rueschemeyer, and T. Skocpol. Cambridge: Cambridge University Press.

Toynbee, A. J. 1946. *A Study of History.* London: Oxford University Press.

Wallerstein, I. forthcoming. "Marxisms as Utopias: Evolving Ideologies." *American Journal of Sociology.*

Part I

How Is Social Order Possible?

2

From Structure to Order

Neil J. Smelser

FOR ALMOST A YEAR—between the time I agreed to chair the session on "How Is Social Order Possible" at the San Antonio meetings of the American Sociological Association in August 1984, and the time I sat down to write this set of introductory remarks—I felt a vague, muffled unease about the enterprise, but in trying to discern reasons for this discomfort, I always came up empty-handed. I finally figured it out, however: The problem lies in the title of the session.

To phrase the question "How is Social Order Possible?" paints oneself into an unwelcome Hobbesian corner in a number of ways. The first thing such a question presumes is that the state of nature is one of disorder, and only "possibly" orderable, and that human beings have to make a special effort to order it; that is very Hobbesian. Second, it is based on that Hobbesian individualism that (Mary Douglas reminds us) is so pervasive in our Western thinking that we have difficulty breaking through it even in our presumably dis-passionate social-scientific thinking about the nature of behavior. And third, the term "order" is a kind of moral one, certainly more moral in its connotations than the more neutral terms "structure" or "pattern"; the *Oxford English Dictionary* (hereafter OED) in one of its 31 renditions of the word "order" defines it as "the condition in which everything is in its proper place, and performs its proper function." The suggestion is that people are individualistic and disorderly by nature; the reason, in short, why I didn't like that question is because it is too ugly in its implications.

One might well have asked with at least equal justification, "How Is Social Anarchy Possible?" What comes to mind are three excellent studies, by Kanter (1972), Zablocki (1980), and Berger (1981), of intentional or communitarian experiments. Most of these experiments are spawned out of some kind of alienation from and rejection of that web of values and norms from which the adherents of the experiments withdraw. Furthermore, in at least a portion of them, a positive utopia is envisioned in which there will be no rules, all will do their own things, and all will be freed from the shackles of a regulated life. The three studies show, in different ways, that these communitarian experimenters cannot bring it off. Before long, understandings and rules begin to emerge (having to do, for example with the division of labor, or with how to deal with very young children); indeed, "orders"—in the classic definition of the term as hierarchical ranks—begin to arise, as exemplary charismatic leaders become the embodiment of usually vaguely articulated norms and standards.

It is true that such communities vary greatly with respect to the degree to which life is hemmed in by norms, rituals, and procedures, and it is true that many of those communities do attain a great deal of freedom for their members. But it is also true that all of them generate some kind of order, even those whose first principle is the renunciation of order. For these little societies, as for societies in general, we need not ask whether order is *possible*; rather, we should simply acknowledge that it *is*. The interesting questions about order, then, are missed by the title of the session; those questions would have to do with accounting for the variability of order, the diversity of means by which it is secured, the consequences of different sorts of order for individuals, and the dynamics of breakdown and restoration of order.

By good fortune the contributors to this little symposium on order are all sufficiently clear-headed that they avoided taking the Hobbesian bait implied in the title, and addressed some of those interesting questions. Douglas nestles clearly in the Durkheimian tradition, assuming social order as a given fact of life, so pervasive that we cannot even think about it without reflecting it. Because we are such prisoners of that order, the only ways to study it are to think about what does not happen in societies and what people cannot think about within societies (this is one of the most interesting arguments for studying counterfactuals and for mental experiments that I have come across), or to see what happens when order is disrupted in some way.

Peter Rossi and Richard Berk also take social order (the normative) as unproblematical in society, but, advisedly and intelligently, they disaggregate the normative phenomenon and regard it as variable along certain lines: whether there is agreement about the behavioral domain to which norms might apply; whether norms are clearly or dimly perceived; how much consensus there is on whether a statement is or is not a legitimate norm; and how much agreement there is if an item of behavior is legitimately to be regarded as an instance ("application") of that norm. Rossi and Berk do not go very far with a next step, namely, to ask what are the consequences for the process of social control that emanate from different combinations of the variables they identify. But surely to pursue that question would generate much light on the ways social order is secured or not secured. William J. Goode comes closest to the issue of how social order is possible, and reviews a number of (mainly individualistic) theories of how some kind of macroscopic continuity (order) can arise out of individual behavior and interaction. He finds most of these solutions wanting, but his evidently preferred candidate is also a Durkheimian one, which views society as a phenomenon *sui generis*, emergent if not transcendent, constraining individuals, and calling for the exercise of social control.

An introduction such as this is constrained to take some kind of overview of the problem at hand, and I shall do so, somewhat in Goode's spirit, though I will slice up the world of sociological thought somewhat differently.

I begin by making a distinction between the idea of "structure" and the idea of "order." The former is a somewhat simpler concept, implying "an organized body or combination of mutually connected and dependent parts of elements" (the OED again). We find this notion of structure everywhere in the sciences: atomic structure, molecular structure, cellular structure, anatomical structure, personality structure, social structure, even the structure of the universe. It seems difficult to conceive of any kind of scientific inquiry without sooner or later invoking the notion of structure. Structure is central to the scientific enterprise because, by tradition, that enterprise is dedicated to discovering (a) *regularities* in whatever part of nature it undertakes to investigate, and regularities mean repeated, nonrandom phenomena, and (b) *systematic relationships* among the things it studies. Consider only the major purposes of almost all statistical techniques as applied in the behavioral and social sciences; they are predominantly devoted to demonstrating that things could be arrayed or have happened by chance alone, or alternately that there is some kind of pattern or structure in evidence.

The notion of structure implies a number of basic units of analysis (items of behavior, persons, roles) that bear some special, nonrandom relationship to one another, a relationship that is repeated in space and time, and a relationship that is qualitatively different from relations with units that are not considered part of the structure (this is necessary if a structure is to have identifiability and integrity); the last ingredient implies the notion of structure-in-environment, and, in addition, the notion that the structure may be relatively closed or open to influences from it. Such a notion of structure appears to be widely if not universally accepted, explicitly or implicitly, by those who are committed to the enterprise of behavioral and social sciences.

It is in the transition from "structure" to "order" where the theoretical fur begins to fly. Most accounts of structure also include some kind of reasons why a structure is a structure, why it hangs together and continues to differentiate itself from its environment, or, what orders the structure. Ideas of survival, adaptation, and function are examples of such reasons. This connotation is contained in the OED's sixteenth listed definition of "order": "a method according to which things act or take place; the fixed arrangement found in the existing constitution of things; a natural, moral, or spiritual system in which things proceed according to definite laws." Most theoretical debates in the social sciences involve competing assertions as to which is (or are) the major ordering principle(s) of organized social life, and assertions about the primacy of one preferred principle over others.

In the theoretical accounts of ordering principles in the social sciences, there appear to be two grand traditions: first, order explained as the effects arising from the interaction of individuals who are interested in one another in some way; and, second, order as emanating from some transcendent source of constraints and opportunities for individuals (and groups), and hence determinative of their behavior and interactions.

In the former tradition, which is usually characterized as microscopic, the following variants can be identified:

- Social structure (and culture) as reflecting the *renunciation* of individual interests in the interests of social order (social contract, the psychoanalytic theory of civilization).
- Social structure (and culture) as *projection* of individual fantasies and conflicts (culture-and-personality accounts of myths, folklore, rituals, and religious belief-systems).
- Social structure as arising from the voluntary *submission* of individuals to leaders (Michels, LeBon).
- Social structure as aggregated effects or *convergences* of multiple individual interactions (neoclassical economic theory, modern exchange theory—in both of which individuals enter relationships for personal reward or gain).
- Social structure as emerging from a multiple of negotiated interactions that establish common *meanings* (ethnomethodology, Berger and Luckman, the symbolic-interactionist notion of "fitting together" of action or "joint action").

Explanations emanating from the second, or macroscopic, tradition are likewise very diverse:

- Structure as arising from some consideration of social *survival*, which calls for differentiation or specialization of parts (Spencer; functionalism generally; Marx).
- Structure as arising from *consensus* on societal values and norms and the ordering of behavior in accord with these cultural forms (Parsons).
- Structure as arising from *social control*, in which positive and negative sanctions are used to regulate behavior and limit deviance (role theory, much of deviance theory).
- Structure as deriving from the introjection or *internalization* of values and norms such that part of the cultural or social structure becomes part of the individual persons, and regulates behavior accordingly (Freud, Durkheim, Parsons).
- Structure as deriving from *coercion* or the application of force (Hobbes, Marx, Dahrendorf).

More examples could be adduced. But the most important point to be made about these notions that arise in the transition from structure to order is the point made by Morris Zelditch, Jr., namely, that they are all metatheoretical in character; none can be proved or disproved by a decisive experiment or event. Even if one goes with Zelditch to say that these ordering principles can be appropriately evaluated according to "how fruitful they are," we remain in some trouble, for there is usually such conceptual slippage between the general principles and the specific hypotheses that are drawn from them—I deliberately refrain from saying derived—that even the confirmation or disconfirmation of such hypotheses is not such as to constitute definitive crediting or discrediting of the general principle. Perhaps this is one reason why it is possible for the theoretical advocates of different principles to cling to them with such persistence and conviction; there is no definitive scientific reason to abandon them.

The other observation to be made about this range of ordering principles is that it seems evident that all of them are present in all societies in some way and in some degree; and, therefore, illustrations for all of them can readily be found (another motive for not giving up any of the principles). Illustrations are not enough, of course, for illustrations alone do not constitute evidence for importance or primacy. It seems to me that a proper sociological strategy for the study of order would be to abandon such a search for primacy or importance, and to treat each of the primary ordering principles enunciated as a variable, both in terms of its presence in a given society and in its combinations with other ordering principles. In general, those with an interest in order in societies make use of multiple ordering principles as a kind of "fail-safe" strategy. Nonetheless, the selection is made among combinations of them that are variable; comparative study should focus on the variable/empirical combinations of ordering principles (including changes of these combinations over time), without making any particular attempt to rank any one of them as important or primary in any wide or universal sense, and to assess the consequences of different combinations for individual and group behavior, and for the working of society.

References

Berger, B. M. 1981. *The Survival of a Counter Culture: Ideological Work and Everyday Life among Rural Communards.* Berkeley and Los Angeles: University of California Press.

Kanter, R. M. 1972. *Community and Community: Communes and Utopias in Sociological Perspective.* Cambridge, MA: Harvard University Press.

Zablocki, B. 1980. *Alienation and Charisma: A Study of Contemporary American Communes.* New York: Free Press.

3

Individual Choice and
the Social Order

William J. Goode

Even the usually pessimistic may sometimes throw off their normal gloom and decide that some progress may be possible. Even sociology may move ahead in the decades to come. Doubtless if that time comes our intellectual descendents will look back and wonder why in this generation we ever tried to wrestle with the slippery topic of social order and, more particularly, the topic of this chapter. That is surely one form of progress: to see clearly that our ancestors were foolish.

For over two millenia wise analysts have pursued the question of individual choice and social order as they might have a will-o-the-wisp. And even though their formulations now sound like clichés to us, we recognize that they are mostly valid, at least in part.

Why then do we keep trying to work on this messy, theoretical problem? Is the guarantee of failure so attractive?

There are, I think, three reasons for pursuing this topic.

The first reason is that human beings perceive order and try to

AUTHOR'S NOTE: *I would like to thank the John Guggenheim Foundation, the Russell Sage Foundation, and the Hoover Institution for facilitating this inquiry.*

explain it. This is a touching element in the arrogance of the human spirit. The human mind perceives system, order, and pattern either before or after it perceives individual units and actions, and does so whether or not that order really exists. Sometimes those patterns can be demonstrated and sometimes not, but the human mind sees them anyway. In the modern view we do not suppose that people add all the individual buffalo in order to perceive a herd, or all the bureaucrats in order to see an organization. Given parts, we perceive a whole. Given a whole, we believe we see its discrete parts. Several generations of experimenters have demonstrated this in great detail.[1] Moreover, it has also been shown experimentally—and here some of our more mischievous colleagues have contributed their share—that people will find meaning, interpretations, causes, and motivations in all sorts of social phenomena, even when these have been artificially constructed so as to have little or no inherent meaning.[2] For example, if a computer gives random responses to the comments of a human being, that person is likely to perceive those responses as meaningful.

Perhaps aside from that psychological bent, this predisposition to perceive order has several other sources: intellectual, of course, but also esthetic and very likely—perhaps even ultimately—religious as well.

As a second stimulus to examine this question, the model of science beckons us. Scientists—just like human beings—also look for order, and they begin with the belief that they already see some order and a faith that the natural world is orderly—the regularities of the parts affect the activities of other parts, and their interrelations constitute the larger order. It is esthetically pleasing to see finally how they fit together. Some pull away, others toward, some are in tension with others, some correct each other or set limits to others. That is so for organisms as well as nonorganic systems.

If we think of biology as a near and inspiring model, we note that keen observers for generations before Darwin discovered small regularities in the workings of the body, or in the relations between a species and its environment. The larger theories of order, as in sociology, were speculations and had little predictive power or precision. Each theory had its faddish hour, but few actually died, just as in sociology. From time to time, however, and this has happened at a faster pace over the past several generations, biologists could see more clearly how smaller relationships fitted with each other and with larger patterns. Those older, less precise grand theories probably did not harm research very much. And, again as in sociology, when a new idea about order appeared, most researchers responded with a moderate to low degree of enthusiasm.

To be sure, the enthusiasm of a response to a theory is not always an accurate measure of the validity of the vision—there are fashions in science, too. However, if there is a solution to the problem of the individual and the larger order, it will probably arrive when the question has been stated correctly and the empirical laws or regularities needed for that new vision have been found. Until that time, we flounder as we do now while continuing to seek. And until that time, we had better enjoy the trip, whatever the destination, for that is most of the fun we shall get.

Thus sociologists tackle this question anew because of a human drive to understand order and its constituents, and because the model of science suggests that the goal might be possible.

A third reason for looking at the connection between individual action and social order is that the very question focuses our attention on what we know—and do not know—and thereby focuses our attention on where we should go next. The question leads us to face the assumptions of our own intellectual orientation, our doctrines as well as the gaps in our knowledge.

We could of course bypass the problem, and there is a philosophical tradition that does so by denying that there is any human order that could be captured by science. Far from fading away, that position is strongly asserted at the present time in France, Germany, and even England, by especially structuralism, critical theory, and many offshoots of Marxism.[3]

It is richly rooted in the humanist tradition as well, to which so many sociologists give some allegiance. Thus a character in a modern novel (Thomas Pynchon's V, 1968) says, "This is life's single lesson: that there is more accident to it than a [person] can ever admit to in a lifetime and stay sane." And even science might have a comment on this, since one inference from the second Law of Thermodynamics is that the statistically most probable condition is randomness.

To be sure, to accept that position would put a quick and perhaps merciful end to this inquiry, which it may not merit. In any event, most commonsense observers report that somehow societies do lurch along from day to day, individuals' choices and actions, however contradictory, cause them to do so, and there is a problem as to how they link together. That problem deserves analysis.

We could also believe in the order, and discard the problem, asserting instead that this is one of those intellectual chestnuts like the connection between nature and nurture, or between conflict and integration, that is not answerable as stated. Almost certainly that view is correct, but an examination of the question should yield greater clarity in our understanding of social theory, and perhaps suggest how the question may be phrased better.

To do this, let us first sketch five formulations of the problem itself. They are mostly not neat hypotheses to be tested easily by empirical data, and inevitably they overlap somewhat. They may be viewed as five different approaches or answers to how individual processes or actions might be the bases of social or any other order. After that, each of these will be considered in more or less detail. They are as follows:

The first is the natural science view, which assumes that the microorder constitutes the macroorder, with nothing left over. For purposes of intellectual convenience and elegance the macro order is used to integrate and explain the microprocess or parts.

The second I shall call the "Benefits" or "Utility" approach, which has a long history in social theory, and is most closely associated with the thought of Locke, the moral philosophers of the eighteenth century, and much of the political philosophy of the nineteenth century. Its answer is that people form and maintain the social order so as to satisfy their individual needs better. Individuals actually support the social order because it yields more benefits to them as to the society as a whole. Social order in this sense, as Dennis Wrong (1984, p. 204) notes, refers to "cooperative relations among individuals and common observance of rules governing their conduct toward one another"—usually for the goals of productiveness and the civil orderliness of the society.

The third approach actually raises a different question: whether the whole—the social order—is qualitatively different from the sum of the individual choices and actions, and must be described by different laws. In recent history, we associate it most closely with Durkheim's thought. The query is, as Jeffrey Alexander (1982, p. xix) puts it, "Are social arrangements or structures the result of individual negotiations, or do they present themselves as collective structures that have *sui generis* or emergent status?"

The fourth approach is that of economics, which gives a negative answer to the Durkheimian question by asserting that we need only sum up or aggregate the individual economic actions and decisions of persons or organizations to arrive at the whole economy. Of course, economics also asserts that because both individuals in a transaction are better off than they were before, the whole is supported by the satisfactions or benefits individuals receive from the larger order, and thus this view overlaps with the Benefits approach.

The fifth version can be called the problem of *transformations*, and it has attempted to work out a basic individual action schema modeled on economics. Those who have followed this approach have either ignored the macrolevel or have suggested paths or transformations by which larger social orders—the class structure, organizations, social institutions—could be derived from the micro-regularities. In the most recent formulation by James S. Coleman (1984a, pp. 1, 23-33) he points out the difficulty of creating "a proper model of micro-to-macro transition, so that we can use microdata to study . . . system-level relations that constitute the major portion of social theory." Let us consider each of these views.

The Natural Science Approach

In the natural science approach, order is a statement of timeless propositions, of regularities and laws about observable phenomena. A system is orderly because its parts—angles in crystals, the exchange of gases in the blood, and so on—are orderly, and they constitute the larger system of order. The microlevel makes up the larger order. There may be no a priori reason to suppose that simply anything we find that is regular at the microlevel will contribute to the regularity of macro order, and certainly it may explain very little of the variance in the order of the larger system, but in fact the history of science reveals that the parts do indeed fit in some fashion. They constitute or are the basis of order in the larger system because there is nothing else out of which the order could be made. The system is ultimately defined by the orderly parts or relations that make it up. In turn, the activities, movements, or forces at the local level are also determined by the whole system.[4]

In this meaning, which is not a theory but an intellectual structure, there is no real problem of the individual and the larger order. There is no gap between them except the theoretical leap needed from time to time in order to envision what the system is and how it works. Such leaps are viewed as new theoretical steps, but that the leap can be eventually made is taken for granted. It is usual that before an intellectually elegant solution is found some less pleasing integrations will be made because the data are not sufficient, or the less relevant relationships have been seized upon, or the new integrating idea is wrong or insufficient. Researchers in the natural sciences do not suppose that there is an inherent contradiction or discrepancy between the micro and the macro order. To the contrary, almost certainly they link together neatly. The intellectual question is how they do so.

The Benefits or Utility Approach

Our second version, the Benefits or Utility approach, is actually an important hypothesis about the bases of order. It is this general hypothesis that especially creates empirical as well as theoretical obstacles to the step from the individual to the social structure. The hypothesis may be an unstated presupposition or perhaps a political assertion, but it claims that members of the society somehow approve the social order because it meets their needs; that ultimately they will it and create it by their individual daily choices because it brings them valuable goals. This last assertion is of course correct in a partial sense because no one else but its members, nothing else but their own acts, could accomplish that. However, because that hypothesis (that people support the social order because it brings them benefits) is implicit in this statement of the problem, classical analysts do not use the idea of order to refer to instability, misery, and inequity, which are also commonly a part of the social regularity. They do not refer to exploitation but to a state or ruler that brings benefits to citizens, and citizens who therefore support the larger system.

Yet that presupposition or implicit hypothesis does pose empirical and theoretical problems. Empirically we simply do not know how strongly over the centuries most human beings have actually supported the social structures they maintained. Through recorded history most people were in fact peasants, and it is highly probable that they believed that the system exploited them and caused much of their misery. Although their individual choices did indeed continue the social order, in a sense they were forced choices, and individuals did not aim at that result. Neither support for nor rejection of the social order was available to them as a choice or action.

That last statement is both empirical and political, but it raises again the theoretical question, for it asserts a gap between the hypotheses we make about individual choices and actions and those about how the social order operates.

At the most elementary levels, where social structure is only a peripheral concern in our research, that gap is most conspicuous though it creates few puzzles. Few people who think of marrying or having a baby, for example, or who face death, consider much whether those acts will increase or decrease the marriage, fertility, or death rates in their country. That is, their individual choices are little concerned with the larger social patterns.

Many acts when aggregated do affect the social structure—choice of occupation, religious conversions, changing one's mix of purchases, joining a political movement, moving to a different region, giving to charity, and so on—but in only a few of our daily acts do we carry it out with the intention and goal of supporting or rejecting the existing social order.

Indeed we might argue that one of the prime bases of social order is precisely that in it we are given almost no opportunities to affirm it or deny it. Our ordinary choices only allow us to select the better among a set of sometimes not very delightful alternatives, but we are not asked whether we would prefer to arrange the whole structures more to our liking.

Still, the hypothesis asserts that in fact the system will not work unless people's aims, needs, and ends are satisfied, and that claim is partly correct in that people have been socialized to accept the values and ends common in their society; that is, there is at least some moral or value base to the social order.

However, this conception focuses on benefits, not ultimate values, and neither contemporary nor historical societies have been much like the relatively prosperous—and politically freer—Western ones out of which that conception or definition emerged. Most human beings in history have not lived in such societies. It is an optimistic constriction of vision to fashion a general idea that fits only the part of humankind that has enjoyed such conditions.

We cannot, without in-depth interviews with those people of the past and present, find out whether they did or do in fact prefer the social structures within which they have lived.[5] Still I would argue, as I have just stated, that most people in the past believed that they were not given justice, were exploited, and were prevented by the social order from getting as much respect, material goods, power, and freedom from fear as they should.

Yet doubtless in their individual worlds they daily affirmed the *cultural* values of their time and place, from manners to religious beliefs; and in their daily *social* interactions they did not fight against the larger system, whether or not they approved it. Yet I do not accept the notion that what has existed and what cannot be altered much by people with little or no power, even over generations, is somehow automatically transformed by mere time into the legitimacy that gives inner allegiance and commitment to the extant social structure.[6] To the contrary, we now know much more about peasants of the past as well as the present than we once did, and their expressed opinions when they revolted or believed they had been given a new social order suggests rather that before the event they had not felt a strong inner belief that their social system was good or moral in itself, or benefited them fairly, even if they felt some commitment to much of their culture.

If that is so, then we cannot simply assert that the ultimate base of the social structure is a deep moral commitment to that larger system—even though much of their daily life expressed such a commitment to some parts of the culture. In more concrete terms, for example, we take for granted that the Polish people do feel committed to much of their culture, from their norms about gender to religious beliefs; and we suppose that applies as well to the English who joined the Peasants Revolt of 1381.[7] That microcommitment to the culture is a good part of the basis of social order, but it is only a part. Another part already noted is that in the microexchanges and interactions of daily life people are wise to focus on what benefits they can obtain from them, for those are their best alternatives and among them is not to be found the choice of a better social structure. These daily benefits are better than nothing, and of course they may be substantial.

Thus if we enlarge our view to consider other great societies in world history, we need to look beyond these three bases of the social structure at the microlevel—that is, some benefits, a commitment to many elements of the cultural pattern, and the lack of choice about the social order. For when we contemplate the vast extensity and near ubiquity of autocracy, racism, religious and subnational persecution, slavery, caste and class oppression, and political corruption throughout human history, we must not only doubt that those untold hundreds of millions of people actually willed those social orders, but we must also accept the pervasive steadying influence of force and force-threat as another major base of the social order—but that rejects the central hypothesis in the utility solution of the order problem.

Although we often use the term "power" to refer to this part of the foundation of the social order, we must not define that term in the Weberian sense so common in contemporary analyses. That usage is much too broad, for it refers to any means whatever by which people or groups impose their will on others. Because these means, as Weber himself pointed out (Weber, 1954/1925, p. 323, 1978/1924, Vol. I, p. 53, Vol. II, p. 920), can and do include esteem, money, affection, or almost any reward or punishment, that realm of action when closely examined in this light becomes coterminous with all of social action and thus it has no discernible qualitative characteristics of its own. By contrast I contend, as I have elsewhere, that the processes of force and force-threat are analytically distinct from others, and deserve an independent formulation (Goode, 1972).

This is not the place to offer such an analysis because we are focusing on one approach to our large problem. All I want to do is to assert that any ongoing social system is also a force-threat system, and most human beings in the past have lived, as perhaps most do now, in a polity where they are aware of its pressures. When the force-threat is strong and predictable enough, people can come to view it as normal even when unjust, and in any event as unwise to be challenged.

Concretely we can claim that the social system cannot rest on force alone, but of course none has to do so; always it has other means of control at its disposal. If it is successful over time, its political forms may seem as solid and invulnerable as much of the physical environment. To be sure, our Western history for the past 300 years seems a vindication of the noble philosophy that the human spirit will inevitably move toward freedom—as Faulkner asserted, it will not only endure, it will also prevail—but much of human history instead appears to be closer to Sorokin's trendless fluctuation in this regard.

We who prefer to think of the human spirit as ultimately free remember the triumphs of rebellion better than its disasters, but the more valid view is that mostly neither occurs. Rather, force and force-threat as it supports the social structure seem to most people over the centuries as immovable, impenetrable, and irresistible. It does change, but not much in their lifetime.

Of course, all concrete systems do fall, but they are not even usually defeated by a new set of rulers who thereupon create a new social order better suited to the inner moral vision of the subjects, based on justice, freedom, or a wider diffusion of benefits. Rather the new system has in the past continued the old with new personnel, with some small changes, not all of them improvements.

Is the Larger Social Order an Emergent?

As noted earlier, the third approach to this problem focuses on quite another question: whether the larger social order is qualitatively different from the individual order, as Durkheim argued. It is recognizable as an ancient philosophical conundrum, and can be easily transformed into a Zenovian type of paradox: Any two things may, taken together, be proclaimed as having new or emergent qualities, or none, because the so-called new or emergent qualities might be instead proclaimed as inherently to be found in a fully adequate description of the original two things. Aristotle remarked that a hand separated from the body is a hand only in an equivocal sense. That is a statement of the former position, but we can as easily take this second position and assert that a complete description of a hand includes its qualities in both separation and integration.

Similarly, it could be claimed that institutions and organizations can be economically described without speaking of individuals, and so may be seen as sui generis or emergent; on the other hand it has been asserted that social institutions are made up of what individuals choose and do in all their complexity.[8]

The question is not, however, only a possible candidate for definitional fiat. It is real because one social science discipline, economics, has built much of its edifice on the notion that by calculating what individuals do in the market it is possible to aggregate those actions so as to produce models of the economy. Even the corporation can be treated as though it were a person, as it was first defined in the law, and described as maximizing its own utility.

Contrary to that view, which we shall consider in more detail later on, is a most ancient position that the person and the state have different goals, rules, and patterns of action. Very likely both kings and priests of all great societies have agreed with Durkheim in part, and imposed their solution long before Hobbes made his formal statement. They could see that their subjects or followers were basically undisciplined and prone to violate the societal rules and needs in favor of their own short-term interests. Without guidance they would make selfish, incorrect choices and the larger society would suffer.[9] To solve that Durkheimian contradiction between individual liberty and social equilibrium (Alexander, 1982, pp. 104-105), they curtailed liberty by slavery, physical threat, religious awe, and the political forces of the monarchy so that people would be docile, hardworking, and at least overtly supportive of the social order.

The preceding sentence also takes for granted that a view of emergence is insufficient if it suggests that our theory and our propositions can be left only at some higher emergent level—hypotheses about groups, societies, or social systems. At some point in our analyses, those explanations must rest on a foundation of individual actions. The "society" may, as in many classic sociological statements, "need" something or another (support in war, protection of the helpless, and so on), but only individuals, real persons, do anything at all. Without their inputs, there are no emergent traits of groups to be analyzed.

It is also to be noted that this more ancient, long-enduring view adds a small but upsetting element to the original statement. Specifically, kings and priests, like Hobbes, agreed that the social order was indeed *sui generis*, but also saw that individual choices and the social order were potentially, perhaps *usually*, in *conflict* with one another and thus the individual had to be curbed.

An additional theoretical point should be added to this older view. Neither Hobbes nor ancient tyrants claimed that human nature alters under such curbs. People simply choose and act differently under different structural arrangements. Left alone they are a danger to each other and to the social order; under curbs they are not.

Sociologists of our era may not have solved the question of the emergent quality of the social order, but we have done the next best thing. We do at least, or most of us do, hold firm doctrines about it.

They are doctrines, orientational statements, or presuppositions that we believe we observe even if we cannot easily put them to the test. Sociologists may wish to qualify each of the following hypotheses to some extent, but they do commonly appear in our courses and textbooks. We believe first that the order or system is somehow willed, or at least created by human actions and not by the accidental play of arbitrary factors, and especially not by a primeval king or godhead; and moreover not by social compact, as our wise eighteenth-century predecessors urged.

Second, we also believe that society is an emergent, with qualities and processes that cannot be deduced or aggragated from individual traits or actions. As Talcott Parsons pointed out nearly half a century ago, Robinson Crusoe may have worked out economic solutions while alone—for example, whether to plant grain or to eat it—but as soon as his man Friday appeared a genuinely new problem arose—the problem of social order, indeed of social control.

However, we now assert in addition that the individual is also an emergent, that we are different as a consequence of the social order. It penetrates and shapes us. Thus our individual choices and actions are different in different societies.

I think we also agree that the whole, the structure of the society, is not the outcome of specific decisions to create or maintain that type of social pattern, but the decisions and actions that people engage in do have that result. In more recent decades we add the corollary notion, that thereby the pattern, the system, is continually being reconstructed, reproduced, and that it can be maintained only by a flow of inputs.

That means in turn that a central foundation of a social order is social control, that is, getting others to do what has to be done if the system is to be held together. Otherwise each person would be more likely to follow his or her own interests, and that is likely to diverge from the needs, wishes, or interests of other individuals as well as those of the whole.

This corollary of course takes for granted that there is disharmony and conflict among individuals as well as between individuals and the larger system.

In these modern statements about the implications of emergence we already see several divergences from our fourth or economic approach. Central is its claim that we need only sum up or aggregate the individual economic decisions and actions of persons and organizations to arrive at the whole economy. Of course, economics also asserts that because both individuals in a transaction are better off than they were before, the whole is supported by the benefits we receive from the economic order. It asserts that market controls are simply instrumental or rational whereas sociology claims that the values, ends, norms, and means always have nonrational components and thus the bases of social control are partly nonrational.

Sociology asserts, then, that people are moved not only by a calculation of gains and losses others rationally impose on them, but they are also moved to act because they feel that some goals, values, norms, or behaviors are good in themselves whether or not directly pleasurable. These elements of action are nonrational. That is, the set of emergents the social order creates in the individual through socialization and resocialization is a necessary part of social control as it is of all action. As Parsons pointed out, it you omit the nonrational, you leave out action altogether.[10] Economics has some problem with this because economists have been unable to discern the difference between the nonrational and the irrational. Because they exclude the irrational in their calculations, they exclude both. Doubtless this is another of the reasons why economics has only a tenuous claim to be a science of action.

It should be emphasized that these last assertions are not definitional but empirical. It is not that we refuse to define behavior as "action" if the nonrational or normative is missing. The assertion is more blunt: We would not do anything at all if we did not want something, if no goals were any more valuable than any others, if we had no evaluative criteria (including the criterion of rationality) by which to weigh the relative desirability of an act or a goal—and all of those elements are nonrational, evaluative, normative. We have no scientific method for "proving" one should live by such standards (including the rational), but they are the core of our motivation to act at all.

These theoretical assertions of sociology add many complexities to the problem of the individual and the social order, but they do give one kind of answer to it. All this is doctrine. We think it is also observation. It is difficult to imagine what form an empirical proof of it would take. At a minimum, however, we can come close to proving—and we shall do so soon—that a purely individualistic view of human action that leaves out institutions, political organizations, bureaucracies, and so on does not fit reality.

Because I have more elaborate comments to make about the fourth approach, that of economics, while the fifth or transformational approach uses part of it, let me postpone that analysis and first briefly state this last mode of addressing our question.

The Transformational Approach

This last approach has attempted to work out a basic individual action schema, and its researchers have either ignored the macro level or tried to suggest paths or transformations by which larger social orders—the class system, social institutions, organizations, and so on—could be derived from it. The most recent formulation of James Coleman points out that much of our research focuses on individual data, but we want to draw conclusions about larger processes and structures. We need to create paths from the individual to the macrostructural, or make transformation rules between the two, so as to create models of the macro order. He also proves how typically even classical research has failed to take this step. He sees the proper way as the utilization of a modified type of economic theory based on an individual action schema.

Coleman's work over the past decade seeks to remedy a gap in theorizing that has emerged with a major theoretical formulation of our time, the resurrection of an older tradition that found the basis of social order in self-interest (Coleman, 1984a, pp. 2, 32). This movement was partially a rejection of what many felt was an overemphasis on norms and values, which came to be seen as an insufficient explanation of social action. Its form was the re-creation and rigorous use of what I call the "Universal Action Schema." A number of writers, among whom I was to be numbered, rediscovered in the late 1950s what George Homans called the oldest social science theory— that is, exchange theory—and some tried to use it to explain larger structures. At about the same time, some economists led by Gary Becker began to move from standard market phenomena to use the econometric scheme to explain many nonmarket processes, such as the use of time, racial discrimination, crime, the family, and so on.[11] Thus much theorizing in social psychology and sociology evolved a type of individual action schema, moving toward some type of economic approach, while economics has been converging with this movement by applying its view to more sociological questions. Then the problem arises as to how and whether that step from micro to macro can be accomplished along this road.

These schema of social action often use different terms, but their elements are similar, and as we shall see that is so for a very good reason. In social action there are only two types of control. Either we get others to want to do something as a pleasure in itself, or as a good in itself even though not very pleasurable; or we get them to do something by altering the balance of valued or disvalued alternatives, that is, through the threatened loss or possible gain of respect, affection, money and goods, or force and force-threat. Thus we get them to see that their better alternative is what we want them to do.

All that has been stated is a variety of formulas that essentially asserted Actor X will do Y, that is, what he or she wants, unless deflected from it by a set of social forces (internal or external) that press X to do otherwise. Obviously that is so for other animals as well. It is almost so for physical objects and forces as well, the difference being that in the physical world such phenomena or things do not themselves, at least so we suppose, much care what they do. (Their lives are doubtless as a result much simpler than ours.)

Whether we couch this Universal Action Schema in the language of dependence theory, exchange theory, Subjective Expected Utility, the comparison of alternatives, marginal utility, or individual voluntaristic choice, it has to be correct. It is not a postulate or even a hypothesis. It is a nonfalsifiable circularity; and we cannot think of ways of disproving it. If Actor X protests he did not want to do it, we can say that is irrelevant because that was his choice, at least among the available alternatives.

Since people do try to choose their better alternatives, and are better off than they would have been had they chosen otherwise, the larger system is supported. Clearly, then, all that we have to do in our analysis is to find out what people want, and the influencing power of the factors that affect them, and we can thereupon easily predict what they and the larger system will do. We would then possess a universal, overarching foolproof theory of social action. To be sure, there seems to be some difficulty in filling in the concrete or abstract factors that will be put in such formulas, but very likely such humdrum details only await careful research on this matter.

The reader who has little faith in such aspirations, and detects an ironic tone in my statements, may agree with me that working at sociology sometimes appears to be a dedication to unraveling life and choice in a continuing quandary. However, that brief analysis of an intellectual approach informs us that what distinguishes economics and sociology is not the use of some form of rational self-interest. A glance at our propositions and findings in sociology will prove that we constantly show how people seek what they want as sensibly as they can.

Manifestly we all make grotesquely erroneous choices at times, but we would have acted differently if we had truly known what would take place. As Herbert Simon (1978, p. 104) comments, "Almost all human behavior has a large rational component." Economics has created a powerful engine for generating hypotheses by simply omitting the social structure as well as the moral order we sociologists think are inherent in all social action. That omission means that its applicability to the real world is severely limited. Its cases are highly specialized, for the market model is only one subtype of social exchange and social action.[12]

Any basic action schema we evolve cannot be as barren as it often is in social exchange theory and as it typically is in economic theorizing. To emphasize this point, let me first note four broad criticisms of the economic approach that make it less than adequate as a model for our own thinking, and then I shall simply list about a dozen specific failures in it that implicitly suggest how different our own basic schema of action must be, from which we might move on to interpret or construct theories of the larger order.

First, the economic actor is fundamentally alone and his or her actions are not shaped by his social relations with others, for the actor is indifferent both to other individuals and to the larger order, being concerned only with his or her own needs. As I have pointed out in great detail elsewhere, this is at a polar opposite from the processes of control in the realm of esteem and prestige (Goode, 1978, Chaps. 1-3). The economic actor cares not at all about others' responses in and of themselves, but only as they will be useful to his or her wants.

In a modern case of economic nonmarket analysis, Gary Becker makes altruism no more than our emotional identification with the person receiving what we give. In that sense, we are still self-seeking because we are really doing something for ourselves. In more technical language, our utility function depends positively on the well-being of others (Becker, 1981, pp. 173-174, and more generally Chap. 8). Or, "The altruist maximizes his own utility." This is a daring extension of meaning, to which one is tempted to respond with the words of two analysts of "perfect beneficence": "Under this stretched notion of utility, martyrdom becomes just another form of hedonism" (Busching and Milner, 1982, pp. 857-869).

As a second broad difference, economics proceeds from the individual to the whole directly, and mostly does that by simple aggregation. The acts of buyer or seller, being unaffected by social structures, can simply be summed up. Economics asks how individual rational self-interested decisions contribute to the whole; sociology is more likely to ask whether the larger order contributes to the individual, and in any event continues to try to state what those links are.

Third, economics insists that we can monetize nonmarket variables, and focus on the contribution to the aggregate, without considering any inherent moral elements. This insistence may stimulate us to consider what a pure market might be without those elements. We might, for example, decide that we can buy the Rumford Medal or the Nobel Prize, though we have pointed out elsewhere that one cannot buy prestige or esteem directly for many reasons, among them being the fact that the person who might be bribed to give a corrupt decision cannot in fact dictate his or her own response of respect. After all, the seller cannot believe in the esteem so purchased because generally people cannot make themselves feel admiration.

Nor can one simply buy love directly, though some do of course pay so much for a kiss, an embrace, and so on. Here too, the person receiving the money cannot make him- or herself actually feel that love. We can go still further, and think of bribery as a perfectly normal part of the market, as indeed it is in some less developed countries, and at various points in our own system. We might bribe the jewelry salesman to reduce our price, for example.

Or we might go still further and note that in a really free market one might be able to buy a murder or two, some amount of race discrimination or slavery, a child, adultery, and so on. One might still attempt to apply Coase's Theorem, and suggest that perhaps total productivity would then be greater.[13] Without moral rules, and only the market, one could buy injuries, and presumably there would be a different price for each kind of injury, set by the normal equilibristic processes with respect to supply and demand. It would, for example, cost us more to purchase harm done to a U.S. senator than to a corner grocer.

Immediately, however, we recognize that our case is already impossible, even hypothetically, because we then would also have to have a legal or moral rule that forbids us such injuries unless they are preceded and authorized by free negotiations and by an agreement on price. A person would not be permitted to kill another, or set fire to another's house, or capture another person for slavery, unless the other has agreed to the market price. Moreover our hypothetical victim would have no right to retaliate by force on his or her own, for example, by killing the person who wants to buy injury or murder. But that requirement too is a legal or moral rule, which must be backed by force or threat, by penalties, and so on.

Thus even the hypothetically pure free market cannot exist without an independent set of moral and/or nonmarket rules to keep it intact, and it cannot rest on money alone. That is, the purely free market without the moral rules does not create enough social order even to be self-sustaining. Even a good computer model has to meet that criterion, because the real world does.

A fourth broad difference is found in the historical irony that economics, aiming at being a science (Bell, 1981, pp. 48 ff.), long ago chose to be rigorous and mathematical, but developed little taste for the reality of the world that might test that rational view. By contrast, sociology has given great weight to the nonrational and to rather loose bodies and nodules of theory, but has remained hopelessly, stubbornly addicted to testing its conclusions in the real world. Thus its hypotheses and its theories are likely to be rather messy, much like real social life.

Moving from such broad differences to the following list of about a dozen criticisms against economic theorizing suggests why in our search for the links between individual choice and the social order we cannot simply borrow the basic mode of economic thinking, which surely is the only alternative to sociology.

First a substantial psychological challenge to the specific economic definition of rationality has been mounted by many people, notably Tversky, Kahneman, Holler, and others. This work is often experimental. It reports, for example, that even third- and fourth-year economics students in the United States and Germany do not come to the rational conclusions found in textbooks; that people have many psychological mechanisms for discounting, in the face of real data, the risks of floods or earthquakes. Cognitive dissonance theory suggests that rather than following an economic pattern of rationality, people may decide that what they have just been buying or doing is more rational (Tversky and Kahneman, 1981, pp. 453-458; 1984, pp. 1124-1131; Holler, 1983, pp. 623-630; Akerlof and Dickens, 1982, pp. 307-319; Simon, 1978, pp. 1-4).

Much of this can be called psychological revisionism, an attempt to show that the actual pattern of psychological choice is different from that in economic analysis. Beyond that it can be shown that in an imperfect market, with rational competitors, there may be no equilibristic solution; that the scarcity of attention itself may shape the decision (Simon, 1978, p. 13); that the complexity of the situation may be too great to permit rational search procedures; and so on.

Granovetter has mounted a sustained sociological attack by noting the absence in economic analysis of the particular history of individuals, whether these are firms or persons; and he has especially noted the absence of networks, a lack that Coleman has also emphasized (Granovetter, 1983a; Coleman, 1984b, pp. 84-88). It is clear, for example, that social networks in the organization will affect search procedures, labor turnover, job search, promotion, and mobility. They lower competition within the firm among workers as well as among subunits of the firm. Granovetter also criticizes the new institutional economics for following a rather out-of-date economic functionalism that proves that whatever is, is ultimately rational. He notes that social networks shape how the various effects of decisions are channeled so that they have different consequences for different sets of employees or different parts of the firm, and none of this is embodied in a marginal utility approach.

He and others also note the importance of trust and esteem processes that affect whether and how business agreements are carried out, and the extent to which the production of services and commodities will be done within the firm or bought outside it. Stinchcombe (1984) has brought together an impressive body of analysis and data to show that the received economic theory of the choice between in-house and contracting out patterns among companies does not fit reality. In this connection, Bell (1981, pp. 72 ff.) has also remarked that marginal utility does not explain wage stickiness.

A more adequate empirical analysis of real economic behavior would require, as Granovetter remarks, more information about power in the market, outside the firm; and more data about social relations within the firm.

Recent experimental data also seem to prove that over a succession of trials with the Prisoners' Dilemma, people who want to win, even at the expense of opponents, and even in competition with others who attempt various strategies of defection and betrayal, will do better than others if they cooperate; or, "nice" rules pay off better[14] just as selfish freeriding is actually less than predicted. Many analysts have pointed out the existence of "flex price" and fixed price subsystems in the economy, which of course could not occur if in fact it were following the rules of self-interested, marginal utility maximization. Each of these dozen or so criticisms is backed by research data.

Conclusion

It is very likely that many of you have made such criticisms yourselves, and have noted that economists do not seem to listen to them. It should be pointed out, however, that it is not only sociologists who make those criticisms. Almost all of them can be found to some extent in the very large critical literature written by economists themselves, some of it written by Kenneth Arrow, Wassily Leontief, Herbert Simon, and by the Hungarian economist Janos Kornai (Kornai, 1971; Arrow, 1974; Shubik, 1970, pp. 405-434; Leijonhu, 1973, pp. 327-337). As Kornai (1971, p. 17) comments, himself a mathematical economist, "Equilibrium theory is merely an intellectual experiment" and it is not a science. Indeed, many of the sneering jokes that sociologists make about economics in their cocktail conversation are duplicates of jokes that economists make to one another, with a more forbearing tone to be sure.[15] I do believe, on the other hand, that the amount of such criticism has increased from both sides, and it is at least possible that some changes are in the offing (for example, an association of "empirical" economists has been formed.)

On the other hand, we cannot wait for that integration of a sociological orientation into standard thinking within economics. Our own forward step must be independent, in part because the factors that we have been noting as being necessary for future theorizing have long been part of the sociologist's intellectual baggage. Perhaps no one is master of it, but we know it better than anyone else. If we turn away from the deficiencies in that approach, and instead build into our basic schema of action itself the variables and factors that economics leaves out, we shall have a richer body of hypotheses for both the micro- and the macrolevels.

It may be objected that thereupon we shall be bypassing our fifth version of the social order problem. For instead of trying to construct the macro from the micro through a suitable transformation model, we would then be reintroducing into the microschema the very social structures and moral order that version aims at constructing at the macro level. I do not wish to defend this solution with great vigor, but I see two justifications for it.

One is that in reality a major part of the forces bearing on individual choice and action does occur within such a social structure, not in an anonymous market made up of people without ties to one another; and those forces are external pressures from networks, structures, groups, and institutions as well as internal feelings, norms, evaluations, or values that arise through socialization and resocialization. Thus they are intrinsically and realistically a necessary part of that basic schema.

The second reason is somewhat more abstract. The relationships we frame as hypotheses at the microlevel describe the processes that are the inputs to the larger system, and ultimately constitute it. We properly build into those microhypotheses the inputs from the macro too, because that is where they come from, in this or any other system.

It is not likely that we can simply make transformation rules for that set of inputs and outputs, for that requires that we know more than we do now, a much more sophisticated level of mastery than we have yet achieved. However, we can at least be more alert to that part of the microprocesses that seem to act as its outputs to the macrolevel and vice versa. To be sure, we do not now have a technique for making that separation, that distinction, but we can perceive at least their general interaction with one another, and possibly work out better techniques for measuring those flows across the boundaries of different social units and orderly relationships.

This analysis has been an exploration, a journey rather than an arrival, but the intricacies of our problem justify our concern with laying out in an orderly fashion a set of theoretical approaches that will continue to challenge our individual and collective creativity in the years to come. Although I came reluctantly to agree with the accusations of one of our then younger sociologists many years ago who charged sociology with being the "littlest science," I do not think we have to give up all of our grand aspirations just yet. And I trust that if I myself cannot solve this problem now, I am a member of one higher social order, made up of my fellow sociologists, that will have a better chance of coming to valid conclusions about the problem than has any other group of scholars. Our findings may be somewhat less than elegant, and so doubtless is life, but if there is order in it, I think we shall eventually find it.

Notes

1. For a brief biographical account of the major group of experimenters on this topic, the Gestalt psychologists, see Coser (1984, pp. 22-46).

2. For various experiments designed in part to counter people's usual assumptions about social meaning, see the accounts in Garfinkel (1967), McHugh (1968), Blum and McHugh (1979), and Sudnow (1972).

3. For a review of some of the principal issues raised by structuralism in its many forms, see Kurzweil (1980) and DeGeorge (1972). Critical theory too has criticized the scientific assumptions of mainstream sociology. See Van den Berg (1980, pp. 449-478), Schroyer (1973), and Horkheimer (1974).

4. Thus with reference to one type of order or system: "Crystallography and structural chemistry [have grown from] observed regularities in the real physical structure of the objects observed. For example, the actual spacing of atoms in different rows and planes of a crystalline

compound determines many of its physical and chemical properties, such as light transmission, elasticity, or how it reacts with other compounds" (Goode, 1975, p. 73).

5. One might suppose nevertheless that revolts, riots, sabotage, and flight do at least suggest discontent, and the historical literature is replete with such events. The modern research of especially Charles Tilly and Ted Gurr has attempted to collect, classify, and analyze riots, overt conflicts, and rebellions of both urban and rural groups. See Moore (1966, pp. 256-257, 332, 335, 497-501, passim) as well as Skocpol (1979) and Paige (1975). For analysis of the reasons why peasants have been less than likely to accept the justice of their systems, see Popkin (1979).

6. Thus, on this important point, I disagree with George C. Homans's (1974, p. 263) assertion that "any distribution of reward, however unjust it may have appeared at one time, that does in fact persist long enough—but how long is that?—to become the expected thing will also become the just thing and cease to arouse resentment."

7. For the opinions of these rebels, see Hilton (1973). See also Scott (1977, pp. 1-38, pp. 211-246). The literature on this point is now very large.

8. One strong voice in sociology has denied the Durkheimian position. See Homans (1974, pp. 12-13, 1964, pp. 817-818, 1975, p. 640). In addition, many expositors of exchange theory have implicitly done so, suggesting that individual self-interest may be enough to account for social behavior.

9. To be sure, rulers often conflated the interests of society and their own interests, and rationalized their self-concern by supposing that was identical to the larger concern of the society.

10. "The elimination of the normative aspect of action altogether eliminates the conception itself" (see David Hume, Concerning the Principles of Morals, Appendix I). We take it as a truism, expressed at least as early as Hume, that when we ask anyone why he or she did something, even if the first answer seems instrumental or rational, the repetition of that question always leads back to an ultimate value or a nonrational goal or standard; see Parsons (1937, p. 732).

11. By now this literature is large. Perhaps the most recent controversial monograph is by Becker (1981). In this connection, the collection edited by Theodore Schultz (1973) offers a wide range of researches. Note also Becker's original work on time (1965, pp. 493-517) and on discrimination (1971).

12. For several empirical and theoretical comments on this, see Goode (1978, pp. 13-15, 28-29, 39-40, Chap. 3).

13. Many economists have utilized Coase's thought, among them especially Becker. See Coase (1960).

14. For a startling series of "experiments" on these matters, see Axelrod (1984).

15. For further comments on such jokes and their meaning, see McCloskey (1984, pp. I, 6-7, 12-13, 19, passim).

References

Alexander, J. C. 1982. Theoretical Logic in Sociology, Vol. II, The Antinomies of Classical Thought: Marx and Durkheim. Berkeley: University of California Press.

Akerlof, G. A. and W. T. Dickens. 1982. The Economic Consequence of Cognitive Dissonance. Institute of Industrial Relations, Reprint No. 451. University of California, Berkeley.

Arrow, K. 1974. The Limits of Organization. New York: Norton.

Axelrod, R. M. 1984. Evolution of Cooperation. New York: Basic Books.

Becker, G. 1965. "A Theory of the Allocation of Time." Economic Journal 75: 493-517.

Becker, G. 1971. The Economics of Discrimination. Chicago: University of Chicago.

Becker, G. 1981. A Treatise on the Family. Cambridge, MA: Harvard University Press.

Bell, D. 1981. "Models and Reality in Economic Discourse." Pp. 48 ff. in The Crisis in Economic Theory. Edited by D. Bell and I. Kristol. New York: Basic Books.

Blum, A. and P. McHugh (Eds.) 1979. Friends, Enemies and Strangers: Theorizing in Art and Everyday Life. Norwood, NJ: Ablex.

Busching, B. and M. Milner. 1982. "Limiting Case Models in Behavioral Sciences: Perfect Competition, Perfect Benevolence, and Perfect Malevolence." *Human Relations* 35: 857-869.

Coase, R. H. 1960. "The Problems of Social Cost." *Journal of Law and Economics* 3: 1-44.

Coleman, J. S. 1984a. *Microfoundations and Macro Social Behavior.* Chicago: University of Chicago. (mimeo)

Coleman, J. S. 1984b. "Introducing Social Structure into Economic Analysis." *American Economic Review* 74: 2.

Coser, A. A. 1984. *Refugee Scholars in America.* New Haven, CT: Yale University Press.

DeGeorge, R. T. (Ed.) 1972. *The Structuralists: From Marx to Levi-Strauss.* Garden City, NJ: Anchor.

Garfinkel, H. 1967. *Studies in Ethnomethodology.* Englewood Cliffs, NJ: Prentice Hall.

Goode, W. J. 1972. "The Place of Force in Human Society." *American Sociological Review* 37: 507-519.

Goode, W. J. 1975. "Homans' and Merton's Structural Approach." In *Approaches to the Study of Social Structure.* Edited by P. M. Blau. New York: Free Press.

Goode, W. J. 1978. *The Celebration of Heroes.* Berkeley: University of California Press.

Granovetter, M. 1983a. *Economic Action and Social Structure: A Theory of Embeddedness.* State University of New York, Stony Brook. (mimeo)

Granovetter, M. 1983b. *Labor Mobility, Internal Markets and Job-Matching: A Comparison of the Sociological and Economic Approaches.* State University of New York, Stony Brook. (mimeo)

Hilton, R. 1973. *Bondmen Made Free.* New York: Viking.

Holler, M. J. 1983. "Do Economics Students Choose Rationally? A Research Note." *Social Science Information* 22: 623-630.

Homans, G. C. 1964. "Bringing Men Back In." *American Sociological Review* 29.

Homans, G. C. 1974. *Social Behavior.* New York: Harcourt Brace Jovanovich.

Homans, G. C. 1975. "What Do We Mean by Social Structure." In *Approaches to the Study of Social Structure.* Edited by P. M. Blau. New York: Free Press.

Horkheimer, M. (Ed.) 1974. *Essays in Critical Theory: Critique of Instrumental Reason.* New York: Seabury.

Kornai, J. 1971. *Anti-Equilibrium.* Amsterdam: North-Holland.

Kurzweil, E. 1980. *The Age of Structuralism.* New York: Columbia University Press.

Leijonhu, A. 1973. "Life Among the Econ." *Western Economic Journal* 11: 327-337.

McCloskey, D. N. 1984. *The Rhetoric of Economics: A Preface to Rhetoric of Inquiry.* Iowa City: University of Iowa. (mimeo)

McHugh, P. 1968. *Defining the Situation.* New York: Bobbs-Merrill.

Moore, B. 1966. *Social Origins of Dictatorship and Democracy.* Boston: Beacon Press.

Paige, J. 1975. *Agrarian Revolution: Social Movements and Export Agriculture in the Underdeveloped World.* New York: Free Press.

Parsons, T. 1937. *The Structure of Social Action.* New York: McGraw Hill.

Popkin, S. 1979. *The Rational Peasant: the Political Economy of Rural Society in Viet Nam.* Berkeley: University of California Press.

Pynchon, T. 1968. *V.* New York: Bantam.

Schroyer, T. 1973. *The Critique of Domination: The Origins and Development of Critical Theory.* Boston: Beacon.

Schultz, T. (Ed.) 1973. *Economics of the Family.* Chicago: University of Chicago Press.

Scott, J. 1977. "Protest and Profanation: Agrarian Revolt and the Little Tradition." *Theory and Society,* 4, 1, Part 1: 1-38; 4, 2, Part 2: 211-246.

Shubik, M. 1970. "A Curmudgeon's Guide to Micro Economics." *Journal of Economic Literature* 8: 405-434.

Skocpol, T. 1979. *States and Social Revolutions: A Comparative Analysis of France, Russia, and China.* New York: Cambridge University Press.

Simon, H. 1978. "Rationality as Process and as Product of Thought. American Economic Association: Papers and Proceedings of the Ninetieth Annual Meeting." *American Economic Review* 68: 1-16.

Stinchombe, A. L. 1984. *Contracts as Hierarchical Documents.* Work Report No. 65. Institute of Industrial Economics, Bergen, Norway.

Sudnow, D. (Ed.) 1972. *Studies in Social Interaction.* New York: Free Press.

Tversky, A. and D. Kahneman. 1981. "The Framing of Decisions and the Psychology of Choice." *Science* 211: 453-458.

Tversky, A. and D. Kahneman. 1984. "Judgment Under Uncertainty: Heuristics and Biases." *Science* 185: 1124-1131.

Van den Berg, A. 1980. "Critical Theory: Is There Still Hope?" *American Journal of Sociology* 86: 449-478.

Weber, M. 1954. *Max Weber on Law in Economy and Society: Edited with Introduction and Annotations by Max Rheinstein.* Translated by M. Rheinstein and E. Shils from Weber's *Wirtschaft and Gessellschaft.* Cambridge: Harvard University Press. (pub. orig. 1925)

Weber, M. 1978. *Economy and Society.* Edited by G. Roth and C. Wittich. Berkeley: University of California Press. (pub. orig. 1924)

Wrong, D. 1984. "Hobbes, Darwinism, and the Problem of Order." In *Conflict and Consensus.* Edited by W. Powell and R. Robins. New York: Free Press.

4

Institutionalized
Public Memory

Mary Douglas

THIS VOLUME INVITES US to think about social order. The idea of social order makes sense. Its possibility is not in doubt. We have often seen and felt it. What is in doubt is the possibility of ever having a thought about social order that is not a direct expression of our experience of a particular social form. Special discipline and contrivance would be needed if we were to think in an independent and sustained way on that subject. For thought depends on the social order. Thought arises out of it, constitutes it, is constrained by it. To expect independent thought on that subject borders on absurdity.

The social order is lived. Thinking about it is the main part of living it. We all accept the impossibility of reason inspecting the conditions for its own functioning. It is one thing to test the link in a chain of logic. It is quite another to examine critically the categories on which the logical operations are being performed. Are they exhaustive? Are they the right ones? What does rightness of categories mean? Apart from the categories we have put into the analysis, what of those we have left out? Some, deliberately discarded as wrong, some, merely overlooked? Thinking about the possibility of social order entails thinking about orders that conceivably could have but did not come into being, and understanding why some never could have existed.

I plan to solve this problem by following Robert Merton's advice. This means following the crowd, for we all do well who take his tips. I am not the first to be interested in his identification, years ago, of a strategic area for research (Merton, 1957, 1962, 1963, 1965). I refer to his discussion of "Priorities in Scientific Discovery," his 1962, "Singletons and Multiples in Scientific Discovery," and the 1963 "Resistance to the Study of Multiple Discoveries in Science." He has elaborated further the pointlessness of asking who said a thing first in a long ironic essay, *On the Shoulders of Giants*. Merton himself, so far from claiming priority, noted that Francis Bacon 350 years ago sketched the outline of a hypothesis to account for the multiple and independent rediscoveries of an idea. The question is why the same fact with its associated hypotheses remains for decades and centuries "in a static condition, as though it were permanently condemned to repetition without extension" (Merton, 1965). I am today going to take seriously Robert Merton's advice that rediscoveries provide a strategic research site for studying resistance to ideas.

To recapitulate briefly, Merton gives a sociological explanation of a recurring blind spot. The star scientists who deny a convergent or earlier discovery are driven by their passions and their passions are driven by the way that science is organized. He links emotion, cognition, and social structure into one system. In science, the big rewards go to accredited innovation. The concept of original discovery is embedded in all the forms of institutional life, along with prizes and naming of facts after scientists. The interpersonal relations of scientists are governed by an institutionalized competition in which everyone loses something: otherwise magnanimous scholars are belittled by their own destructive anger when they learn of a competitor to their claim to be first; they are baffled to meet untruths to which they have consented; the profession loses from practices of secrecy that contradict intellectual openness; science policy is misled by the fallacy of wasteful duplication. Standing coolly outside the rivalry, Merton shows how a distinctive social order generates its pattern of values, commits the hearts of its members, and creates a myopia that certainly seems to be inevitable.

The analysis is relevant to our dilemma. Because he is not in their social order, Merton can think thoughts about it that are impossible for insiders. How could those scientists give credit to the idea of multiple discoveries? Even when told about them, how could they ever keep them in mind? Their thoughts are held in the grip of their social order as ours are held in our own. They cannot reflect calmly upon it, nor can we. Perhaps we could find a way of standing aside from our society by developing Merton's little cybernetic model into a big one, with several compartments each dealing with the passions that are inherent in different forms of social organization and analyzing the control that socially reinforced motivations have upon the vision of individuals.

Note that Merton has made a back door approach to the problem. He is not asking, "How do people think about the social order?" He asks, "How are they prevented from thinking? What are the impossible thoughts?" He shows what thoughts are discarded by the system. This is another clue to how we might do well to proceed. I like back door approaches to difficult questions. They can be formulated in a way that escapes the self-referencing dilemma. Ask people what foods they eat and they will answer what they think you think they ought to eat. A team of Arizona anthropologists once imitated archaeologists by getting their information from domestic garbage heaps (Harrison and Rathje, n.d.). The food rejects tell more surely about the diet than answers to questionnaires. The theory of social deviance is another kind of back door approach to cognitive sociology. I myself used a back door approach to social values. Too much interpretation can be put upon positive statements about what behavior is most honored. A sociological theory of cultural value must remain elusive. Much clearer evidence comes from studying aversion. The rules for avoiding reprehensible behavior, punishing and purifying after disapproved contact, are more clearly known and easier to elicit. A sociological theory of disgust can be more securely based than a sociological theory of value (Douglas, 1966). Likewise for our problem. The thinkability of the social order is beset with infinite regress. Merton's example invites us to focus on unthinkables and unmemorables in a system.

In themselves the multiple discoveries are not so interesting. They are only important as an instance of socially structured forgetting. Let us focus on the process of forgetting and let us distance ourselves by using anthropological examples, of which there are many. The topic of structural amnesia arrived in British social anthropology in 1940 with the publication of Evans-Prichard's (1940) book , The Nuer. The fieldwork on which it was based belongs to the early 1930s. Both Merton and his precursor were alerted to the relation between the social order and thinking about the social order by the French school of *L'année Sociologique* and particularly by Halbwachs's work on collective memory. Of course, Marx and Hegel were there before. However there are several differences between anthropologists and sociologists. Anthropologists ask different questions and make different assumptions. For one thing, we do not ask, "Why do they keep forgetting?" (which is roughly Merton's question about the scientists).

For us, traditionally, the wonder has been that people with only clubs and spears for weapons ever remember anything at all. Anthropology has inherited an ancient criterion of intellectual advancement, based on technology. It is not such a bad criterion. There are engineering achievements that could not be performed before differential calculus was invented, administrative triumphs that depend on double entry bookkeeping. Some basic techniques of discrimination, calculation, and holding in memory may be prerequisite for any particular form of knowledge. Anthropologists have always paid attention to the available counting skills. They have been specially fascinated by people who seem to do well without being able to count beyond three. Early psychologists were very interested in feats of memory that could be performed by people enjoying only a low level of technical competence. It was generally thought that rote learning was the secret.

The Nuer can generally recall nine to eleven generations of their ancestors. How do they remember all that? Closer study shows that they forget more than they remember. Their personal genealogies claim to run back to the beginning of time, but eleven generations do not cover even their history in the region. A lot of forgetting has been going on. Despite the continual growth of new generations, the number of known progenitors stays constant. Somewhere along the line a lot of ancestors are being dropped off the list. Somewhere after the tribal founder and his two sons and his four grandsons and his eight great grandsons, the tribal memory has developed a yawning hole, and multiple ancestors are tumbling into it. They are not being forgotten randomly. Just as with our modern scientists who remember so much but cannot remember the fact of multiple past discoveries, the strengths and weaknesses of recall depend on a mnemonic system that is the social order. If it were appropriate to make such claims, I would like to say that the Nuer study was the first fully explicit analysis of an idea that was in the air.

A second difference in the approach of anthropology to this subject is a caution not to invoke a pathological state to explain forgetting. In 1957 Robert Merton explained the resistance to multiple discoveries as the normal response to a badly integrated institution. Using Freudian terms, he defined the resistance as motivated denial of an accessible but painful reality. In later writings, that part of the argument has been modified—correctly, I think.[1]

The career of a successful fact is explained by four principles. First, and foremost, a fact that is going to gain a permanent place in the public repertoire of what is known will need to interlock with the cognitive procedures that guarantee other kinds of facts. At the foundation of any large cognitive enterprise there are some basic formulae, equations in common use, and rules of thumb. In science such shared techniques of validating spread across different subdisciplines. For example, the mathematics of seepage is used in mineralogy and ophthalmology. The anchoring of a set of facts in one field imparts authority to a set elsewhere, anchored by the same procedures. This is just as true for social forms of validation as for scientific ones.

For example, the Nuer use one fundamental equation: 40 head of cattle ratify a marriage. If they wavered on that fixed amount, transactions based upon its rightness would have to be renegotiated. Graded on this basis, all other rights are computable. To reckon the right compensation for killing a man, the formula is extended: 1 woman and her progeny = 40 head of cattle = 1 man's life. Several legal fictions sprout from this basic formula. Under specified conditions, 1 woman = 1 man, so that a female link can be treated as a male one. Gaps and lumps in the genealogy are smoothed so that it presents an unbroken succession of males. A similar fiction allows a dead man to count as a legal father to a child begotten after his death. The rules of accounting allow flexibility without ambiguity or contradiction.

The first principle that the Nuer public memory illustrates is the power of interlocked formulae of ratification. The second is that the successful facts get their longevity from their service in promoting private claims. A few accepted procedures control a society's knowledge of its own past. Nuer marriages are nodal points in a regular pattern of exchange that sorts and collapses previous claims into an intelligible form. There is an incentive to turn up at weddings and to work out in public one's precise relationships. A Nuer who goes to a wedding either expects to get a cow or will have contributed a cow. One who contributed to the groom's expenses will claim cows when his daughter gets married a generation later. One of the cattle distributed at a marriage is allocated to a relative connected at the fifth generation, after which no further claims are recognized. Weddings and cattle distributions order the memory of the past up to the father's father's father in all directions—an impressive feat of memory if one had to do it alone, but the repeated patterns give plenty of incentive not to forget. This is what I mean by saying that a set of facts, such as the names of my father's father's father, his sisters and brothers, and their offspring, will not be lost if they are worked into the strategies for validating private claims.

The third quality of a successful fact is that it can serve individual strategies to create a public good. Nuer memory of ancestors does that service too. The Nuer family depends on men for herding duties, women for dairying; it needs to belong to a village; the village needs to recruit men to conduct raids and to provide defense. Young men can only get the cattle they need to marry with if they can prove links to the right ancestor. They are compelled to make clear their group loyalty. Their political coalitions are based on the principle of descent from the four generations of the founding ancestor, his son, grandsons and great grandsons, each of whom founded a political unit. This level of their organization further prompts their memory of their ancestors. The top-down reckoning of political allegiance anchors the names of four to six remote generations. The strategies for individual claims anchor five proximate generations on a bottom-up reckoning. In-between there lies the open gap into which successive generations of ancestors keep disappearing. It is not merely that there is no special reason for remembering them. There is strong pressure against remembering them. The successful fact is predatory. Sheer consistency of use endows the well-tried formula with might and it will swallow up competitors if they do not join it.

The Nuer idea of ancestry has all three of these qualities. It also matches well with their political feeling. The Nuer are fiercely egalitarian, individualistic, and independent. The disappearing ancestor trick puts everyone on a par with everyone else. It suits them not to know more about individual past history. If the political system that suited them had been a hereditary chieftaincy, they would have remembered more ancestors, or rather, certain of them would have. Royalty needs long lineage to vindicate dynastic claims. Students of Evans-Pritchard developed the subject of institutionalized public memory by comparing social structures that could and could not sustain genealogical depth.[2] The most fascinating part of that research lays bare the procedures by which genealogical history is clipped and stretched and smoothed out. I would like to claim that body of work for the sociology of science, for it supports later work on textbook writing in science that follows Merton on self-fulfilling prophecies and Thomas Kuhn on normal science. For reasons that I am mustering now, there is a low probability of my getting you to remember my claim.

It will be easier to explain the import of this sociological research on mnemonic structures by leaving the Nuer example. Let us return to the physical scientists and their disbelief when confronted with convergent discoveries.

Robert Merton has shown how the strategies to validate scientists' claims use originality as a main criterion for prizes and positions. This immediately gives a major advantage to the originality idea and a disadvantage to the fact of rediscovery. What seems dysfunctional when enraged scientists make a public display of their vanity may be counted as the cost of keeping the race open to the swift. Competition is always costly in human terms. In respect of serving to build up collective benefits for science, rediscovery has no strong qualification for being remembered. Robert Merton did not mention its failure to latch on to an accepted cognitive infrastructure. As Bernard Barber (1961) could have emphasized more than he did in his article on scientific discovery, many of the cases in which a new scientific discovery has been rejected and left to lie inert until a later rediscovery are precisely cases that lacked formulaic interlocking with accepted procedure of validation. It appears that the fact of mulitple discoveries also misses out on this third qualification for success. And it misses out on political feeling as well. Competitive social systems are weaker on memory than ascriptive ones.[3]

Forgotten ancestors and forgotten scientific discoveries are in the same case. None of them passes the four tests of a successful fact. Scientific precursors disappear from view because they never had an earthly chance of making their way to the surface of public memory. Forgotten discoveries are a lot of facts that failed. It ought to be useful to know the pattern of failure in advance, before we ourselves get committed to a hopelessly unfashionable fact.

We have been examining the accessibility of the social order to the thought of persons living in remote societies. Physical scientists are almost as remote as Nilotic pastoralists. I will now bring the question closer by turning to some precursors of Merton's structural analysis of forgetting. Psychologists are apparently incapable of remembering what they discover intermittently about humans as social beings. They often remind one another of how artificial the parameters are that they have set around their subject matter. Famous psychologists keep upbraiding their fellows for despising or ignoring institutional factors in cognition. The literature of the social sciences is sprinkled with rediscoveries of that idea. I pick on a few to illustrate the case.

Leon Festinger wrote in 1948 on the relation between the spread of information and the degree of integration in a group. The measure of integration has not become a successful fact. What Festinger said seemed to be true nearly 30 years later when James Coleman rescued the lost idea. Festinger had said, "There would seem to be a sufficient accumulation of studies to show that social relationships are important factors in the flow of information, but very little evidence on what kinds of social relationships make what kinds of differences" (Coleman et al., 1977). There is the nub of it: No systematic synthesizing theory has been developed.

More recently, J.M.F. Jaspers (1981) writes about the use made in cognitive psychology of the concept of attitudes. He discovers that the social nature of "attitudes" has been completely overlooked. He traces the current increase of dissatisfaction with attitude research:

> We have lost sight of the collective nature of attitudes because attitudes have been impounded by social psychology and made into individual response dispositions of an evaluative nature. . . . Recent developments in attitude research and scaling techniques have led to a complete individualization of the study of attitude.

There must be hundreds more of such isolated complaints, insights, and independent discoveries. They have been doomed. I sense very strongly the rightness of Donald Campbell's diagnosis. There is a professional dislike of control models that inevitably smack of social engineering, sociological determinism, and Big Brother's 1984 apotheosis. In 1975 Donald Campbell put his finger on the spot. Psychologists, he said, are so committed to the assumption that individual psychic development is restricted by social conventions that they see all conventional and institutional constraints as wrongful. He makes the psychologists sound like a romantic band of knights errant seeking to deliver the weak and infirm from the claims imposed by life and society. The idea that stabilizing factors could be useful for cognitive and emotional development is unthinkable. He says in so many words that it is professionally impossible in psychology to establish the notion that institutional constraints can be beneficial to the individual. The notion can be scouted, but it cannot enter the memorable corpus of facts. To counteract this bias, he strongly recommended that institutional sources of stability be given priority in research. But then he proved his point by instantly forgetting his good advice. Now he is seeking stabilizing factors in our biological makeup. However, his finger is pointing to the one idea we need to exploit to understand why knowledge of our knowledge of the social order is so elusive. His case suggests that it is an inherently unstable idea and we should surely expect as much. We could start by going more deeply into the sources of its weaknesses.

Let us see what we can learn from the life work of a very distinguished precursor who was strongly committed to that very idea. Frederick Bartlett was born in 1886, became director of the Cambridge Psychology Laboratory, and was long-time editor of the *British Journal of Psychology*. His research and teaching successfully established a major insight—the importance of selective and constructive elements in human awareness—but that was only half of what he set out to do.

When Bartlett first went to St. John's College, W.H.R. Rivers was there, a very influential anthropologist, physiologist, and psychologist. Rivers had been editor of the *British Journal of Psychology* from 1904-1913. Earlier, he had been a member of the great Cambridge Expedition to the Torres Straits, 1898, one among other famous psychologists and doctors, C. S. Myers, McDougall, and C. S. Seligman. The object of the expedition was to base a many-fronted evolutionary study of human cognition on the population of Melanesia. The team was led by A. C. Haddon, originally a marine biologist, now Melanesian ethnologist and specialist on the evolution of primitive art (Haddon, 1895).

Bartlett always claimed his own research to have been deeply influenced by Rivers and Haddon, two anthropologists. From Rivers he adopted the idea that individual emotions and cognition are institutionalized in social forms. From Haddon's work on Melanesian art he adopted the idea that an experimental study of cognition should focus on the process of standardization or conventionalization. In 1913 he was actually under contract to the Cambridge University Press to write a book on conventionalization. I maintain that both these intentions were doomed from the outset.

I may need to work hard to convince you that this established psychologist was ever looking for a sociological theory of perception. Most of the evidence depends on the use made by Bartlett of Rivers's (1920) *Instinct and the Unconscious*. In an appendix added in 1922 Rivers adapted Freud's conception of censorship to both the nervous system and the social system, all within an evolutionary framework. He taught that each was arranged so "far as function is concerned, in a number of levels, one above the other, forming a hierarchy in which each level controls those beneath it and is itself controlled by those above." The life history of a human psyche Rivers assumed to be the growth of a similar hierarchy of controls over unconscious experience. Hysteria was to be explained by a process that puts the higher levels into abeyance and allows rein to the lower, instinctual levels. This is very close to the current model of growth to moral maturity still credited in developmental psychology. But Rivers's strength was that he tried to add the social dimension: He held that in every form of human society higher ranks control the lower and inhibit or suppress activities belonging to earlier phases of culture.

This is a cybernetic idea of the relation between psyche and society. As a political model, it is admittedly conservative. There is no necessity to place so much value on strength of the controls. When Bartlett (1927) wrote *Psychology and the Soldier*, he based it on Rivers's *Instinct and the Unconscious* and used Rivers's main terms: instincts, group tendencies, and inhibitory mechanisms. He was reaching toward a feedback theory of the relation between individual cognition and society, in which the control by the higher orders was democratized.

> In the nature of the society there is something that predisposes the individuals concerned to accept and act upon hints and half expressed views and commands conveyed through other members of a group. There is thus facilitated a unity of thought, feeling and action which may run through a whole community [Bartlett, 1927].

In his earlier book, *Psychology and Primitive Culture*, Bartlett (1923) had taught emphatically that the individual is always a social individual and that social influences selectively control cognition and emotion. He was already drawing heavily on Rivers's work and comparing something he and Rivers called "primitive comradeship" and the collective conscience of the *L'année Sociologique* writers. He described how in primitive society conflict is averted by instituted separation and how curiosity is brought under institutional control.

One reason why this interest in the social order's control on thinking never became more than a speculation lies undoubtedly in certain current evolutionary assumptions. Both Bartlett and Rivers thought that social control of the free-ranging curiosity of individuals was stronger in primitive society. Their evolutionary theory, itself quite congenial to the period of colonial empire, made it self-evident to them that modern humanity had lost this sensitivity to group signals just as the human race in general has lost the sense of smell so useful in lower animal orders. Bartlett's (1932) account of memory among contemporary African peoples suggests a mysterious osmotic process unlike the pure ratiocination of moderns. Because this faculty was clearly in his opinion less well-adapted to modern life, he tacitly exonerated himself from trying to study it, though he continued to the end emphasizing the importance of social input to perception.

So much for Rivers's influence on this sociological interest. Now we turn to Haddon, the other anthropologist whom Bartlett specially acknowledged for his influence on the choice of research site. The power of cultural convention to control perception and recall was initially Bartlett's prime problem. Solving it would relate the perceptual processes of the individual to the individual's deepest emotions, which, according to Rivers, were determined by the form of institutions. Bartlett seems to have been on the verge of a nervous collapse trying to write his promised book on "Conventionalization." He had read all of the Gestalt work on memory and decided that the German psychologists could go no further along the route they were pursuing. He wanted to experiment on perception of a whole instead of experimenting on the faculty of memory exercised on jumbled nonsense parts. James Ward had advised him to research sequences of perceptions. But clearly he was stalled for a long time on an experimental design. In 1913, Norbert Wiener, than aged 19 with a Harvard Ph.D. in philosophy, came to Cambridge to work with Bertrand Russell. Bartlett confided his research block to the young man and Wiener suggested the experimental method that was to make Bartlett famous: the method of serial reproduction or "Russian scandal." The technique was to use perceptual sequences with some element missing from or added to a pattern and then to score how the observers "constructed a terminating design before they had reached it and reported having seen detail which in fact was not there" (Bartlett, 1958).

Bartlett's work was to continue in this line. He became a great designer of experiments. We can read how they became more and more strict, subtle, and amenable to objective scoring. The design of the research focused, true enough, on the process of conventionalization, but Rivers's original hypothesis could never be tested. Experimental stringency required the particular differences of emotional interest affecting each subject to be strictly excluded. The social dimensions of their experience were peeled away from the subjects. Broadbent (1970), who wrote the notice of Bartlett in the *Dictionary of National Biography*, recorded that Bartlett's special contribution to psychology was to show perception and remembering to be controlled by some process sensitive to the purposes and interest of the perceiver. But all of the ambitions Bartlett had earlier expressed about analyzing the selective process were frustrated.[4] His story is full of ironies. The expert on memory had himself managed to forget his own teachings. He who taught that intentions guide cognition forgot his own intentions. Looking for a cybernetic system, he had the extraordinary luck to meet the future inventor of cybernetics. Something was always happening to distract his vision. Those fragile good ideas fell plop into the waters of oblivion, waiting for the next phase in the cycle of rediscovery.

If we run his forgotten discovery through our four-fold prescription for a successful fact, we find it was wrecked on the first requirement. There was not and never has been since a way of latching that insight onto the accepted formulae of validation. The analytic tools that Rivers bequeathed to him were about as sharp as jelly. Those ideas of Bartlett that did succeed well exploited an existing set of tools. He would not have needed to change C. S. Myers's (1911) chapter on statistical method in *Textbook of Experimental Psychology* greatly. The analysis of variance, already powerful in other branches of psychology, demography, sociology, and economics, was there at hand and becoming increasingly sophisticated. One hard, sharp tool naturally wins against a softer one. One well-connected unifying method can drive out an idea that does not use its accredited formula. At a narrow professional level, Bartlett's contribution was completely positive. However, the loss of the initial insight about the social control of cognition has been counterproductive for our understanding of the social fabric.

At this point I know how good sociologists are going to react. First, you will be tempted to feel smug about the narrow perspectives of psychology. Then you will divide into two camps: Some will report that what I say is quite wrong, and others that it is true, well-known already, and too obvious to keep repeating. I must deal with both of these positions, mutually contradictory though they are.

Who would seriously maintain that it is wrong for sociology to try to develop a systematic approach to social factors influencing cognition? The assumptions that underpin our sociological theorizing impinge too heavily on this topic for it to be brushed aside as trivial. It seems fair enough for the applied disciplines, such as market research, to think from the seat of their pants about connections between attitudes and social pressures. It even seems fair enough for the economists to leave motivations to other specialists—but to whom, if not to the sociologists? Do I need to belabor the point that this is a socially structured forgetting?

I need more explicitly to address those who would maintain that I have overlooked a vast amount of work on the very subject that I maintain is neglected, that the problem is well known and that active steps are being taken to remedy it. Please tell me about this work. Spot-on research that connects one social factor to one kind of bias does not qualify. Nor does research that shows local blank spots in cognition without a sustained theoretical scheme. It is true that there is a lot of that kind of inquiry. I have also already met research that embarks on this very problem without identifying a bounded social system as Merton identified that of science and as anthropologists identify a tribal society. What I am describing as a failed fact connects the social order in a systematic way with the cognitive processes of its members.

I should pass in review the four qualities that enable speculation to become an established fact. Of these only the first seems to be of crucial importance. The interlocking methodology that holds clumps of scientific activity together is the one essential requirement. With this secure, all else will be added. Every time the sociological analysis of cognition has surfaced, it has failed to use the normal ratifying procedures, so no wonder it has been forgotten. If it were not for this, I might despair of the prospects for this important insight so central to anthropology dealing with exotic peoples, and so ignored by sociology dealing with ourselves. If it were not for this, I would be wasting your time on unmemorable memorabilia. All that is needed is a shift in the underlying technology of thinking about society. A precise tool for describing institutional structures has been lacking to match the precise psychological tools for assessing emotional and cognitive bias.

Notes

1. For a later account of the idea of dysfunction, see R. K. Merton (1975).

2. This section repeats much of what I have written in "Evans-Pritchard," (Fontana, *Great Masters*, 1980). The main references to this research tradition are listed there.

3. This is by definition.

4. In 1939 Bartlett edited a volume: *The Study of Society: Methodology and Problems*, (R.K.P.) in which anthropologists and sociologists again joined with psychologists. But it was not a bridge

successfully built between disciplines. When he considered how his life work could be carried on by younger psychologists, he looked with satisfaction to future achievements from J. Bruner and G. Humphrey; neither of them had shown signs of interest in the fact that Rivers had rediscovered and to which he, Bartlett, had committed much effort—the fact that individual cognition submits to institutional control.

References

Barber, B. 1961. "Resistance by Scientists to Scientific Discovery." *Science* 134: 596-602. (republished 1962 in *The Sociology of Science*)

Bartlett, F. C. 1923. *Psychology and Primitive Culture.* Cambridge: Cambridge University Press.

Bartlett, F. C. 1927. *Psychology and the Soldier.* Cambridge: Cambridge University Press.

Bartlett, F. C. 1932. *Remembering, An Experimental and Social Study.* Cambridge: Cambridge University Press.

Bartlett, F. C. 1958. *Thinking, An Experimental & Social Study.* New York: Basic Books.

Broadbent 1970. *Dictionary of National Biography, 1961-1970.* Oxford: Oxford University Press.

Campbell, D. 1975. "On the Conflicts Between Biological and Social Evolution and Between Psychology and Moral Tradition." *American Psychologist* 30: 1103-1126.

Coleman, J., E. Katz, and H. Menzel. 1977. "The Diffusion of an Innovation Among Physicians." *Sociometry* 20: 253-270. (republished, 1977, in Lienhardt, Samuel, *Social Networks, A Developing Paradigm.* New York: Academic Press).

Douglas, M. 1966. *Purity and Danger: An Analysis of Concepts of Pollution and Taboo.* London: Routledge & Kegan Paul.

Evans-Pritchard, E. E. 1940. *The Nuer, the Political Institutions of a Nilotic People.* Oxford: Clarendon.

Festinger, L., et al. 1948. "A Study of a Rumor: Its Origin and Spread." *Human Relations* I: 464-486.

Haddon, A. C. 1895. *Evolution in Art as Illustrated by the Life Histories of Designs.* London: AMS Press.

Harrison, G. and W. Rathje. n.d. "Monitoring Trends in Food Utilization: Application of an Archaeological Method." *Federation Proceedings* 37: 1. (Federation of American Societies for Experimental Biology).

Jaspers, J.M.F. and C. Fraser. 1981. "Attitudes & Social Representations." Chapter in *Social Representations.* Edited by S. Moscovici and R. Farr. Cambridge: Cambridge University Press.

Merton, R. K. 1957. "Priorities in Scientific Discovery: A Chapter in the Sociology of Science." *American Sociological Review* XXII: 635-659.

Merton, R. K. 1962. "Singletons and Multiples in Scientific Discovery: A Chapter in the Sociology of Science." *Proceedings American Philosophical Society* CV: 471-487.

Merton, R. K. 1963. "Resistance to Multiple Discoveries in Science." *European Journal of Sociology* (Archives) IV: 237-282.

Merton, R. K. 1965. *On the Shoulders of Giants, A Shandean Postscript,* New York: Harcourt Brace Javonavich.

Merton, R. K. 1975. "Structural Analysis in Sociology." In *Approaches to the Study of Social Structure.* Edited by P. Blau. New York: Free Press.

Myers, C. S. 1911. *A Textbook of Experimental Psychology.* London: Longmans.

Rivers, W.H.R. 1920. *Instinct and the Unconscious.* London: Century Bookbinders.

5

A Conceptual Framework for Measuring Norms

Peter H. Rossi
Richard A. Berk

THIS CHAPTER ASPIRES to develop specific criteria for the identification and measurement of differing normative orders. The empirical study of norms has been hampered by inadequate conceptualization. As a result, the bases for recognition and interpretation of norms remain ambiguous.

We will not be especially concerned with differences among sociological thinkers on the nature and function of norms. It suffices that all authors who use the concept recognize that norms are important social phenomena consisting of widely acknowledged rules specifying what a society or social group considers to be appropriate and inappropriate behavior in specified circumstances. Thus some norms govern the behavior of all members—for example, the prohibition against murder and theft of property—some concern only some members—for example, norms concerning roles of

AUTHORS' NOTE: A somewhat different version of this chapter has been published in Rossi and Berk (1985). Reprinted with permission. We wish to acknowledge the very helpful comments made on earlier drafts of this chapter by Professor Ronald Burt of Columbia University, Professor Andy Anderson of the University of Massachusetts/Amherst, and Professor JoAnn Miller of Purdue University.

husbands, wives, neighbors, and so on—and some establish values of objects, roles, and individual qualities—for example, rules concerning the prestige of roles, preferred qualities of individuals, or standards of beauty. That is, norms may prescribe, proscribe, or establish the relative or absolute values of social objects.

Note that certain key elements are common to most definitions of norms; there is agreement, first of all, that norms are statements of obligatory actions or evaluative criteria. Some norms are statements about how all persons are obligated to behave or think under specified circumstances. They are thus distinguished from attitudes, opinions, and personal preferences. The norms dealing with relations between the sexes, for example, prohibit rape (as specified in the norm) no matter which individuals are involved. In contrast, people may hold varying opinions about the kinds of individuals with whom they prefer to associate, because opinions are expressions of personal preferences rather than norms.

The second common thread running through definitions of norms is that they are recognized as binding by members of the society to which they apply. Hence the definitions imply consensus concerning normative content, and possibly also on the degree of obligation imposed. That is, the concept of norm implies that members of the society in question know what the norm is and agree on the strength of the obligation accompanying the rule involved.

Note that neither of these common threads requires that all members of a society must internalize all norms or even agree with all of them. Some large degree of consensus about the content of at least the central norms of a society is implied, but how much consensus there need be over the extent to which norms are binding on individuals or over which are the central norms are both open questions.

Note further that because norms must necessarily be stated in general terms, in the sense of applying to classes of circumstances, defined fairly generally, there are still many ways in which disagreement may arise over whether a norm is applicable in a specific circumstance. Thus, although all Americans may believe that rape is prohibited behavior, questions arise over whether specific instances of sexual intercourse constitute rape; for example, can a husband rape his wife? Indeed, a large part of the work of our legal system lies precisely in making determinations about whether the legal norms apply to specific instances of behavior. Hence, by the very nature of norms, we can expect greater consensus about them when they are stated in more general terms and lesser degrees of consensus over the application of norms to specific instances of behavior.[1]

This chapter focuses on two of the central issues in the empirical study of norms, namely, how to *conceptualize normative structures* and how to *operationalize consensus about norms*. We will proceed by describing a number of different models of consensus that in principle can be extracted from data.

To an outside observer of our discipline, it must seem strange that the direct empirical study of norms has not been one of the favorite research endeavors of sociologists, especially in light of the centrality of the concept in many sociological schema. The neglect, we contend, is in part a product of a missing conceptual framework for the operationalization of the phenomenon. Here we attempt to provide such a framework by merging two intellectual strands: (1) attempts to operationalize normative orders and (2) statistical models consistent with that operationalization.

The Problem of Consensus

Measurement practices of sociology and social psychology seem designed to avoid the discovery of norms for which there is popular consensus. When we find measures upon which individual subjects agree, we tend to discard them either as having serious measurement faults or as pertaining to a domain of little substantive interest. Perhaps we are following too blindly the practices of psychometricians who, when they develop a cognitive test, usually discard those items that are of very low difficulty (everyone answers correctly) or very high difficulty (everyone answers incorrectly). Similarly, survey items with highly skewed marginals are discarded because they can tell us little about interindividual variation. Items with maximum variance are preferred; hence, with corresponding minimum agreement among subjects, a strategy that makes good sense in measuring interindividual variation may not make good sense for sociologists who wish to understand the patterning of human behavior.

Sociologists and social psychologists often are puzzled when they find data sets that show the characteristics of normative order. Some well-known complex data sets, for example, show signs of relative invariance over method, population, and time. These data sets become controversial because they do not yield to our favorite form of analysis, that is, finding sources of interindividual variation. Thus crime seriousness (U.S. Department of Justice, 1984; Rossi et al., 1974) and occupational prestige (Hodge et al., 1966; Reiss et al., 1961; Treiman, 1977; Goldthorpe and Hope, 1974) data make us uncomfortable because the measures of crime seriousness and occupational prestige appear to be so steady over population subgroups and over time; they also survive changes in measurement method. In addition, although these data sets show an appreciable amount of interindividual variance, that variation appears to be only weakly related to the characteristics of the individuals studied.

We suspect there are many such examples that have been ignored or even discarded in the belief that the data were either defective or uninteresting. Undoubtedly, there are also domains (such as sexual preferences) that have not been studied because "everyone knows" that the resulting data sets would be relatively invariant over many characteristics of the individuals studied. (For example, for most Americans, sexual preferences are highly likely to be invariant within gender.)

A major reason for the neglect of the empirical study of normative domains is the failure to consider the measurement of norms within a clearly operationalized perspective, especially with the concept of random (i.e., stochastic, unsystematic) error clearly in mind. For example, crime seriousness studies all show remarkable amounts of "steadiness" in mean seriousness scores, but considerable intersubject variation around the means, a finding that has led some social scientists to spend an inordinate amount of CPU time searching for the correlates of what is essentially the noise of the disturbance term. As will be elaborated below, sources of random variation may contribute to the superficial appearance of systematic variation. What is required is systematic attention to specific manifestations of "shared agreement" or "consensus" in the actual data sets.

Some Basic Ideas

It is necessary to set forth a few elementary concepts in order to lay a foundation for the remainder of this chapter. An important starting point is the concept of a domain, used here to designate a content area that on theoretical and empirical grounds appears to be coherent. *A normative domain is a set of norms all pertaining to a relatively homogeneous area of behavior.* Thus one may conceive of a

TABLE 5.1: Schematic Representation of a Multimeasure Data Set Pertaining to a Normative Domain

Subjects, i,	A_m Applications (Items)					Mean
	a	b	c	d $\cdots\cdots\cdots$ m		
1	J_{1a}	J_{1b}	J_{1c}	J_{1d} $\cdots\cdots\cdots$ J_{1m}		$\overline{J}_1$
2	J_{2a}	J_{2b}	J_{2c}	J_{2d} $\cdots\cdots\cdots$ J_{2m}		$\overline{J}_2$
3	J_{3a}	J_{3b}	J_{3c}	J_{3d} $\cdots\cdots\cdots$ J_{3m}		$\overline{J}_3$
4	J_{4a}	J_{4b}	J_{4c}	J_{4d} $\cdots\cdots\cdots$ J_{4m}		$\overline{J}_4$
.	. .	. .	. .	. . $\cdots\cdots\cdots$ . .		. .
.	. .	. .	. .	. . $\cdots\cdots\cdots$ . .		. .
.	. .	. .	. .	. . $\cdots\cdots\cdots$ . .		. .
.	. .	. .	. .	. . $\cdots\cdots\cdots$ . .		. .
.	. .	. .	. .	. . $\cdots\cdots\cdots$ . .		. .
n	J_{na}	J_{nb}	J_{nc}	J_{nd}	J_{nm}	$\overline{J}_n$
Mean	$\overline{J}_a$	$\overline{J}_b$	$\overline{J}_c$	$\overline{J}_d$	$\overline{J}_m$	$\overline{J}$

normative domain consisting of those norms that specify the role behaviors of spouses, or those norms that define such crimes as "theft" or "rape." Corresponding to a domain are a multiplicity of "applications," each consisting of specific situations to which norms apply. Thus the normative domain covering teacher-student role relationships may be viewed as a number of applications, each dealing with some specific aspect of teacher-student relationships. Empirical study of a normative domain necessarily involves "sampling" such applications.[2]

In order to simplify the discussion, we assume that a single, homogeneous domain has been identified, bypassing for this discussion the very difficult issue of how such domains may be identified. For present purposes, all that is required is that a set of norms pertaining to an area of behavior (for example, norms pertaining to cross-gender behavior or seriousness of criminal acts) and a set of applications and specific situations to which the norms in question be envisaged.

The matrix in Table 5.1 is a schematic representation of a normative domain studied via m applications of the domain considered by n persons. An application, A_m, of a norm produces a judgment response, J_{im}, from each individual, i. The m by n cells of the matrix contain all the basic information, that is, all the judgments made by the n persons studied. The bordering row and column contain summary measures (means) derived from calculations performed respectively on the adjacent columns and rows; row means are the average responses given by the individual represented in the row, and column means are average responses given to each of the "applications" in question.

Examples of the kinds of items that might be analyzed by this means are readily at hand. A test of kinship obligation norms currently being studied consists of a set of items, of which the following are examples:[3]

> Your married brother is going to have a birthday. How much of an obligation would you feel to give him something appropriate to the occasion? (Response scale runs from 0 to 10.)

> Your widowed grandfather has lost almost everything he had in a household fire. It will take a few weeks for the insurance company to settle. This problem is straining his financial resources. How much of an obligation would you feel to offer him some financial support? (Response scale runs from 0 to 10.)

In these examples, response J_{im} is recorded in the form of degrees of felt obligation to act toward the kin in question in the manner specified in the item. The essential features of such a test of norms is that it be composed of a number of items and that the responses may be transformed into numerical values.[4] All of the observations resulting from the administration of such a test can be contained in an $n \times m$ matrix, similar to the scheme shown in Table 5.1. Note that each respondent's, i's, responses, and J_{im}'s, occupies a row and all the responses given to an item, m, are contained in a column.

Models of Normative Structures

From the perspective of this chapter, however, the critical issue is not measurement but rather how to think about such a matrix. An essential place to start is with a model of underlying mechanisms that generate responses. The equation shown in Table 5.2 provides one framework, based on the standard regression formulation, but with two kinds of disturbance terms (e.g., Kmenta, 1971, pp. 514-516; Judge et al., 1985, pp. 341-342).[5]

$J_{im} = M_0 + a_i S_i + b_m A_m + e_i + e_{im}$
  where J_{im} is the response of individual S_i to the A_mth item.
    M_0 is the intercept value for all J_{im}
    a_i is a coefficient specific to individual i

TABLE 5.2: **Formal Model of Individual Responses to Applications**

$$J_{im} = M_0 + a_i S_i + b_m A_m + e_i + e_{im}$$

where: J_{im} is the response of individual S_i to the A_m th item.

M_0 is the value of J_{im} when all subsequent terms are 0.

a_i is a coefficient specific to individual i.

S_i is a dummy variable, one for each individual i.

b_m is a coefficient specific to application m.

A_m is a dummy variable, one for each m application.

e_i is an error term associated with each individual i.

e_{im} is an error term associated with each combination
of an individual and an item.

S_i is a dummy variable, one for each i
b_m is a coefficient associated with each application, m
A_m is a dummy variable, one for each m application
e_i is a disturbance term associated with each individual i
e_{im} is a disturbance term associated with each application m and each
individual i

Note that in this equation each individual and each application is represented as a dummy variable. The equation simply states that a response of an individual to an application is a function of an intercept applicable to all individuals and applications, a weighted characteristic response of the ith individual, a weighted characteristic response to the mth application, and stochastic disturbance associated with the ith individual and the unique crossing of each individual, i, and item, m. Note that in order to simplify the discussion, the equation does not consider sampling or measurement errors.

The equation may also be regarded as another way of stating that the (fixed) main effects are represented by row and column effects. The two types of disturbances are stochastic variations in response associated with particular individuals and combinations of items (applications) and individuals. Following statistical conventions, the two kinds of disturbances will be assumed to produce chance perturbations in judgments that in the aggregate have expected values of zero. We also assume that the disturbances are uncorrelated both within and between terms. Other assumptions will be considered later under particular models of data sets. Indeed, at this point the inclusion of both the dummy variables and the disturbances associated with individuals leads to perfect collinearity; under variance components formulations, the disturbances associated with individuals are simply stochastic representations of the fixed effects captured by the dummy variables for individuals. That is, one asserts that the dummy variables originally associated with individuals behave as if drawn at random from some (often normal) density and can, therefore, be conceptualized in the aggregate as nothing more that chance effects with expected values of zero.

In practice, the model will be specified without redundant terms. For example, within the usual variance components framework, the dummy variables for individuals and applications are replaced by substantively interesting regressors that presumably summarize important aggregate effects. For the individual dummy variables one might substitute education, gender, and race. For the applications one might substitute variables describing the applications along certain conceptual dimensions along which applications vary. For example, specific kinship terms in the items shown above may be replaced with more descriptive terms such as gender and marital status of the kin in question along with the number of degrees removed from the respondent. In addition, it is assumed within these formulations that both sets of disturbances are uncorrelated with these summary regressors (which is true under the correct specification), and the redundancy disappears.

These technical issues are of more than passing interest. Indeed, it is precisely by means of the ideas contained in the representation of Table 5.2 that we propose to reconceptualize the problem of understanding normative structures. Consider Table 5.3, which contains some of the many possibilities, each labeled as a "model."

Model I: Absolute Consensus and Uniformity

The first possibility is one in which the coefficients a_i and b_m are 0 and the error terms are 0. Under these conditions, all the entries in the matrix are identical (or could be made identical by converting all of the entries in a column or columns into their complements). Statistically, this would imply that there is no variance within any column and any row. Hence all the column means and all the row means would be identical.

An outcome of this sort would be a truly remarkable example of complete consensus in a society, both on the content of the norms and on the strength of adherence to each and every statement of the norm. It would also imply that each and every person has identical amounts of knowledge of the norms of the society and not only subscribes to each and every aspect, but with the same degree of

TABLE 5.3: Heuristic Models for Normative Domain Data Sets

Model and Description	Conditions Holding For				Consequences
	a_i	b_m	e_i	e_{im}	
A: Unrealistic Models					
I: Absolute consensus and uniformity	0	0	0	0	$J_{im} = M_0 = \bar{J}$
II: Absolute consensus and uniformity with error	0	0	0	≠0	$(J_{im}) = M_0 = \bar{J};\ J_{im} = \bar{J}_m;\ J_{im} = \bar{J}_m + e_i + e_{im}$ $= M_0 + e_i + e_{im}$
III: Absolute consensus, differentiated judgments, and no error	0	≠0	0	0	$J_{im} = \bar{J}_m$
B: Realistic Models					
IV: Absolute consensus, differentiated judgments, and error	0	≠0	≠0	≠0	$E(J_{im}) = \bar{J}_m;\ J_{im} = \bar{J}_m + e_i + e_{im}$
V: Relative consensus, differentiated judgments, and error	≠0	≠0	≠0	≠0	$J_{im} = M_0 + a_i + b_m + e_i + e_{im}$
VI: Modified model V: Error variance correlated with individual characteristics	same as Model V				$r^2_{e_i k_i} \neq 0$
VII: Modified model V: a_i Values correlated with individual characteristics	same as Model V				$r_{a_i k_i} \neq 0$
VIII: Segmented normative structures	Model V conditions obtain locally				$r_{b_i k_i} \neq 0;\ r^2_{e_i k_i} \neq 0;\ r_{a_i k_i} \neq 0$
IX: Structureless domains	0	0	≠0	≠0	$J_{im} = M_0 + e_i + e_m$

NOTE: k_i is some characteristic of individuals, i (e.g., age, ethnicity, socioeconomic status, etc.).

intensity. In practice, one can also expect that the responses given will tend to be located at the extremes of any range of response categories. In survey research terms, the items on a data set characteristic of Model I would produce marginals in which all the responses would be found in only one of the response categories. If there are several categories available for use in responding, the categories used would most likely be at one extreme or the other. Consensus implies some degree of endorsement and hence the piling up of response at the extremes. Another way of stating this is that a society in which there is a strong consensus is also a society that tends to see norms in black and white terms.

Clearly, were anyone to run across a data set with these characteristics, only the very naive would not suspect wholesale data forgery. It is virtually inconceivable that all members of a society would have perfect understanding of the norms, that all would subscribe to them to the same degree, and that the subjects would record those judgments without some random error. However, Model I is relevant because, in searching for normative structures, some researchers impose conditions on data sets that are nearly equivalent to the qualities just discussed, and hence never find either normative structures or consensus. To such persons, any sign of departure from identical entries in a data matrix is looked upon as evidence of weakness in the normative structure involved.

Model II: Absolute Consensus and Uniformity with Error Only

This is a condition that obtains when there is absolute consensus (i.e., a_i and $b_m = 0$), but respondents and/or instruments are subject to unsystematic, stochastic perturbations. That is, the expected values for all items are identical and all respondents have the same expected values, but random fluctuations intervene. If such perturbations are allowed, then the entries in the data matrix will differ one from the other, but these differences result solely from chance effects. Model II is relatively easy to detect because a two-way ANOVA on judgments normalized along rows and columns would on the average reject the hypothesis that the column and row variances and means were different.[6]

What kinds of processes would generate random perturbations? Perturbations for individuals are easy to envisage. All we require is that there be variations across individuals that have an expected value of zero and that they be unrelated to the dummy variables for individuals. As illustrations, transitory moods, understandings, or confusions would tend to produce variations that would obscure stable normative predispositions. For example, the content of the morning paper would temporarily alter (in either a positive or negative direction) an individual's commitment to a particular prohibition, and hence an individual might vary his or her response, acting on the temporarily altered agreement with the norm in question. Under such circumstances, consensus across individuals would also temporarily disappear.

Random perturbations associated with crossing individuals and applications are also easy to imagine. Given the ambiguities that exist in every language, it is not possible to have a "pure" measure of anything as an item in a test or survey. Reactions to this "extraneous content" differ from individual to individual. For example, an item that mentions an impending birthday may tap idiosyncratic attitudes toward birthdays as well as degrees of felt obligations toward kin. Individual respondents might therefore rate obligations differently depending on how much they like or dislike birthdays.

In practice, it may be difficult to distinguish data generated by this model from one in which the major underlying judgment generating process is simply random. A randomly generated data set would have marginal distributions on each of the items that asymptotically reflect the generating random process involved. Given human tendencies not to produce random processes resulting in flat distributions or with central tendencies at the extremes of a range, we can detect data generated by Model II because central tendencies of responses will tend to be at the extremes. That is, in Model II, M_0 will tend to be toward one or the other extreme of the response scale.

Model III: Absolute Consensus and Differentiated Judgments with No Error

This is the case when the J_{im}s are identical within a column but varying across columns ($b_m = 0$). Column variances are zero, but row variances are nonzero and identical across rows. That outcome would occur, for example, if all persons in the society agreed that some types of kinship relations impose greater degrees of obligation than others and on the degrees of "obligation" involved; they might believe that more is "owed" to uncles than to aunts, but agree on the amount of obligation owed to each.

In Model III, judgments are differentiated in the sense that respondents acknowledge that the norms take into account differences among moral situations. In short, for example, not all kin are judged to have equal claims to help, or not all crimes are judged as equally serious. Judgments are not identical for each instance of possible applications of the norms—as represented in individual items on the norms test—but are instead differentiated according to applications.

Data that have the characteristics of Model III can be detected by simple inspection of row and column means and variances. Inspection of rows would indicate uniformity from row to row with zero variance across rows. Inspection of columns would indicate differences among columns but zero variance within columns. Although more realistic than either Model I or Model II, Model III nevertheless lacks important features that are almost universally found in "real" data sets, namely, random disturbances.

Model IV: Absolute Consensus, Differentiated Judgments, and Error

If one adds the two kinds of random disturbances to the previous example (III above), then a more likely and more realistic case appears (i.e., e_i and e_{im} are nonzero). Model IV reflects a society in which there is effective agreement among members about both the content of norms and the intensity with which members should endorse or reject particular applications of those norms. However, judgment responses inevitably have noise (i.e., e_i and $e_{im} \neq 0$) and hence there is variation from individual to individual within each of the columns of the data matrix, despite the fact that persons are "truly" identical. Hence, in principle, a one-way ANOVA of rows will yield insignificant F-ratios. Noise associated with the applications and individuals (i.e., e_i and e_{im}) will tend to obscure the true differences between column means, but in principle an ANOVA will yield statistically significant F-ratios. We say "in principle" because there are technical complications involved in a specification in which are included dummy variables for individuals and applications coupled with disturbances for individuals and interactions between individuals and applications. We will not worry about such complications here in part because in realistic applications, the dummy variables would be replaced by a more substantively instructive regressor (e.g., race, sex, properties of the application).[7]

Although the introduction of chance perturbations makes the model more realistic, there is still the very serious constraint that everyone should on the average feel the same way and with the same intensity about each of the applications. Note that this condition is obviously one in which there is effective consensus among members of the society or group under study. In the resulting data set, there is variability from person to person, but this variability is both unstructured and does not obscure the norms. If the distribution of the disturbances takes on the usual forms, conventional measures of central tendency will yield unbiased estimates of group norms. Hence, it is tempting to declare that Model IV data ought to be the standard for whether or not a normative structure exists in a group; any set of data that does not approximate this criterion does not reflect a normative structure. However, Model IV conditions appear to be too demanding for any empirical data set. Under Model IV rules, few domains in any society would qualify as fulfilling the criteria for normative structure. We will need to relax some of these conditions if we are to approximate real data sets addressed to normative domains.

Model V: Relative Consensus, Differentiated Judgments, Varying Thresholds, and Error

Model V introduces the idea of relative consensus, in which individual members of a group or society need not agree on the specific judgment to be rendered on each moral situation, but each individual can be different from others by an individually specific constant amount represented by the coefficient a_i.[8] Persons agree with each other in their differential responses to applications, but differ from each other by amounts characteristic of specific individuals; hence the term "relative consensus." In addition, as in Model IV, the two error terms (e_i and e_{im}) are nonzero.

The a_i coefficients can also be seen to be linearly related to the difference between an individual's judgment of an application and the mean judgment of the society, J_m. From this perspective, a_i can be given an interpretation similar to individual "thresholds," a characteristic, if not universal, finding in psychophysical research. Borrowing from that field, we will use the term "threshold" for a_i coefficients. Because each coefficient represents the systematic way in which individuals vary one from the other in their degree of endorsement, the coefficients can be regarded as individuals' thresholds of endorsement of the norms in question.

Put differently, persons agree on the norms but hold to them with varying intensity. Thus, for example, everyone might agree that negligent manslaughter is a more serious crime than burglary but some would give the crimes scores of 95 and 40, respectively, on a 0 to 100 scale, whereas the corresponding scores given by others might be 80 and 25. The latter persons have higher thresholds than the former, indicating perhaps an overall view of crimes as generally less serious.

The statistical qualities of a data matrix corresponding to Model V are relatively simple. Each row correlates highly and positively with the column sums, the "coefficient of alienation" corresponding to the amount of unsystematic variation in the judgments. In principle, ANOVA of raw scores by rows would indicate significant differences among respondents, but if judgments are normalized within rows, ANOVA results would become insigificant. Similarly, in principle, ANOVA by columns of raw scores would indicate significant differences among items used in the norms test in question. Normaling raw scores within columns should reduce the ANOVA F-ratios by columns to statistical insignificance.

It turns out that there are actual data sets that appear to have the requisite characteristics of Model V. One such data set resulted from a pilot factorial survey of the normative structure of welfare entitlements (Rossi and Pereira, 1984). The research attempted to uncover the normative structure of popular views of who should be entitled to welfare payments and how large (in dollar amounts) such payments should be. About 200 respondents in the New York metropolitan area were asked to indicate the dollar level of weekly financial support they thought each of 50 simulated welfare applicants deserved to get. Each of the hypothetical applicants was described in short vignettes in terms of age, gender, marital status, labor force status, number of dependent children in the home, reasons for dependency, and so on through a list of some eighteen different dimensions. Each dimension was represented in each description (vignette) by a level chosen at random from each dimension. For example, one of the dimensions, marital status, had four levels, each describing a welfare applicant of different marital status.[9] Within the present framework, each of the hypothetical persons described in the vignette was an "application" of the norms concerning welfare payments, with respondents being asked what they thought various persons should get in the way of welfare payments given a description of such persons' fortunes and deprived conditions.

Respondents tended to agree on the characteristics of individuals that justified welfare payments and also on the characteristics that merited receiving larger or smaller amounts. However, there was considerable variation from respondent to respondent in the actual dollar amounts respondents accorded to the welfare applicants. These differences seemed to be characteristic of the respondent, some being relatively generous in the payment they thought the applicants should receive and others being less generous. Indeed, a major portion of the total variance in the data was contributed by the a_i coefficients.[10] Respondent thresholds for support payments were different, although they appeared to be subscribing to a set of commonly held norms about who are deserving applicants.

Similar patterns appeared in less striking way in a 1972 study of the perceived seriousness of crimes (Rossi et al., 1974). Each respondent was given a set of 80 crimes, described in behavioral terms, to rate along a 9-point scale of seriousness. By and large, respondents agreed about the relative order of the seriousness of the crimes in question but varied in thresholds, with some respondents seeing all crimes as on the average more serious and with others giving a lower average rating. However, threshold differences did not dominate as in the case of the welfare entitlement study.

An important conceptual issue presented by data sets fitting Model V is the extent to which threshold differences indicate substantively important degrees of dissensus in the society or group under study. Certainly, threshold differences among members of a society can generate considerable conflict within the society, as evidenced in the two substantive areas from which our data set examples are drawn. Perhaps everyone in the United States agrees about what kinds of persons are more and less entitled to transfer payments under a public welfare system, but the fact that they disagree over thresholds that rule over the issue of the level of payments to welfare clients is sufficient to make public welfare a perennial issue in national and local politics. Similarly, the controversy over capital punishment appears to be generated by threshold differences among Americans. Apparently, no one believes that cold-blooded murder ought to be condoned. However, considerable disagreement exists over whether murderers should be subjected to capital punishment or punished to some lesser extent.

Indeed, it appears likely that Model V more or less describes the majority, if not most, of normative domains. In most domains, people by and large agree on what the norms are but differ in their degrees of attachment to the normative structure so defined. Controversies over norms appear to be not so much over whether or not some behavioral practice ought to be valued or prohibited but over the degree to which it should be valued or prohibited. For example, almost everyone agrees that children ought not to be abused, but disagreements arise over what constitutes abusive treatment, what sanctions should be applied, and whether child abuse should be defined as a criminal offense. Such disagreements lie at the heart of current moral confusion in this domain.

Our own inclination is to regard a domain in which there are widespread threshold differences among individuals as a domain that lacks threshold consensus. In other words, a normative domain that, when measured, produces data sets that have the qualities described for Model V is a domain characterized by consensus over normative content but dissensus over thresholds.

There are other ways in which a normative domain may exhibit lack of consensus, some of which are discussed below.

Model VI: Modified Model V; Error Variances Correlated with Individual Characteristics

Model V appears to be a useful and realistic data set model. However, that model assumes implicitly that the disturbances variances for respondents, e_i, were (a) homoskedastic across respondents or, if not homoskedastic, (b) unrelated to the individual by application disturbances. That is, it was assumed either that all individuals exhibited the same amount of chance variation or that the amount of chance variation was not systematically related to properties of those individuals.[11] We now relax those two assumptions.

Substantively, varying error variances have several interpretations, depending in part on whether a normative domain is conceptualized as having some sort of independent-of-people existence or whether norms are conceived simply as central tendencies. From the first viewpoint, differences in disturbance variances across respondents means that some people perceive the norms in question more accurately than others. From the second perspective, varying individual disturbance variances may connote a variety of processes at work, including, for example, varying degrees of contact with other persons and hence varying abilities to estimate accurately central tendencies in the rest of the population. Substantive interpretations aside, varying individual disturbance variances would be manifest in a matrix of the sort shown schematically in Table 5.1, via varying R^2s for the regressions of column sums on row entries. Alternatively, regressions for each individual across applications would reveal different R^2s. In short, some respondents would come closer than others in their responses to the central tendencies shown by the entire sample.

Instances in which the disturbance variances are related to individual characteristics can also be substantively instructive. A good example can be found in the crime seriousness data, cited above. In an extension to that study (Rossi and Henry, 1984) in which the 1972 study was replicated with samples of judges, probation officers, and prosecuting attorneys in the Chicago area, it was found that these occupational groups had considerably lower error variances, indicating higher correspondence between the ratings given by members of these occupational groups and the mean ratings computed from pooling data from several replicated studies. In addition, persons with higher educational attainment also had higher R^2s, indicating that their responses were closer to the central tendencies than those of less well-educated respondents.

It is quite understandable that persons professionally engaged in law enforcement (i.e., who are norm enforcers) would be more familiar with descriptions of crimes and also more accurate in their perceptions of the relevant norms. Formal education also provides appropriately differentiated vocabularies to understand rating tasks, as well as providing knowledge about the norms.

Quite similar findings characterize occupational prestige data sets (Hodge and Rossi, 1978): The more formal education attained by a respondent, the more highly correlated his or her ratings are with the mean ratings of the national sample. A similar interpretation thus is plausible: The more formal education attained, the more knowledge about the occupational system and, hence, the more knowledge about how prestige is allocated to various occupational groups.

Model VII: Modified Model V; Thresholds Correlated with Individual Characteristics

As defined above, an individual's threshold, a_i, is the "constant bias" in his or her judgments, a set difference between the individual's judgments and those of other individuals. The alteration to Model V of interest here is a model in which the a_i values are correlated with some characteristics of individuals and hence may be regarded as "structured." A few examples may help to illustrate. In the study of welfare entitlement norms, referred to above, respondent thresholds dominated responses. That is, the amount of money that a respondent would allow as a fair payment to any welfare applicant was more closely related to that individual's threshold than to any characteristics of the application in question. Respondents apparently approached the judgment task with strong ideas concerning appropriate levels of support for welfare recipients.

However, the thresholds were related fairly strongly to two individual level variables: (1) the respondent's estimate of the weekly cash income necessary for a family of four in New York to live a "comfortable existence," and (2) whether or not the respondent had experienced episodes of "bad luck." The higher the respondent's estimates of the amount needed for a "comfortable existence" and the more bad luck episodes in his or her life, the more the respondent was willing to allow in the way of welfare payments. In short, a person's normative stance in this domain was strongly affected by personal perceptions of need and experiences, due in part, we suspect, both to differences in identification with deprived persons and to cognitive assessments.

We encountered still another example of structured thresholds in our recent study of the appropriateness of sentences given to convicted felons. Some respondents were consistently more severe in prison sentences they deemed appropriate. Correlates of threshold amounts included gender—women were harsher in their sentencing judgments than men—and education—persons of lower educational attainment were harsher in their judgments than persons of higher educational attainment. The thresholds in this domain were small but nevertheless consistent, statistically significant, and robust enough to survive all the tests for competing explanations that we could perform with the existing data set. Convincing explanations for these two correlates were beyond the limits of our imagination to construct, although we are fairly well convinced that the findings are real and not simply spurious.

Model VIII: Segmented Normative Structures; Global Dissensus and Local Consensus

Up to this point, the discussion has centered on models in which dissensus is more a matter of degree than of kind. In contrast, Model VIII is concerned with the possibility of more structured dissensus, in particular, data indicating the existence of more than one consensus about a domain's normative structure. In terms of the framework of Table 5.2, correlations would exist between the b_m and individual characteristices and/or between e_{im} values and individual characteristics.[12] Furthermore, the relevant individual characteristics would be those that conventionally identify social groups. In such cases, the weights given applications systematically vary by groups of individuals and/or groups of individuals react differently to the various applications. Thus, let us say, young persons tend to regard marijuana possession as a less serious crime than do older persons. This difference is reflected in the judgments of younger and older persons when measuring the seriousness of marijuana possession.

The importance of Model VIII is obvious. Sociologists often assume the existence of subpopulations with markedly different normative systems. Thus some forms of conflict theory predict that the normative domains of oppressed groups will be different from those of oppressor groups. Distinctive normative structures are postulated in such concepts as the "Culture of Poverty" (Rossi and Blum, 1969) or in the notions of ethnic and delinquent subcultures.

A useful and productive approach to the problem of detecting Model VIII is to postulate that a data matrix generated by Model VIII conditions would be composed of several submatrices, each of which would separately show the characteristics of Model V normative structures whereas the entire matrix considered as a unit might have no clear structure. If those local regions under which Model V would obtain were also composed primarily of persons from some identifiable social group, then the condition of segmented consensus obtains. That is, consensus is obtained within but not between submatrices. For example, if different normative structures pertained to the family and kinship norms of blacks and whites in the United States today, then blacks and whites considered separately would show, say, a Model V consensus pattern, but when combined into a single matrix would show either confused patterns or none at all.

The same reasoning can be applied positively in attempts to detect inductively the existence of segmented consensus. If a data matrix with no particular patterning could be rearranged by shifting rows and columns, so that there were local regions wherein the data satisfied the conditions for Model V, a good case could be made for having uncovered segmented consensus, providing those local regions also comprised members from largely distinctive social groups. Several conventional methods for systematically rearranging rows and columns of data matrices could be fruitfully adapted to this task.

Model VIII is designed to characterize data sets pertaining to domains composed of sets of conflicting norms (as many sets as there are recognizable segments). Societies likely to generate such data sets are not difficult to imagine. For example, antebellum United States probably had subpopulations that differed widely on norms governing slavery. Or, Mormon family and marriage norms must have contrasted sharply with family and marriage norms of most other Americans in the latter half of the nineteenth century. Similar contrasts concerning private property norms undoubtedly divide socialist societies from capitalist societies.

Current normative divisions within the United States seem unlikely to produce Model VIII data sets. Some Marxists would like to believe that if persons were classified by their relationships to the means of production, segmented consensus would reveal contrasting value systems of workers and bourgeois. The worker submatrix would show a different normative structure than the bourgeois submatrix, if appropriate normative domains were studied. More likely, however, are domain divisions along gender lines concerning appropriate gender role behavior.

Consensus segmentation can take a variety of forms, following the previous discussion:

(1) Judgment segmentation: indexed by a correlation between b_m and/or e_{im} and some individual characteristic k.
(2) Threshold segmentation: indexed by correlations between a_i and some individual characteristic k.
(3) Error variance segmentation: indexed by correlations between e_i^2 and some individual characteristic k.
(4) Combinations of the above.

Some of the potential forms of segmentation listed above are put forth as logical possibilities, for which there are few empirical illustrations.

Our researches have yet to uncover a normative structure that shows a strong degree of judgment segmentation. However, judgment segmentation along gender lines was encountered in our study of sexual harassment norms (Rossi and Weber-Burdin, 1983). Men and women students and faculty at two public universities were given short descriptions of instances of potential sexual harassment of females of subordinate status by superordinate males. Analysis of the resulting data matrix showed that there was considerable agreement on the overall gross ordering of such instances of potential harassment. More careful examination of the data showed areas of the domain in which there was some disagreement between male and female respondents. In particular, the gender difference centered around specific applications judged as less serious instances of sexual harassment by men as compared to women. For example, men tended to regard incidents as less likely to qualify as sexual harassment if the man and woman involved had some relationship prior to the incident being discussed. In contrast, for women respondents, prior relationships made no difference in their assessment of sexual harassment. Men saw prior relationships between a man and a woman as justifying more aggressive approaches to the woman; women did not. This disagreement was only apparent in one portion of the domain that referred to incidents between males and females who had known each other fairly well before the encounter in question.

Another study found that young black men manifested different thresholds than did others for crimes of violence, tending to view such crimes as less serious. This disagreement occurred almost entirely over assaults and homicide. In contrast, young black males and others largely agreed on the seriousness of other crimes.

For the normative domains that we have studied so far, and for U.S. society in the 1970s and 1980s, widely divergent normative structures within population subgroups seemingly do not exist. Even when we asked convicted felons in a Massachusetts maximum security prison about the normative bases for just prison sentences, their responses were different only by small threshold amounts from those of a sample of Boston metropolitan area adults. Nor were the felons' judgments radically different from those of Boston area police. All agreed on the principles used in meting out sentences, although the prisoners called for shorter sentences than the other groups studied (Rossi et al., 1985).

Although our results do not preclude finding strong judgment segmentation in domains yet to be studied or in other historical periods, the findings suggest that disputes over norms do not often take the form of opposing normative systems. Normative disagreements instead appear to be more frequently centered around degrees of adherence to an agreed upon normative system. Thus the most frequently encountered form of subgroup segmentation consists of threshold differences among subgroups.

An important issue with which we cannot deal in this chapter is whether a subgroup that defines segmentation is or is not a "social group." For present purposes, our stance is liberal, accepting all sorts of social characteristics as defining social groups, including characteristics such as age and gender that are not universally accepted as defining qualities. Indeed, gender threshold differences appear to be pervasive, though usually small; as noted, consistent and small gender threshold differences have been found in the normative domains of appropriate punishment for convicted felons, and definitions of child abuse and sexual harassment. Others forms of frequently encountered threshold segmentation involve socioeconomic levels, educational attainment levels, and geographic regions.

Threshold segmentation is perhaps the most pervasive form of dissensus in our society. This generalization is based on less than a dozen studies, however, all undertaken over the past decade in a society that is not plagued by deep and rancorous social conflict. Although there are fault lines in the American social structure, we are a long way from the tragic conditions that prevail, for example, in Northern Ireland or in Israel's West Bank.

Error variance segmentation is a logical possibility that we have not encountered frequently, possibly because we have not looked specifically for it. But a few examples can be cited; Hodge and Rossi (1978) found error variance segmentation in occupational prestige. Respondents from higher socioeconomic levels had less error variance in judging prestige positions of occupations, a finding that we have interpreted to mean that the upper socioeconomic levels have more of an "interest" in a structured prestige system and hence "learn" it more thoroughly. Similarly, the lower error variance among court personnel in judging the seriousness of crimes is a manifest of much the same knowledge and interest in a domain.

Normative domains that have smaller amounts of error variance may be regarded as more clearly defined. That is, members of the society are more certain about how to answer questions on normative issues, make fewer inconsistent and more reliable judgments. Extrapolating the findings discussed above, we expect that professional groups would show stronger normative structures when questioned about professional normative domains than will the general public. Occupational groups whose vocational duties involve dealing with the normative issues in a domain should also manifest lower amounts of error variance. This is to say no more than that, let us say, ministers of the cloth should be expected to know more theology and be more internally consistent and reliable on theological issues than sociologists. Indeed, error variance segmentation may simply mark off portions of the social structure in which special concerns arising out of special life situations lead to structured perceptions of the norms and to more firmly held views regarding them.

Model IX: Structureless Normative Domains

The eight models described above are positive models in the sense that they attempt to describe what qualities data sets may assume when they reflect some empirically defined normative domain. To round out the full range of possibilities, we now consider matrix conditions if no normative structure exists. Substantively, such conditions might be encountered when the structure of a domain has not yet formed, or when normative structure has disintegrated. For example, there is likely no structure to norms that would govern behavior toward extraterrestrials (except perhaps among that handful of persons throughout the world who have devoted some attention to the issues involved). Similarly, there likely is no structure to the prestige evaluations of archaic and obsolete occupations, for example, ship's chandler, drayman, cooper, and so on, about which popular knowledge is slight or nonexistent.

Structureless domains should have several distinctive statistical properties, the most important of which is that the regression of column means on any row's entries would be negligible (essentially zero). Second, column means, on the average, are not likely to fall at response scale extremes.

The first condition indicates that central tendencies among answers to specific items are not governing individuals' normative responses. Substantively, this means that respondents are not sensitive to the expected values of the responses in the society; in short, the responses are not socially determined or influenced. Consequently, data under an absence of normative structure should have the following statistical properties: ANOVA across normalized rows and across normalized columns should produce F-ratios indicating no significant statistical differences among rows and columns. However, raw score analyses may produce significant row ANOVA values, possibly showing very generalized response sets held by respondents as, for example, would be generated by "social desirability." Significant column ANOVA values might be related to the specific content of individual items. For example, items that contain affect-laden words might produce distinctive response levels generated more by the appearance of those words than by the norms adhered to by the respondent.

The second condition for Model IX has been partially discussed under Model II. It seems likely that if the applications items used in the text are meaningless, the column means on the average would be identical and also identical to central tendencies generated by the kinds of guessing processes employed by respondents. For example, if respondents' guessing produced a symmetric distribution of responses, the mean of those responses might well approximate the midpoint of the response scale employed in the test. Although this is not a necessary result (people might group their guesses at any part of the response scale), it is perhaps the most likely outcome. And midpoint responses for all items in a test of a normative domain are simply not to be expected because the essence of a normative domain is that it is composed of rules about which members of the society feel strongly one way or the other. Skewed responses are to be expected in normative domains.

In our researches, we and our colleagues have yet to encounter an empirical example of structureless domains. However, we strongly suspect that this is the case because we have had good a priori reasons to believe that the domains we wanted to study had some structure. If we had thought otherwise—that is, that there were good reasons to believe the domain to be unstructured—we would have studied them. Indeed, it is not likely that anyone might undertake to study a structureless domain because it is of the essence of a normative domain that most members of a society be aware of the norms in question. This assumes the validity of a priori expectations. We thought one of the tasks of social science was examination of the "taken for granted."

Nevertheless, it is important to note Model IX's characteristics because structure is a matter of degree and some domains have been found to be almost without structure. The important message to take from this discussion is that structureless domains give rise to data that are dominated by chance perturbations and little else. To the extent that a given data set approximates these qualities of a structureless domain, then that domain is not normative.

Varieties of Consensus in Normative Systems

The preceding discussion provides the foundation for the development of a multidimensional scheme for the description of normative domains. The multidimensional system is based upon four dimensions: (1) strength of domain structure: the degree to which a domain is structured; (2) threshold dissensus: the degree to which existing dissensus concerning a domain is a matter of threshold differences; (3) domain dissensus: the degree to which existing dissensus revolves around disagreements about norms; and (4) segmentation of dissent: the extent to which dissensus coincides with critical social groups within a given society.

Strength of Domain Structure

A "strong" domain structure is one in which there is considerable agreement among the members of a society over the norms of the society and, consequently, individual members perceive the norms in a relatively error-free fashion; in statistical terms, systematic effects dominate unsystematic effects. A "weak" domain is one with the opposite characteristics. The critical indicator of the strength of a domain is the amount of stochastic error in individuals' judgments. In a domain with a lot of noise, the norms are only dimly perceived by members; hence, members' responses are poorly correlated with measures of the central tendency within the data set. At the extremes of weakness, a normative system resembles data encountered in Model IX; that is, a nonnormative content area.[13]

Threshold Dissensus

Domains differ in the extent to which interindividual differences in judgments are accounted for by threshold differences among societal members. At one extreme, a domain in which threshold differences are essentially zero is characterized by a very high degree of consensus on the intensity with which normative statements are endorsed. At the other are domains in which there is maximum disagreement over how seriously the norms should be ruling principles of behavior.

Although the potential for intrasocietal conflict is greatest for domains with large amounts of threshold dissensus, whether or not that potential is realized depends on the degree of segmentation of dissensus, a point to which we will turn. Nevertheless, we are inclined to view a data matrix with large interindividual differences in thresholds as troublesome because there is little agreement on how strongly the normative prescriptions should apply. This is likely what is going on in the U.S. today vis-à-vis kinship obligations. There is agreement that, say, one has more obligations to one's mother than to one's mother's sister, but there may be strong disagreement concerning obligations to one's mother: do they extend only to sending a birthday card, or to calling her on the phone once a month; do they include personally providing nursing care when she is sick or financial support in her old age? The consequences of such dissensus may entail only deeply disappointed mothers and harassed children, or they may result in serious deterioration of the quality of some lives. To the extent that threshold differences are correlated with respondent characteristics, they may be the basis for political mobilization. As such, the amount of dissensus in the society may be cause for concern about societal stability.

Threshold differences are particularly important when they are correlated strongly with some population characteristic. As such, they may represent major fault lines in the society. Thus, for the contemporary U.S., threshold differences correlated with race, ethnicity, religion, socioeconomic level, or geographical region are possible sources of acrimony. Such fault lines are capable of generating concerted political action and open conflict.

Domain Dissensus

This dimension captures the extent to which dissensus in a domain centers around some portion of the domain, representing at the one extreme alternative value systems that are not consonant one with others. The other extreme represents modest differences in emphasis on some norms in the domain rather than others. For example, the domain of norms identifying crimes is well ordered if one only considers crimes against the person and property crimes committed against individuals and households as victims. Disagreement of a threshold variety centers around so-called victimless crimes (e.g., drug usage, homosexuality) and white-collar crimes, (e.g., violations of occupational safety laws, laws against deceptive advertising). Another example might be the current controversy over access to legal abortions in which a domain concerning reproductive rights may very well consist of separately organized sets of norms that view the rights of adults in this area quite differently.

Segmentation of Dissent

Whatever form dissensus may take, it makes a great deal of difference whether or not dissent is structured along social group lines. Individuated dissent characterizes those domains in which dissent is uncorrelated with any social characteristic. Persons disagree, say, about how seriously the norms should be upheld, but such disagreements appear to be uncorrelated either with personal characteristics of individuals or with their locations in social space.

Such a domain would be one in which personal preferences apparently reign supreme. In contrast, "social" dissent occurs when such disagreements are correlated with individual characteristics that identify members of critical social groups. As noted earlier, a society in which normative dissent coincides with important social groupings capable of political mobilization is vulnerable if those groups square off against each other in political struggle.

Conclusion

This chapter has attempted to lay the foundations for exploring normative structures based on both technical and conceptual tools. On the technical side, we have specified some of the observable properties of normative domains. On the conceptual side, we have provided a richer menu of meanings for consensus and dissensus. We have, in addition, discussed the social implications of various structural features of normative domains.

We have placed special emphasis on the static side of normative domains, especially on the attributes that various domains may evidence. How normative domains arise and are transformed are issues of enormous importance to sociology and the social sciences generally. Although we have not directly addressed these topics, the analysis provides a foundation for systematic and concerted study of normative change in the future.

Notes

1. It is over difference between general statements and particular applications that some schools of sociology have parted company. Traditional survey researchers, for example, have focused on the broader issues (i.e., general normative principles) in writing survey items. Symbolic interactionists and ethnomethodologists have concentrated on how norms are played out in particular situations. It is more than an ecumenical gesture to assert that both perspectives are required.

2. It is, of course, important that the domain be properly identified and that the sample of applications be representative of all the applications that constitute that domain.

3. These items come from a scale developed by Alice S. and Peter H. Rossi, currently being used in a study of relations between parents and their adult children funded by National Institute on Aging Grant #1 RO1 AG0426301, entitled "Parent-Adult Child Relations in Three Generations." The full "test" is a factorial survey composed of items in which kin terms are systematically rotated, along with the kind of obligation and the occasion that activates the obligation.

4. Numerical representation can include binary (1, 0) or dummy variable representations.

5. In principle, a third type of disturbance term associated with each application, e_m, may be distinguished under the circumstances that items are being sampled from some universe of items belonging to a domain, as for example in a cognitive test in which each item in a given administration of a test is drawn randomly without replacement for each such administration.

Under those specified circumstances each item would produce an error associated with it that varied from one administration to another. However, in the usual sociological or social psychological research, items are ordinarily "fixed" and are constant within each of the tests in question. Hence the error term, e_m, is not defined here.

6. Normalization of raw scores is made necessary by the fact that error variances for items and individuals are unlikely to be identical either within or between applications and individuals.

7. In brief, within the usual data set, it is impossible to distinguish between the role of the dummy variables for individuals and the individual-level perturbations.

8. Actually, the a_i coefficients in the model of Table 5.2 represent the deviation of each individual respondent from the response of the individual respondent serving as the "omitted category" in the dummy variable representation.

9. In a factorial survey, respondents are given sets of vignettes, constructed by randomly sampling from the set of all possible combinations of a fixed set of dimensions and levels within dimensions. Each respondent is given a separately drawn sample. See Rossi and Nock (1982) for a fuller description of the factorial survey approach.

10. In this case the a_i coefficients were represented by the mean responses given by each individual, a measure that is linearly related to the a_i coefficients for dummy variable representations of the respondent.

11. Recall that we earlier followed the usual conventions by assuming that both kinds of disturbances were unrelated with properties of individuals or applications.

12. There are additional forms of systematic error structures with which we will not deal in this chapter, for example, the possibility of correlated disturbances. We have already allowed for certain possibilities through disturbances linked either to individuals or applications. Clearly, if all of the judgments of a particular individual are increased or decreased by a single random shock, there will be within-person disturbance correlations. The same holds for applications. However, there are other possible structures for autocorrelation within individuals or applications. For example, one might postulate an autoregressive model in which the correlation between the within-person disturbances dissipates as more applications are considered. This might reflect a fading response set as the individual becomes sensitive to the judgment task. Or one might postulate an autoregressive model in which the correlation between within-person disturbances decreases with the amount of time that has elapsed from judging application m to judging application n. Such patterns have not been especially salient in the relevant research to date and perhaps need not be discussed further here. This interpretation assumes that other types of errors (e.g., measurement errors) are similar in size across the substantive domains in question, a matter on which we have no evidence.

13. A comment on cross-domain differences in e_i and e_{im} disturbance variances is appropriate at this point. Among the several normative domains on which our colleagues have collected data sets, there appear to be considerable differences in average error variances. At the one extreme, the normative domains of child abuse (Garrett and Rossi, 1982), welfare entitlements (Rossi and Pereira, 1984), and mental health (Thurman and Lam, 1984) all had high error variances to the extent that these domains scarcely appear to have any structure at all; whereas other domains— crime seriousness (Rossi and Henry, 1984), sexual harassment (Rossi and Weber-Burdin, 1982), household socioeconomic levels (Rossi and Nock, 1982), and appropriate punishments for felons (Rossi et al., 1985)—appeared to have very firm structures. Our interpretation is that the normative domains for the first set of substantive areas are less clearly defined than the latter set. In other words, there is more agreement among respondents over what constitutes sexual harassment than over what constitutes child abuse. However, because any empirical data set also contains measurement errors (a topic with which we will not deal here), the amounts of error found in the data sets may be a function of poorer or better measurement devices.

References

Garrett, K. and P. H. Rossi. 1978. "Judging the Seriousness of Child Abuse." *Medical Anthropology* 2.

Goldthorpe, J. H. and K. Hope. 1974. *The Social Grading of Occupations.* London: Oxford University Press.

Hodge, R. W. and P. H. Rossi. 1978. *Intergroup Consensus in Occupational Prestige Ratings.* Sozialwissenschaftliche-Annalen, Band 2.

Hodge, R. W., P. M. Siegel, and P. H. Rossi. 1966. "Occupational Prestige in the United States: 1925-1963." In *Class, Status and Power.* Edited by R. Bendix and S. M. Lipset. New York: Basic Books.

Judge, G. G., W. E. Griffiths, R. C. Hill, and T. Lee. 1985. *The Theory and Practice of Econometrics.* New York: John Wiley.

Kmenta, J. 1971. *Elements of Economics.* New York: Macmillan.

Meudell, B. 1982. "Household Social Standing: Dynamic and Static Dimensions." In *Measuring Social Judgments: The Factorial Survey Approach.* Edited by P. H. Rossi and S. Nock. Beverly Hills, CA: Sage.

Reiss, A. J. et al. 1961. *Occupations and Social Status.* New York: Free Press.

Rossi, P. H. and A. Anderson. 1982. "The Factorial Survey Approach: An Introduction." In *Measuring Social Judgments: The Factorial Survey Approach.* Edited by P. H. Rossi and S. Nock. Beverly Hills, CA: Sage.

Rossi, P. H. and R. A. Berk. 1985. "Varieties of Normative Consensus." *American Sociological Review* 50: 333-347.

Rossi, P. H., R. A. Berk, C. A. Bose, and E. Waite. 1974. "The Seriousness of Crime: Normative Structure and Individual Differences." *American Sociological Review* 39.

Rossi, P. H. and Z. Blum. 1969. "Class, Status and Poverty." In *On Understanding Poverty.* Edited by D. P. Moynihan. New York: Basic Books.

Rossi, P. H. and J. P. Henry. *Occupational Influences On Crime-Seriousness.* Unpublished paper.

Rossi, P. H. and S. Nock. 1978. "Ascription Versus Achievement in the Attribution of Social Status." *American Journal of Sociology* 84.

Rossi, P. H. and S. Nock. (Eds.) 1982. *Measuring Social Judgments: The Factorial Survey Approach.* Beverly Hills, CA: Sage.

Rossi, P. H. and J. Pereira. 1984. *Entitlement Norms: A Pilot Study.* Amherst, MA: Social and Demographic Research Institute.

Rossi, P. H., J. Simpson, and J. Miller. 1985. "Beyond Crime Seriousness: Fitting the Punishment to the Crime." *Quantitative Studies in Criminology* 1.

Rossi, P. H. and E. Weber-Burdin. 1983. "Sexual Harassment on the Campus." *Social Science Research* 12.

Treiman, D. J. 1977. *Occupational Prestige in Comparative Perspective.* New York: Academic Press.

U. S. Department of Justice. 1964. *Bureau of Justice Statistics. The Severity of Crime.* Bulletin, January.

6

The Problem of Order

Morris Zelditch, Jr.

The Question

"Individual choice and the social order" is the question of order in its classic form: It is concerned not with empirical, that is, testable, hypotheses but with what questions to ask in and what presuppositions are required by empirical inquiry. Goode (Chapter 3) comes to two conclusions: No theory of action can be as barren of institutions and structure as contemporary exchange, even social exchange, theory; but structure cannot be understood only in holistic terms, that is, without actors, without giving up the task of understanding how structure is created and maintained. Goode's chapter is the record of his sometimes painful struggle to reconcile the actor and the emergent in a single framework.

The correct question to ask about this position is how fruitful it is. Goode's chapter is metatheoretical rather than theoretical or empirical. It is concerned with the presuppositions required by empirical inquiry, not with empirical answers. I do not mean to derogate it by saying this because metatheory is the inescapable foundation of any empirical inquiry. I mean to say merely that it makes no sense to ask of Goode's position whether it is true or false any more than it makes sense to ask whether Parsons was empirically correct that all action is normatively oriented, or utilitarians that all actors maximize utility, or conflict theorists that all systems are reducible to only two (collective) actors.

Tests of all such premises are circular: Any empirical test of them also presupposes them in the way it deduces inferences from observations. In any case, they are pure tautologies. If action is not normatively oriented, it is not "action." Maximizing utility means only that people prefer to do what they prefer to do. Bilateral conflict is not a hypothesis about observable class relations; it is an analytic device. In view of the infrequency of bilateral structures, it would have long since been abandoned if it were about observable class relations. Such premises are directives, not empirical hypotheses. They instruct theorists in how to pose questions and formulate hypotheses. It makes little sense to ask if they are true or false but it makes good sense to ask how fruitful they are.

What is most fruitful about Goode's position is that it does not fall into easy but false dichotomies. His purpose is essentially to reconcile strategies that emphasize voluntarism with those that emphasize coercion and force, and strategies that emphasize structure with those that emphasize action. The history of the problem of order, whether you begin it with Plato or with Hobbes, has been a history of arid, irreconcilable conflicts over the horns of false dilemmas such as force (or conflict) versus consent (or consensus) and structure versus action. Goode manages, I believe, to avoid both these false dichotomies, to unite both force with consent and structure with action.

Goode's argument is founded on two articles of faith: that there is factual order—that is, empirical regularities of behavior—and concerted action—that is, actors who coordinate joint action for collective purpose. A social system that concerts action toward some collective end commits resources to accomplish it, implying both that it mobilizes resources from members and makes decisions that bind them to unitary courses of action. It is evident from the way the problem is stated that it makes little sense to suppose either that (1) any system except the most transient and smallest can be entirely mobilized by force alone or (2) that any system except the most transient and smallest can be entirely mobilized by voluntary consent alone. It is unreasonable to think of any except the most transient and smallest groups mobilizing resources by force alone because it is mobilization that creates force of the kind that controls the members of any large-scale, institutionalized social system. It is unreasonable to think of any except the most transient and smallest groups mobilizing resources by consent alone because consent is so undependable. What it is reasonable to suppose is that mobilization depends on consent somewhere but not necessarily everywhere in any large-scale institutionalized social system. The consent of a sufficient number, or of a number with sufficient resources, provides any system with the organizational capacity required to enforce its rules and decisions on those members who do not voluntarily consent to them. But without voluntary consent at least somewhere, a system is incapable either of organization or institutionalization on any scale.

Goode avoids a second false dichotomy by refusing either to reject pregiven structure or to regard it as complete. No one has ever supposed that the "state of nature" actually exists, hence no one has ever conceived of the possibility that a sociologist will actually observe the emergence of a wholly new order out of perfect anomie. It follows that one necessarily presupposes that some pregiven structure exists and that it determines any actually observable interaction. This is a basic thesis of Goode's argument, and applies as much to interactionism and ethnomethodology as to exchange theory. But he also points out that the pregiven is never complete. Rules do not guarantee their own application, there are often multiple rules and they often conflict, and rules in any case, because they must be general to be rules, never fit every conceivable circumstance. Little crises of order must therefore be very common, and new rules, or elaborations of old rules, must be emerging all the time.

Interaction must therefore be conceived of as a process in which some pregiven structure is input to every particular situation, constituting one of the conditions that governs interaction in that situation; but actors are also actively creating particular orders out of particular circumstances in many, if not all, particular situations, the outcomes of each interaction being the further elaboration of the pregiven structure. The conditions under which such elaboration is maintained in subsequent interaction will presumably depend on, and hence be a useful way to study, the process of institutionalization. Thus in Goode's sociology people are neither passive, oversocialized emanations of the pregiven social order nor wholly free to affirm or deny it.

Methods of Answering the Question

Rossi, Berk, and Douglas are concerned not with what question to put but how best to put it. Their question is not Goode's question; it is Parsons's. Both chapters presuppose that "order" is a pregiven normative structure. Each brilliantly solves the problem of how to find such order, but they solve it in opposite ways. The Rossi and Berk chapter is the best example I have ever read of the direct method of inferring order: It is lucid, elegant, exact, and systematic; altogether beautiful. Douglas's chapter is a profound, subtle, insightful theory of how cognitions are determined by the social order: "Facts" that are remembered are facts the methods of ratification and implications for structure of which interlock with those of other facts and are used in private and public action. The theory provides a tool for thinking about order that Douglas refers to as a "back door," that is, an indirect method. By contrast, Rossi and Berk's method is a "front-door" method. The two methods are not only different; each implies that the other is insufficient. Douglas argues that no direct method solves the self-referencing problem and that such methods are reactive. Rossi and Berk, somewhat less explicitly, imply that Douglas's method presupposes rather than measures the extent of order.

The self-referencing problem is the problem of asking questions about order independently of the categories provided by a particular social order for asking questions. Thought, even the thought of sociologists, constitutes, but also is constituted by, social order. What is in doubt, Douglas argues, is the possibility of ever having a thought about social order that is not a direct expression of the experience of one particular social order. It requires special contrivances if people created by a particular social order are to think in general ways about order. The special contrivance it requires is the study of silences, of what social orders cannot say, cannot ask, cannot think, and cannot remember.

Thus Douglas offers an analysis of structural myopia and amnesia in place of Rossi and Berk's front-door method. Her argument implies that their method is severely limited in scope. But a second argument that Douglas derives from the first does not, I think, have the same force. Douglas derives from her argument that direct methods are reactive, obtrusive measures. For example, she argues, instead of asking people for positive statements about food values one ought instead to study their garbage. The purpose is to find out what they really honor, which is more tellingly told by their behavior than their words. What they tell an interviewer in a survey is what they believe they ought to say, not what they do.

But normativity bias is a strange objection to make to a method of inferring norms. It in the first place does not follow from the self-referencing argument. It is undesirable only if one accepts the entirely separate premise that "real" order exists only in behavior. Certainly one wants to distinguish between real and ideal values, to penetrate behind a society's verbiage about charity and saintliness to what it "really" values, but Douglas's assumption that only behavior permits the inference of order is too strong. It requires that action emanate from norms when in fact there are multiple causes of action of which norms are only one. If one relaxes Douglas's assumption that "real" order exists only in behavior, then the normativity bias of the front-door method is undesirable only if the purpose is to predict behavior rather than to discover norms.

A more important implication of Douglas's concept of order is that order has features often neglected by the conventional sociological concept of a rule that is adopted by Rossi and Berk. Rossi and Berk take rules to be what is prescribed, permitted, or prohibited. They argue that this is what most sociologists mean by "rule" and in this they are probably right. But Douglas has a different concept of "rule," a concept deriving from Wittgenstein and the ordinary language philosophers, that distinguishes constitutive from regulative rules. Regulative rules exactly fit Rossi-Berk's paradigm of a rule: Thus a dealer playing bridge deals the cards clockwise, a player moving a pawn in chess moves it exactly one space except on the first move, a baseball player scoring a run must touch the plate, and so on. If the individual does not conform to the rules, he or she is in error; it is assumed that the individual will correct the error, and, if not, that there are penalties for being wrong.

Not all rules fit this paradigm of the regulative norm. Some rules, in fact, define rather than regulate, create rather than constrain. They constitute acts, empower actors. Thus the rules of bridge, chess, and baseball also establish what a player is, what moves count as moves in the game, what the goals of play are, what circumstances differentiate the conditions of play. They are usually not, as regulative rules are, in the imperative. They are declarative, they are "is" and "in order to" rather than "must" or "must-not" rules, they describe how an action is done if one is doing the action, and the mark of such rules is that if one does not follow them one is not doing X wrong; one is simply not doing X.[1]

The difference between the two kinds of rule affects what conformity to a rule means, what motivates it, and how social controls regulate it. The definition of a constitutive rule is that if one does not follow the rules of X, one is not doing X. One is not playing baseball if one is not on a diamond, one is not playing chess if one is moving pieces around a blank table, one is not playing bridge if one is fiddling with cards scattered on the floor. What motivates conformity to constitutive rules is the desire to do X, not the promise of incentives for conformity of the fear of sanctions for nonconformity, and what controls the actor is not reward or punishment but the fact that not following the rules is a nonact, one has not done what one wanted to do. Thus institutions control behavior not only by constraining it but also by the ways in which they empower it, and insofar as empowering does constrain it the constraint lies not in sanctions but in the absence of a choice of ways of doing X.

It would be a valuable addition to their method if Rossi and Berk could extend it to constitutive rules. But from Rossi and Berk's perspective, Douglas's method has its own limits: What Rossi and Berk want to do is analyze consensus, infer its pattern from observed responses. The entire method depends on the fact that disorder is admitted as a possibility. This is not true of Douglas's method, although she has certainly reckoned with disorder in other places, as in *Natural Symbols* (1973). The back-door method is not Douglas's only method. But clearly one must think of the back-door method as one limited to that kind of order that is consensual. It is, like Garfinkel's breaches of order, a method of exposing to view what is so taken for granted that no one except a sociologist has questioned it. It is not very suitable for the study of disorder, dissensus, or conflict.

The Challenge In the Question

One thing all three chapters agree on is that order is not only a metatheoretical question; it is also an empirical question. Order is, of course, one of the fundamental metatheoretical issues in sociology. It is fair to say that a sociology without a concept of order is not a sociology. Even conflict sociologies have a concept of order, a concept of how a society is possible, of how pluralities of actors are related to each other—norms are not the only way to conceive of order. But it is equally fair to say that a metatheoretical concept of order is not enough. It is necessary, but it is not a sufficient condition for the growth of knowledge, a beginning but not the end of the tasks of an empirical sociology.

There is no paucity of empirical questions about order, and taken together, the three chapters in this section imply a rich agenda for research. One exploitable area, for example, is to study how controls differ for different kinds of rules. Another is implied in the distinction made by both Goode and Rossi and Berk between belief in and acknowledgment of social order, a distinction implicit also in Douglas because constitutive rules do not require internalized commitments; they require only knowing how something is done. Control processes may work differently not only for different kinds of rules but also when (1) individuals believe in the rules held by the group, (2) individuals do not believe in the rules held by the group, and (3) individuals believe in rules not held by the group. In the first case, which corresponds to the kind of consensus that creates Douglas's silences, the fundamental question is the conditions under which people are awakened from them. In the second case, of which Prohibition was a notable example, what one wants to know is whether Prohibition exhausts the possibilities of the question. In the third case, which corresponds to something like the desire to enforce affirmative action policies in surroundings in which they are not the norm, the question is whether individuals attempt control over others when their beliefs are not supported by group norms and what the consequences are if they do.

A third exploitable topic of research is emergence. Here the task is only hinted at, in Goode, and the hint is perhaps too undifferentiated. Emergence is not a unitary process. There are at least six, perhaps more, distinct ways that rules emerge: (1) tacitly and informally; (2) informally, but out of explicit agreements; (3) contractually, in formal agreements; (4) out of the rule-making activities of specialized bodies, such as legislative assemblies; (5) from judges; (6) from executive authorities, making ordinances out of commands.

Rossi and Berk complain that there is a paucity of research about norms, and the study of emergence is a good example. Political scientists have studied legislation extensively, but usually they have studied allocative rather than regulative issues. Organizational sociologists have also studied rule-making activities of authorities fairly extensively. And there is a very small body of work on judge-made law and the sociology of contracts. But there is almost nothing about tacit emergence or informal agreements, and even less has been done to integrate what we know into a coherent body of knowledge. Nevertheless, it would be a mistake to view all this too pessimistically. What should be emphasized is the richness of the subject, and the challenge implicit in how much of it is ahead rather than behind us.

Note

1. Both kinds of rules are binding rules, to be distinguished from a third, strategic, kind of rule consisting in contingent, instrumental maxims or rules of thumb that are guides to how to do X better; including how to choose the best opening gambit in chess, what the percentages of a given hand are in poker or of a given substitution in the batting order of a baseball game, and so on. These also extend the conventional sociological notion of a rule, but neither Douglas nor Rossi and Berk touches on strategic rules and I therefore omit them from the discussion.

Reference

Douglas, M. 1973. *Natural Symbols.* London: Barrie and Jenkins.

Part II

Utopian and Dystopian Views of the Social Fabric

7

Orwell as Macrosociologist

Morris Janowitz

GEORGE ORWELL'S REPUTATION rests mainly on his two books on the modern totalitarian state. These two books, *Animal Farm* and *1984*, represent powerful writing. Saul Bellow considers George Orwell one of the most distinguished literary figures of the contemporary period. Current critics express the view that the passage of forty years has not downgraded the "humanistic worth" of these volumes. Interest in *Animal Farm* and *1984* has been widespread. I am told that each of these books sold more than ten million copies. Even if that figure is a gross overstatement, for a serious literary work to sell more than five million copies in the United States is an awesome achievement. This figure was facilitated by many high school and college teachers who made the purchase of these titles mandatory for their courses. Others "pushed" the sale of the books where it was not mandatory. There is no other work written in the contemporary period that has had such massive exposure. Margaret Mead's reputed one million copies of *Coming of Age in Samoa* pales by comparison.

Orwell's books deal with the basic issue of the future of the totalitarian state. George Orwell is in error about the durability of the totalitarian state. He is wrong in his implication that the nation-state that experienced this form of government would necessarily persist as a totalitarian state. In particular, the USSR, Germany, Italy, and Japan have had different political histories, but since 1945 they all converge in moving away from the totalitarian models as used by George Orwell.

It is possible for totalitarianism to engulf any nation-state. However, the distinction between the totalitarian states and authoritarian states helps the macrosociologist to offer a more subtle analysis. An authoritarian regime is much less brutal and repressive than a totalitarian one. I shall return to this theme.

Of course, the democratic nations of Northwest Europe are subject to the threat of totalitarianism, and this includes Great Britain. The probability of this group becoming totalitarian is much lower. For Orwell, the modern police state is a very general category, so all nations are threatened in various degrees. In fact, Great Britain is so vulnerable that it becomes the central case in his analysis.

George Orwell's writing on the totalitarian state appeared at the end of all too short a career. He died soon after the end of World War II at the age of 47. He had completed at least six titles that deserve examination in order to assess his two centerpieces. Of these titles, two are particularly noteworthy: *Down and Out in Paris and London* and *The Road to Wigan Pier*. The central theme of these volumes is the description of poverty, sickness, old age, and "social-economic" misery at the bottom of society.

George Orwell was born into a middle-class family without money. He grew up in a Tory atmosphere and moved to the left. But he was no stereotyped intellectual radical. As a young man, he held various low-paying jobs. These experiences enlarged his outlook and sharpened his sense of reality. In fact, his intense work experience helped his literary efforts and development. In effect, he was engaged in meaningful sociology. However, he wrote without concern for sociological formalisms. He gradually achieved reasonable and adequate economic conditions for his writing. He deeply engaged himself in writing and achieved a solid reputation. Of his social realism books, the book I know best is *Down and Out in Paris and London*.

George Orwell was hardly a typical writer-radical. He had too much experience to accept the cliches of the period, and he was more an observer-writer than a political activist. His "fieldwork" enabled him to be realistic in his writing and to maintain a deep sense of sympathy for the underdog. In *The Road to Wigan Pier* he expresses his negativism toward the blindness and arrogance of many left-wing writers. For example, in *The Road to Wigan Pier*, he is explicitly fearful of a collectivist society. He is concerned with the consequences of any social arrangement into which all members of society would fit in their "proper" place. Such a society would carry the threat of repression and be limited in what I would call the looseness required for personal freedom. Likewise, his doubts and implied criticism of "collectivist" solutions are laid bare in *Hommage to Catalonia*. This book, which deals with the Spanish Civil War, hardly glorifies the leaders of the militant left.

These two books on the police state are markedly different in style from the novels based on social realism. The difference between the two styles of writing offered by Orwell is so immense that one wonders if the same person wrote both. The splendid style and richness of detail utilized to describe social conditions gives way to a highly condensed type of prose. It is important to remember that Orwell calls both *Animal Farm* and *1984* novels. If they are novels, they are a unique type of novel; this is the case especially for *Animal Farm*.

The terse style is most appropriate. It permits and facilitates "packing in" an immense amount of material. His detailed explication of the techniques of the totalitarian state are presented with immense force. Even on rereading, it is nervewracking. Moreover, it is necessary for the reader to keep in mind that the book was written in the late 1940s. The academic study of totalitarian and authoritarian states in depth was just getting under way. Orwell jumps in without any disclaimer to present a picture that, despite important omissions, is spectacular. In effect, he offers an "ideal type of analysis." The view he presents is not mainly derivative but of his own construction. It is brilliant, but not without fundamental flaws.

George Orwell focuses heavily on a social portrait of the "mass media" and their personnel. The result is a mixture of description and ruthless satire. Orwell is basically in a polemical mood. In both volumes, he seeks to spread an understanding of the vast human destruction that total repressive control permits and generates. In the police state the media officials have among their goals the separation of the individual from his or her past. For this purpose, a new language is gradually developed.

The mass media machinery is highly developed and subjected to daily supervision and review. But how effective are the mass media?

Orwell believes that they are very effective, but I believe that he overstates the effectiveness of the mass media.

It is essential that we make a distinction between the role of the mass media in the rise and seizure of power and the impact of the mass media once there has been an installation of a totalitarian regime. Despite popular beliefs, the mass media are of limited effectiveness in the totalitarian setting. In the rise to power of totalitarian movements, mass propaganda is more effective than it is after the seizure of power. This observation appears to be a paradox, but it is not. Under the totalitarian state, the mass media's power is derived from coercive agencies of the state. The mass media contribute to repressive behavior precisely because they are backed by a "reliable" armed force. Lack of accurate information among the population is probably more important than propaganda campaigns under totalitarianism.

Orwell's analysis spells out the details of the propaganda system, but he fails to provide a picture of the institutional pattern of repressive machinery in a totalitarian state. In particular, he avoids probing the living arrangements, especially of the "proles" by which the ordinary "citizen" works out a system of survival. His outlook is essentially psychological microanalysis and not social institutional analysis. We encounter such an emphasis at many crucial points in *1984*.

Orwell is not a futurologist; his success in predicting the future is not crucial. Like many trained sociologists, he is seeking an understanding of a complex set of issues. His overemphasis on the psychological process and underemphasis on social organization prevents a broad understanding of the limits of the police state. There was no inherent reason why Orwell should have worked within this imbalance, but he did and the results influence and distort his conclusions.

In essence, Orwell does not come to grips with the central issue concerning the diffusion and relative durability of the totalitarian state. It is clear that Orwell anticipated a spread of repressive governments. He seemed to believe that World War II would hardly eliminate totalitarian states. They would persist and expand. In the simplest language, Orwell was wrong. In three totalitarian societies, the reverse took place: Germany, Italy and Japan. Comparative study—that is, cross-national analysis—is a complex and difficult task. These three societies emerged from World War II with difficult sociopolitical problems. It could happen that one or another could produce a "police-type" regime in the future, but I doubt that such a reversal will take place.

The case of the USSR is different but of particular interest. The impact of World War II was immense and one might have expected the result to be a continuation of a totalitarian regime. But again, such an outcome has not been the case. The Russians have not produced a democratic society, but they are no longer operating as a full-scale totalitarian society. The full-scale return to such a regime does not seem likely in the next decades. The important point is that, compared with the 1930s, the Russian regime has moved toward a limitation of its most repressive features. My view is that the drive to increased industrial goals has limited the degree of repression that can be tolerated. An industrial society such as the contemporary USSR can no longer function in the political atmosphere of the 1930s.

The most important of George Orwell's predictions, or rather, expectations, was that Great Britain, along with the rest of the English-speaking nations, would move away from a "democratic" format. Orwell uses the term *Insoc* to characterize the new ideology. Great Britain would follow the master trends of post-World War II, and there would be a changed British society.

In short, the population living under a full-fledged totalitarian regime has declined. In fact, the postwar period is best described in terms of the decline and, in fact, at least a temporary elimination of totalitarian political systems and the rise of authoritarian ones. An authoritarian regime has some element of repression, but we are dealing with a different threshold. In particular, the massive reliance on the police force and especially on the concentration camp is strikingly absent or limited in most authoritarian regimes.

The extension of political independence after World War II was not accompanied by the spread of democratic political processes but rather by that of authoritarian regimes. The authoritarianism of the colonial powers was replaced by locally based authoritarian leaders. This has been a profound disappointment, but the level of repression and coercion was relatively limited and there have been cases in which the level of authoritarianism has decreased. However, George Orwell is not sensitive to these trends. I believe that he would argue that the social scientist is making distinctions of little importance.

When these books first appeared, they rapidly developed widespread audiences. The interest and sharp debate was refreshing to teachers in various disciplines from the social sciences to English and the humanities. Many teachers had a special, positive response: They

believed that advanced industrial society developed a mass bureaucracy that alienated and dehumanized both the teacher and the
student. The bulk of teachers interested in such books were not
political, but saw in the books an opportunity to raise questions about
U.S. education. I see no evidence that the interests of the teachers
produced any relevant social change in educational practices. It
permitted letting off steam, and served as a form of catharsis. Social
reform requires more than catharsis; it requires an agenda as well.
The elements of an agenda are missing.

In the decades of the 1950s and 1960s, these books became
standard curriculum. There has been a slow erosion of interest in
them as teaching materials, but they still are appealing to many
students. I am not certain that the impact, because of the absence of
an agenda, was on the whole beneficial. I would like to stress that I
believe that the novelist, the humanistic writer, must or should
present his or her sociopolitical position. Such a position is easily
misunderstood. I am not expecting the writer, and especially the
novelist, to offer an elaborated political agenda. I am requesting the
humanistic writer to present at least a suggestion indicative of the
direction of political change, or nonchange, that appeals to him or
her.

It must be remembered that the combination of *Animal Farm* and
1984 appealed both to the liberal and conservative student. My
colleague, Paul Baker, a careful student of the teaching of the social
sciences, believes that students who read these books divide sharply
between those who accept the main thesis and those who reject it.
Few students are indifferent. I agree with Baker that these books
cannot be said to contribute to creating political consensus. Those
who accept Orwell's sociopolitical writing emphasize that the world
is already slipping into a system of repression. Those who reject
Orwell speak of the long-range ability of U.S. society to solve
problems up to a point, including the problem of balance of
individual rights versus group obligations. But it is my estimation that
Orwell did contribute to the political education of the new generation by posing questions. But to pose questions without presenting
social and political alternatives is indeed unsatisfactory and even
dangerous.

8

War and Peace in Oceania

Kai Erikson

OCEANIA, YOU WILL REMEMBER, was perpetually at war, although the face of the enemy was subject to instant change. The signs of war were not hard to find. Solitary rocket bombs landed on London from time to time in what seemed a lazy and random pattern. Images of the enemy were flashed on the telescreen with some regularity. Public executions were staged every now and then. And passers-by occasionally caught a glimpse of prisoners being transported to whatever fate awaited them—"little yellow men in shabby greenish uniforms" with "sad Mongolian faces" (Orwell, 1983, p. 96).

For the most part, however, everyday life in Oceania was not greatly affected by the fortunes of war. There were no cycles of mobilization and demobilization, of destruction and rebuilding. Rationing was a constant. Surveillance was a constant. Only those who, like Winston Smith, managed somehow to retain a few rags and bones of memory, had even a fleeting sense of the difference between peace and war. For the rest, such a distinction had largely disappeared.

It was the *emotions* of the citizenry that were mobilized. People were kept at a constant pitch of excitement—poised, as it were, on the edge of fury—and the excitement would reach momentary peaks during the daily Two Minutes Hate, and erupt into a kind of mad frenzy, a true "delirium," during Hate Week.

In one sense, at least, this was war in its pure state, the absolute essence of war. In "real" history, enemies appear on the horizon or within our own borders who offend us, and war becomes the agency by which the ensuing quarrel is settled. However often we go to war, we experience it as a puncturing of the peace. We say that it "broke out," and we give it an identifying name. But in Oceania it was the other way around. The state of war was a given, and enemies and causes had to be found for it after the fact. Oceania's Emmanuel Goldstein wrote in The Book that "it is a warfare of limited aims between combatants who are unable to destroy one another, have no material cause for fighting, and are not divided by any genuine ideological difference" (Orwell, 1983, p. 153). Why, then, does it take place?

One reason is implicit in the text, and it is sound sociology as well. The people of Oceania are not bound to one another by kinship, culture, or a sense of shared history, and such fellow feeling as there is comes almost wholly from common loathings. Community is created at the center of group space by supplying a hard outer edge of fear and hate. "The social atmosphere," Goldstein explains, "is that of a besieged city . . . the special mental atmosphere that a hierarchical society needs" (p. 158).

Another reason, according to Goldstein, is that the constant fighting discharges whatever surpluses the hard-worked people of Oceania manage to create. "The primary aim of modern warfare," he writes, "is to use up the products of the machine without raising the general standard of living" (p. 155).

> War is a way of shattering to pieces, or pouring into the stratosphere, or sinking into the depths of the sea, materials which might otherwise be used to make the masses too comfortable, and hence, in the long run, too intelligent. . . . In principle the war effort is always so planned as to eat up any surplus that might exist after meeting the bare needs of the population [p. 157].

It might be noted in passing, although the thought does not figure in Orwell's novel, that other surpluses are discharged in warfare as well: a surplus of vigor, a surplus of unneeded skills, a surplus of resentment—a surplus, in short, of all those youthful ingredients that, fused in the right way, can mean rebellion.

There has been quite some discussion over the years about the literary species to which 1984 belongs. Orwell insisted, if in a somewhat oblique way, that the book was not so much a prophecy as a warning—a distortion of tendencies that seemed to him all too evident in the present. He called it "a fantasy . . . in the form of a naturalistic novel" (Hynes, 1971, p. 14), and he lived long enough to see it described as fable, parody, satire, nightmare, cautionary tale, and allegory. Orwell had written a few years before turning his energies to *1984*:

> This business of making people *conscious* of what is happening outside their own small circle is one of the major problems of our time, and a new literary technique will have to be evolved to meet it [1968, IV, p. 270].

Whether *1984* was that new literary technique or not, the novel is not only a glimpse at the future but an invitation to take a few brisk historical paces away from the present in order to look back at the place one has just vacated, with the clearer vision that distance provides. Orwell was deeply concerned about what was happening to the English language and to the moral temper of those people who not only expressed themselves in it but learned to think through it. He was deeply concerned about what was happening to the character of the State. Both of those concerns, clearly, are reflected in *1984*: the language and the political structure of Oceania are grotesque exaggerations of a disturbing present.

War was not a subject much discussed in Orwell's novel if one counts the lines devoted to it, but it is a dominating fact of the world portrayed there all the same. And it would be a natural response to Orwell's invitation to ask the same question of *our* 1984, as we did of Orwell's 1984. Why? Why war? Why do the nations so furiously rage together? A naive question, to be sure, but one that sounds much more natural when Orwell's work lies before us on the table. And it happens that some thought has been given to the subject in our discipline.

The social science literature, for example, is full of hypotheses about what used to be called, in a less delicate time, the "functions" of war. War, it has been said, is a device by which wealth, in the form of horses or camels or other objects of value, is redistributed. War is a device by which human beings are redistributed as well—captured in raids or scattered by the force of some offensive. War is a device by which pent-up irritations are directed outward, as was the case for the New Guinea native who told John Whiting (1944, p. 143) that he had organized a raid because his wife had made his "belly hot with anger." War is a device by which people in power diffuse the energies of other people whose bellies, for different reasons, are also hot with anger. Shakespeare's Henry IV, canny in the ways of statecraft, advised his son:

> Therefore, my Harry,
> Be it thy course to busy giddy minds
> With foreign quarrels.

And so on. The modern uses of war—if our literature is any measure—all have to do with increasing the size of a territory, increasing the reach of a sovereignty, increasing the richness of a purse. The literature on war in the social and behavioral sciences is, by now, fairly extensive, but the part of it that touches on the origins of warfare seems to trace to one or the other of two fundamental notions, both of them rather old.

The first is that warfare is built into the very tissues of humankind as a species. William James (1911, p. 272), himself a devoted pacifist, put the matter bluntly: "Our ancestors have bred pugnacity into our bone and marrow, and thousands of years of peace won't breed it out of us." The seeds of war, then, are in the human germ plasm itself. We are aggressive and combative and full of explosive rages as the result of our animal nature. Thus Hobbes. Thus Freud. Thus William McDougall. Thus Konrad Lorenz.

Now this may or may not be biological nonsense, but it makes a wholly unsatisfactory theory of warfare in any event. Even when a war has reached its emotional crest, only a small proportion of the populace is under arms; and only a small proportion of the persons under arms ever see combat; and, if S.L.A. Marshall and other observers are correct, only a small proportion of those who reach the combat zone ever fire their weapons or aim them at human targets. And that is to speak only of soldiers at the front; those who drop bombs from a mile in the air or fire artillery shells at targets two miles away can hardly be said to be acting out of anger. If aggression is general to the species, it is amazing how few of us are able to express it in wartime! Samuel A. Stouffer (1949, p. 108) and the other authors of *The American Soldier* reported that only 2% of the enlisted men interviewed listed feelings of revenge as the most important factor in "keeping them going" in combat, one of several reasons why the authors concluded "that hatred of the enemy, personal and impersonal, was not a major element in combat motivation" (1949, p. 166).

In modern times, moreover, wars are declared by old men and old women who never see a minute of combat, and they are fought—for the most part, at least—by young men who, according to their own report, would rather not be there at all. If the old men and women who declare war are overwhelmed with rages seething from within, we can cite that fact in support of the biological argument if we want; but it makes no sense at all to assume that the same rages can be found in those who do the actual fighting.

The second of the two fundamental notions about the origins of war—this one being sociology's main contribution to the discussion—is that warfare is a natural counterpart to the emergence of human societies. The basic idea, expressed most sharply in the early years of the discipline by such as Herbert Spencer and William Graham Sumner, begins with what was taken as a biological truism: War is the natural way for human beings gathered into collectivities of one kind or another to compete, and competition, in its turn, is the one fixed law of nature. "War arises from the competition of life," wrote Sumner (in the first issue of *The Yale Review*), which can be seen as "a fundamental condition of human existence. . . . It is the competition of life, therefore, which makes war, and that is why war always has existed and always will" (1911, pp. 5, 6). This view was widely held until the early years of World War II, not only by Spencer and Sumner, both of them hard-core social Darwinists, but also by sociologists whom we like to remember as of a gentler and more reflective cast of mind—such as Robert E. Park (1941).

War, then, is the inevitable outcome of human grouping, but it is also the fire in which the bonds that obtain within the group are tempered and made stronger. By joining hands in opposition to an enemy "they," the members of the group cohere ever more closely together and develop a more secure and more lasting sense of "we." "So it has been with war," wrote Sumner (1971). "While men were fighting for glory and greed, for revenge and superstition, they were building human society" (p. 9). And William James (1911), echoing much the same general thought, described war as "the gory nurse that trained societies to cohesiveness" (p. 272). When war was "frequent and fierce," Sumner continued, the discipline of the group became harder and "the whole societal system was more firmly integrated." When there "was little or no war," on the other hand, "the internal organization remained lax and feeble," and "a societal system scarcely existed" (p. 8).

That is a fact of social life that the recruiting sergeant in Bertholt Brecht's *Mother Courage* understood perfectly:

> What they could use around here is a good war. What else can you expect with peace running wild all over the place? You know what the trouble with peace is? No organization. And when do you get organization? In a war. Peace is one big waste of equipment. Anything goes, no one gives a damn. See the way they eat? Cheese on pumpernickel, bacon on the cheese? Disgusting! How many horses have they got in this town? How many young men? Nobody knows! They haven't bothered to count 'em! That's peace for you! I've been in places where they haven't had a war for seventy years and you know what? The people haven't even been given names! They don't know who they are! It takes a war to fix that [1966, pp. 23-24].

That is also a social fact of life that a reflective citizen of Oceania, had the times allowed such a person to emerge, would have understood. The first of the three Party slogans in Oceania was WAR IS PEACE, the "inner meaning" of which, according to Goldstein (1983, p. 164), is that "by becoming continuous war has ceased to exist" and is thus indistinguishable from the inner zone of peace that the outer war helps shore up and keep intact.

Orwell, incidentally, who distrusted the social sciences so passionately, would probably have been amazed to learn how old an insight the Party slogan really represented. William James (1911, p. 273):

> "Peace" in military mouths today is a synonym for "war expected." The word has become a pure provocation, and no government wishing peace sincerely should allow it ever to be printed in a newspaper. Every up-to-date dictionary should say that "peace" and "war" mean the same thing.

And William Graham Sumner (1911, pp. 6, 7):

> We can now see why the sentiments of peace and cooperation are complementary to sentiments of hostility outside. It is because any group, in order to be strong against an outside enemy, must be well disciplined, harmonious, and peaceful inside. . . . It is no paradox at all to say that peace makes war and war makes peace.

Now the "competition" of which Spencer and Sumner spoke is of a rare sort, because it takes the form of creatures slaughtering members of their own species in very large numbers. It is unlike anything encountered elsewhere in nature with the possible exception of a few odd strains of ants—for most creatures, whatever the furies that burn within them, have built-in inhibitions against killing their own kind. All creatures fight, to be sure. At times of mating and nesting and drawing territorial boundaries in particular, the sounds of puffing and gnashing and snorting, the pounding of hooves and the clatter of horns, are heard widely in nature. But these collisions—for the most part, at any rate—are a kind of ritual combat from which both winner and loser retire alive, with their bodies—if not always their dignity—intact. Only human beings engage in simple brawling—a flailing about with fists and feet, thumbs and teeth—for no other apparent reason than to inflict harm and discharge anger. And only humans engage in organized warfare with creatures of their own kind, again with the exception of those fierce and obdurate ants I mentioned a moment ago. Nature may truly be "red in tooth and claw," as Tennyson thought, but the color is almost always provided by the blood of a different species. So war in any form is a rare biological phenomenon. It is probably even rare in our own history, for the earliest indications of organized hostility appear quite late in the human record, at least as evolutionary time is normally reckoned.

People war because they manage to persuade themselves that those they call "the enemy" are something less than entirely human, not quite worthy of whatever the usual civilities and decencies are that prevent neighbors from casually slaughtering each other.

Erik H. Erikson (1984, pp. 481-482) calls this "pseudospeciation," and means by use of the term to draw attention to the fact that

> mankind from the very beginning has appeared on the world stage split into tribes and nations, castes and classes, religions and ideologies, each of which acts as if it were a separate species created or planned at the beginning of time by supernatural will. Thus each develops not only a more or less firm sense of identity but even a kind of historical immortality . . . created superior to or at least unique among all others. . . .
>
> At its friendliest, "pseudo" means only that something has come to appear to be something it is not; and in the name of pseudo-species man could endow himself and his universe with tools and weapons, with roles and rules, with legends and myths and rituals, all of which would bind his group together and give to its existence the kind of super-individual significance that inspires not only hard work and sacrifice but loyalty, heroism, fellowship, and poetry. . . . What renders this "natural" process a potential malignancy of universal dimensions, however, is the fact that in times of threat and upheaval the idea of being the foremost species tends to be reinforced by a fanatic fear and hate of other pseudo-species. The feeling that those others must be annihilated or kept

"in their places" by warfare or conquest can become a periodical and reciprocal obsession of man.

The concept of "pseudospeciation" has received a biological seal of approval from such as Julian Huxley, Konrad Lorenz, and Stephen Jay Gould, and it is rich in psychoanalytic subtleties as well. In order not to be taxed by either the biological or the psychoanalytic implications of that concept here, however, it might be useful for the time being to speak of "social speciation" (as we pour through a thesaurus looking for something better) and end our definition with something like the following: social speciation, at its worst, can become a process by which one people manages to neutralize the humanity of another to such an extent that the inhibitions that normally prevent creatures of the same kind from killing one another wantonly are relaxed.

If it is the task of psychology to describe a tendency of which the human mind is capable, it is the task of sociology to describe the social and cultural scaffoldings that frame and give shape to that tendency. At the very least, social speciation lies at the outer edges of what we normally mean by "differentiation," and it clearly involves a supreme example of distancing. This is presumably what Raymond Aron (1962, p. 361) had in mind when he wrote, "Nonrecognition of one's own kind in the foreigner is one of the social and psychic roots of the distance between collectivities, hence of war."

What are the social forms that lend support?

Language, first of all, is certainly one of them. Glenn Gray (1959), who wrote a compelling memoir of men in combat, points out that we almost always use the definite article in speaking of wartime adversaries. It is rarely *our* enemy or *an* enemy, but *the* enemy—a usage that seems to hint darkly of something impersonal, something fixed and immutable, something abstract and evil. In a similar way, the words we use to refer to the enemy often involve a sharp denial of his humanity. Vietnam is so widely cited an example that it has almost lost its value as an illustration: slope, dink, slant, gook, zip—such terms, sounding almost like curses when said aloud, describe a landscape without real people. A Vietnam veteran said to Robert J. Lifton (1973, p. 204):

It's the good against the bad. It's always gooks. In every war we've ever fought, we haven't killed *people*. Even when we killed whites of the same religion and they looked like us, they were Krauts.

Second, dehumanization of enemies, both actual and potential, is a clear theme in the myths of people everywhere. The legends people tell of their own origins describe them as living at the center of the universe, specially blessed by God or nature or history or something else, and more human by far than those other creatures with whom the surface of the world must be shared. Joseph Campbell (1972, p. 171) writes,

> For it is a basic idea of practically every war mythology that the enemy is a monster and that in killing him one is protecting the only truly valuable order of human life on earth, which is that, of course, of one's own people.

Third, the dehumanization of the enemy is sometimes encouraged by the communalities of combat itself and the sheer numbness of spirit that it can bring about. The distinguished French biologist Jean Rostand said in an interview with the New York Times, "In war, man is much more a sheep than a wolf. He follows. He obeys" (Montagu, 1976, p. 272). And what he follows is not so much the orders of a superior as the momentum of the larger fellowship to which he belongs. It is difficult to find a battlefield memoir that does not speak of these bonds, although it may have been said best by a writer who had never been within a thousand miles of a front line when he wrote the following:

> There was a consciousness always of the presence of his comrades about him. He felt the subtle battle brotherhood more potent even than the cause for which they were fighting. It was a mysterious fraternity born of the smoke and danger of death. . . .
>
> He suddenly lost concern for himself, and forgot to look at a menacing fate. He became not a man but a member. He felt that something of which he was a part—a regiment, an army, a cause, or a country—was in a crisis. He was welded into a common personality which was dominated by a single desire. For some moments he could not flee no more than a finger can commit a revolution from a hand.

That was Stephen Crane in The Red Badge of Courage (1952, p. 41), but the same theme is sounded again and again in the reports of others. Here is the same Glenn Gray (1959, p. 121) quoted a moment ago:

> In mortal danger, numerous soldiers enter into a dazed condition in which all sharpness of consciousness is lost. When in this state, they can be caught up into the fire of communal ecstasy and forget about death by losing their indivi-

duality, or they can function like cells in a military organism, doing what is expected of them because it has become automatic.

Fourth and finally, hatred of the enemy, like any other enmity, has to be carefully taught, and that might be the longest chapter in any sociological account of this peculiar process in human life. In classrooms, in training camps, this kind of socialization goes on remorselessly in countries at war—or, as we have reason to know, in countries tuned for war.

And that's how it was in Oceania, too. To speak of *the* enemy in such a context makes better linguistic sense, for the country's adversaries were really more of a concept than a people, but enemy soldiers were portrayed as only marginally human. Behind Goldstein's (1983, pp. 14-15) head in the first glimpse we get of a telescreen,

There marched the endless columns of the Eurasian army row after row of solid-looking men with expressionless Asiatic faces, who swam up to the surface of the screen and vanished, to be replaced by others exactly similar.

And later, during Hate Week:

A new poster had suddenly appeared all over London. It had no caption, and represented simply the monstrous figure of a Eurasian soldier, three or four meters high, striding forward with expressionless Mongolian face and enormous boots, a submachine gun pointed from his hip. (1983, p. 123)

In Oceania, moreover, a citizen is forbidden to learn other languages or to encounter the people of Eurasia or Eastasia—this on the wholly sensible ground that

if he were allowed contact with foreigners he would discover that they are creatures similar to himself. . . . The sealed world in which he lives would be broken, and the fear, hatred, and self-righteousness on which his morale depends might evaporate [1983, p. 162].

To live in a world of such distances can be a wondrous, awesome, frightening thing, freeing the human imagination for projects that other creatures, cramped and inhibited, cannot even begin to undertake. As I draw these remarks to a close, having stirred up water I have no idea how to settle, let me give you a sample.

On May 3, 1982, the British fleet, thousands of miles from home, sank an Argentinian battleship. Three hundred young men—steaming for home, as it happens—were blown apart by the initial blast or drowned. The headline of the London *Sun* of May 4 read in its entirety: GOTCHA!

A poem had been written on an occasion much like that more than 80 years earlier by a person who found that kind of distancing hard to understand. The author was named Ernest Crosby (1906, pp. 13-14). The occasion was the sinking of the Spanish fleet by American warships in 1898:

> There is "great rejoicing at the nation's
>   capital." So says the morning's paper.
> The enemy's fleet has been annihilated.
> Mothers are delighted because other mothers have
>   lost sons just like their own;
> Wives and daughters smile at the thought of new-
>   made widows and orphans;
> Strong men are full of glee because other strong
>   men are either slain or doomed to rot alive in
>   torments.
> Small boys are delirious with pride and joy as
>   they fancy themselves thrusting swords into
>   soft flesh, and burning and laying waste such
>   homes as they themselves inhabit;
> Another capital is cast down with mourning and
>   humiliation just in proportion as ours is
>   raised up, and that is the very spice of our
>   triumph.

Now *there* is a problem that belongs on the research agenda of the social and behavioral sciences. If we could learn how that bit of human chemistry is done, how that cast of mind is created, we would stand on the edge of something very important.

References

Aron, R. 1962. *Peace and War: A Theory of International Relations*. Translated by R. Howard and A. Baker Fox. London: Weidenfield and Nicholson.

Brecht, B. 1966. *Mother Courage*. Translated by E. Bentley. New York: Grove.

Campbell, J. 1972. *Myths to Live By*. New York: Viking.

Crane, S. 1952. *The Red Badge of Courage and Selected Stories*. New York: New American Library. (pub. orig. 1895)

Crosby, E. 1906. "War and Hell." In *Swords and Plowshares*. New York: Funk & Wagnalls.

Erikson, E. H. 1984. "Reflections on Ethos and War." *The Yale Review* 73: 481-486.

Gray, G. J. 1959. *The Warriors: Reflections on Men in Battle*. New York: Harcourt Brace Jovanovich.

Hynes, S. L. 1971. *Twentieth Century Interpretations of 1984*. Englewood Cliffs, NJ: Prentice-Hall.

James, W. 1911. "The Moral Equivalent of War." In *Memories and Studies*. New York: Longman.

Lifton, R. J. 1973. *Home from the War*. New York: Simon & Schuster.

Lifton, R. J. and N. Humphrey. 1984. *In a Dark Time*. Boston: Harvard University Press.

Montagu, A. 1976. *The Nature of Human Aggression*. Oxford: Oxford University Press.

Orwell, G. 1968. "As I Please." In *Collected Essays, Journalism and Letters*. Edited by S. Orwell and I. Angus. London: Secker & Warburg.

Orwell, G. 1983. *Nineteen Eigthy-Four*. New York: New American Library.

Park, R. E. 1941. "The Social Function of War." *American Journal of Sociology* 46: 551-570.

Stoufler, S. A. et al. 1949. *The American Soldier* (Vol. II). Princeton, NJ: Princeton University Press.

Sumner, W. G. 1911. "War." *Yale Review* 1: 1-27.

Whiting, J.W.M. 1944. "The Frustration Complex in Kwoma Society." *Man* 44: 140-144.

9

The Iron Fist and the Velvet Glove: Totalitarian Potentials Within Democratic Structures

Gary T. Marx

Discovery and invention have made it possible for the government, by means far more effective than stretching upon the rack, to obtain disclosure in court of what is whispered in the closet.

—*Justice Brandeis*

As a polemical warning of what could happen, Orwell's *1984* is masterful. By the criteria of public awareness and mobilization for preventive action, it is an unparalleled success. Rather than judging the book by how accurately it describes current social reality, the comparision should be reversed; that is, how closely does society approximate the conditions envisioned in 1984?

AUTHOR'S NOTE: *I am grateful to Stan Cohen, Glenn Goodwin, Nancy Reichman, Jim Short, Steve Spitzer, and Ron Westrum for critical comments. In addition to the ASA meetings, some of the material was presented at a 1984 conference on George Orwell sponsored by the Council of Europe, and appears in* Dissent *(Winter 1985). The title is inspired by* The Iron Fist and the Velvet Glove *(Crime and Social Justice Associates, 1982). Police lyrics reprinted with permission of Hal Leonard Publishing Corporation.*

In Orwell's Oceania,

(1) the state is all powerful and the citizen has neither rights nor input into government;
(2) there is no law;
(3) mass communication is rigidly controlled by, and restricted to, the state;
(4) there are no voluntary associations (all such organizations are directly sponsored and controlled by the state)
(5) society is hierarchically organized, but there is little differentiation, diversity, or variety; everything possible is standardized and regimented;
(6) political and economic systems are merged;
(7) there is little social mobility and a low, and declining, standard of living; all surplus goes into war preparations rather than consumption;
(8) individuals are isolated from, and do not trust, each other;
(9) private communication is discouraged and writing instruments are prohibited;
(10) learning a foreign language and contact with foreigners are prohibited;
(11) individuals are increasingly bored, indifferent, and intolerant, and memory of past liberties fades with each year;
(12) proper attitudes and feelings are as or more important than proper behavior.

Empirical data on communications, social participation, and support for civil liberties in the United States today hardly fit this characterization. On most conventional measures of domestic affairs, this country is far from the society Orwell described. Much of the trend data suggest even further movement from it.[1]

Indeed in many ways the society sketched in *1984* is the opposite of contemporary Western democracies, especially with respect to physically coercive forms of oppression and the social conditions supporting such a repressive society.[2] This would be cause to celebrate, were it not for the fact that new, and potentially repressive, social forms and technologies have appeared.

Traditional social supports working against totalitarianism are strong, and perhaps growing stronger in the United States; an educated citizenry committed to democratic ideals, a variety of independent channels of mass communication, a plethora of voluntary organizations, and constitutional protections for civil liberties. I would not wish to be characterized, following Brecht, as a man smiling because he "has not yet heard the terrible news," however. For if the news is not terrible, it does not follow that it is good. To judge the state of freedom and liberty and their social supports only by the standard set by Orwell (and previous theorists such as Burke and Tocqueville who were concerned about the growth of the

Leviathan state), results in too narrow a vision and unwarranted optimism.

There is reason for concern about the state of privacy, liberty, and autonomy in Western democracies. Orwell's state used both violent and nonviolent forms of social control. In linking these, Orwell described only one of several possible totalitarian models: a model based on his experiences during the Spanish Civil War and his observations of the USSR, Germany, and Italy. Orwell's image of the future ("a boot stamping on a human face" and Big Brother watching) was drawn from those societies. Today, violent and nonviolent forms of social control are becoming uncoupled, with the latter increasing in importance. Therein lies the current danger. Over the last four decades subtle, seemingly less coercive, forms of control (some of which Orwell anticipated) have emerged. Their existence within societies that have not become less democratic, and in which the state makes less use of domestic violence, may obscure and blind us to their ominous potential.

Orwell's powerful vision needs to be updated. Threats to privacy and liberty are not limited to the use of force, or to state power, and indeed they may appear in the service of benign ends. It is important to examine control by other means, and by groups other than the state.[3] New forms of control and surveillance represent a profound break with the past, posing great challenges to students of society and all citizens.

The velvet glove is replacing, or covering, the iron fist. Orwell hints that the decline of physical coercion is consistent with the rise of liberty:

> The heirs of the French, English, and American revolutions had partly believed in their own phrases about the rights of man, freedom of speech, equality before the law, and the like, and had even allowed their conduct to be influenced by them to some extent. But by the fourth decade of the twentieth century all the main currents of political thought were authoritarian . . . and in the general hardening of outlook that set in round about 1930, practices which had been long abandoned, in some cases for hundreds of years—imprisonment without trial, the use of war prisoners as slaves, public executions, torture to extract confessions, the use of hostages and the deportation of whole populations . . . became common again.

Many of the major ideas associated with the French, English, and American revolutions have crept forward. Despite ebbs and flows, the rebirth of the domestic use of physical force for social control purposes has not occurred. The kinds of harsh empirical indicators Orwell implies (some of which Amnesty International and related groups use) are an appropriate, but incomplete standard. It does not follow that the absence of physical oppression guarantees liberty. Orwell did not anticipate, or develop, the possibility of significant inroads on privacy, liberty, and autonomy, even in a relatively nonviolent environment with democratic forms, and with presumed bulwarks against totalitarianism in place.

Given democratic political values, Orwell identified the right set of terrible outcomes for his dystopia: absence of privacy, freedom, and liberty, lack of individuality, mindless conformity, misinformation and disinformation, rampant fear, insecurity, and hatred, and the equation of morality and truth with power. Some of these conditions are possible, however, within the framework of traditional democratic societies.

In the United States there are clear limits on the use of coercion by control agents. But there are few limits on efforts to shape behavior through culture and public relations campaigns that seek to create the impression of police omnipresence and omnipotence.

Modern technology offers an alternative set of causal mechanisms of social control beyond those so frightfully described by Orwell. Indeed, the decline of violent means seems ironically to be associated with increased use of manipulation and deception. Two major forms of manipulation and deception involve efforts to control culture through the mass media and new technologies of surveillance. We will briefly consider the former before turning to an extensive discussion of the latter.

The Control of Culture

The velvet glove comes in various sizes and shapes and is more likely to hold what looks like a carrot than a stick. Our psyches are more invaded by the economy's need for consumers than by repressive political needs of the state. An economy and state oriented toward mass consumption has a more benign view of workers and the public than did nineteenth-century laissez faire capitalism. The masses are motivated not so much by scarcity or fear of punishment (as in Orwell's society), as by the promise of ever-increasing abundance. For the affluent, a dazzling array of consumer goods is available. For the poor, direct and indirect supports are offered by the welfare state. However minimal relative to the more affluent sectors of society, in absolute terms these supports are vastly superior to those available to the poor historically, and they may serve to mute dissent.

The self-conscious shaping of culture (and thus of behavior) through the manipulation of language and symbols, propaganda, and the rewriting of history is a major theme for Orwell, and one that has inspired much scholarly research. In Orwell's society, the state dominated the mass media and carefully designed media messages as an important nonviolent form of control.

Culture is invisible and usually taken for granted; we generally accept its myriad dictates unaware that we are doing so, or that a choice has been implicitly made for us. In the past, to a much greater extent than today, culture tended to develop nonpurposively from thousands of diverse sources, in an anarchic process of nondirected evolution. We are moving closer to the manufacture and control of culture found in Orwell's society, though private interests are involved to a much greater extent than is the state.

Since Orwell wrote, new varieties of professionals have appeared— media specialists, market researchers, political consultants, and public relations and advertising experts. They invent needs, package products (entertainers, politicians, public issues, or breakfast food), and sell the public. These skills are continually improving, though much art and guesswork remain (see, e.g., Fox and Lears, 1983, Schudson, 1984). Their influence may be experienced automatically and unreflectively. Even when we are aware that a choice has been made (for a political candidate, a foreign policy, an underarm deodorant, or a lifestyle), the technologies seek to make us feel that the choice is rational and voluntary.[4]

The state cannot watch everyone all the time. It is far more efficient to have all eyes riveted on common mass media stimuli offering messages of how to behave. Mass media persuasion is far more subtle and indirect than a truncheon over the head. Though the force involved is psychological rather than physical, it is not necessarily less coercive. Both violence and manipulation seek to counter informed consent and free choice. An adequate consideration of Orwell's vision and contemporary society must devote attention to culture and the mass media.

Another prominent form of the velvet glove involves medical and therapeutic responses to deviance, dissent, and disorder. By defining subjects as sick and in need of treatment (e.g., some psychotherapies, psychosurgery, pharmacology, genetic engineering), attention is diverted from structural bases for problematic behaviors and conditions. Here my attention must be limited to more direct forms of nonviolent control involving surveillance.[5]

The New Surveillance

The hit song "Every Breath You Take," recorded by a popular rock group, The Police, includes the following lyrics (my notes of available technology are in parentheses):

every breath you take	[breath analyzer]
every move you make	[motion detector]
every bond you break	[polygraph]
every step you take	[electronic anklet]
every single day	[continuous monitoring]
every word you say . . .	[bugs, wiretaps]
every night you stay . . .	[light amplifier]
every vow you break . . .	[voice stress analysis]
every smile you fake	[brain wave analysis]
every claim you stake . . .	[computer matching]
I'll be watching you	[closed circuit tv]

This song suggests that popular culture is more attuned to the social control implications of the "new surveillance" than is academic analysis.[6]

The surveillance component of social control is changing in subtle and often invisible ways, the elements of which are voluntary and not defined as surveillance.[7] For younger persons, especially, computerized dossiers, x-rayed luggage at airports, video cameras in banks, lie detector tests for employment, and electronic markers on consumer goods, and even library books, have always been the normal order of things. But their elders, too, are often unaware of the extent to which surveillance has become embedded in everyday relationships.

The new surveillance is related to broad changes in both technology and social organization. The rationalization of crime control that began in the nineteenth century has crossed a critical threshold as a result of recent technical and social developments. Technical innovations permit social control to penetrate and intrude in ways that previously were imagined only in science fiction. As digital information has become central to the working of the modern industrial state, traditional notions of privacy have been torn asunder. The information-gathering powers of the state and private organizations have been extended deep into the social fabric. The ethos of social control has expanded from focused and direct coercion used after the fact and against a particular target, to anticipatory actions entailing deception, manipulation, planning, and a diffuse pan-optic vision. The rough-and-ready cowboys of an earlier era have been replaced by new technocratic agents of social control and decentralized forms of monitoring.

Gigantic data banks made possible by computers raise important surveillance questions. The computers of the five largest credit reporting companies control more than 150 million individual credit records. Health records are increasingly computerized: More than nine out of ten working Americans have individual or group health insurance policies. Even pharmacies have begun to keep computerized records on patient's drug use and health characteristics. Individual financial transactions increasingly involve electronic tellers and electronic check and credit card authorization. Electronic Funds Transfer has become central to banking. The size and reach of criminal justice data bases, such as the FBI's National Criminal Justice Information Center, continue to grow.[8]

Surveillance is qualitatively altered with computers, as well. Bureaucratic checking of records before the advent of computers tended to be for errors, internal consistency, and missing information. Cross-checking vast data bases was simply not practical. With computerization, surveillance is routinized, broadened, and deepened. Bits of scattered information that formerly posed no threat to privacy are now joined. Organizational memories are extended over time and across space. Observations have a more textured dimensional quality. Rather than focusing on the discrete individual at one point in time and on static demographic data, surveillance increasingly involves more complex transactional analysis, relating persons and events (e.g., the timing of phone calls, travel, bank deposits; Burnham, 1983).

A thriving new computer-based, data-scavenging industry now sells information gleaned from sources such as drivers' licenses, vehicle and voter registration lists, birth, marriage and death directories, and census-tract records.

Many issues of privacy, civil liberties, uses of and control over information, unauthorized access, errors, and the rights of persons about whom information is gathered are raised by computer matching and profiling operations (see, e.g., Marx and Reichman, 1984).

Matching involves the comparison of information from two or more distinct data sources. In the United States more than 500 computer matching programs are routinely carried out by government at state and federal levels, and the matching done by private interests is far more extensive. Profiling involves an indirect and inductive logic. Often clues are sought that will increase the probability of discovering violations. A number of distinct data items are correlated in order to assess how closely a person or event approximates a predetermined model of known violations or violators. Consider the following examples:

A Massachusetts nursing home resident lost her eligibility for government medical assistance because of a bank and welfare records match. The computer correctly determined that she had more than the minimum amount permitted in a savings account. What the computer did not know was that the money was held in trust for a local funeral director and was to be used for her burial expenses. Regulations exempt burial contracts from asset calculations. Another woman was automatically cut off welfare because a loan for her son's college education had been temporarily deposited in her bank account pending payment of his tuition.

A welfare recipient in Washington, D.C., obtained employment and notified the welfare department. Despite repeated notifications of her new status, her welfare checks continued to come in the mail. She eventually cashed the checks to pay off doctor bills incurred from a serious illness. A computer match linking employment and welfare records resulted in her indictment on a felony charge. Before her trial, her name (along with 15 others) was listed in a newspaper story describing the successful results of a computer match. Her case was dismissed.

The Educational Testing Service uses profiling to help discover cheating. In 1982 it sent out about 2000 form letters alleging "copying" to takers of its scholastic aptitude tests based partly on computer analysis. The letters note that a statistical review "found close agreement of your answers with those on another answer sheet from the same test center. Such agreement is unusual and suggests that copying occurred." Students were told that in two weeks their scores would be cancelled and colleges notified, unless they provided "additional information" to prove they had not cheated.

In New York City, because of computer matching, persons cannot purchase a marriage license or register a deed for a new home if they have outstanding parking tickets.

Some of fiction's imaginary surveillance technology, such as the two-way television that George Orwell described, is now reality.

According to some observers, video-telephone communication is likely to be widespread in private homes by the year 2000. One-way video and film surveillance has expanded rapidly into shopping malls, banks, and other places of business. Cameras, with complete 360-degree movement and the ability to tape record are often concealed in ceiling globes.

The telescreen surveillance in *1984* is a wonderful representation of the pan-optic eye envisioned by social theorists such as Bentham. Orwell wrote, "Always the eyes watching you and the voice enveloping you. Asleep or awake, working or eating, indoors or out of doors, in the bath or in bed—no escape." Yet it had limits. It could not hear "a very low whisper" nor could movements "in darkness" be seen. And the "few cubic centimeters inside your skull" were "your own." Aircraft surveillance was limited to "Police Patrol" helicopters that, when "snooping into people's windows," had to skim "down between roofs." Surveillance is no longer limited by darkness, whispers, or distance. Given the claims made by increasingly sophisticated forms of physiological monitoring, even the "few cubic centimeters inside your skull" may not be one's own.

Recent developments permit intrusions that until recently were in the realm of science fiction, not envisioned even by Orwell: new and improved lasers, parabolic mikes and other bugs with powerful transmitters, subminiature tape recorders and video cameras, remote-camera and video and audiotape systems activated by sound or motion, a refrigerator sized tape machine that can record up to 40 conversations at once; means of seeing in the dark, detecting heat, motion, air currents, and vibrations; odor, pressure, sound, and contraband sensors; tracking devices and voice stress analyzers and techniques for reading mail without opening it.

Surveillance technology need not rely on relatively primitive helicopters skimming between buildings to permit peering into people's windows. "Mini-Awacs" that can spot a car or a person from 30,000 feet up have been used for surveillance of drug traffickers. Satellites may soon be used for this purpose as well, from 180 miles up. The CIA has apparently used satellite photographs for "domestic coverage" to determine the size and activities of antiwar demonstrations and civil disorders. Computer-enhanced photography can identify vehicles moving in the dark and detect camouflage.

The "starlight scope" light amplifier developed for the Vietnam War can be used with a variety of film and video cameras or binoculars. It needs only starlight, a partial moon, or a street lamp 500 yards away. By amplifying light 85,000 times night turns into day. Unlike earlier infrared devices, it gives off no tell-tale glow. The light amplifier can be mounted on a tripod or worn as goggles. Attached to a telescopic device, its range is over a mile.

The National Security Agency uses 2,000 staffed interception posts throughout the world, satellites, aircraft, and ships, to monitor electronic communication from and to the United States. Its computer system permits simultaneous monitoring of 54,000 telephone calls and cables. The agency is beyond customary judicial and legislative controls and can apparently disseminate information to other government agencies without a warrant (Bramford, 1983; Krajick, 1983).

The transmission of phone communication in digital form via microwave relays and satellites along with "cellular" automobile and cordless telephones using radio waves for transmissions and communication between computers offer new possibilities for eavesdropping.[9] Automatic telephone switching technology now records when, where, to whom and for how long, a call is made. A person whose phone rings now may see a digital display indicating where the call comes from before the phone is picked up.

A 400-pound, bullet-proof mobile robot "guard" has been developed. Equipped with a sonar rangefinder, sonic and infrared sensor, and an odor detector for locating humans, the robot can find its way through a strange building. Should it encounter an intruder, a stern synthesized voice intones, "You have been detected." Another "mobile robotic sentry" (the Prowler, for Programmable Robot Observer With Logical Enemy Response) resembles a miniature tank. It patrols an area and identifies intruders. Users can choose the robot's weaponry and whether or not human command (from a remote monitoring station) is needed before it opens fire. But not to worry. The manufacturer assures us that in the United States, "We don't foresee the Prowler armed with lethal weapons"; or if it is, "there will always be a human requirement in the loop."

Telemetric devices attached to a subject use radio waves to transmit information on the location and/or physiological condition of the wearer, permitting continuous remote measurement and control. Together with new organizational forms (e.g., halfway houses and community treatment centers) such devices diffuse the surveillance of the prison to the community. Offenders in at least four experimental jurisdictions are serving court-supervised sentences that stipulate wearing a monitoring anklet containing an electronic transmitter. Radio signals are picked up by a receiver connected to the telephone in the wearer's home. The receiver relays a signal to a central computer. If the wearer strays beyond 150 feet from the receiver or tries to remove or unplug the device, the interruption of the signal is displayed on a computer. A judge receives a daily printout from the system and any errant behavior must be explained.

In other proposed systems subjects are not restricted to their residences; however, their whereabouts are continuously known. A radio signal is fed into a modified missile-tracking device that graphs the wearer's location and can display it on a screen. The electronic leash can be attached to nonhuman objects as well. In some police departments, an automatic car-locator system (Automated Vehicle Monitoring) has been tried to help supervisors know exactly where patrol cars are at all times. Various hidden beepers can be attached to vehicles and other objects to trace their movements.[10]

The Hong Kong government is testing an electronic system for monitoring where, when, and how fast a car is driven. A small radio receiver in the car picks up low-frequency signals from wire loops set into streets and transmits the car's identification number. The system was presented as an efficient means for applying a road tax to Hong Kong's high concentration of cars. It can also be used to enforce speed limits and for surveillance. In the United States, a parking meter has recently been patented that registers inserted coins and then radios police when time has run out.

Surveillance of workers on assembly lines, in offices, and in stores, has expanded with computerized electronic devices. Factory outputs and mistakes can be more easily counted, and work pace controlled. Employee theft of expensive components or tools may be deterred by embedded sensors that emit a signal when taken through a barrier. Much has been written of the electronic office, where the data-processing machine serves both as work tool and monitoring device. Productivity and employee behavior thus are carefully watched (Marx and Sherizen, 1986; OTA, 1986). Even executives are not exempt. In some major American corporations communication flows (memo circulation, use of internal phone systems) are closely tracked.

In some offices, workers must inform the computer when they are going to the bathroom and when they return. Employees may be required to carry an ID card with a magnetic stripe and check in and out as they go to various "stations." The computer controls access to restricted areas, while continuously monitoring employee location.

A New Jersey hospital has what its director calls "a people-oriented system," designed to make the hospital more secure and also "to make the most efficient use of vital health care skills." Thus if a person stays too long at one place (e.g., the parking lot or the water cooler) the computer can alert a guard for possible assistance. The information is also used to "evaluate tardy employees."

Integrated "management systems" are now available that offer visual, audio, and digital information about the behavior of employees and customers. At many convenience stores information may be recorded from cash register entries, voices, motion, or from persons standing on a mat with a sensor. Audio and/or visual recordings and alarms may be programmed to respond to a large number of "triggering devices."[11]

Means of personal identification have gone far beyond the rather easily faked signature or photo ID. One new employee security-checking procedure involves retinal eye patterns. Before gaining access, or a benefit, a person's eyes are photographed through a set of binoculars, and an enlarged print of the retina pattern is compared to a previous print on file. Retina patterns are said to be more individual than thumbprints, offering greater certainty of identification. There is also a much improved technique for footprint or footwear identification. Signature verification technology, which analyzes the pressure and direction of a signature as it is being signed, can be automatically compared to data stored from previous signatures. A video camera that can distinguish guards from intruders has been developed and a camera able to identify particular persons by comparing the current image to one stored in its computer memory is being developed. These may be combined. A "hybrid multisensor system" developed by the Air Force examines voice, fingerprints, and handwriting before permitting entry to sensitive areas.

Scientists in the society Orwell described were "a mixture of psychologist and inquisitor, studying with extraordinary minuteness the meaning of facial expression, gestures and tones of voice, and testing truth producing effects of drugs, shock therapy, hypnosis and physical torture." The last decade has seen increased use of "scientific inference" or "personal truth technology," based on body clues (such as the polygraph, voice stress analysis, blood and urine analysis, and dogs and machines that "smell" contraband). There are claims that brain waves can be "read" as clues to certain internal states.[12] These highly diverse forms have at least one thing in common—they seek to verify an implicit or explicit claim regarding identity, attitudes, and behavior.

Although precise data on polygraph use are not available, indirect evidence suggests that its use is increasing (Hayden, 1981; Lykken, 1984). The number of persons trained to operate polygraphs has significantly increased. The most common use is not in criminal settings, but to screen job applicants. Such tests are used disproportionately by retailers, fast food franchises, drug stores, and nonunionized companies.

Conversations with pathologists and media reports suggest that use of "toxic drug screens" (of broad populations and particular suspects) has increased. According to one estimate, four million persons were required to undergo urinalysis tests in 1983.[13] Private citizens may play an increased role. A commercially available at-home urinalysis kit (with the lovely double-think name of "U-Care") makes it possible for parents to mail a child's (or other suspect's if they can get it) urine sample for analysis.

Increased public concern over drunk driving has led to broad population screens using roadblocks. A recent development for determining the amount of alcohol in a person's system permits easy assessment. All the officer needs to do is hold a microphone-like device or a special flashlight in front of the suspect, it is not even necessary for the person to agree to breathe into a breathalyzer.

Voice stress analyzers—of questionable reliability—are also in increased use. One firm offers an "ultra miniaturized" hand-held system that "in business or personal meetings" helps "determine if your employees are stealing . . . if your associates are cheating . . . if your friends are really your friends." The device is said to analyze a person's voice electronically for subaudible microtremors that, it is claimed, occur with stress and deception. A person need not know that he or she is being tested and "even your telephone conversations can be analyzed for truth." The CIA has reportedly used microwave lie detectors that measure stomach flutters from a half a mile away (*Christian Science Monitor,* 1984).

Undercover practices—those old, traditional means of surveillance and investigation—have drastically changed in form and expanded in scale during the last decade. Aided by technology and imagination, police and federal agencies have penetrated criminal, and sometimes noncriminal, milieus in utterly new ways (Marx, 1982; U.S. Congress, 1982, 1984). The individual undercover worker making isolated arrests has been supplemented by highly coordinated and staged team activities involving technological aides and many agents and arrests. Fake organizations beyond the imposter or infiltrator are key elements in many operations.

In the United States, the most involved agency is the Federal Bureau of Investigation. In the past, the FBI viewed undercover operations as too risky and costly (for both individuals and the agency's reputation) for use in routine investigations of conventional criminal activity. Now, however, in the words of an agent, "Undercover operations have become the cutting edge of the FBI's effort to ferret out concealed criminal activity." The number of such investigations steadily increased from 53 in 1977, to 239 in 1979, to 463 in 1981.

Beyond well-known cases (Abscam, the fake consulting firm run jointly by IBM and the FBI that sold "stolen" data to Japanese companies; the John DeLorean case; police posing as derelicts with exposed wallets or as fences purchasing stolen property), recent cases have involved policewomen posing as prostitutes and then arresting the men who propositioned them; tax agents stationed in banks and businesses posing as prospective buyers or clients in order to gain information; phony cases entered into the criminal justice system to test if prosecutors and judges would accept bribes; "bait sales" in which undercover agents offer to sell, at a very low price, allegedly stolen goods to merchants or persons they meet in bars; agents acting as guides for big game hunters and then arresting them for killing protected species or animals out of season.

Less costly investigative means involve informing and citizen surveillance. These decentralized and inexpensive forms have expanded significantly in the United States. A good example are hot lines for anonymous reporting. These range from a turn-in-a-poacher program in Connecticut to a Washington state program that encourages motorists to report individuals driving in expressway lanes reserved for car pools by dialing 764-HERO. Federal cabinet agencies are required to have hot lines where citizens can report abuses. All 19 federal inspector general offices have hotlines for receiving allegations of fraud, waste mismanagement, and other abuses.

Many private companies maintain an internal hotline for anonymous reporting, WeTiP, Inc., a nonprofit organization, offers a general, nationwide 24-hour toll-free hotline for reporting suspicious activity. One of the largest groups is TIP (turn-in-a-pusher) found in hundreds of communities. The video equivalent of the old reward posters is a program called "crime stoppers-USA, Inc.," now in over

450 cities. Televised reenactments ("the crime of the week") are used to encourage witnesses to unsolved crimes to come forward. There are also radio and newspaper versions. There is even a new mass circulation publication called *Reward Magazine*, the pages of which are designed to look like wanted posters. It offers cash for information that leads to the location of wanted suspects. There are also more generalized forms. One sheriff's department gives out leaflets that ask, "Do you know something the Sheriff should know?"

Other resources have been made available to support the flow of information from citizens to the state. The Federal Witness Protection Program provides relocation and a new identity to informants. Increased legislative and judicial protections are provided for whistle-blowers. Some legislation also makes it a crime not to report certain kinds of violations such as hazardous working or environmental conditions.

More open-ended and organized citizen crime-watching groups that report suspicious activity also should be noted. According to one estimate 20,000 communities have from 5 million to 10 million members of such groups. The National Sheriff's Association sponsors a group called "Neighborhood Watch" that exists in 2,500 communities. Detroit has groups on 4,000 of its 12,000 city blocks. The Citizens Crime Watch in Dade County, Florida, has 175,000 members and, like many such groups, has extended its operations into schools.

What were once scattered and isolated groups are nationally organized. Some of these programs are quite vigorous and have a social movement-like proselytizing quality. National staffs hold conferences aimed at starting new groups. Federal funds have also been provided for such programs.

Distinctive Attributes of the New Surveillance

Although the causes, nature, and consequences of the various new surveillance methods differ, they share to varying degrees nine characteristics relative to most traditional forms of social control. The new surveillance:

(1) TRANSCENDS DISTANCE, DARKNESS, AND PHYSICAL BARRIERS. As many observers have noted, the historic barriers to the old, Leviathan state lay in the sheer physical impossibility of extending the rulers' ideas and surveillance to the outer regions of vast empires; through closed

doors; and into the inner intellectual, emotional, and physical regions of the individual. Technology makes these intrusions easier. Technical impossibility and inefficiency have declined as the unplanned protectors of liberty.

(2) TRANSCENDS TIME AND ITS RECORDS CAN EASILY BE STORED, RETRIEVED, COMBINED, ANALYZED, AND COMMUNICATED. Surveillance information can be "socially freeze-dried" (Goodwin and Humphreys, 1982). When stored, it is available for analysis many years after the fact and in totally different interpretive contexts. Computer records, video- and audio-tapes and disc, photos, and various "signatures"—like workers or parts used in mass production—have become increasingly standardized and interchangeable. Information can be converted into portable forms, easily reproducible and transferable through telecommunications. Data thus can migrate to places far removed from original locations.

(3) IS CAPITAL- RATHER THAN LABOR INTENSIVE. Technical developments have dramatically altered the economics of surveillance. Information is easily sent back to a central source, making possible economies of scale. A few persons can monitor a great many persons and places (in contrast to traditional forms, such as the gumshoe tailing a suspect or manually searching records). Economy is further enhanced because persons become voluntary or involuntary consumers of much surveillance—indeed they participate in their own monitoring.

(4) TRIGGERS A SHIFT FROM TARGETING A SPECIFIC SUSPECT TO CATEGORICAL SUSPICION. In the novel Gorky Park the police inspector asks a central character who she suspects of having stolen her iceskates. She replies, "Everyone," to which the inspector responds, "So do I." In the technical implementation of Kafka's nightmare, modern society, too, suspects everyone. The camera, the tape recorder, the identity card, the metal detector, the obligatory tax form that must be filled out even if one has no income, and the computer make all who come within their province reasonable targets for surveillance. These "softer" forms of control tend toward the creation of a society where people are permanently under suspicion and surveillance. The Napoleonic assumption that everyone is guilty until proven innocent is facilitated by technologies that permit continuous, rather than intermittent, monitoring. As Michel Foucault observed, what is central is not physical coercion—but never-ending "judgements, examinations, and observation."

(5) HAS AS A MAJOR CONCERN THE PREVENTION OF VIOLATIONS. As Gordon Liddy observed in justifying the Watergate operation, "Closing the

barn door after the horse has gone" does no good. Anticipatory strategies seek to reduce risk and uncertainty. Bureaucratic organization and modern management, consistent with the idea of rationality, attempt to make control more predictable, reliable, and effective. As little is left to chance as possible. Control is extended to ever more features of the environment. Publicity about omnipresent and omnipowerful surveillance seeks to deter violations. Where violations cannot be prevented, the surroundings may be so structured that violators are either caught in the act or leave strong evidence of their identity and guilt.

(6) Is DECENTRALIZED—AND TRIGGERS SELF-POLICING. In contrast to the trend of the last century, information can now in principle flow as freely from the center to society's periphery as the reverse. National data resources are available to widely dispersed local officials. (The power of national elites, in turn, may also increase as they obtain instant information on those in the farthest reaches of the network.)

Those watched become (willingly, knowingly or not) active partners in their own monitoring, which is often self-activated and automatic. Persons often are motivated to report themselves to government agencies and large organizations and corporations in return for some benefit or to avoid a penalty. Subjects may directly trigger surveillance systems by, for example, talking on the telephone, turning on a TV set, checking a book out from the library, entering or leaving controlled areas.

(7) Is EITHER INVISIBLE OR HAS LOW VISIBILITY. It becomes ever more difficult to ascertain when and whether one is being watched and who is doing the watching. There is a distancing (both socially and geographically) between watchers and watched, and surveillance is increasingly depersonalized. Instruments are often difficult to discover, either because they are something other than they appear to be (one-way mirrors, or cameras hidden in a fire extinguisher or mannequin) or, as with snooping into microwave transmissions, there often are few indications of surveillance. Evidence may be hidden until some special process identifies it, as with fluorescent dust markings, hidden marks on currency and stocks, or a tiny beeper placed in a vehicle.

(8) Is MORE INTENSIVE—PROBING BENEATH SURFACES, DISCOVERING PREVIOUSLY INACCESSIBLE INFORMATION. Like drilling technology boring ever deeper into the earth, today's surveillance is able to probe ever deeper into physical, social, and personal areas. It hears whispers, penetrates clouds, walls, and windows. With blood and urine analysis and

stomach pumps it "sees" into the body—and with voice stress and polygraph analysis it attempts to "see" into the soul, claiming to go beneath ostensible meanings and appearances to real meanings.

(9) GROWS EVER MORE EXTENSIVE—COVERING NOT ONLY DEEPER, BUT LARGER AREAS. Previously unconnected surveillance threads now are woven into gigantic tapestries of information. Or, in Stan Cohen's (1985) imagery, the mesh of the fishing net has not only become finer and more pliable, the net itself now is wider. Broad new categories of person and behavior have become subjects for information collection and analysis, and as the pool of persons watched expands, so does the pool of watchers. Anyone may be watched: everyone is a potential watcher. The creation of uncertainty about whether or not surveillance is present is an important strategic element. Mass surveillance has become a reality. The increased number of watchers (human and electronic) and self-monitoring have re-created some of the dense controls characteristic of small, closely watched villages.

The awesome power of the new surveillance lies in the paradoxical, never before possible combination of decentralized and centralized forms. Forms of monitoring traditionally used only for criminal and espionage suspects, or prisoners, now are used for categorical monitoring of broad populations.[14]

The new surveillance has been generally welcomed by business, government, and law enforcement. It has many attractive features, examples of which are easily cited: the life of an elderly heart attack victim who lived alone was saved when her failure to open the refrigerator sent an alarm through her telephone to a centralized monitor; a corrupt (or corruptible) judge was caught when he took a bribe from a police agent pretending to be a criminal; serious crimes have been solved as a result of tips received on hot lines. Advanced emergency communications systems, which flash a 911 caller's whereabouts and phone number the instant an operator answers the phone, have saved lives. Satellite photography can monitor factory compliance with pollution emission standards. Credit cards ease consumer goods purchases; taxpayers' dollars are saved because of computer-matching programs; citizens may feel safer when video surveillance is present. Increasingly, Americans seem willing, even eager, to live with intrusive technologies because of anticipated benefits.

We are not hapless victims of technological determinism. Technology is created and used in social contexts, and choices are possible. Errors and problems of data tampering and misuse can be lessened by legislation and policies, good program design, and sensitive and intelligent management. To a greater extent than in most countries, the United States restricts the use of surveillance technologies, though there is often a significant lag between the appearance of a technology and its regulation; and regulation is often weak. Furthermore, in a free-market economy, some surveillance can be neutralized by countersurveillance devices.

My point is neither to advance a romantic neo-Luddite worldview nor to deny the enormous complexity of the moral judgments and trade-offs involved. I do not argue that more harm than good has resulted from these innovations. Absent a better statistical picture of extensiveness and consequences, and agreement as to how conflicting values are to be weighed, any such conclusion is unwarranted. But the eagerness to innovate and infatuation with technical progress and gimmickry may obscure real dangers.

There is nowhere to run or to hide. There is no exit from the prying eyes, ears, and data-processing machines of government and business. Citizens' ability to evade surveillance is diminishing. Participation in the consumer society and the welfare state requires personal information.

The new surveillance goes beyond merely invading privacy, as this term has conventionally been understood. Many of the constraints that made privacy possible are now irrelevant. Traditionally, privacy depended on certain technically or socially inviolate physical, spatial, or temporal barriers—varying from distance to darkness, to doors, to the right to remain silent. Invasion of privacy required crossing an intact barrier. The new technology transcends these barriers.

Individual freedom and liberty prosper when detailed information about a person's life, for the most part, is private. The idea of starting over in the new world or moving West to a new frontier, is a powerful one. The optimistic belief that people can change and improve, and the belief that once a debt has been paid to society it ought to be forgotten, are important American values. American popular culture prides itself on looking at what a person does today rather than what they may have done in the past. Devices such as sealed or destroyed records, prohibitions on certain kinds of record keeping, and constant requirements for the release of information reflect these concerns.

With massive computerized "jackets" on everyone so easily accessible, the past is likely to become increasingly important in structuring individual opportunities. Persons may never cease paying for earlier misdeeds. Aside from the possibility of locking in erroneous or sabotaged data, this may have the unintended consequence of permanent stigmatization. It might even increase commitment to rule breaking. Those who wish to lead law-abiding lives may face increasing difficulties as a result of electronic branding. Starting over may prove to be much more difficult.

The issues go far beyond criminal records and faulty computer banks. As records of education, work, health, housing, civil suits, and the like become ever more important in administering society, persons may decline needed services (as for mental health), avoid conflictual or controversial action (filing a grievance against a landlord), shun taking risks and experimenting for fear of what it will look like on the record. Conformity and uniformity may increase, squashing diversity, innovation, and vitality.

A related point concerns the changing nature of the things we wish to keep private. In 1930 much of what an individual wished to keep private could be kept in a desk drawer or a safe deposit box. But the location of personal information has shifted from the person to the large organization. Property in the form of information is less tangible. It can be seen or sent without a trace, and often without consent. Because the Fourth Amendment was designed for more tangible forms of property, and at a time when persons had much greater physical control over the things they wished to keep private, it does not cover recent incursions. The intrusive search behavior characteristic of the new surveillance is inconsistent with the spirit, if not the letter, of the Bill of Rights.

In the face of such intrusions, and the changing nature of property, it is important to rethink the nature of privacy and to create new supports for it. Some of these, ironically, must rely on new technologies (such as encrypted or scrambled communications, antiradar and debugging devices). Legislation and heightened public awareness are also important. Less than one state in five has laws requiring written standards for the collection, maintenance, and dissemination of personal information.

Yet more is at stake than privacy. The right to be left alone and to remain anonymous, so highly valued in modern society, is diminished. Vast publicly available data bases can be mined to yield precise lists, for example, of suspects or targets for sales pitches and solicitations. When they are linked with automatic telephone dialing equipment, or word processors, protection against invasion is increasingly difficult. Aside from annoyance, "personalized" yet standardized word processed solicitations may be threatening: "What do they know about me? how did they find out? what else do they know? who are they?"

The fragmentation and isolation characteristic of totalitarian societies result not only from the state's banning or absorption of private organizations, but because individuals mistrust institutions, organizations, and each other. The social bonds among individuals, organizations, and government are weakened. In a society where everyone is suspect and a target for temptation and investigation, trust—the most sacred and desirable element of the social bond—is damaged. To be sure, in modern society suspiciousness is often a prudent response. But what of its unintended consequences and its proportionality to the threat?

The new surveillance may actually increase fear of victimization. If the government and large private organizations feel they must take such intrusive steps, is there not a great deal to fear? Legitimacy thus may be unintentionally damaged. Corruption in Congress or the judiciary may lead people to the cynical conclusion that all participants in basic institutions are corrupt. Surveillance practices of businesses may encourage alienation on the part of employees. Employees in the large retail firms serviced by a leading private detective agency received a memo stating that "systematic checkings are made of every employee; you never know what day or hour you are being checked." Such warnings, together with practices previously discussed, communicate mistrust that may be cynically responded to in kind.

Making means of anonymous denunciation too easily available may also encourage distrust and lead to false and malicious accusations.[15] Because much surveillance is of low visibility or covert, accountability is lessened and exploitation and coverups are enhanced.

Distrust is furthered to the extent that social control seeks to perpetuate the "myth of surveillance." Advocates argue that creating the impression that persons are always being watched, or that they can never tell when they are being watched, results in deterrence. But it may also deter legitimate behavior such as political expression or applying for entitlements.[16]

The perception that surveillance is more powerful than it really is also deceives. The deception lies in the claim that people are being watched when often they are not (there is no one behind the one-way mirror, there is no monitor behind, or film in, the surveillance camera, there are no radar-equipped aircraft to monitor speeders). Deception occurs also when control agents and situations are disguised (e.g., police posing as elderly persons or alcoholics in the hope of attracting robbers, or as priests, journalists, lawyers, or doctors in the hope of eliciting information, or as private police posing as customers while testing cashiers or watching customers).

Efforts to convince people that techniques involving the polygraph, voice stress analyzer, and computer are more powerful than they actually are also deceive. Many people stand in fear of supposedly scientific investigative techniques. Nixon's remarks on the Watergate tapes are instructive: "Listen, I don't know anything about polygraphs, and I don't know how accurate they are, but I do know that they'll scare the hell out of people." Lie detectors are thought to be most effective when persons being tested believe that they work. This gives rise to a variety of ruses.[17]

Freedom of speech and action are inhibited when deception becomes official policy. Deception may increase in the society in self-defense and because it comes to be seen as acceptable and easier to rationalize.

Proliferation of the new techniques may create a lowest-denominator morality. In order to protect privacy and autonomy, the tactics against which one seeks protection may be adopted in self-defense.[18] The new surveillance may create an electronic climate of suspiciousness.

The new surveillance increases the power of large organizations. There is hardly equal access to these means, even if, in principle, most are available to any individual or group. Except in totalitarian countries, intrusive technologies do not long remain the exclusive property of the state.[19] Countermeans may reduce the impact of surveillance for those with the resources to employ them. The tables may also be turned as private citizens or public interest groups use computers and other surveillance means to monitor government and corporate activity.[20] Yet the availability of such technology gives little cause for optimism. Although it may serve to neutralize some intrusions, on balance the technology is not likely to be used only defensively or in the public interest.

The scale is still overwhelmingly tipped toward government and large organizations. In spite of the spread of home computers and mail-order snooping devices, individual consumers, renters, political dissenters, loan applicants, and public interest groups clearly do not have the surveillance and data analysis capabilities of credit card companies and marketing research firms, landlords' associations, police intelligence units, the NSA, banks, or large corporations. As a result the new surveillance technologies are an important factor in decreasing the power of the individual relative to large organizations and government.

Some other negative aspects of the new surveillance can be briefly mentioned:

IT IS CATEGORICAL in nature, involving "fishing expeditions" and "searches" absent any evidence of specific wrongdoing, thus violating the spirit of the Fourth Amendment. The presumption of innocence can be undermined—shifting the burden of proof from the state to the accused. There is also a danger of presumption of guilt (or an unwarranted innocence) by association or statistical artifact. And, because of the technical nature of the surveillance and its distancing aspects, the accused may (at least initially) be unable to face the accuser. The legal basis of some of the new surveillance's crime-prevention actions is also questionable.

THE SYSTEM'S FOCUS on prevention entails the risk of wasting resources on preventing things that would not have occurred in any case, or, as sometimes occurs in undercover activities, of creating violations through self-fulfilling affects.

POWERFUL NEW DISCOVERY mechanisms may overload the system. Authorities may discover far more violations than they can act upon. There is a certain wisdom to the ignorance of the three monkeys. Having information on an overabundance of violations can lead to the misuse of prosecutorial discretion or demoralization on the part of control agents. Charges of favoritism and corruption may appear as only some offenses can be acted upon.

IN ORWELL'S AND OTHER science fiction accounts, control is both highly repressive and efficient. There is perfect control over information (whether the ability to discover infractions with certainty or to manage beliefs). As the examples cited suggest, the new surveillance has great repressive potential (in actuality or via myth). But it is invariably less than perfectly effective and certain, and it is subject to manipulation and error.[21]

ALTHOUGH DETERRING OR DISCOVERING some offenders, the routinization of surveillance, ironically, may grant an almost guaranteed means for successful violations and theft to those who gain knowledge of the system and take action to neutralize and exploit it. This suggests that, over time, many of these systems will disproportionately net the marginal, amateur, occasional, or opportunistic violator rather than the master criminal. The systematization of surveillance may grant the latter a kind of license to steal, even while headlines hail the effectiveness of the new techniques.

A problem of a different order is the *apocalypse someday* argument, calling attention to future disasters rather than current problems (Rule et al., 1980). The potential for harm may be so great, should social conditions change, that creating surveillance systems may not be justified to begin with (e.g., creating linkages between all federal and state data banks and a mandatory national identification system).

Because there is as yet no catastrophe and there are many benign examples to point to, this argument is usually not given much credence. From this perspective, framing the policy debate around the reform of surveillance systems is misguided. The issue, instead, is whether the system should be there to begin with. Once these systems are institutionalized and taken for granted, even in a democratic society, they can be used for harmful ends. With a more repressive government and a more intolerant public—perhaps upset over severe economic downturns, large waves of immigration, social dislocations, or foreign policy setbacks—these same devices could easily be used against those with the "wrong" political beliefs, against racial, ethnic, or religious minorities, and those with lifestyles that offend the majority. A concern with prevention of disorder could mean a vastly expanded pool of "suspects."

Should totalitarianism ever come to the United States it is likely to occur by accretion rather than by cataclysmic event. As Sinclair Lewis argued (*It Can't Happen Here*), it would come in traditional American guise, with the gradual erosion of liberties.

Voluntary participation, beneficent rationales, and changes in cultural definition and language hide the onerous aspects of the new surveillance. As Justice Brandeis has warned:

> Experience should teach us to be most on our guard when the government's purposes are beneficent. Men born to freedom are naturally alert to repel invasion of their liberty by evil-minded rulers. The greatest dangers to liberty lurk in insidious encroachment by men of zeal, well-meaning, but without understanding [Olmstead, 1927].

The first task of a society that would have liberty and privacy is to guard against the misuse of physical coercion on the part of the state and private parties. The second task is to guard against the softer forms of secret and manipulative control. Because they are often subtle, indirect, invisible, diffuse, deceptive, and shrouded in benign justifications, this is clearly the more difficult task.

Notes

1. Supporting empirical data may be found in Marx (1983). Evaluating how closely data characterize a work of art is similar to a Rorschach test, where observers offer very different interpretations depending on their social locations, needs, and starting assumptions. Whether a glass of water is half empty or half full, and whether its purity should be judged by the highest standard imaginable or the worst known case, are hardly scientific questions, however precise and valid our measurements. Yet optimism with respect to civil rights and civil liberties seems warranted when contemporary Western democracies are compared to their checkered pasts, to contemporary totalitatian countries, or to the gap between technically possible surveillance capabilities and what is done in practice. The ratio between what those in authority do and what they are in principle capable of doing may not have increased and may even have decreased as technology has advanced, even if there is greater intrusion land use of state power than in the past.

2. These observations are restricted to domestic affairs, rather than to international relations, where elements of Orwell's description of broad superpower conflict may be more fitting.

3. The image of an all-powerful repressive state comes easily to Americans, whereas the image of equally powerful and repressive private groups does not. The novel *1984* focuses attention on the destruction of liberty, the invasion of privacy, and manipulation by government. In the United States there is much less awareness of threats from the private sector. From a civil liberties standpoint this narrowing of emphasis is unfortunate, given the size of the private sector, its self-seeking goals, and the fact that it has access to much of the technology that is available to government, while in many ways being subject to fewer restrictions.

4. By offering escapism and an unrepresentative picture of society, the media may also focus attention away from problems and avoid political challenges.

5. This discussion is at the level of political theory. I do not suggest that these are somehow equivalent in the pain and suffering they cause, even if the goal of control is similar. Forced to choose, the newer forms of control are likely less unattractive, although to some observers such as Paul Goodman, the choice between "the lesser of two evils" is not a choice between a half and a full loaf, "but between a more and less virulent form of rat poison."

6. A song by Rockwell contains the lines "I always feel like somebody's watchin' me and I have no privacy . . . can the people on tv see me or am I just paranoid?" Similar themes are sounded in a song by Hall and Oates, "Private Eyes": "They are watchin' you, they see your every move."

7. By surveillance I mean watching or monitoring persons, events, records, or places in order to discover violations, means of violation, or violators. Its goals include apprehension, intelligence, and prevention. Other aspects of social control include various forms of socialization, reward and punishment, rehabilitation, opportunity reduction, target hardening, and suspect weakening. By social control I mean the effort to see that others conform to rules. These forms of course may occur simultaneously or be intertwined. For example, eligibility for rewards or punishment may in principle be allocated on the basis of surveillance-determined eligibility. But they are distinct forms.

8. Expansion occurs in numbers of persons included and kinds of information. A 1984 proposal to expand that system to include data on "suspicious" person was defeated—this time. The validity and completeness of criminal record files varies significantly. They include records of persons who were not charged, or who were found not guilty; information on court disposition may be lacking. An analysis of the FBI's automated criminal history file found that 54% of the records disseminated had data quality problems. See Laudon (1986).

9. Laws are unclear or contradictory here. A 1934 Federal Communications Commission law protects voice transmissions that are sent over wires. In a recent case the Kansas Supreme Court

ruled that police may lawfully monitor and record cordless telephone conversations heard over an FM radio.

10. More generally EAS (electronic article surveillance) systems are constantly being extended. Now even in many supermarkets, should a customer go through a checkout stand with a concealed item, a buzzer sounds and lights flash.

11. In one system they operate randomly for 15 seconds of each two minutes. In addition they start running whenever the cash register drawer is opened or closed for longer than a specified time, when particular keys on the cash register are hit or hit "too often" (clear or no sale keys), when more than fifty dollars is in the cash register, or when the last bill is removed (suggesting robbery).

12. Burnham (1983, p. 255) refers to research seeking to "read" brain waves as indications of internal states such as surprise or confusion.

13. *Clinical Chemical News*, as reported in *Privacy Journal* (March 1984, vol. X, no. 5).

14. For a discussion of parallel developments in Norway see Mathiesen (1983). Brodeur's (1983) discussion of the expansion of a more absorbent style of "high" police makes an equivalent point.

15. In a useful discussion Gross (1984) stresses informing as the principal mechanism by which totalitarian states penetrate the private domain. "The real power of a totalitarian state results . . . from its being at the disposal, available for hire at a moment's notice, to every inhabitant."

16. Like dolphins unintentionally caught in fishing nets set for tuna, persons eligible for benefits may be hurt as well. Thus many persons withdrew from a food stamp program after publicity about a computer matching program. Whether all those who withdrew were in fact ineligible, and others who were eligible subsequently did not apply, is an interesting question. The perception that benefits are difficult to receive, and that persons are constantly being checked, may mean underutilization of welfare programs. With their focus on fraud and abuse, government computer matching programs have rarely looked to see if persons are not receiving benefits to which they are entitled.

17. To this end a trick sometimes used before an interrogation begins is to show the subject a monitor with a dial. The subject is then asked to tell a lie and sees the dial go up, supposedly indicating that the lie has been detected. What the subject doesn't know is that the operator causes the dial to move, independent of what the subject has said. Appropriately impressed, the examination begins. Another device is to ask the subject to pick a card from a marked deck or a deck where all the cards are the same. After a series of questions the examiner then identifies the card.

18. For example the office of the Special Prosecutor set up to investigate Watergate had vibration detectors, closed circuit television, alarm tape on windows, venetian blinds closed at all times, heavy drapes on windows that were drawn whenever sensitive conversations took place, periodic checks for electronic bugs and wiretaps on phones, and 24-hour security guards.

19. In the best free market tradition some firms are adept at playing both ends of the street—they help develop and sell new surveillance devices, as well as the countermeasures needed to thwart them. Through advertisements in major national periodicals (not simply esoteric security publications) and mail-order catalogues a vast array of control and counter-control devices have been brought to mass markets. One large company offers a "secret connection briefcase" that among other things includes a "pocket sized tape recorder detector that lets you know if someone is secretly recording your conversation," a "micro-miniature hidden bug detection system which lets you know if you're being bugged," a "miniature voice stress analyzer which lets you know when someone is lying," a "built-in scrambler for total telephone privacy," and an "incredible 6 hour tape recorder—so small it fits in a cigarette pack."

20. This is nicely illustrated by the USSR's unwillingness to make personal computers available to its citizens. In offering accessibility (whether legitimately or illegitimately) to data bases, a means of creating alternative communication networks via electronic mail and bulletin boards, links to international telecommunications, and a private printing press, the personal computer can break the state's monopoly of information. The seeming paradox of computers perceived in the United States as a symbol of big brother and in the USSR as a symbol of liberation is partly

resolved by separating large, institutionally controlled, main frame computers, from small, privately controlled microcomputers.

21. The source of the limitations vary. Computer matching may find valid correlations but can be no better than the data. Data may be dated or wrong to begin with. The data are often rather blunt and acontexual. Chemical analyses that may be valid in suggesting drugs in a person's system can not reveal how they got there (thus THC may appear in the bloodstream because a person smoked marijuana or simply because they were around people who were smoking it). Nor does such analysis determine whether a drug was used on or off the job. The inquisitor in *1984* tells the frail Winston, "I am always able to detect a lie." No such certainty can be claimed by current truth detection devices. Lie detectors and voice stress analysis are pseudosciences relying primarily upon intimidation, deception, and salesmanship (see Lykken, 1984; see also Saxe et al., forthcoming).

References

Bramford, J. 1983. *The Puzzle Palace.* New York: Penguin.

Brodeur, J. P. 1983. "High Policing and Low Policing: Remarks about the Policing of Political Activities." *Social Problems.*

Burnham, D. 1983. *The Rise of the Computer State.* New York: Random House.

Christian Science Monitor. 1984. April 16.

Cohen, S. 1985. *Visions of Social Control.* Cambridge: Polity Press.

Fox, R. and T. Lears. 1983. *The Culture of Consumption.* New York: Pantheon.

Goodwin, G. and L. Humphreys. 1982. "Freeze-Dried Stigma: Cybernetics and Social Control." *Humanity and Society* 6.

Gross, J. 1984. "Social Control under Totalitarianism." *Toward a General Theory of Social Control,* Vol. 2. Edited by D. Black. New York: Academic Press.

Hayden, T. 1981. *Polygraphs and Employment: The Myth of Lie Detection.* New York: New York Civil Liberties Union.

Krajick, K. 1983. "Electronic Surveillance Makes a Comeback."; *Police Magazine* (March).

Laudon, K. C. 1986. "Data Quality and Due Process in Large Record Systems: Criminal Record Systems." *Communications of the Association for Computing Machinery.*

Lykken, D. 1984. "Detecting Deception in 1984." *American Behavioral Scientist* (March/April).

Marx, G. 1982. "Who Really Gets Stung? Some Issues Raised by the New Police Undercover Work." *Crime & Delinquency* (April).

Marx, G. 1983. *Fragmentation and Cohesion in American Society.* Washington, DC: Trend Analysis Program, American Council of Life Insurance.

Marx, G. and N. Reichman. 1984. "Routinizing the Discovery of Secrets: Computers as Informants." *American Behavioral Scientist* (March).

Marx, Gary T. and Sanford Sherizen. 1986. *Some Social Aspects of Privacy and Security Practices in Computer and Telecommunication Work Environments.* Washington, DC: Office of Technology Assessment, U.S. Congress.

Mathiesen, T. 1983. "The Future of Control Systems." In *The Power to Punish.* Edited by D. Garland and P. Young. Atlantic Highlands, NJ: Humanities Press.

Office of Technology Assessment (OTA). 1986. *Automation of America's Offices, 1985-2000.* Washington, DC: Office of Technology Assessment, U.S. Congress.

Olmstead v. U.S. 438 (1927).

Orwell, G. 1973. *Nineteen Eighty-Four.* New York: New American Library.

Rule, J., D. McAdam, L. Stearns, and D. Uglow. 1980. *The Politics of Privacy.* New York: New American Library.

Saxe, L., D. Dougherty, and T. Cross. forthcoming. "The Validity of Polygraph Testing." *American Psychologist.*

Schudson, M. 1984. *Advertising, The Uneasy Persuasion.* New York: Basic Books.

U.S. Congress. 1982. Select Committee to Study Undercover Activities of Components of the Department of Justice, 97th Congress, Second Session, *Final Report, December 1982* Washington DC: Government Printing Office.

U.S. Congress. 1984. Subcommittee on Civil and Constitutional Rights of the Committee on the Judiciary, House of Representatives, 98th Congress, Second Session, *Report: FBI Undercover Operations* Washington, DC: Government Printing Office.

Part III

Population, Resources, and the Social Fabric

10

To What Degree Is a Social System Dependent on Its Resource Base?

William R. Catton, Jr.
Gerhard Lenski
Frederick H. Buttel

Sociology Within a Cocoon

As members of a technologically advanced society, sociologists today are surrounded with products of human ingenuity—cities, highways, air transport systems, hotels, offices, factories, corporations, universities, professional associations, and so on. These products so insulate us from the biophysical environment that an effort is required to recall how the success and survival of social systems depend on a continuous, voluminous, and diverse flow of natural resources.

The humanmade cocoon we call modern industrial society is characterized by a complex division of labor; only a minute fraction of the adult population (about 3% in the United States) is engaged in the production and extraction of raw materials. For the ever-growing majority of us who are employed in the service sector, reality consists

165

largely of words, ideas, abstractions, social relationships, activities, records, careers, and countless other things having little or no material substance. Small wonder, therefore, that so many sociological theories and so much of our research have so little to say about the material bases of human life.

It is time to recognize how seriously misleading this perspective has become. The first premise of every sociological theory should be that human societies are a part of the larger world of nature and dependent on it for their welfare and their very survival. The relation of societies to their environments should be a matter of central concern.

If the relation of societies to their environments is so important, how has it been possible for most sociologists to ignore it so successfully for so long? This was made possible, in large measure, by the paradigmatic shift that occurred in sociology near the beginning of the present century; sociologists abandoned the comparative method and the evolutionary perspective and substituted for them studies of their own societies viewed synchronically or in a very limited time frame. Emile Durkheim (1912) provided an intellectual justification for this shift in the important final chapter of his famous volume, *The Elementary Forms of the Religious Life*. He argued that the essence of religion is universal and can be observed as readily in modern French society as in the societies of the Australian aborigines. Thus the comparative method and the evolutionary perspective became unnecessary in social research, or so it seemed to some adherents of the Chicago school that dominated American sociology between the two world wars, and so it seemed also to the functionalist school that became so influential after World War II.

This departure from the older comparative method and evolutionary perspective might have been less harmful if the society that was to become the focus of attention had been fairly representative of the total universe of human societies. Unfortunately, though, American society in the twentieth century was hardly an "average," "typical," or "representative" society. Instead, sociology preoccupied itself with the most powerful, most complex, and wealthiest society in history (and one of the largest as well). If the forces and circumstances responsible for this society were exceptional, it is unsafe to construct a theory of human societies as a whole based largely on observations and analyses of this one atypical case.

Resource Dependence in Ecological
and Evolutionary Perspective

Considering American society in a comparative and evolutionary light belatedly, we can see that members of our society have come closer to experiencing the Garden of Eden than anyone since Adam and Eve. In the Garden of Eden, the material needs of our first parents were amply met—and without special thought or effort on their part. Until recently, much the same was true of our society. Its rivers and streams teemed with fish, and vast forests provided a seemingly inexhaustible supply of cheap energy and raw materials with which to fuel a rapidly expanding economy. Before these resources were exhausted, enormous quantities of readily accessible coal, iron, petroleum, natural gas, and other resources were discovered. With the clearing of forests, the supply of farmland steadily increased, and much of it proved to be of exceptional quality. The population that consumed these resources was still strikingly small but technologically advanced—far more advanced than the Indian population they were displacing.

Because of these circumstances, it is not surprising that Americans in general, and social scientists in particular, have largely been indifferent to the resources base of our society. It was taken for granted, like the air we breathed or the water we drank. Until the oil crises of the 1970s, natural resources never seemed problematic. When one resource began to be depleted—for example, cheap wood—there were others to take its place. Technological innovation combined with resource substitution could always solve the problem.

Through trade and commerce, European societies also benefited from the vast untapped storehouse of natural resources in the New World. Thus they also experienced growth and expansion and acquired some of the same positive and optimistic world view that has been especially characteristic of Americans. American scholars would have developed a very different world view had they turned to the scholars of China, India, or other Asian societies for guidance and inspiration. Or, if the comparative method and the evolutionary perspective had not been discarded early in this century, sociologists might have been much more aware of the exceptional character of the relationship between U.S. society and its environment. Thus they might have realized sooner that this Eden-like relationship was deteriorating rapidly with significant consequences for the social system.

A comparative and evolutionary perspective could have revealed that countless societies in the past had come to grief because they failed to recognize in time their dependence on the biophysical environment or were unable to preserve a relationship that was compatible with wholesome living conditions for their members. A classic instance has recently come to light (Deevey et al., 1979). Archaeologists examining the ecological foundations of Mayan societies discovered that population growth in the centuries preceding the collapse of that civilization had apparently led to almost total deforestation, which, in turn, led to serious soil erosion and declining crop yields. The eventual collapse seems to have been brutally swift; archaeological evidence suggests that within decades the population dropped to less than a tenth of what it had been previously. Consider also the decline of societies in the Sahel region of Africa in recent years. Introduction of modern medical technology reduced the death rate and led to significant population growth. This, in turn, necessitated larger herds of livestock to support the human population, but the enlarged herds so overgrazed the fragile ecosystem in the area that the Sahara began to expand southward. The resource base on which the human population had been dependent for centuries has been severely diminished.

Growth of human population in the distant past, and its resultant impact on the resource base, caused a profound and far-reaching transformation in conditions of life for humans who have lived since. Seen from the perspective of twentieth-century American society, the sequence of events in the latter part of the Old Stone Age that forced nomadic hunters and gatherers to turn to farming has looked like a triumph of the human intellect. We have conventionally viewed those remote ancestors as extending their mastery over the world of nature, improving their own lot and that of all their descendants. But if we extricate ourselves from this seriously distorted view of what happened (and of its meaning for subsequent human generations), we see instead that the shift from hunting and gathering to farming was not a matter of choice but rather an unavoidable, often unwanted, adaptation to pressure of population upon limited resources. Small, mobile, egalitarian societies of hunter-gatherers were gradually transformed into larger, more sedentary, less egalitarian, horticulture-based societies. Eventually they evolved into the huge, highly stratified, and exploitative agrarian societies of more recent history. The vast majority of their population became peasant drudges toiling to produce an economic surplus—providing luxuries, palaces, and other monuments at the command of a harsh and tiny elite. These societies also produced a surplus of children for whom there was no permanent employment—a vast pool of expendables for whom life was indeed "poor, nasty, brutish, and short." If the shift from hunting and gathering to farming appears to us today as a triumph of human creativity and innovativeness, it is only because our noncomparative and nonevolutionary sociology has allowed us to neglect all of the generations between then and now.

Once the dependence of societies on their environments and on the resources they contain is acknowledged, several basic principles quickly become obvious. First, both for biological and cultural reasons, societal demand for resources is virtually limitless. Biologically, human populations, like other animal populations, are able to multiply exponentially unless environmental constraints intervene, or unless human foresight and restraint are exercised (Appelman, 1976; Birdsell, 1957). Culturally, too, there is no inherent limit on the human appetite for resources. Increased production seems to multiply human needs and desires. Currently, about half of the growth in Gross World Product (and, hence, in consumption of natural resources) is due to simple population growth, and about half to rising standards of living and expanding needs and desires.

But if the demand for resources is limitless, the supply is much less expandable. In fact, the most basic resources of our planet—land, water, minerals—are not expandable at all. They have only seemed expandable because technolgical advance has made available added portions that were previously inaccessible or unusable. Thus the invention of the steam engine in the eighteenth century made vast deposits of coal minable that previously had not been accessible, just as other inventions more recently have provided access to deeper and less easily recovered oil deposits. But these technological advances do not actually increase the earth's stock of such mineral resources, and when the finite supply has been exhausted, there is no more to be had.

Long before that point is reached, societies have to find substitutes for declining resources—substitutes that are not prohibitively expensive. Modern societies have been slow to shift from petroleum and natural gas to solar energy and other alternatives despite the rising cost of petroleum and natural gas, chiefly because the alternatives have been more expensive (but see Etzkowitz, 1984). Further advances may reduce the cost of some of these technologies and make them competitive. Increased production may lead to economies of scale once the shift to the newer energy sources begins in earnest. But even if these things happen, there is no assurance that they will happen quickly enough to prevent serious social dislocations.

It is easy to forget that timing is extraordinarily important. It is not enough to know that human ingenuity could eventually find a solution to this problem or that. The modern industrial system is extremely complex and interdependent. The failure of one essential part of the system, such as the energy supply, for even a short period could produce a domino effect that could lead to a system crash—not just in a single society but throughout all or most of our now highly interdependent world system of societies. Complex systems such as this have little tolerance for component breakdowns unless backup elements are in place and can be brought on-line quickly, and this does not appear to be the situation in the modern industrial world. Were the entire system to crash, the magnitude of human suffering that would result (with world population now numbering nearly 5 billion) is difficult to exaggerate.

Dependence on Former Dependents

Let us consider, then, what sort of complex world system was emerging as industrial dominance set the stage for recent upheavals. At the time of World War I, just over one-fourth of the nearly 1.7 billion people on earth lived in the "great powers"—nations that were (or were becoming) industrial. Almost another one-third of the world's people lived in colonies ruled by these great powers, and one-fifth lived in semicolonial countries. Thus, with fewer than 300 million others living altogether outside the orbit of colonialism, it is little wonder that Lenin (1939/1917, p. 80), writing in Zurich on the eve of the Russian revolution, saw domination of preindustrial continents by industrial capitalist nations as the world's basic structure. Following Marx, Lenin believed that division of the planet's raw materials-producing colonies among the industrial ruling powers would become increasingly integral to twentieth-century imperialism.

Integral it may have been on the eve of World War I, but by 1965 the world economy and its geopolitics were not what Lenin had described or predicted. Between the two world wars certain segments of the European colonial empires had gained independence, and a wave of resistance to European rule began, especially in India. Independence movements spread quickly among the colonies after World War II. By 1965, colonial rule was largely a thing of the past. The United States, a country that never had a large colonial empire, emerged as the dominant industrial power in the world economy. Foreign investments in the former colonies and semicolonies were no longer dominated by raw materials investments (i.e., investments in agriculture, mining, forestry, and the infrastructure for exporting these materials). By 1978, for example, 44.1% of U.S. overseas investments were in manufacturing; only 4.2% were in mining and 19.8% in petroleum (Syzmanski, 1981, p. 108).

Further, it was widely recognized that neither the receipt of large foreign investments nor the freedom from colonial bondage had produced the robust development of the Third World anticipated by Lenin, by the classical Marxists, and by modernization theorists. A literature began to appear (e.g., Baran, 1957) that argued that the flow of capital between the metropolitan powers and the Third World was not as Lenin had described it; data and theory emerged suggesting that the net flow of capital was from the Third World to the First World (rather than the reverse, as Lenin had expected). Influential theories of "dependency" and "world systems" arose.

If much of Lenin's theorizing about the dynamics of the global expansion of capitalism was rendered doubtful by developments from World War I to the mid-1960s, was he wrong as well about the role of the flow of raw materials in the world economy? More specifically, to what degree are the United States and other industrial powers dependent upon imports of raw materials from former colonies and semicolonies, and with what effects?

Post-World War II Raw Materials
Consumption and Imports

Largely because of the destruction of European and Japanese industry in World War II, the United States emerged as the world's hegemonic industrial power in the postwar period. At the same time the former colonies and semicolonies in Asia, Africa, and Latin America exhibited generally slow rates of economic growth up to the mid-1960s.

There were two major raw materials consequences of these divergent trends. First, the United States shortly after World War II accounted for startlingly high proportions of world mineral consumption and fuel consumption. It consumed 66% of world crude oil output, 93% of natural gas output, 99% of the uranium, and 10% of world coal production (Tanzer, 1980, p. 17). Of the major nonfuel minerals, U.S. consumption as a percentage of total world extraction was as follows: aluminum, 60%; copper, 60%; zinc, 50% lead, 50%; tin, 70%; iron ore, 50%; and nickel, 75%. Moreover, total world output of fuels, nonferrous minerals, and ferrous minerals skyrocketed after World War II (Tanzer, 1980, p. 16). This surge of production and consumption of major raw materials was due not only to U.S. economic expansion but also to expansion in the other advanced industrial countries as they recovered in the late 1950s and 1960s from the devastation of World War II. Moreover, many former colonies and semicolonies in what came to be known as the Third World began to experience rapid economic growth in the 1960s and, as a bloc, came to account for larger shares of world mineral production and consumption. U.S. consumption of total world production of minerals and fuels slowly diminished as a percentage of increasing world totals. For example, U.S. consumption of crude oil dropped from 66% of total world output in 1947 to 32% in 1978; the comparable percentages for copper and iron ore were 60% and 23%, and 50% and 22%, respectively (Tanzer, 1980, p. 17). In absolute terms, U.S. consumption of fuels and minerals increased during this period, but with global economic expansion and a growing world population, U.S. increases became a smaller percentage of the world total.

Nations such as the United States and other advanced industrial countries import raw materials for either or both of two reasons. First, a particular natural resource may be unavailable in a given country; if it is critical to production, importing it is the only option. Second, even when a resource is physically available within a country, it may be of lower quality or have higher extraction costs than imported materials.

By comparison with other advanced industrial societies, the United States remains relatively self-sufficient in the resources it consumes. Krasner (1978, p. 9), for example, has pointed out that "in the mid-1970s the United States was dependent on foreign sources for only 15 percent of its supply of critical nonfuel minerals while Western Europe and Japan had to import, respectively, 75 and 90 percent of their supplies." Table 10.1 shows, however, that the United States has become increasingly dependent on imported minerals. Dependence on imports of fuels has grown more rapidly than dependence on

TABLE 10.1: Imports as a Percentage of U.S. Consumption (by value)

	All Minerals	Fuels
1900	11	1
1930	11	6
1950	17	9
1969	21	17
1982	32	27

SOURCES: 1900 to 1969 data derived from figures in U.S. Department of Commerce, Bureau of the Census, **Historical Statistics**, pp. 584-585 (reported in Krasner, 1978, p. 9). 1982 data calculated from figures given in Mangone (1984, p. 60).

TABLE 10.2: Trend of U.S. Net Import Reliance for Selected Minerals (percentage imported)

	1950	1960	1970	1980	1990
Columbium	100	100	100	100	100
Manganese	83	89	95	98	99
Bauxite	NA	74	88	94	NA
Cobalt	90	66	98	93	92
Chromium	89	85	89	91	91
Platinum group	74	82	78	88	80
Tin	88	82	81	79	75
Nickel	90	72	71	71	76
Potassium	NA	E	42	65	NA
Zinc	41	46	54	60	54
Cadmium	NA	13	7	55	NA
Tungsten	61	32	50	53	62
Petroleum	14	21	26	45	NA
Vanadium	4	E	21	35	27
Titanium	NA	22	24	32	NA
Iron ore	11	18	30	25	18
(Iron and Steel)	NA	E	4	15	NA
Copper	31	E	E	14	15

SOURCES: 1950 data (except petroleum), and 1990 projections, from Mangone (1984, pp. 34-35); all petroleum figures, and all other 1960, 1970, and 1980 data from Statistical Abstract (1984, p. 721).
NOTE: NA = data not available. E = net exports.

imports of other mineral resources. Dependence on imported metals was already high in 1900 (Krasner, 1978, p. 9).

There is, however, broad variation from one mineral to another in terms of the inability of domestic resources to meet total demand. The United States does import a considerable percentage of several minerals, but it is not always clear whether this demand for imports is due to the substance's unavailability in the United States or only to the tendency for imports to be cheaper than domestic supplies. Table 10.2 provides information on trends in and projections of U.S.

dependence on imports of various minerals of industrial importance. In several instances imports have come to constitute far more than half of domestic demand. In some cases, the proportion of domestic demand supplied by imports has fluctuated as time has passed, but there are no solid trends away from import dependence and toward self-sufficiency. Further, the projections of domestic demand and of the ability of domestic resources to meet these demands at the end of the present decade show few expected reversals of the major trend toward increasing import dependency. (These data indicate the plausibility of attributing the actions of multinational firms or of makers of foreign policy to the search for scarce raw materials).

Data on overall imports of raw materials of course include imports from other developed countries as well as from the less-developed countries (LDCs) of South America, Asia, and Africa. Table 10.3 provides information on which minerals entail the most notable U.S. dependence upon sources from those three continents. It is clear that U.S. imports of natural resources do not all derive from Third World countries.

Projections of domestic reserves of key industrial raw materials in relation to estimated domestic demand suggest the need for even larger increases in import dependence in future decades. Whereas many mineral commodities are imported from advanced industrial societies, the Third World is the major or only source of supply of several critical industrial raw materials for which U.S. reserves are inadequate. It should be stressed, however, that the United States, by comparison with the other major industrial countries (especially Japan), contains a remarkable abundance and diversity of raw materials and is the least dependent on foreign sources. Nevertheless, it appears that the developed industrial world as a whole and the once Eden-like United States in certain respects are dependent on imports of raw materials to a substantial and inexorably increasing extent. A number of these raw materials originate primarily in the LDCs.

Scarce Resources Theory:
What Can It Account for?

It was not until the rise of the environmental movement in the 1960s that the social sciences paid any significant attention to the influence of flows of raw materials on global economic and geo-political phenomena. But during the late 1960s and early 1970s, analysts such as Kolko (1969), Magdoff (1969), Dean (1971), and

TABLE 10.3: Location of Leading Source of U.S. Mineral Imports, 1978-1981

	Asian, African, or South American Nation	Elsewhere
Columbium	X	
Manganese	X	
Bauxite		X
Cobalt	X	
Chromium	X	
Platinum-group	X	
Tin	X	
Nickel		X
Potassium		X
Zinc		X
Cadmium		X
Tungsten		X
Vanadium	X	
Titanium		X
Iron ore		X
Copper	X	

SOURCE: Statistical Abstract (1984, p. 721).

Meadows et al. (1972) came to see (in various ways) that raw materials flows are at the heart of global political-economic and environmental trends. Whereas academic social science had largely ignored the raw materials sector and international trade in raw materials, U.S. status in world raw materials consumption was well known to government officials. There had been a continuing flood of federal reports since the 1940s that highlighted the importance of imported raw materials to the U.S. economy and advocated various domestic and foreign policies to ensure their continued availability (see, for example, U.S. Congress, Senate, 1945, 1969; U.S. Council on International Economic Policy, 1974; U.S. President's Cabinet Committee on Minerals Policy, 1954; U.S. President's Materials Policy Commission, 1952; see also Krasner, 1978, Chap. 2).

There was a crucial difference between the "environmental movement era" theorists of geopolitical dynamics and Lenin: whereas Lenin gave virtually no attention to the adequacy of supplies of raw materials in sustaining the expansion of industrial capitalism, Dean (1971), Kolko (1969), and Magdoff (1970) premised their analyses to varying degrees on the scarcity of these materials as a key explanatory factor.

This scarce resources theory of imperialism has been criticized on two grounds. The first objection has been that the United States only imports 33% of its minerals from Third World countries and thus the

Third World is not as important a source of minerals as are other developed countries (Syzmanski, 1977). Given the limited dependence on Third World sources, critics suggest that scarce resources really cannot account for economic imperialism. Scarce resource theorists have responded, however, by noting that (1) Third World sources are especially important for the largest (i.e., multinational) firms, which are most able to influence government policy, and (2) certain rare but absolutely indispensable materials, including manganese, nickel, tungsten, titanium, and tantalum, are largely located on or under Third World soil.

The second criticism of the scarce resources theory has stressed that raw materials imperialism was not really necessary because substitutes (either somewhat more expensive U.S. sources, or other minerals) would have been adequate for U.S. industrial growth (Miller et al., 1970; Goldthorpe, 1975). Magdoff (1970) has countered this criticism on two grounds: first, several key raw materials have no known inexpensive substitutes, and, second, the ultimate interest of U.S. multinationals is a compelling desire to maintain market control, and not merely an absolute requirement for natural resources from the Third World.

Although the scarce resources theory may not suffice to explain all facets of imperialism, it does emphasize resource-related imperatives of international economic and geopolitical relations in an era when declining availability of resources has begun to penetrate the national consciousness. Resource considerations may at certain points be decisive in state policy determination. For the United States, policy decisions related to raw materials are a significant component of foreign policy determination. Substantial investments of American capital in raw materials extraction have been and continue to be made. For several decades, the U.S. government has stockpiled strategic raw materials for military and national security purposes. As has become apparent in recent years, the U.S. foreign policy tightrope in the Middle East has been premised at least in part on maintaining access to petroleum.

First World countries, especially the United States and Japan, are becoming more dependent on imported energy resources and ores, from Third World and other sources. The United States and Japan dominate world consumption of industrial raw materials and account for disproportionate shares of raw materials traded in international markets. These two resource-hungry industrial giants have achieved their dominance in access to raw materials in very different ways, however. Japan has been poorly endowed with raw materials relative to other advanced industrial countries. Thus during the entirety of its post-World War II industrialization period, Japan has been heavily dependent on imports of raw materials. The Japanese state has exhibited a long-standing policy thrust oriented toward increasing the security of Japanese access to imported raw materials (Vernon, 1983). In contrast, the abundance of raw materials within U.S. territory has given this country a policy option that most other advanced industrial countries cannot have. The principal U.S. response to actual or feared shortfalls in raw materials supplies has been to encourage domestic production. This policy, especially in the case of energy resources during the period following the Arab oil embargo, has had the effect of diminishing the U.S. inventory of nonrenewable raw materials to a greater degree than would otherwise have been the case (Vernon, 1983, p. 121). An incidental effect has been that U.S. industry has faced the disadvantage of higher raw materials costs, compared to its foreign competitors.

Problems of Diachronic Competition

What matters even more than the extent to which the United States, Japan, or any other industrial nation depends on resources imported from someone else's piece of this planet is the extent to which we all have committed ourselves to dependence on stocks of resources that are by their nature nonrenewable. More important sociologically than the fact that so much of the world has to obtain oil from the Middle East is the fact that the world has to obtain so much oil—at all, from anywhere. The distinction between domestic versus foreign resources is less basic to our analysis of forces threatening the social fabric than is the distinction between renewable and nonrenewable resources.

Sociology needs to break away from Durkheim's rules enough to take explicit account of certain facts of geology and ecology that shape social facts. It simply is not true any more, if it ever was, that the cause of a social fact is always another *social* fact. The nonrenewability of resources upon which human societies became dependent through industrialization is too important to overlook. Because of it, human efforts to hold today's social fabric together make tomorrow's social fabric still more fragile. To understand this, we must acquire a clear grasp of the concept of *carrying capacity*. Unfamiliarity with this ecological concept allows illusions about the social fabric's durability to persist. Conditions of our time put us (to an unfamiliar degree) in competition with posterity. Learning to study the human condition from a more ecological perspective will highlight diachronic competition. Resisting that perspective will not alleviate such competition.

Deceptive Folk Geology

In 1983, the world's human societies consumed 18 billion barrels of oil, or about 2.7% of the world's "proven reserves" of 670 billion barrels (Brown et al., 1984, p. 9). "Proven reserves" comprise just the oil that is both definitely established as being in place and is so located as to be profitably extractable by present technology at present prices. Oil company officials don't mind, however, if references to a larger quantity called "ultimately recoverable reserves" appear to raise in the public's mind the total stock of oil humankind can hope ever to burn—from a mere 670 billion barrels to an ostensibly reassuring 2,100 billion barrels.

We humans act as if we mean to continue indefinitely a social order based on rates of resource consumption at least comparable to recent rates. In effect, by living as if our rates of resource use were sustainable—by trying to suppose an oil-based system is anything but temporary—we seriously misconstrue that "ultimately recoverable reserves" figure. We behave as if petroleum were being replenished by nature's processes at a rate that is geologically impossible—a pace that would have sufficed to put all we now think is there into the earth just since 1867 (the year of publication of the first volume of Das Kapital).

By acting according to such false geological premises, however, we are making it impossible for our descendants to live as we do. That is sociologically the most important consequence of our dependence on nonrenewable resources. It is a great sociological irony of our time that lifestyles about which we can be so ethnocentric are so inexorably temporary. Satisfaction of often trivial desires by members of our own generation is purchased at the expense of future generations. For them we are leaving a legacy of resource depletion that will preclude for them a way of life comparable to our own. Such diachronic competition is the inevitable result of our insistence on exceeding our environment's carrying capacity.

For any particular environment there is some maximum amount of use (of a given kind) that the environment can endure year after year without degradation of its suitability for that use. The name given to that maximum sustainable use level is "carrying capacity." In this defining statement, the word "use" is intended broadly enough to encompass what is done to an environment by a particular occupation, such as farming or copper mining, by a recreational activity such as wilderness exploration, or by the whole gamut of activities involved in supporting and maintaining a vast and intricate human society.

Confusion About Carrying Capacity

Concern about the dependence of human societies upon a shrinking resource base was heightened by publication of *The Limits to Growth* (Meadows et al., 1972). In the following year, when OPEC boosted crude oil prices, this not only dramatized the industrial world's dependence on this nonrenewable energy resource but also aroused anxieties regarding future prospects for our own continuing economic progress. Further, it began to seem uncertain whether the so-called developing countries would ever attain full industrial stature. More recently, famines have again become news stories. All of these events have heightened concern about the long-range human outlook. An important manifestation of such concern was the 1980 publication of *The Global 2000 Report to the President*, which foretold serious stresses involving population, resources, and environmental conditions, if then-current trends were to continue. Its writers were convinced that we live in a world profoundly altered from the one familiar to us in the long sweep of previous human history. Human population had doubled within one lifetime. Use of many resources had accelerated in a pattern that, each decade or so, doubled the total amount already extracted and used. *Global 2000* told of already serious stresses that will worsen because "the earth's carrying capacity . . . is eroding" (Council on Environmental Quality [CEQ], 1980, pp. 3-4, 40-41).

Within four years, however, the Heritage Foundation funded a cocksure rejoinder (Simon and Kahn, 1984). Entitled *The Resourceful Earth*, it insisted that continuation of present trends would produce in 2000 A.D. a world "less crowded (though more populated), less polluted, more stable ecologically, and less vulnerable to resource-supply disruption." "Mineral resources," it said, "are becoming less scarce rather than more scarce," a claim its authors acknowledged was an affront to common sense. The nature of the physical world, they confidently asserted, "permits continued improvement in humankind's economic lot in the long run, indefinitely" (Simon and Kahn, 1984, p. 3).

One important key to the difference in thinking between *Global 2000* and *The Resourceful Earth* is their opposite view of carrying capacity. On the single page where Simon and Kahn (1984, p. 45) deigned to mention the concept, they wrote, "Because of increases in knowledge, the earth's 'carrying capacity' has been increasing throughout the decades and centuries and millenia to such an extent that the term 'carrying capacity' has by now no useful meaning."

Clarifying the Concept

Rather than dismissing the concept as meaningless, its meaning needs clarification. Let us, accordingly, rephrase the principle of maximum environmentally tolerable use:

> Carrying capacity means, for a given environment, the amount of use that can be exceeded only by impairing that environment's future suitability for that use.

Here, then, is a concept that is relevant in assessing user loads on a local fishery or a particular farm, on a recreational site, on an entire continent or even a planet. Whatever the scope of the environment (or resource base) we want to consider, it is important to consider the consequences of its possible overuse. In essence, the consequences of overuse come down to reduced opportunities for future users. In other words, carrying capacity limits can put present and future generations into a competitive relation to one another.

Years ago, the essence of competition was defined as "a clash of interests of such a sort that gratification on the part of one individual or unit precludes gratification on the part of another individual or unit" (Fairchild, 1944, p. 54). The same sociological dictionary went on to note that the basis of competition was found in, among other things, the finite character of the earth. Elaborating, "ecological competition" was defined as "that form of ecological interaction in which two or more organisms, each striving to obtain some limited supply of an environmental resource, decrease the amount of that supply obtained by others." However, the idea that two or more competitors might belong to different times was not yet apparent. Nor have later definitions acknowledged *diachronic* competition (see Theodorson and Theodorson, 1969, p. 66; Sills, 1968, pp. 181-186).

Writers such as Simon and Kahn who deny the meaningfulness of carrying capacity are especially likely to neglect the problem of diachronic competition. They miss the intergenerational significance of modern society's reliance on so many nonrenewable resources. As we deplete the existing stock of a nonrenewable resource we are necessarily changing the environment in which our posterity will live, making it less possible for them to behave as we have behaved. Future generations will have to get by with less of certain resources the abundance of which has been a major condition of our lives. Conversely, insofar as a human society lives by using renewable resources, and uses them at no greater than sustainable yield rates, members of a given generation are then not competing with their descendants.

Various nonsociologists have addressed explicitly this problem of diachronic competition. When Aldo Leopold (1933) called for a "land ethic" or "conservation ethic" that would restrain humans from doing things to our environment that reduce its capacity to support us or to sustain humanly desirable ways of living, he was writing an essentially sociological essay even if he published it in a forestry journal. Later, a Congressman from Tennessee, saying our society has "pillaged the past and pawned the future," lamented,

> It is as if our civilization has lost a sense of the future. We are so busily engaged in making miracle products for our present enjoyment from substances deposited in the earth over millions of years, we don't stop to consider the environmental burdens we are placing on future generations [Gore, 1982, p. x].

Policies of conservation are ways of mitigating diachronic competition. The International Union for the Conservation of Nature and Natural Resources (quoted in Eckholm, 1982, p. 78), by defining conservation as "management of human use of the biosphere so that it may yield the greatest sustainable benefit to present generations, while maintaining its potential to meet the needs and aspirations of future generations," has implied that we ought to recognize diachronic competition as a fact and deliberately try to devise resource policies to minimize it.

How might sociologists participate in such recognition and contribute to constructive policymaking?

One thing we must do is soften the tendency to read only our own literature. By allowing ourselves to delve into the literature not only of anthropology but also of history, we can discover examples of human societies that were actually facing imminent collapse just when they seemed to be (as we tend to see our own society today) resoundingly successful. The Polynesian social fabric on Easter Island, for example, came violently apart at the apparent height of its cultural florescence because the island's human load had overshot the carrying capacity of its finite environment, causing a legacy of resource scarcity (Mulloy, 1974). In Mesopotamia, the cradle of Western Civilization, the once legendary fertility of the region's land was destroyed by cumulative side effects of the very irrigation schemes that once enabled its alluvial soil to support millions more people than can now live in that area (Jacobsen and Adams, 1958; Hughes, 1975).

Instead of citing recent dramatic improvements in our own standard of living as a basis for confidence that the road ahead leads onward and upward, we should take a careful look at the curve representing Ireland's population history (Catton, 1982, p. 249). After more than two centuries of population growth in response to enlargement of Ireland's apparent capacity after introduction of the potato, a fungus infection destroyed in 1845 what had come to be Ireland's main source of sustenance. What we should note for our own enlightenment is that the population curve (which strikingly approximates the logistic growth pattern) had barely passed its inflection point—and was still rising steeply—on the very eve of an abrupt episode of demographic collapse.

Escalation of oil imports by industrial nations in the 1960s and 1970s was functionally equivalent to Irish emigration after the blight. Both were instances of relying on overseas resources when domestic resources ceased to be adequate for supporting an enlarged load. (For the industrial nations, of course, "load" was enlarged not just by population growth but also by marked increases in per capita resource appetites.) The excessive reliance of industrial societies on one energy resource that cannot last parallels Ireland's excessive reliance on one food resource they did not foresee failing them.

Now, almost six generations after the Irish catastrophe, in a world with four times the number of human inhabitants that there were then, many of whom are members of industrial societies that make them voracious and prodigal consumers of nonrenewable resources, economic headlines frequently reflect the fact that the present generation is finding it difficult to live within its means. "Eager to maximize output today, we are borrowing from tomorrow" (Brown et al., 1984, p. 2). American agriculture, for instance, provides crop surpluses that Brown suggests are not so much signs of thriving success as of the extent to which we are "mining" the soil. Projecting the erosion patterns now observable, total world topsoil per capita will be reduced between 1980 and 2000 A.D. by some 38%. As such examples indicate, by reading certain nonsociological (but sociologically relevant) literature—with the carrying capacity concept in mind—sociologists can begin to see diachronic competition as a recurrent human experience, and we can become sensitized to indicators that it is happening today.

A second thing sociologists can do is to recognize that carrying capacity is not simply the maximum supportable *number of people*. It is the maximum permanently supportable *load*—where load has two dimensions: number of resource consumers times per capita resource appetite. Technology has enlarged our per capita resource demands (and our per capita environmental impact)—so that even a nongrowing population can impose a rapidly increasing load. And technology has rendered us dependent on nonrenewable resources. We must see that carrying capacity can be overshot in several ways: (1) by a growing population, (2) by a burgeoning technology employed even by a no-longer-growing population, or (3) by reliance upon and depletion of nonrenewable resources (incapable of permanently supporting a given load).

A species with as long an interval between generations as there is for humans, and with cultural as well as biological appetites for resources, can be *expected* to overshoot carrying capacity. Our largest per capita demands upon a resource base are not asserted until decades after we are born. The discipline in which the concept of cultural lag originated ought not to be the last discipline to recognize this instance of lag and appreciate its importance.

If we are a species with a special likelihood of exceeding sustainable carrying capacity, we are a species especially likely to induce conditions of diachronic competition. This being so, sociologists have reason for reading critically the literature (produced mainly by economists) in which the concept of the "discount rate" provides a rationale for depleting exhaustible resources (see, e.g., Baumol, 1968; Clark, 1976; Mueller, 1974; Solow, 1974). We also have reason for exploring creatively the extensive literature in philosophy and ethics that has sought to grapple with problems of intergenerational equity (e.g., Hubin, 1976; Kavka and Warren, 1983; Williams, 1978). We especially need to contemplate as open mindedly and perceptively as we can the literature of ethology, in which animal behaviors are described that appear to serve the function of preventing (or correcting) overshoot, and thus protecting carrying capacity (e.g., Cohen et al., 1980; Wynne-Edwards, 1962).

Conclusion

Some important benefits would accrue to sociology if more of us were to adopt an ecological and evolutionary perspective in our study of human societies. First, this perspective would compel us to pay much closer attention to the dependence of human societies on the biophysical environment and on the vital resources it provides. Early in this century, Sumner and Keller (1927, p. 4) declared that the ratio of resources to population size "is the fundamental consideration in the life of any society." This is a lesson that most contemporary sociologists have forgotten—or never learned.

Second, we would gain strikingly new insights into our own society and that part of the world system with which it has been most closely linked, namely, western Europe. We would see that the wealth and power of this set of societies have been the products of a unique set of circumstances that can never be repeated: the sudden acquisition by a small number of societies (with then-small populations) of the almost untapped resources of an entire hemisphere—30% of the land surface of the planet and presumably at least 30% of the planet's then-remaining resources. We cannot assume that societies that did not share in the great bonanza that resulted from conquest of the New World will share in the other experiences of those that did (e.g., material affluence, democratization, and so on). Anomalies that vex traditional theorists (both Marxist and non-Marxist) can become understandable. Thus modernization theorists may expect less than they have heretofore expected from introduction of modern educational systems, mass media, and other accoutrements of Western societies into Third World societies. Without a favorable ratio of carrying capacity to load, there are real limits to what social institutions and modern technology can accomplish. From this perspective, world system and dependency theorists may blame the world capitalist economy somewhat less exclusively for the poverty and other problems of Third World countries.

Sociologists must become more cautious than we often have been in using the American experience during the first 200 years of nationhood as a model for anticipating developments here and elsewhere in the next 200 years. Now that the cream has been skimmed from the world's supply of natural resources, we would be wise to anticipate changes in the years ahead. High economic growth rates may be increasingly difficult to sustain. Standards of living may decline, especially if political leaders cannot or will not stem the flow of immigration. Problems in an era of resource scarcity may put American political institutions to a sterner test than any they have encountered since the Civil War. Human rights issues may be understood differently as we increasingly recognize problems of diachronic competition.

Although the optimists among us may discover that not all stories can have happy endings, ecologically realistic sociological analyses could sustain a measure of optimism by helping decision makers understand the basic forces that shape societal systems, better anticipate impending problems, and more effectively struggle to preserve and extend the resource base of our own and other societies.

References

Appelman, P. (Ed.). 1976. *An Essay on the Principle of Population: A Norton Critical Edition*. New York: W. W. Norton.

Baran, P. A. 1957. *The Political Economy of Growth*. New York: Monthly Review Press.

Baumol, W. J. 1968. "On the Social Rate of Discount." *American Economic Review* 58: 788-802.

Birdsell, J. B. 1957. "Some Population Problems Involving Pleistocene Man." *Cold Spring Harbor Symposium on Quantitative Biology* 22: 47-69.

Brown, L. R., W. Chandler, C. Flavin, S. Postel, L. Starke, and E. Wolf. 1984. *State of the World 1984*. New York: W. W. Norton.

Catton, W. R., Jr. 1982. *Overshoot: The Ecological Basis of Revolutionary Change* [Illini Books edition]. Urbana: University of Illinois Press.

Clark, C. W. 1976. *Mathematical Bioeconomics: The Optimal Management of Renewable Resources*. New York: John Wiley.

Cohen, M. N., R. S. Malpass, and H. G. Klein (Eds.). 1980. *Biosocial Mechanisms of Population Regulation*. New Haven, CT: Yale University Press.

Council on Environmental Quality, and the Department of State. 1980. *Global 2000 Report to the President*. Washington, DC: Government Printing Office.

Dean, H. 1971. "Scarce Resources: The Dynamic of U.S. Imperialism." Pp. 139-154 in *Readings in U.S. Imperialism*. Edited by K. T. Fann and D. Hodges. Boston: Porter Sargent.

Deevey, E. S., D. S. Rice, P. M. Rice, H. H. Vaughan, M. Brenner, and M. S. Flannery. 1979. "Mayan Urbanism: Impact on a Tropical Karst Environment." *Science* 206: 298-306.

Durkheim, E. 1912. *Les Formes elementaires de la vie religieuse*. Paris: Alcan.

Eckholm, E. 1982. *Down to Earth: Environment and Human Needs*. New York: W. W. Norton.

Etzkowitz, H. 1984. "Solar Versus Nuclear Energy: Autonomous or Dependent Technology?" *Social Problems* 31: 417-434.

Fairchild, H. P. 1944. *Dictionary of Sociology*. New York: Philosophical Library.

Goldthorpe, J. E. 1975. *The Sociology of the Third World*. Cambridge: Cambridge University Press.

Gore, A., Jr. 1982. "Foreword." Pp. ix-xii in *Hazardous Waste in America*. Edited by S. S. Epstein, L. O. Brown, and C. Pope. San Francisco: Sierra Club Books.

Hubin, D. C. 1976. "Justice and Future Generations." *Philosophy and Public Affairs* 6: 70-83.

Hughes, J. D. 1975. *Ecology in Ancient Civilizations*. Albuquerque: University of New Mexico Press.

Jacobsen, T. and R. M. Adams. 1958. "Salt and Silt in Ancient Mesopotamian Agriculture." *Science* 128: 1251-1258.

Kavka, G. S. and V. Warren. 1983. "Political Representation for Future Generations." Pp. 21-39 in *Environmental Philosophy.* Edited by R. Elliot and A. Gare. University Park, PA: Pennsylvania State University Press.

Kolko, G. 1969. *The Roots of American Foreign Policy.* Boston: Beacon.

Krasner, S. D. 1978. *Defending the National Interest: Raw Materials Investments and U.S. Foreign Policy.* Princeton, NJ: Princeton University Press.

Lenin, V. I. 1939. *Imperialism: The Highest Stage of Capitalism.* New York: International Publishers. (pub. orig. 1917)

Leopold, A. 1933. "The Conservation Ethic." *Journal of Forestry* 31: 634-643.

Magdoff, H. 1969. *The Age of Imperialism.* New York: Monthly Review Press.

Magdoff, H. 1970. "The Logic of Imperialism." *Social Policy* 1: 20-29.

Mangone, G. J. (Ed.). 1984. *American Strategic Minerals.* New York: Crane Russak.

Meadows, D. H., D. L. Meadows, J. Randers, and W. W. Behrens III. 1972. *The Limits to Growth.* New York: Universe Books.

Miller, S. M., R. Bennett, and C. Alapatt, 1970. "Does the U.S. Require Imperialism?" *Social Policy* 1: 13-19.

Mueller, D. C. 1974. "Intergenerational Justice and the Social Discount Rate." *Theory and Decision* 5: 263-273.

Mulloy, W. 1974. "Contemplate the Navel of the World." *Americas* 26: 25-33.

Sills, D. L. (Ed.). 1968. *International Encyclopedia of the Social Sciences.* New York: Macmillan and Free Press.

Simon, J. L. and H. Kahn. 1984. *The Resourceful Earth: A Response to Global 2000.* New York: Basil Blackwell.

Solow, R. M. 1974. "Intergenerational Equity and Exhaustible Resources." Pp. 29-45 in *Symposium on the Economics of Exhaustible Resources.* Edited by G. M. Heal. Special issue of *Review of Economic Studies.*

Statistical Abstract. 1984. U.S. Bureau of the Census. Washington, DC: Government Printing Office.

Sumner, W. G. and A. G. Keller. 1927. *The Science of Society.* New Haven, CT: Yale University Press.

Syzmanski, A. 1977. "Capital Accumulation on a Global Scale and the Necessity of Imperialism." *Insurgent Sociologist* 7: 35-53.

Syzmanski, A. 1981. *The Logic of Imperialism.* New York: Praeger.

Tanzer, M. 1980. *The Race for Resources.* New York: Monthly Review Press.

Theodorson, G. A. and A. G. Theodorson. 1969. *A Modern Dictionary of Sociology.* New York: Thomas Y Crowell.

U.S. Congress, Senate, Special Committee Investigating Petroleum Resources. 1945. *American Petroleum Interest in Foreign Countries.* Hearings, 79th Congress, 1st Session. Washington, DC: Government Printing Office.

U.S. Congress, Senate, Committee on Public Works. 1969. *Toward a National Materials Policy.* Committee Print, 91st Congress, 1st Session. Washington, DC: Government Printing Office.

U.S. Council on International Economic Policy. 1974. *Critical Imported Materials.* Special Report. Washington, DC: Government Printing Office

U.S. President's Cabinet Committee on Minerals Policy. 1954. *Report of the President's Cabinet Committee on Minerals Policy.* Washington, DC: Government Printing Office.

U.S. President's Materials Policy Commission (Paley Commission). 1952. *Resources for Freedom.* Washington, DC: Government Printing Office.

Vernon, R. 1983. *Two Hungry Giants: The United States and Japan in the Quest for Oil and Ores.* Cambridge, MA: Harvard University Press.

Williams, M. B. 1978. "Discounting Versus Maximum Sustainable Yield." Pp. 169-185 in *Obligations to Future Generations.* Edited by R. I. Sikora and B. Berry. Philadelphia: Temple University Press.

Wynne-Edwards, V. C. 1962. *Animal Dispersion: In Relation to Social Behavior.* Edinburgh: Oliver and Boyd.

Part IV

Institutions, Systems, and Processes

11

The Limits and Possibilities of Government: A Perspective from Sociology of Law

Richard D. Schwartz

THE LIMIT OF GOVERNMENT is reached when, in the metaphor of this book, the basic fabric of the society unravels. The maximum possibility for government, in most circumstances, is that it preserves and strengthens the existing social fabric. As societies become more complex, the government's burden of maintaining its authority by securing the consent of the governed becomes increasingly difficult. To do so, government must reflect, draw on, and reinforce the fabric of society. Failing that imperative, it is driven to maintain control by naked repression,[1] a mechanism that has not so far provided enduring stability for any major society.

When an old order collapses, the fabric of society must be repaired or rewoven. If traditional patterns cannot be restored, a new fabric of society necessarily takes its place. The process by which such changes occur is both difficult to predict and extremely important. Whether

AUTHOR'S NOTE: I acknowledge with thanks the comments of Manfred Stanley, Cathy Thau, Margret Ksander, Michael Haberberger, Donald T. Campbell, Elliot Lehman, and Arnold S. Feldman. Mr. Haberberger also provided valuable research assistance.

peaceful or violent, gradual or sudden, social revolutions have profound significance for the way of life of a people. A new social fabric may emerge, created in part by changes in the governmental loom on which that fabric is woven. To the extent that government and society reinforce each other, stable patterns tend to develop, which, in the complex societies of the past, have continued basically unchanged for millenia.

In our times, we see the signs of a new society and culture emerging. Like the great social revolutions of the past, this one seems to result from changes in technology that have greatly expanded our capacity for production, communication, and transportation. In this revolution, more than the others, new weaponry also plays a crucial role. These changes converge to increase the potential for human interaction (constructive and destructive) in ways that require new patterns of culture and social organization. This time, the evolving fabric of society will be not regional but global.

Understanding government's relation to society is particularly crucial in a revolutionary age. We live in such a time when the first world society may be coming into existence. Although the nature of the fabric of that society is as yet unknown, it will undoubtedly be quite varied, comprising in part existing elements. Because we are participants in that process, it is difficult for us to understand what is happening or how we can contribute to the outcome. Emerson remarked that individual silkworms can hardly know how much they contribute to the beautiful material that is made from their waste products. Humans have a better, although still limited, chance to glimpse at our role in an era of revolutionary change. If consensus emerges on the future society, we may be able to build a world social order based on common aspirations. Failure to achieve even a minimal consensus may result in intolerable violence, if not in suigenocide—the self-destruction of the entire human race.

How, then, to discharge our obligation? Some have turned to social history as a way of forecasting and promoting a particular version of the future. In our field, macro sociologists such as Andre Gunder Frank (1967), Immanuel Wallerstein (1974), and Charles Tilly (1984) have made especially important contributions. In every other field of the social sciences inquiries are under way aimed at trying to understand, forecast, and, in most cases, affect the emergent world society. This chapter—my first effort to contribute to this body of thought—is based on my growing conviction that sociology of law offers a useful perspective on these questions.

My objective is to search for the value assumptions that might provide the normative basis for world society. Every historic revolution has been based on a set of value premises and interpretations of reality. These ideas help to bring about change by discrediting the old order (see Brinton, 1938; Edwards, 1970) and plausibly promising a new order that will cure the society's existing difficulties and achieve widely shared objectives.

The value premises of a society vary widely from one culture to the next (see Benedict, 1934; Kroeber, 1952). In isolated, homogeneous, technologically simple societies studied by ethnographers, one finds a marvelous array of "patterns of culture." In legal anthropology, Hoebel (1954, p. 13) has described these divergent normative premises as "jural postulates."

Jural postulates constitute abstract descriptions derived from explicit statements (and from behavior) of what is widely thought to be good, proper, and necessary in a given society. As used by Hoebel, the set of jural postulates also forecasts the actions of officials in positions of governmental authority. A regime that follows jural postulates exercises power legitimately, thereby maintaining "authority" (Weber, 1957/1922) or hegemony (Gramsci, 1971).[2]

What jural postulates might provide the basis for an emergent world society? When and how are they likely to develop? What implications do they carry for the conduct of government before, during, and after the establishment of world society?

The best available basis for addressing these questions, I believe, is through the study of the great historic societies. In this chapter I focus on three historic cultures: Chinese, Indian, and Western. With apologies in advance to specialists in each, I urge that they help me to correct any inaccuracies in my analysis.

These cultures exhibit two striking features: each is socially and culturally very different from the others, and their distinctive characteristics have endured through thousands of years.[3] As a first approximation, let me describe the three cultures this way:

From its origin to the present, China has had a central government, maintaining authority for periods of three to four centuries. Most of these periods, known until this century as dynasties, were followed by a transition period in which conflict and chaos replaced central authority. These times of disorganization, typically briefer than the dynastic periods, were regularly followed by new regimes that established central authority with a commitment to the restoration of traditional values. These values (or jural postulates) included harmony, respect for the dignity and well-being of the peasantry, merit-based opportunity for upward mobility through civil service, and toleration for diversity of beliefs.[4]

India has followed a very different pattern. In 3,000 years of Indian history, there have been only three brief periods during which India was unified. Each time this occurred, unity lasted for less than a century and was followed, after chaos, by decentralization into smaller governmental units. These units tended to be linguistically and religiously homogeneous, with fissions occurring regularly, bringing additional conflict (see Thapir and Spear, 1965). The three periods of all-India unity had one striking characteristic in common: The three leaders who established authority over the entire sub-continent were ideologically committed to a belief system that *denied* the jural postulate, fundamental to Hinduism, that society must be based on innate inequality, as ascribed by caste origin. Specifically, Asoka was Buddhist, Akbar was Muslim, and the British Raj was Christian.

Finally, Western society has been characterized from its inception, more than 2,000 years ago, by disunity. During this time, common governmental authority was achieved only once, at the time of the Roman Empire. Efforts at the creation of Western unity before that time were undertaken through conquest. When successful, the resultant empire lasted a relatively limited period of time, soon to be toppled or replaced by a rival. In the Fertile Cresent, which I include because of its contribution and similarity to downstream Western culture, one nation typically managed in a given era to establish through military means its dominance over the others. One empire succeeded the next relatively rapidly, each failing to establish its authority over the conquered peoples. As far as can be determined, neither Sumer nor Assyria nor Babylonia nor Persia persuaded the others to accept, as legitimate, incorporation into their empires. Persian hegemony lasted longest, but faltered as it extended its ambitions toward Greece and Egypt. Macedonia then undertook to unify the known world, again by conquest, but that effort collapsed into three separate empires upon the death of its extraordinary founder, Alexander the Great.

The Roman Empire achieved unity in the Western World for about 200 years. Like the Chinese Empire, Rome adopted the principle of toleration of diverse beliefs and the extension of rights to all citizens of the Empire, regardless of origin, under Roman law.

Although Rome permitted ethnic diversity, it failed to check the concentration of wealth and power, with the result that it faced attack by external invaders and demoralization in its own ranks. Efforts to restore its authority by embracing Christianity postponed decline, but destroyed the basis of toleration on which the earlier Empire rested. With the adoption of Christianity, Western society incorporated the sectarian belief that there is only one God, superior to all others, and that salvation depends on finding the proper way to serve Him. This principle of intolerance, traceable to the Hebrew concept of the Chosen People, was built into the Judeo-Christian tradition. Its importance in contributing to fission has been manifest in the endless chronicle of religious schisms and heresies (e.g., Arian, Waldensian, Albigensian). Efforts to unite Christendom failed massively with the split between Rome and Byzantium. Even Roman Christianity was unable to achieve more than nominal unity under the Holy Roman Empire, which, in the words of an old cliché, was neither holy, Roman, nor an empire. The fissioning tendencies of Western society, based on religious intolerance, were further manifested in the rise of Islam in opposition to Christianity. Although tolerant words can be found in the scriptures of each, Christianity and Islam built on the Hebrew foundation of intolerance, serving one God enthusiastically by slaughtering, if they could not convert, infidels. The same tendencies were found within each religion, as evidenced by the enthusiasm with which Catholics and Protestants, Sunnis and Shiites have from time to time massacred each other.

Nor does the story end with conflicts explicitly based on religion. The Western taste for intolerance, deprived of theological support in a less religious age, found an alternative rationale in the growth of nationalism. To this day, the antagonism between republicanism and communism, both explicitly secular systems of thought, continues to be used as a fervent justification for violence and the threat of violence.

I have spent more time describing the durable features of Western, than Chinese or Indian, society because familiarity with our own cultural history may encourage us to overlook its characteristics, no matter how obvious to outside observers. Moreover, I have emphasized features that may be most difficult to admit and I have understressed others in which we take pride. Lest this be misleading, I believe some features of Western society are very important as potential building blocks for an emergent world order.

Western society differs from Indian, and resembles Chinese, in its openness to upward mobility. The capacity of the individual to achieve beyond parent generations has been emphasized in the West in many ways. Unlike traditional India, hardly any Western society has been organized totally in terms of ascribed status. Slavery has of course existed from time to time in Hebrew, Arabic, Greek, Roman, and U.S. societies. But these arrangements have been relatively short-lived and always open to reconsideration. In the Old Testament, for example, explicit instructions are given for the freeing of slaves in the forty-ninth, that is, Jubilee Year, with provision for stigmatizing the slave who insists on voluntarily retaining servitude. Rome also treated slaves with such sympathy that the institution produced substantial opportunities for mobility and achievement.[5]

The Western disinclination to accept ascribed status as a basis for social position has been repeatedly demonstrated. In the nineteenth century, for example, the U.S. Emancipation Proclamation and the freeing of the Russian serfs by Czar Alexander virtually coincided in time. Both had something to do with parallel economic developments, to be sure, but (as Weber pointed out) this in turn was not unrelated to the religious ideology of the West. In this century, the impulse to provide opportunity regardless of accidents of birth is manifest in policies condemning discrimination according to race or gender. The widespread Western campaign against apartheid in South Africa is further evidence of the vigor of the jural postulate against ascribed status.

These two characteristics of Western society—ideological intolerance and an emphasis on freeing achievement from the fetters of status ascription—may be linked in some significant way. In opening the doors of opportunity, Western society creates for its members expectations of achievement that are likely to be unfulfilled. As Robert Merton (1957) suggested, the gap between expectation and achievement generates frustration that seeks an outlet.[6] Whereas Merton focused on domestic manifestations of this frustration (e.g., crime, drugs, ritualism), another outlet is found in ethnocentric antagonism (see LeVine and Campbell, 1972). Mobility frustration can lead to aggression at home or abroad. Because prejudice against others within the society tends to be disruptive, contradicting the jural postulate against ascribed status and threatening social order, antagonism tends to be focused on other societies. Hatred of a suitable foreign target is readily interpretable as excessiveness in the defense of liberty, a course explicitly recommended by presidential candidate Senator Barry Goldwater twenty years ago, and successfully practiced by other American leaders. It may be no mere coincidence that politial figures who encourage hopes for mobility and redistribution at home often turn out to be the most vigorous leaders of foreign wars as well.

I turn now to a more detailed consideration of China and India with some comparison with the West. I shall then return to the question with which the chapter began, namely, how might the themes and histories of these major cultures be used to identify a potential set of jural postulates that might serve as a basis for consensus and integration for an emerging world society?

Before going on to these subjects, I should make clear my value perspective in this chapter. I have, of course, some personal values about the kind of world I would like to see emerge from this process. This said, however, I believe my analysis goes beyond personal preference.

In discussing possible characteristics of a world order, I am trying to identify jural postulates and organizational patterns that seem to be (a) emergent and (b) viable. By looking at recent changes in the great cultures, after millenia of stability, powerful trends are revealed. We can then ask which of these emergent characteristics constitutes a viable response to our new circumstances, that is, to the conditions that are promoting change—the conditions to which the new culture will have to adapt.

The inquiry acquires special significance in light of the terrible price to be paid if some minimal level of adaptation to new circumstances is not achieved. For example, efforts to retain a racist basis of social order in a society whose subordinate members can obtain lethal weaponry is likely either to fail utterly or to require unacceptably high levels of repression. I do not insist that we cannot survive in a state of extreme repression (though I have my doubts). I do suggest, however, that viable patterns are emerging that do not require repression because they rest on consensus. Similarly, although we might survive despite an increase in intolerance, I believe toleration is a more stable adaptation in emergent world society. The norm of toleration (which is personally preferable to me) appears to be better adapted and more viable, though not yet emergent. By pointing to its viability, I hope to foster thought and action that contribute to its emergence, despite its present problematic character.

My thesis starts with the proposition that in complex societies government embodies and reinforces patterns of culture and social organization that become and remain the very fabric of society. Once these patterns are established, they permeate social life with a persistence that is truly remarkable. Their persistence may well depend on the mutual support of these patterns by government and society. A complex society depends on government to embody and reinforce its pattern. A ruler, to maintain power, must accommodate to the pattern of society.

Even in the face of an apparent revolution, these sociogovernmental patterns have a way of reasserting themselves. In that light, it is not surprising that determined revolutionaries devote intense, sometimes frenzied, attention to rooting out ancient regimes, whether they be Imperial French, Czarist-Orthodox Russian, or feudal Chinese. Their success in doing so, however, is problematic because the structure of government tends to be deeply rooted in the society. Even the ideology of an earlier period, often the target of revolutionary attack, often survives to reassert itself. Napoleon certainly acquired powers to match or exceed those of Louis XIV, the Sun King. Bonaparte's nephew, Louis Napoleon, converted his title from President to Emperor Napoleon III after four years of republican incumbency.

In the Soviet Union, the rise of Andrei Vyshinsky as the leading governmental theorist signaled the rejection of Samuel Pashukanis, who had taken seriously the Marxist theory that after the Revolution the state would wither away. As the power of the Soviet state was increased and consolidated through purges, show trials of dissidents, and a burgeoning of the role of the secret police, few could doubt that the paramount Soviet leader, Josef Stalin, intended to use instruments of government reminiscent of Czarist Russia to ensure that the new regime survive and flourish. Reinstatement of old styles of government is more than an expression of preference, habit, or culture of the new leaders. It reflects the underlying fabric of society, which is culturally commited, often through centuries of experience, to habits of organization, deference, and—in Gramsci's term—hegemony.

The second step in my thesis is that these recurrent patterns of culture and interaction between government and society seem to go back to the earliest history of the society. I want to suggest that the great culture areas are deeply affected by their birth experiences.

The history of China is illustrative. The Chinese empire goes back at least 2,200 years to the conquest of China, from Outer Mongolia in the north to Tonkin in the south and 4,500 miles across the east-west length of China. This remarkable feat was accomplished by a provincial prince who, following his conquests, took to himself the name of Shih Huang Ti (First Emperor). In eleven years of his imperial reign (221-210 B.C.), the Ch'in emperor completed the great Wall, instituted a standard script, broke the power of the feudal lords by exiling more than 120,000 aristocratic families, and built a system of roads to facilitate communication. Notwithstanding these efforts, he had time to burn the works of Confucius, whose original writings seemed to support feudal relations without making place for the citizen's obligation to the emperor.[7] Four years after the death of Shih Huang Ti, his son was overthrown and replaced by Liu Pang, a peasant who successfully led an army of peasants and lower-ranked soldiers against an aristocratic Ch'in general. Liu founded the Han dynasty, which consolidated the Empire, revised Confucian philosophy to include obedience to the state, and instituted the civil service system to maintain a cadre of imperial officials, chosen by examination, to govern the country. These features, literally emerging in the first century of the Chinese empire, persisted for 2000 years (see Fitzgerald, 1961, pp. 135-173, 213-229; Gladden, 1972, pp. 148-174).

The pattern of Chinese government preserved the features of a centralized state: headed by an emperor and his court, and served by officials selected in part through examinations, who moved from post to post through the Empire maintaining fealty to the emperor. These officials manned a bureaucracy that administered each province, enforced criminal law, and collected taxes. Taxes came from the labor of the peasantry by way of the landlord. Taxes were sent to the imperial capital, often in the form of grain shipments, where they were used to maintain power (see Fitzgerald, 1961; Gladden, 1972).

During the millenia that followed, dynasties came and went, typically lasting 300 to 400 years. Even the pattern of dynastic rise and fall was similar. A new emperor would consolidate power, reform the bureaucracy, moderate the tax burden, and gain the popular support that signaled the Mandate of Heaven. The foundation of the new dynasty would lead to a new period of energy and organization, a peak period of splendor, a decline of support (as taxes and corruption grew), and a descent into chaos. In the interim periods, separate kingdoms often flourished, but after another few centuries a centralizing leader would arise (often a man of the people) who would reestablish the centralized state, paving the way for another dynastic era.

Meanwhile, the pattern of society remained relatively fixed, based on a large peasant population and centering around the villages in which wealthy landlords related to their tenants in a symbiotic way. Some mobility was possible from the village level to the bureaucracy, by the route of adoption or sponsorship, and successful study. The village gained some influence and protection through the placement of one of its own in government service.

In the main, however, the village lived in a world apart. Villagers tried to fulfill their obligations to the landlord, the bureaucracy, and the emperor. Courts were particularly to be avoided because a court appearance before a governmental official typically meant a judgment of guilt, followed by one or another excruciating modes of torture. None of the protections known to Western societies operated—neither a presumption of innocence, a concept of rights, the idea of due process, an independent judiciary, nor legal representation (see van der Sprenkel, 1962; Ch'u T'ung-tsu, 1961; Unger, 1976). Judgment was administered by officials as one of several bureaucratic duties. To avoid a presumption and finding of guilt, village patterns of informal dispute resolution served to reduce the likelihood of involvement in the social control system of the state. Even at present, the mediation of disputes is found in the residential quarter, the neighborhood, and the work place. Other features that persist in the People's Republic of China are a centralized government and recruitment of good students for leadership. On the other hand, current Chinese leadership seems to be moving toward the adoption of Western ideas in the development of its legal system (see O'Callaghan, 1984; Cohen, 1980, pp. 1533-1535). Whether that innovation will survive may prove to be an important determinant of the success of some of the other efforts by China's current leadership to modify the traditional pattern of society.

The fabric of Indian society, tracing back to the Upanishads and the Laws of Manu, described and enforced a system of strata that, unlike the Chinese system, permitted no individual upward mobility. A detailed set of sumptuary requirements kept the members of these castes, or broader groups known as Varnas, apart from each other. Instead of a merit basis for rising in the governance structure, literacy was the privilege of the priestly caste, the Brahmins. Others were precluded by birth from governmental power. Military and merchant castes were also differentiated. The mass of the population was born into the agricultural castes. Later, there evolved the designation of untouchability to describe hereditary outcastes who were consigned to carry out the most contemptible functions of the society.

The Hindu system also persisted for more than 2000 years. The Laws of Manu were used, until Indian independence, to preserve caste distinctions. Only with the adoption of the new Constitution have these formal requirements changed.

These requirements have not only persisted, they continue to give form to the fabric of Indian society. The very units of Indian society were related to one's caste rather than to units of governance.

As a corollary, perhaps, Indiawide governance by a central state proved virtually impossible. A dominant national regime has not succeeded for any sustained period in India. Instead, loyalty to the caste and (to a lesser extent) the local princeling was the usual pattern. These patterns persisted in India into the modern era, when Indian culture, like Chinese, shows signs of major change.

This brings me to the third point of my thesis: We live at a time when traditional units of government and society, so persistent in the past, are subject to major change. If the emergent society follows the precedent of Chinese, Indian, and Western society, its early characteristics once established may well set the pattern for millenia to come. That prospect adds further to the importance of the inquiry into initial features of the emergent society.

Although we cannot predict what those features will be, they will undoubtedly be deeply affected by the experience of government and society in the great societies of the past. As intensive students of Western culture, sociologists have a particular obligation to understand its fundamental characteristics and to compare and contrast these with other great cultural traditions. We must try to understand Indian, Chinese, and other societies equally well in order to learn how these different traditions may be reconciled, so that each can contribute to an emergent world cultural system.

Even at this early stage in the development of world culture, some cross-cultural norms are beginning to emerge. For example, a norm against discrimination based on ascribed status is advancing steadily. On this matter, Chinese culture has long been favorable, as has Western society, with some effort and exceptions. Indian society, although traditionally committed to the opposite approach, has moved very far, very fast. Under the influence of B. R. Ambedkar and Mahatma Gandhi, India's constitutional provisions for compensatory education and representation, as implemented, constitute a serious effort to adopt and institute what for India is a major step toward the norm of China and the West. In its efforts to do so, India has provided a major lesson in how judicial decisions can combine with administrative process to work toward major change in the fabric of society. A recent study by an American sociolegal scholar shows in detail how that process has worked (Galanter, 1984).

Within the area of stratification, Indian culture contains some elements that could be useful to the other two. Neither China nor the West has demonstrated a noteworthy capacity to limit the acquisition of wealth, or its transmission, by those in positions of privilege. One consequence for Chinese society has been mentioned in the account of factors affecting the fall of dynasties. In China, the traditional culture pattern has accorded extraordinary wealth to the emperor, his court, and the landlords—even when the burden tended to crush the peasantry. Also, the use of power in China to maintain control reached extremes of torture that became notorious around the world. In the Heavenly City, for example, the emperor was reportedly regularly entertained in his bejewelled throne room by the shrieks of miscreants being tortured and executed on the palace grounds for any of a variety of offenses.

In traditional India, power was somewhat less concentrated, in part because of the very disunity that kept state size small. The Indians, moreover, separated wealth and power through the specialization of castes. Brahmins, members of the Varna with the highest prestige and learning, were not as wealthy as the Vaisyas (Baniya) who were the merchants. Moreover, the ideal of Indian society provided that men at the height of their attainments retire from active affairs to contemplate, and to live a life of poverty, as *sinyasi*. The concept of sinyasi is known in the West from the example of Gautama when he abandoned his power and princely possessions to become the enlightened one, the Buddha.

This Indian concept does not by any means guarantee substantial reduction in the distance between strata in Indian society. Poverty among the untouchables (harijans) and peasants is frightful, and self- or family-imposed disability is often used to facilitate begging that will relieve poverty. But the concept of humility through asceticism may have salutary effects worth considering for all of the cultures, none of which is immune to the danger of limitless appetite together with complacent toleration of the misery of the less privileged.

The life of Mahatma Gandhi illustrates the potential value of this idea for emergent world culture. In adopting an ascetic way of life, Gandhi eschewed wealth and carefully limited his authority. His ascetic way led him to practice the spinning of cotton cloth in his own home, urging that others throughout India do the same. In this way, he intended to help the poor raise themselves from deepest poverty to some degree of self-sufficiency, not dependent on the wealthy or powerful. For societies such as ours, where the "curse of bigness" prevails, this approach deserves some thought. When projected on the world scene, with its countless starving people unaided by adequate self-support systems, it may provide a vital idea for the emergent society. The West has encountered this idea (see Schumacher, 1973; Toffler, 1980), but thus far does not seem to have taken it seriously.

Gandhi's attitude toward power also merits attention. Demonstrating himself to be a superb political tactician, he regularly outmaneuvered experienced and professional British civil servants. Yet he refused, when India became independent, to accept any formal position in the new Republic. In his renunciation of formal power, he illustrated a message very difficult to explain to Westerners: that there are alternatives to formal power, that moral leadership may usefully complement or even substitute for national-bureaucratic authority, that there is an important difference between (as Koestler, 1945, put it) the yogi and the commissar.[8]

On the matter of intersocietal conflict, all cultures must go far beyond present norms. Learning in this sphere must include a capacity to evolve a new norm in which sovereignty of the state, of every state, is constrained. This will require the development of new mechanisms and a new spirit of reconcilation, as well as the evolution of a taboo against nuclear war, and other kinds of violence that might lead in that direction.

To reach that point will require a sustained, intelligent effort at mutual understanding and trust. The West, with its tradition of holy war, has perhaps the most to learn in this sphere. In that light, Chinese toleration of differences in belief and Gandhian pacifism may contribute to tempering of the belief, held by both Western superpowers, that each of their ideologies is unmistakably superior.

One final illustration will suffice in this setting. It concerns organization. In the West, as Weber repeatedly and skillfully asserted, the bureaucratic organizational form was developed to a high degree. It has served to overcome some problems of inefficiency and corruption that have plagued other societies. Nepotism is specifically ruled out in theory and, effectively, in practice.

The spread of bureaucratic organization to almost all areas of social life in the West, and its influence on the remaining ones (e.g., the family), has been truly remarkable. The emergence of a common structure in corporations and governmental agencies is impressive. To some extent, this model is found in close to ideal-typical form in the military and the church. Even universities, schools, charitable institutions, political parties, and unions take this form in Western societies. With the decline of small business and the family farm, areas of life not subject to bureaucratic organization have been limited largely to family and informal associations.

Comparable trends in other societies may also be observed. The Soviets have shown no lesser tendency than we to organize matters in this way. If anything, their system of state socialism rationalizes industry and government in a single hierarchical organization, thus reducing such difference and space as exists between economic and political bureaucracies in a capitalist democracy. Evidence from these Western societies, and non-Western ones as well, suggests that the trend toward bureaucratization continues in a way that might add efficiency and uniformity—at the cost of individuality and self-direction. Whether that trend can be tempered by countermeasures, such as citizen participation, remains to be seen.

In these examples, reference has been made to a number of areas in which a common world culture may be emerging. Each self-standing society can in this period contribute to the fabric of the new world order. None of us can tell at this stage what its norms will be. But inventions capable of implementing emerging common values, or meeting palpable needs, may be of particular importance at this stage. We are developing, through channels of international exchange, methods of sharing our cultures, including the results of research and other scholarly pursuits. Some of these mechanisms are intergovernmental, often in the context of the U.N. and its agencies. Some are through nongovernmental organizations (NGOs) that vary in their official status. (NGO's may not be official, but acquisition of an acronym suggests they have already taken on a quasi-governmental role.)

In every sphere, such sharing may contribute to a process of norm formation. The development of norms, both procedural and substantive, may help to emphasize commonalities in a way that moves toward the concept of world citizenship. This process can counteract ethnocentrism and enhance readiness of people to take additional steps toward a world government. Examples of these developments include formal arrangements—such as the Geneva Convention on prisoners of war—and unofficial activities—such as those of Amnesty International—that tend to develop uniform standards for the treatment of political prisoners. As such efforts increase, they may establish the frame and set the design for an emergent world government.

The final point in my thesis is that activity at all levels, within as well as between nations, is potentially important in this process of forming a world society. In a bureaucratized world, we tend to exaggerate the capability of those in positions of formal authority and to minimize unduly the importance of processes that take place among ordinary people (Dahl, 1985). This bias can detract from norm formation, which occurs chiefly at the grass roots. It also places an undue burden on enacted laws, rules, and regulations. Positive law, diverging sufficiently from the norms, can readily become deadlettered compared with what Ehrlich (1936) called "living law." Positive law, faced with normative conflict or normlessness, also encounters difficulty. In the aggregate, positive laws that are collectively devoid of normative support hardly merit designation as laws, and are unlikely to play an effective role in the formation of world society.

What this suggests is that activities at all levels of a given society, as well as between societies, are relevant to the emergence of a world society. If the peaceful management of conflict, for example, is a vital requisite of the emerging world society, methods developed and successfully practiced in the resolution of microconflicts may affect the handling of such problems at the macrolevel between nations. Too complex to explore in this context, these micro-macro level exchanges need the benefit of close and systematic study. Not only can we learn from the microlevel methods of use at the macro and vice versa, we may also acquire through experience or praxis at one level habits and commitments that are transferable to the other. Thus, as a general matter, those concerned about an emerging world society who seek ways of contributing to it might wish to consider the significance of day-to-day activities for larger contexts.

In the emergence of any new society, the problem of authority inevitably is central. When a society is in transition, norms are bound to be tenuous. In the present world situation, this creates the greatest kind of danger. People who become aware of subordinate status, relative to others, and who acquire the capacity to use force, create a potential for disturbance that cannot be readily allayed. Altering relations between dominant and subordinate groups, while maintaining order, presents a difficult problem at all levels within a society and between societies.

Illustrations of this problem abound. Absent agreed-upon norms, and ways of enforcing them, groups with grievances utilize the force available to them, undeterred even by massive counterforce. In Western culture, particularly, the culture of self-assertion, conflict, and intolerance promotes the tendency to fight for the interest of one's group, armed with the conviction of righteousness. Those tendencies, acted out, do not lead necessarily toward common norms of what is right or of how to compose differences. Procedural models for dispute resolution, established in one nation, do not easily or inevitably transfer to a world rule of law. On the contrary, national differences may mobilize ethnocentrism and violence as a means of settling conflict.

The task, then, of evolving substantive and procedural norms for governance in an emerging world order is difficult indeed. Until we recognize how badly this evolution is needed, international order, even survival, is dangerously at risk.

I have suggested here that recognizing the stability of the great cultures of the past might enable us to turn our efforts toward analyzing the conditions of order for an emergent world culture and society. As a start, we might select from the great cultures some characteristics of each for all of us to cultivate. Several merit consideration: the tolerance of the Chinese tradition, the tempering of authority and the reverence for life of India, the protection of human rights and opportunity cultivated in the West.

As such postulates give rise to particular norms, we will need to know how best to identify them and to provide opportunity for their expression at micro and macro levels. For example, in the current South African dispute over apartheid, the world reaction in opposition seems to draw on a larger jural postulate: that biological origin is not a sufficient basis in itself for denying one group of people in society the privileges and immunities that a second group of people in that society enjoys.

The emergence of this kind of principle, when widely accepted, can provide opportunities for developing procedures by which the international community, acting in a quasi-governmental manner, may adjudicate the issues and plan for the orderly, authoritative, nonviolent if possible, perhaps gradual, elimination of the practice. Thus in enunciating and implementing substantive norms, cooperative international intervention may help to illustrate and promote orderly resolution of disputes, if not reconciliation among disputants. If this can be done in a manner that affords some potential benefits for the parties to disputes, as well as to interested bystanders, it may demonstrate the possibility that government might aid in the establishment of jural postulates for an emerging world order.

Notes

1. For a classic discussion of the potential damage to social order of increasingly repressive sanctions, see Montesquieu (1949/1748) *The Spirit of the Laws.*

2. Regarding Weber, "authority" here refers to "legal-rational" (or, "bureaucratic") authority. See Weber (1957/1922, pp. 325-328). For Gramsci, "hegemony" means the interdependent nature of the economic, cultural, and political relationships entailing the direction (*direzione*) and domination (*dominazione*) of the ruling class over society. For a detailed development of this concept, see Gramsci (1971, pp. 242 ff.).

3. In this analysis, I have drawn substantially on the work of Turner (1941).

4. Except where otherwise noted, the discussion of China draws heavily on Fitzgerald (1961).

5. Even so, Rome relied heavily on slaves for military purposes and as a source of labor. Its practice of drawing slaves from increasingly remote boundaries suggests a conflict between the extension of citizenship and this reliance on slavery. See Anderson (1978).

6. It is Merton's (1957, p. 132) "central hypothesis that aberrant behavior may be regarded sociologically as a symptom of dissociation between culturally prescribed aspirations and socially structured avenues for realizing these aspirations."

7. Although the book burning is reported by Fitzgerald (1961), this assertion has been challenged by Needham (1954, p. 101).

8. "The real issue remains between the Yogi and the Commisar, between the fundamental conceptions of Change from Without and Change from Within" (Koestler, 1945, p. 4).

References

Anderson, P. 1978. *Passages from Antiquity to Feudalism.* London: Verso.

Benedict, R. 1934. *Patterns of Culture.* Boston: Houghton Mifflin.

Brinton, C. 1938. *The Anatomy of Revolution.* New York: W. W. Norton.

Ch'u T'ung-tsu. 1961. *Law and Society in Traditional China.* Vancouver, B.C.: Institute of Pacific Relations.

Cohen, J. 1980. "China's New Lawyer's Law." *American Bar Association Journal* 66: 1533-1535.

Dahl, R. A. 1985. *Controlling Nuclear Weapons: Democracy Versus Guardianship.* Syracuse, NY: Syracuse University Press.

Edwards, L. P. 1970. *The Natural History of Revolution.* Chicago: University of Chicago Press.

Ehrlich, E. 1936. *Fundamental Principles of the Sociology of Law.* Cambridge, MA: Harvard University Press.

Fitzgerald, C. P. 1961. *China: A Short Cultural History.* New York: Praeger.

Frank, A. G. 1967. *Capitalism and Underdevelopment in Latin America: Historical Studies of Chile and Brazil.* New York: Monthly Review Press.

Galanter, M. 1984. *Competing Equalities: Law and the Background Classes in India.* Berkeley: University Presses of California.

Gladden, E. N. 1972. *A History of Public Administration, Vol. I, From Earliest Times to the Eleventh Century.* London: Frank Cass.

Gramsci, A. 1971. *Selections from the Prison Notebooks.* Translated and edited by Q. Hoare and G. N. Smith. New York: International Publishers.

Hoebel, E. A. 1954. *The Law of Primitive Man: A Study in Comparative Legal Dynamics.* Cambridge, MA: Harvard University Press.

Koestler, A. 1945. *The Yogi and the Commisar, and Other Essays.* New York: Macmillan.

Kroeber, A. L. 1952. *The Nature of Culture.* Chicago: University of Chicago Press.

LeVine, R. A. and D. T. Campbell. 1972. *Ethnocentrism.* New York: John Wiley.

Merton, R. K. 1957. *Social Theory and Social Structure.* New York: Free Press.

Montesquieu, C. L. 1949. *The Spirit of the Laws.* Translated by T. Nugent. Introduction by F. Neumann. New York: Hafner Press. (pub. orig. 1748)

Needham, J. 1954. *Science and Civilization in China, Vol. I. Introductory Orientations.* Cambridge: Cambridge.

O'Callaghan, M. L. 1984. "Let a Thousand Lawyers Bloom." *Japan Times* (May 26).

Schumacher, E. F. 1973. *Small Is Beautiful: Economics as if People Mattered.* New York: Harper & Row.

van der Sprenkel, S. 1962. *Legal Institutions in Manchu China.* London: Athlone.

Thapir, R. and P. Spear. 1965. *A History of India,* Vols. I and II. Baltimore, MD: Penguin.

Tilly, C. 1984. *Big Structures, Large Processes, Huge Comparisons.* New York: Russell Sage Foundation.

Toffler, A. 1980. *The Third Wave.* New York: Morrow.

Turner, R. E. 1941. *The Great Cultural Traditions: The Foundations of Civilizations, Vol. I, The Ancient Cities; Vol. II, The Classical Empires.* New York: McGraw-Hill.

Unger, R. N. 1976. *Law in Modern Society: Toward a Criticism of Social Theory.* New York: Free Press.

Wallerstein, I. M. 1974. *The Modern World-System: Capitalist Agriculture and the Origins of the European World Economy in the Sixteenth Century.* New York: Academic.

Weber, M. 1957. *The Theory of Social and Economic Organization.* Edited by Talcott Parsons. New York: Oxford University Press. (pub. orig. 1922)

12

Government and the Making of Social Structure

Thomas S. Moore
S. M. Miller

THE PAST SEVERAL DECADES have witnessed a worldwide trend toward an increased share of government in GNP. As long as economic growth rates remained high and prices remained stable, this trend was frequently portrayed as part of the "logic of industrialism." With the advent of declining growth rates and rising prices in the mid-1960s, however, the Keynesian underpinning of the logic of industrialism began to collapse. Once again, the expansion of the public sector was widely criticized for its supposed corrosive effects upon the norms and incentives essential to a competitive market economy, and democratically mandated programs became increasingly vulnerable to the charge that they jeopardize material progress.

This conservative opposition to "big government" is neither new nor unique to the American experience. Debate on the role of government in a private economy, both in this country and elsewhere, has traditionally emphasized the trade-offs between the regulative and redistributive goals of the public sector and the efficiency and freedoms of market allocation. But if the conservative emphasis upon the limits of government is not new or unique to this country, its claims that government spending is wasteful, that the tax burden is excessive, and that intervention in the economy is generally unnecessary and counterproductive have been singularly effective in shaping our contemporary political debate. The historical precedents that legitimized the growth of government, and especially its social welfare components, in Continental Europe and Japan have been largely absent from the American experience (see Reich, 1983, Chap. 1). As a result, the connection between economic prosperity and social justice was necessarily forged on the basis of Keynesian principles of aggregate demand management. In the Keynesian model, growth is constrained by effective demand, and social welfare programs are defended as a means of accelerating economic activity by supplementing the income of those with a high marginal propensity to consume. Keynesian theory thus gave legitimacy to popular demands for redistributive justice and to the liberal social policies originating in response to those demands.

As economic growth slowed despite increased social welfare spending, the narrow legitimacy of American liberalism became apparent. Criticism of both the democratic impetus and the Keynesian rationale behind social welfare spending intensified. Neoconservatives such as Brittan (1975), Buchanan and Wagner (1977), and Kristol (1979) argued, for example, that the extensions of the franchise and the growing popular awareness that government can influence economic outcomes together result in a sense of entitlement and the displacement of distributional conflicts from the marketplace to the political arena. This escalation of redistributive demands and the taxation and spending programs to which they give rise are alleged to constitute a system of disincentives to work effort, saving, and entrepreneurial risk-taking. Nor has criticism been confined to the supposed effects of government spending upon economic performance. Because equity claims based upon "citizen rights" do not generate partisan loyalties, social welfare spending is also faulted for contributing to the emergence of weak parliamentary regimes and the contemporary crisis of political legitimacy. As distributional claims upon the state come to dominate the political arena, they bring in their train a volatile electorate, independent and distrustful of the major parties (Janowitz, 1976). Presumably exacerbating this electoral instability is the limited success of Keynesian theory and the Employment Act of 1946 in politicizing unemployment, a matter dealt with less explicitly by conservative commentators.

The conservative critique of government is not all-inclusive. Criticism of defense spending and of public subsidies to business is either absent or muted whereas that of business and personal taxes, government regulation, and social welfare spending is usually present and strident. But if the particular objects of criticism are not fully representative of the activities of government, the anti-Keynesian theme of contemporary conservatism is that the expansion of government spending per se has become a drag upon the rate of economic growth and a threat to the stable political affiliations that are the basis of social control under parliamentary regimes. More successful in altering the composition than in reducing the share of government in Gross National Product, the impact of this critique of government is undeniable. Its validity appears more doubtful. We begin our evaluation of this conservative thesis, therefore, by examining the relationship between public and private sector growth in the major Organization for Economic Cooperation and Development (OECD) countries.

Big Government and Economic Growth

From 1953 to 1973 per capita real GNP increased in the United States at an annual rate of 2.1%. The following decade, 1973 to 1983, it grew at a yearly rate of .9% (Dornbusch and Fischer, 1984, p. 580). The first problem with attributing this slowdown to the expansion of the public sector is one of timing; the increase in total government spending has closely followed the growth of the economy itself. Total government spending grew 2.5% a year from 1948 to 1966 before slowing to 1.2% from 1966 to 1973 and then to .3% from 1973 to 1979 (Bowles et al., 1983, p. 38).

Nor does the accumulated burden of government offer a credible explanation for slower U.S. growth rates when viewed in relation to the governmental share of other industrial capitalist economies. Measured in terms of both outlays and revenues, all of the major OECD countries except Japan devote a larger share of their economies to government (see Table A-1 in the Appendix). Even in the case of Japan, the ratio of government spending to Gross Domestic Product (GDP) now rivals that of the United States. Between 1960 and 1981 government spending here rose from 27.6% to 35.4% of GDP; that of Japan grew from 18.3% to 34.0% (OECD, 1982, Table 6.5).

Throughout the postwar period the other major OECD countries—West Germany, France, the United Kingdom, Italy, and Canada—consistently spent a larger share of GDP on government and increased that share more rapidly than has the United States. Yet despite the relatively small and slowly growing proportion of government in the U.S. economy, the other major OECD countries experienced more rapid labor productivity growth, measured in terms of real GDP per person employed. During the postwar period labor productivity in West Germany, France, and Italy more than doubled and that of Japan increased more than fourfold relative to the U.S. (Kendrick, 1981, p. 136).

Prior to the 1970s the rapid productivity growth of Europe and Japan was largely attributable to the transfer of technology from a much more advanced American economy. This diffusion of technology from abroad could arguably be said to have offset the adverse effects of rapid public sector expansion. But "the penalty of taking the lead" does not explain the relatively poor economic performance of the United States after 1973. Our patent balance turned negative with West Germany in the mid-1960s and with Japan in the mid-1970s, and both those countries had by then achieved technological leadership in many industries (Magaziner and Reich, 1982, p. 52). By the end of the decade the gap in labor productivity between the United States and its principal competitors had narrowed to the point where there was very little of a lead to be transferred. Yet their economic growth rates continued to exceed that of the United States.

Both timing and cross-national comparison suggest that the expansion of the public sector does not account for the slower U.S. growth rate. Compared to our major trading partners, the relative size of the government and of the taxing and spending programs most criticized by conservatives is not large. This conclusion is supported by recent analyses of the U.S. productivity decline.

In conventional economic theory there are two sources of labor productivity growth: either the rate of capital-labor substitution (i.e., change in the capital-labor ratio times the capital share of factor costs) may increase or the productivity of the factors themselves may rise. The latter is variously referred to as the "rate of technical progress" or "total factor productivity" and includes such unmeasured inputs as advances in knowledge, improved resource allocation, and economies of scale. Ever since Robert Solow's (1957) study of the sources of growth, it has generally been acknowledged that most of the historical rise in output per labor hour is due to technical progress, that is, to factors other than the capital-labor ratio. A decline in this rate of technical progress also appears to be primarily responsible for the worldwide economic slowdown since 1973 (see Appendix).

If the way in which resources are used is of greater consequence for long-term growth than the aggregate level of inputs, it seems curious that public attention has been directed almost exclusively to the adverse effects of government policy upon factor supplies. This supply-side focus becomes more curious when we look for evidence of the detrimental effects of policy upon the growth of the capital stock. Despite changes in inflation, interest rates, and tax policy the U.S. saving rates—the initial determinants of capital stock growth— have remained stable throughout the postwar period. Saving behavior appears to be singularly unresponsive to fiscal and regulatory policy shifts, including interest rate hikes designed to encourage saving. In an exhaustive accounting of the sources of growth, Denison (1979, p. 56) concluded that the stability of the private saving ratios relative to GNP indicates that slower growth of the capital stock cannot be ascribed to changes in the private propensity to save. Nor did budget deficits, which reduce the volume of saving available for investment, account for the slowdown. In neo-Keynesian fashion, Denison attributes the decelerating growth of the capital stock to weak investment demand and the underutilization of existing capacity. Other analysts (e.g., Clark, 1982, pp. 149-154) attach greater importance to the oil price shocks and attendant inflation that raised the rental price of capital (by eroding tax deductions), thereby contributing to the shift to more labor-intensive production. In either case, slower growth of the capital stock is not a consequence of the size of government.

Analysts have been less successful in explaining the drop in total factor productivity. Particularly puzzling is the finding that much of the productivity decline can be traced to seven quarters in 1974-1975, a fact that is hard to reconcile with the lagged effects of both policy changes and oil price hikes. In a recent article Michael Darby (1984) offers a solution to this productivity puzzle that confounds claims that the growing burden of government is the source of economic decline. Dividing the twentieth century into three broad periods— 1900-1929, 1929-1965, and 1965-1979—on the basis of changes in the labor supply, Darby found no substantial variation over the course of the century from a 1.75% annual rate of increase in total factor productivity. Insofar as broad trends go, the U.S. productivity slowdown appears to be a case of "statistical myopia."

Further analysis of the variations in hourly productivity growth within the 1929-1965 and 1965-1979 periods suggested reasons for this myopia. The rapid growth rate of 2.4% for 1948-1965 followed a much slower 1.2% rate for 1929-1948 and was primarily due to the recovery of the capital-labor ratio from its abnormally low level at the end of World War II. The very sharp drop in hourly productivity in 1974-1975, on the other hand, was found to be the result of measurement error. The seven quarters in which the decline is concentrated coincide with the relaxation and removal of price controls, and measured output was biased by corporate evasion of those controls. Aside from this substantial measurement bias, the principal cause of the decline in productivity growth over the 1965-1979 period was the trend to a more youthful labor force, an effect that now operates in the opposite direction.

If Darby's analysis is correct, there has been no substantial, inexplicable decline in total factor productivity growth. The size of government and the effects of specific policies and programs combine with numerous other determinants of the growth trend, but they do not explain its apparent decline since 1965.

The Social Construction of Limits

Several decades ago the distinguished economist Colin Clark asserted that no economy could devote more than 25% of its GNP to public expenditures. Today all of the major OECD countries and most of the smaller ones as well exceed this figure. And in the early 1960s, then secretary of Health, Education, and Welfare, Abraham Ribicoff, declared that the United States would never tax more than 10% of the wage bill for social security (both employer and employee contributions). Today the joint social security tax is about 14% and rising.

Falsified by subsequent events, these predictions about limits can be seen today to reflect the value judgments of the speakers. Without a historical record similarly qualifying or discrediting the claims of contemporary conservatives, we have attempted to show that the expansion of the public sector, as a whole, has neither undermined the growth of the capital stock nor caused the decline in factor productivity. Government policies can adversely affect economic performance, especially that of particular industries, and the U.S. economy has declined relative to its major competitors. But the size of government is not the source of that decline and does not represent an obstacle to continued economic growth.

Above all, the size of government controversy is a political strategem, which is not to deny that it is motivated by a real concern. The engine of growth in a private economy is the profitability of individual firms, and there is some evidence that both before- and after-tax corporate-profit rates fell throughout the 1970s (Council of Economic Advisers, 1980, p. 303). Whether this falling rate of profit reflected short-term difficulties or long-term trend, heightened international competition and increased capital mobility undoubtedly gave added impetus to efforts to reduce the wage share of net domestic corporate income. Any reduction in the wage share would increase profitability, if only temporarily, by shifting the burdens of competition and relative decline onto labor. Of course, such a reapportionment of the domestic corporate income ultimately depends upon the effectiveness of unemployment in reducing wage claims, and here the growth of government becomes a problem. In the form of countercyclical policy, the institutionalization of collective bargaining, and a partial redistribution of the social product via increased social welfare spending, government has lessened the vulnerability of wage earners to the pressures of unemployment (see Bowles and Gintis, 1982).

The expansion of the public sector has not created a system of disincentives that act as a drag upon productivity growth, but it does appear to have undercut the effectiveness of unemployment in reducing wage levels. By curbing and redirecting government spending, conservatives hope to reestablish the normative framework of an earlier economic era, a framework conducive to the upward redistribution of corporate income in particular and of the social product in general. Unfortunately, this backward-looking agenda fails to acknowledge the changing realities of economic competition and risks the long-term prosperity that it seeks to secure.

Changing Realities and the Possibilities of Government

Emphasizing the antagonisms of market and government and the trade-offs between economic prosperity and social justice, neoconservatives deny the increasing interdependence of both. Yet today every major industry is heavily involved with and dependent upon government—so much so that we cannot identify industrial or occupational structures based solely upon the market and existing independently of government actions. Consequently, we cannot empirically isolate and measure the concept of a pregovernment income distribution. Government is inevitably and increasingly involved in the creation of social structure, and prosperity inevitably and increasingly depends upon the equity of the social arrangements that are being created.

In an evermore open and competitive world economy, laissez-faire notions about the role of government pass from being an anachronism to becoming a threat to our standard of living. The diffusion of high-volume, standardized production techniques throughout much of the world has placed approximately 70% of all U.S. manufactured goods in direct competition with foreign-made products (Reich, 1983, p. 121). The heightened mobility of capital and the speed with which technology now diffuses throughout the capitalist world economy have made a skilled and flexible work force the only real alternative to low-wage competition as the key to continued prosperity. Unless we wish to compete through an absolute immiseration of the American work force, a sustained level of public investment in human infrastructure and a deeper public commitment to equitable industrial and social relations is imperative.

The increasing interdependence of state and civil society can be illustrated by identifying the several ways in which governmental expansion has contributed to the standard of living. For if by living standard we refer not only to the amount of goods and services produced but also to the availability of goods that do not enter into GNP and to the equity with which all goods are consumed, then our standard of life is essentially the product of deliberate social action. Only by appreciating the extent to which the social arrangements under which we live reflect public choice can the construction of possibilities replace the current preoccupation with limits.

First and foremost among the areas of governmental expansion is the control over taxing, spending, and the money supply that coalesce in macroeconomic management. Today Keynesian doctrine and its activist conception of government are criticized within and outside the economics profession for the failure to ensure both full employment and stable prices. In their stead, monetarists call for less government and less active government. However, the inability of economists to predict the velocity with which money circulates, and their consequent failure to manage a gradual expansion of the economy through the growth of the money stock, has led important segments of the business press to question the viability of the monetarist prescription of a noninterventionary role for government (see *Business Week*, 1983). For those like ourselves who view the private economy as inherently unstable and capable of self-depressing, an activist role for government seems inescapable. There can be no doubt that "automatic stabilizers," such as the income tax and unemployment compensation, have dampened the business cycle. Mitigating the hardships and instability imposed by economic fluctuations, government narrows the gap between potential and actual GNP and reduces both unemployment and the degree of vertical inequality.

Of course, the greater stability of aggregate demand bolsters union-organizing efforts and the ability of labor to resist wage reductions. In advocating tax cuts and a balanced budget amendment, many conservatives seek not only to reduce the size of government but also to curtail stabilization policy. This short-sighted pursuit of bargaining advantage through greater cyclical instability risks long-term growth and does so for at least two reasons. First, the most important determinant of productivity growth within a given industry is the state of its industrial relations (Freeman and Medoff, 1984, pp. 162-180), and deep recessionary downturns are not conducive to good industrial relations. Second, prolonged recessions mean long periods of low gross investment, which also undermine productivity advances and the competitive position of firms within international markets. A necessary condition for equitable industrial relations, public management of aggregate demand stabilizes the growth trend while dampening the cyclical fluctuations around the trend.

Interlinked with the management of effective demand is a second dimension of state expansion—the development and maintenance of minimum standards of economic well-being. Comparatively late in establishing most social welfare programs, U.S. government cash and in-kind benefits amounted by 1980 to an annual equivalent of $2,500 for those otherwise below the poverty threshold and provided half of the income of the bottom quintile (Piven and Cloward, 1982, p. 15). These expanding benefits and the national standards governing their distribution are blamed for the growing sense of entitlement among the disadvantaged and, like social spending in general, for limiting the disciplining effects of unemployment upon labor.

The problem with this welfare effort is not its size but the fact that it is perceived as a form of charity divorced from and antagonistic to economic development. In order to minimize the labor market effects of social welfare, many U.S. programs are means-tested with eligibility restricted to the most unfortunate citizens. We thereby define and stigmatize a category of welfare recipients segregated from the economic mainstream instead of making social services available to the population as a whole. Our major competitors more readily acknowledge the connection between social welfare programs and economic development, and spend a greater proportion of their GNP on them. West Germany, France, Sweden, and Japan all have national health insurance, wage insurance, and prior notification requirements in the case of plant shutdowns, and retraining programs that enroll between 1% and 2% of their work forces—the comparable percentage for the United States is .1 (Reich, 1983, pp. 220-221). Emphasizing the relation between social welfare and productivity, rather than that between unemployment and wage demands, these policy initiatives lessen the insecurities of the job market. We cannot demonstrate a causal relationship between this social welfare effort and productivity growth, but sometimes circumstantial evidence can be very compelling.

A third direction of state growth is the regulatory effort. The detailed regulation of economic activity has become one of the most visible, and resented, aspects of government. Critics range from those who view all regulations as necessary hindrances to the efficient operation of the market to those who argue that, inevitably, regulations are subverted from their original purposes and regulatory agencies are co-opted by their regulated industries, thus providing the illusion rather than the reality of reform. Despite these criticisms and the element of truth to both, we believe that the regulatory effort will increase over the long term. Frank Ackerman (1982, p. 120) cites four reasons for the success and probable continuance of recent regulatory legislation. First, most of the newer regulations are worthwhile when measured by the rigid standards of cost-benefit analysis. Second, the off-cited burden of paperwork has been shown to be quite small for most industries. Two-thirds of the time spent filling out forms for federal regulators is accounted for by businesses—mostly radio and television stations—monitored by the Federal Communications Commission. For other industries paperwork consists primarily of tax forms that have not increased in complexity since 1963. Third, many businesses have developed profitable production lines or, as in the case of the automobile industry, have avoided a self-destructive commitment to older lines in response to regulators. Finally, there is direct evidence of declining levels of pollution in the years since environmental regulation began. To these specific reasons we can add a fifth: The costs of regulation account for only a small part of the decline in GNP growth and are far less consequential, for example, than demographic shifts. But the real force behind the regulatory effort is the awareness that deliberate public action can be a source of benefit. Every regulation that is perceived as beneficial, whether or not its benefits are included in the GNP, contributes to a sense of collective efficacy and thus to the legitimacy of regulation itself.

A fourth and overlapping area of governmental expansion King (1983) terms "social engineering." Through the enactment of civil rights and equal opportunity legislation as well as through the expansion of public sector employment, government has played a crucial role in improving the opportunities available to women and minorities. Criticized for undermining traditional family roles and meritocratic norms, this governmental effort has proved indispensable in combatting the discriminatory practices that restrict employment opportunities in the private sector. To the extent that these discriminatory barriers are overturned, government ensures the increased labor force participation of disadvantaged groups, channeling their talents and energies into the economy.

This concept of "social engineering" extends beyond civil rights and equal opportunity efforts to encompass virtually all government activities insofar as they affect the equity of social arrangements. As an analytic distinction, it points up the failure of liberal social policy to confront the particular interests served through the composition, as opposed to the level, of taxation and spending programs. Nowhere is this shortcoming more evident than in the purchase of public goods. The various levels of government together are by far the largest source of demand for goods and services in our society. Approximately half of the federal budget alone goes to purchase such public goods as military and police, transportation and infrastructure.

In neoclassical economic theory a public good or service is one that people cannot be excluded from consuming (e.g., a lighthouse). Because the market will not produce that for which it cannot charge, government must provide these necessary goods and services. The flaw in this neoclassical logic is that we do not all participate in decisions regarding the composition of public goods purchases, nor do we benefit equally from their consumption. Unfortunately, public awareness of the unequal benefits emanating from public goods expenditures in general and military spending in particular is likely to remain quite limited. Compared to social welfare expenditures, public goods spending is unpoliticized. The lack of unity on this issue within the major party coalitions constrains party competition to relatively minor differences while the resulting absence of debate and information available to the public facilitates the domination of policy by monolithic military and corporate interests (see Page, 1983).

The social structural consequences of this policy domination are several. Consuming a large part of the budget, military spending in particular limits transfers and income redistribution. It similarly undercuts spending on more democratically consumed goods and services. Finally, it is directed to the most capital-intensive industries and therefore offers limited employment benefits while supporting industrial and occupational wage differentials. But if the outlook for the redirection of public goods spending is not encouraging, neither is it altogether bleak. As the increasing levels of military spending threaten to make it a political issue, the pressure of international economic competition strengthens the position of those who would reallocate public resources to more productive ends. This needed reallocation represents the greatest challenge to those desiring a more equitable and democratic society. For contrary to the claims of many conservative commentators, the trend in public goods spending, as in the growth of government, is not likely to be reversed. What is to be contested, therefore, is the speed and composition of that growth rather than its continuance.

Appendix

Tables A-1 and A-2 document several of the international trends cited in the text. Table A-1 presents total government outlays and revenues as a percentage of GDP as well as annual growth rates in per capita real GDP for the major OECD countries; Table A-2 shows their income distributions. It should be noted that the rapid growth rates of Japan and many of the European countries throughout the 1960s were due in part to the diffusion of technology from abroad (primarily from the United States). Also important was the continuing recovery of their capital-labor ratios, a recovery spurred by relatively high rates of saving and investment. As "steady state" growth (the point at which saving is sufficient to offset depreciation while maintaining a given capital-labor ratio) is attained, growth rates return to their long-term trend.

Probably the most dramatic example of decelerating growth is Japan. In addition to diminishing gains from imported technology, total factor productivity in Japan fell as a result of smaller contributions from the "shift effect" (the reallocation of labor from agriculture), as well as from economies of scale and advances in knowledge. And although it remains comparatively uncontroversial, the regulatory effort is estimated to have reduced Japan's growth rate by a full percentage point, 2.5 times its effect upon the U.S. growth rate (Kendrick, 1981, pp. 140-141). Exacerbating the effect of these proximate determinants were the oil price shocks, which had a particularly severe impact upon the oil-importing nations of continental Europe and Japan. Despite these setbacks, Japan has sustained a high rate of growth while enjoying a relatively equal distribution of income. By comparison, the United States has experienced both slow growth and greater income inequality than any major competitor except France. Our small and slowly growing share of government in GNP has brought neither relative prosperity nor greater equality.

TABLE A-1: **Public and Private Sector Growth in the Major OECD Countries**

	1960-1967	*1967-1973*	*1973-1979*	*1960-1981*
A. Government Outlays as a Percentage of GDP				
U.S.	29.9	31.7	34.0	31.5
Japan	19.1	20.5	29.8	23.4
Germany	35.8	39.9	47.9	41.3
France	37.4	39.0	44.7	40.5
U.K.	35.0	40.0	45.3	40.1
Italy	31.9	36.0	44.3	37.5
Canada	29.8	35.3	40.2	35.1
Smaller OECD	27.7	33.2	42.5	34.6
B. Government Revenues as a Percentage of GDP				
U.S.	27.6	30.5	32.1	30.0
Japan	20.4	20.9	25.7	22.4
Germany	36.3	39.6	44.1	40.0
France	37.2	38.8	42.8	39.7
U.K.	32.8	38.4	40.2	37.0
Italy	29.7	30.8	34.6	31.8
Canada	27.8	34.8	37.1	33.1
Smaller OECD	28.9	34.5	40.9	34.8

(continued)

TABLE A-1 Continued

C. Average Annual Growth Rates of Per Capita Real GDP

U.S.	3.1	2.2	1.6	2.2
Japan	9.4	7.3	2.5	6.4
Germany	3.3	4.1	2.6	3.0
France	4.2	5.0	2.7	3.6
U.K.	2.4	2.9	1.4	1.8
Italy	5.0	3.9	2.0	3.5
Canada	3.7	3.6	2.1	3.1
Smaller OECD	3.7	4.1	1.3	2.8

SOURCE: OECD (1982; Tables 6.5, 6.6, 3.2).

TABLE A-2: Size Distribution of Post-Tax Income in the Major OECD Countries

	Year	Quintile 1	2	3	4	5	Gini	Ratio 5/1
U.S.	1972	4.5	10.7	17.3	24.7	42.9	.381	9.53
Japan	1969	7.9	13.1	16.8	21.2	41.0	.316	5.19
Germany	1969	6.5	10.3	15.0	21.9	46.1	.312	7.09
France	1970	4.3	9.8	16.3	22.7	46.9	.414	10.91
U.K.	1973	6.3	12.6	18.4	23.9	38.7	.318	6.14
Italy	1969	5.1	10.5	16.2	21.7	46.5	.398	9.12
Canada	1969	5.0	13.8	17.9	24.3	41.0	.354	8.20

SOURCE: Sawyer (1976, Tables 4, 6).

References

Ackerman, F. 1982. *Reagonomics: Rhetoric Vs. Reality.* Boston: South End.

Bowles, S. and H. Gintis. 1982. "The Crisis of Liberal Democratic Capitalism: The Case of the United States." *Politics and Society* 11: 51-93.

Bowles, S., D. M. Gordon, and T. E. Weisskopf. 1983. *Beyond the Wasteland: A Democratic Alternative to Economic Decline.* Garden City, NY: Doubleday.

Brittan, S. 1975. "The Economic Contradictions of Democracy." *British Journal of Political Science* 5: 129-159.

Buchanan, J. and R. Wagner. 1977. *Democracy in Deficit.* New York: Academic.

Business Week. 1983. "The Failure of Monetarism." April 4, pp. 64-66.

Clark, P. K. 1982. "Inflation and Productivity Decline." *American Economic Review* 72: 149-154.

Council of Economic Advisors. 1980. *Economic Report of the President.* Washington, DC: Government Printing Office.

Darby, Michael R. 1984. "The U.S. Productivity Slowdown: A Case of Statistical Myopia." *American Economic Review* 74: 301-321.

Denison, E. F. 1979. *Accounting for Slower Economic Growth: The United States in the 1970s.* Washington, DC: The Brookings Institution.

Dornbusch, R. and S. Fischer. 1984. *Macro-Economics.* New York: McGraw-Hill.

Freeman, R. B. and J. Medoff. 1984. *What Do Unions Do?* New York: Basic Books.

Janowitz, M. 1976. *Social Control of the Welfare State.* New York: Elsevier.

Kendrick, J. W. 1981. "International Comparisons of Recent Productivity Trends." In *Contemporary Economic Problems*. Edited by W. Fellner. Washington, DC: American Enterprise Institute.

King, A. 1983. "The Political Consequences of the Welfare State." In *Evaluating the Welfare State: Social and Political Perspectives*. Edited by S. Spiro and E. Yuchtman-Yaar. New York: Academic.

Kristol, I. 1979. *Two Cheers for Capitalism*. New York: Basic Books.

Magaziner, I. C. and R. B. Reich. 1982. *Minding America's Business*. New York: Vintage.

OECD. 1982. *Economic Outlook, Historical Statistics, 1960-1981*. Department of Commerce, Bureau of the Census.

Page, B. I. 1983. *Who Gets What from Government*. Berkeley: University of California Press.

Piven, F. F. and R. A. Cloward. 1982. *The New Class War: Reagan's Attack on the Welfare State and Its Consequences*. New York: Pantheon.

Reich, R. B. 1983. *The Next American Frontier*. New York: Penguin.

Sawyer, Malcolm. 1976. "Income Distribution in the OECD Countries." *OECD Economic Outlook, Occasional Studies* (July): Tables 4, 6.

Solow, R. 1957. "Technical Change and the Aggregate Production Function." *Review of Economics and Statistics* 39: 312-320.

13

Wheeling and Annealing:
Federal and Multidivisional Control

Eric M. Leifer
Harrison C. White

WHILE SERVING AS acting assistant secretary of state for security and consular affairs, Philip Heymann conceived the idea that it would be good if U.S. visa policy were liberalized. The regular renewal of visas was an unnecessarily tedious process and not really useful to internal security. The best that the frequent traveler could obtain was a four-year visa. Heymann could not see why a free society would want to put up an unnecessary barrier at its borders.

Heymann arrived at the assistant secretary's job in 1964, following the departure of Abba Schwartz. Schwartz had been driven out by his subordinate, Frances Knight, the bureaucratically and politically powerful head of the Passport Office. It was an era when J. Edgar Hoover was still powerful at the FBI, and anti-Communism was a salient agenda issue. In the setting Heymann entered, there was general uneasiness over prospects for the easier entry of potentially disloyal foreigners and unregistered aliens, the potential loss of consular jobs, or a bureaucratic flap with Hoover or Knight, with the

AUTHORS' NOTE: We thank Dr. Ramon Alonso for bringing up the annealing metaphor and Dr. James F. Short, Jr., for editing our chapter.

State Department vulnerable to charges of being "soft on Communists." Few had reason to be positive about Heymann's ideas.

As Heymann saw his situation, the involved players were his superiors in the State Department, including Secretary Dean Rusk; the Justice Department, including the FBI and the Immigration and Naturalization Service; the consular affairs bureaucracy; the White House staff, and those members of Congress interested in trade, foreign affairs, and the Communist threat—especially the oversight subcommittee responsible for the budget of the State Department.

Heymann was able to have a new policy of an "indefinite visa" approved by (1) getting the proposal studied by his career subordinate so that it would be put forth in a technically sensible fashion, and enlisting that subordinate's commitment by naming the proposal after him; (2) using high-level friends at the Justice Department to neutralize potential objections of Hoover; (3) changing the face of the issue for the White House so that it could be proposed as a protourism move that would be included on a list of steps being taken to improve the balance of payments; (4) exploiting the long-standing relationship of the now committed career subordinate with the key subcommittee chairman so that the conservative could be informed and reassured that this was a step in favor of efficiency; and (5) informing the secretary of state of the action under way with a memo explaining that certain regulatory language would be changed from one form to another on such and such a date unless the secretary disapproved (account taken from Bower, 1983, pp. 28-29).

Across the border and a few years later, Part III of the National Transportation Act of 1967 was implemented in Canada. Part III put responsibility for the regulation of interprovince trucking in federal hands; prior to that, all trucking regulation had been left to provinces. The act specified that the implementation of Part III was to involve consultation with the provinces, leaving all other specifics open. In the long and ultimately unsuccessful effort to implement Part III, the major federal actors were (1) Pickersgill, president of the Canadian Transportation Commission, a commission responsible for advising the Ministry of Transport on policy issues; (2) Peel, director of the Highways Branch in the Department of Transportation, primarily concerned with operational issues; (3) the ministers of transport, first Hellyer then Jamieson, ultimately responsible for the implementation.

Pickersgill, who supported the NTA passage as minister of Transport, opposed implementing Part III when he shifted over to the CTC. The workload of the CTC was already too great in Pickersgill's view, and federal regulation of the over 2,700 trucking concerns would be a bureaucratic nightmare. Peel, with backing from the trucking industry, pushed for Part III implementation while courting provincial support, something gained only at the cost of provincial involvement in the regulatory process (something Pickersgill was strongly against).

Pickersgill was an extremely skilled politician, with many connections in the federal government. His position was delicate, however, as he could not publicly oppose implementation. Part III was, after all, the law. Pickersgill exercised the "power of sitting still," not hiring any staff, which made the minister's position weak in facing the provinces. In addition, Pickersgill displayed his "enthusiasm" for Part III by advocating numerous spurious plans that were obviously unworkable and thus frustrating to those who were in a position to respond to them. Finally, Pickersgill refused to recommend a conference with the provinces, something advocates of Part III felt was a necessary first step for implementation.

Peel initiated an ingenious manuever, arranging a meeting between the minister and the Canadian Trucking Association, in which complaints over provincial regulations were aired. This prompted the minister himself to recommend a federal-provincial conference in a Cabinet memorandum, thus circumventing Pickersgill. Before the memorandum could be acted upon, however, Minister Hellyer resigned and was replaced by Jamieson, a long-time friend of Pickersgill. Jamieson, however, fell into the habit of passing "strictly confidential" letters from Pickersgill down to career subordinates for comment, and these subordinates were not opposed to Part III and eventually persuaded the minister to arrange a conference.

The conference, however, was only the beginning of a long struggle between Pickersgill and advocates such as Peel in the Department of Transportation (and even some members of Pickergill's own commission). The struggle drew in many groups and individuals in and outside of government, extended across a major reorganization, and had many twists and surprises. It ended in an unresolved standoff over the role to be played by the provinces in the regulatory process, and hence in the failure of Part III to be implemented. This account is drawn from Schultz (1980, pp. 81–146).

There is little remarkable in these accounts of governmental process. The wheeling and dealing they describe are part of the daily reality in the upper echelons of government, or any other large-scale organization (e.g., Bower, 1983). Accounts of wheeling and dealing satisfy the insider's effort to explain policy outcomes or the lack of an outcome, as in the second account. Or, perhaps more accurately, they serve as a standard by which someone is judged an insider. Paperback bookstores are full of insider accounts, varied in names and places, but remarkably consistent in the rough contours of wheeling and dealing they depict. They offer outsiders a glimpse of organizational process, one so readily available that it could hardly be surprising.

The remarkable thing over which we are concerned here is that we sociologists, who are collectively confused over our insider or outsider status, do not know what to do with this wheeling and dealing in our theories of large-scale organization. When we describe it, we usually do a poor job of what journalists can do better. More often we ignore it with our ideal type models of bureaucracy, its business organization successor, the multidivisional, or, closest to present concern, federalism. These ideal type models give wheeling and dealing a residual status as "friction" in an otherwise smoothly functioning mechanism. The widely used term, "informal organization," is only a fancy label for this residual status. It does not resolve the problem of figuring out the role of wheeling and dealing in (as part of) large-scale organization.

We argue that wheeling and dealing is core, and not frictional, in the nature of control at the upper echelons of large-scale organization. Effective control does not come with a position, but is largely dependent on the skill of the position holder in effecting control. Positions are defined in only the vaguest terms so as to unencumber the position holder's quest for control. The use of authority associated with a position signals the failure of effective control, and not its basis. Unlike authority, which pushes its originator into public view, control in the upper echelons is by its nature diffuse. Effectively exercised control obscures its originator. It is this very quality that makes control the basis for a bond between people. As Crozier (1964) and Edwards (1979) have incisively shown, authority relations are accompanied by the absence of interaction. Wheeling and dealing is found where control is the issue, not authority.

There is a need for new kinds of ideal types, ones built on relations rather than nonrelations between people in organizations. Descriptive accounts of wheeling and dealing in organizations point out an important phenomenon, but cannot satisfy our theoretical needs. We need ideals to evaluate the description against. The ideal we are interested in is that of skill, or the effective exercise of control in organizations. The ideal type model we have in mind is one in which control is diffuse. The term "decentralized" can be used for our model, though this risks the false image of a coming out from centralization through intentional design. We refer to "decentralization" as the logical consequence of the effective exercise of control, which serves to diffuse control away from any distinguishable center. A formally centralized system may be highly "decentralized" in this sense.

We shall pull together a variety of findings to underscore the need for ideal types of organization that admit control relations between position holders into their core mechanism, and push toward developing such an ideal type. The key will be to link effective control with its diffuseness in a setting. This will lead to the paradoxical conclusion that skill, as the ideal in our ideal type, is tied to the diffusion of control rather than its concentration. Control will accordingly have no one-to-one linkage with "getting what you want," a result consistent with the interesting work of Endurud (1976) on perceiving power in organizations. The common ex post interpretations of outcomes in terms of actor preferences will be what they are, purely ex post constructions as March and Olsen (1976, p. 21) have warned.

We draw our materials from the literature on federalism, mostly American, with an excursion to the business analogue, multidivisional organizations. These are both formally decentralized structures, which makes our task easier, though formal decentralization is certainly no prerequisite for finding the forms of control we wish to illustrate (see Ashford, 1982, for a rich study of "decentralization" in the unitary governments of Britain and France).

National-State Relations in the Old and New Federalism

The federalism laid down in the U.S. constitution resolved some difficult problems. It provided a model for intergovernmental relations where the autonomy of established and heterogeneous state governments was not threatened by the newly established national government. Autonomy was ensured through assigning different functions to national and state governments. The independence of these functions ensured independent operation and a clear criterion for the encroachment of one governmental body into the domain of another. Though the residual power of the national government to take over functions not explicitly given to the states had much import for the future scope of the national government, the distinct functions assigned to state governments made them complementary rather than subordinate to the national government. They had full autonomy in their own domain. The intergovernmental relations of American federalism were nonrelations, where complementarity of function performance is more of an issue than the power balances or imbalances that can grow from direct competitive relationships. American federalism effectively defused the issue of relative power of the national and state governments.

The "dual" federalism found in the American Constitution (and explicated by James Madison) is a poor model for actual U.S. intergovernmental relations, unquestionably in this century and arguably in the last also (Elazer, 1967; Grodzins, 1967). The crucial fact, as Reagan (1981) notes, is that the functions are shared. The national government has always been involved in the domestic functions constitutionally assigned to the states. This involvement has taken many forms. In the nineteenth century, Joint Stock Companies, in which the national government shared an interest in a state-initiated project, were common. The national government was additionally involved in public education, finding many indirect ways to support this explicit state function such as overreimbursing the states for military contributions and, more commonly, through the Land Grant in the expanding West. The Army Corps of Engineers, in addition, was instrumental in state highway, railway, and waterway construction. In the state of Minnesota, revenues from federal sources, including direct federal payments to the state and income from federal grants, represented over 40% of the total annual revenue of Minnesota, and after 1865, never fall below 20%. The analogous percentage in 1959 was 25.3% (Elazer, 1967, p. 212).

In this century, the categorical grant-in-aid has become the dominant vehicle through which the national government involves itself in official state functions. A total of $91 billion of federal funds were distributed to the states in grants-in-aid in 1982, through over 490 programs (accounting for over 30% of state and local revenues). The most recent Block grant and general revenue-sharing funds, which ostensibly give the state more autonomy in carrying out its functions (with federal funds), have received much press but are minor relative to the categorical grant. From 1972 to 1976, under $7 billion was transferred annually in revenue-sharing funds, whereas 200 new grant-in-aid programs were started in the 1970-1980 decade.

Since the New Deal, scholars have recognized national-state government collaborating in function sharing as a core feature of American federalism, and not just as "friction" in an otherwise adequate dual federalism model. The term "cooperative federalism" has come into vogue (Meisel, 1973; Reagan, 1981), and the very flexible and reusable term "New Federalism" has also received much press. The "cooperative" or "New" descriptors acknowledge the interdependencies that can arise in sharing function performance. With this acknowledgment, there has arisen much concern over the relative power of national and state governmental units. If operative federalism, as opposed to federalism in theory, approximates our envisioned ideal typic interdependent system, then the issue of relative power should be difficult to resolve. Effective control, we argue, hides its source.

It is commonplace to hear of the growing encroachment of the federal government on state and local government. The new minimum-age drinking law being currently pushed on the states with the threat of highway fund withdrawals has brought with it many complaints of federal omnipresence. Less topical, the apparently irreversible trend of increasing federal domination of public revenues seems to paint a gloomy picture for state autonomy in the future. The federal government received 56.5% of all public revenues in 1976, with 24.5% and 19% going to state and local governments, respectively. In 1902, the comparable figures were 38%, 11%, and 51% (Reagan, 1981). Coupled with the growing number of strings attached grant-in-aid programs, these figures can and have been enlisted to point out increasing centralization and, hence, a definite power advantage of the federal government over state and local governments. We would find such a clear advantage troublesome from our theoretical point of view.

Fortunately, some writers much more knowledgeable than ourselves about the intricacies of American federalism have come to our rescue. These writers have recognized that interdependence is not a reliable situation for domination. Rather, the effective handling of interdependence yields the decentralization, or diffusion of power, that safeguards the autonomy of state and local governments. Weidner (1967, p. 229), writing in the 1940s, notes that the "disagreements and conflicts that do arise and that may be encouraged by federalism's structural features are not basically clashes between state and national governments. Instead, they are clashes between much smaller groups of people and the opposing groups are located within a single governmental level as often as not." He observed little conflict between national and state professional administrators, noting that "in general the *political* officials feel that professional employees engaged in administering national grant-in-aid programs tend to play off supposedly rigid national standards against state political control they do not like . . . reading somewhat more into national minimum standards than is actually there" (p. 243). Political (legislative) officials felt more constraint from the national government than administrators. These results came from a survey of 650 legislative officials and administrators in Minnesota.

From the same study, Weidner found that both national and state administrators stressed nonauthoritative means in their interrelations (nation-state and state-local). "Advice, consultation, technical assistance, information—these were the devices that had an appeal alike to the state and national administrator. . . . The more authoritative devices went unused, or were *used only with the advice and consent* of the officials to whom they were to apply, or were used as an unwelcome last resort in one or two *rare* cases" (Weidner, 1967, p. 251, our emphases). Weidner explains the use of nonauthoritative devices in terms of "political and administrative realism":

> The success of a program depends in most instances on the lack of use of authoritative devices in carrying it out. Politically, the superior unit of government is open to attack. If a national administrative official were to offend unduly the administrators from a state, there might be immediate repercussions in the congressional delegation of the state as well as official protest. . . . State officials have powerful political levers over national action just as local officials have a real check over state administrative supervision [Weidner, 1967, p. 251].

These passages point out some subtleties in assessing the power relation between interdependent levels of government. Weidner (1967, p. 253) goes on to discuss how the cooperative development of program policy alleviates potential conflict between levels, where "state administrators will recommend a course of action to national officials, usually with prior knowledge that their suggestion will be acted upon without substantial change."

Writing a decade later, Grodzins (1967, p. 258) offered his now classic "marble-cake" metaphor for the intermingled levels of government. Even in the absence of joint financing, Grodzin points out, "Federal-state-local collaboration is the characteristic mode of action. Federal expertise is available (in a wide variety of areas). . . .

States and localities, on the other hand, take important formal responsibilities in the development of national programs for (a wide variety of areas)." At the behavioral level, Grodzins (1967, p. 268) argues, "The politics of administration is a process of making peace with legislators who for the most part consider themselves the guardians of local interests. The political role of administrators therefore contributes to the power of states and localities in national programs." With the numerous domains of collaboration and the delicacies of "administrative and political realism," the levels of government get swirled together instead of being clearly distinct as in a layer cake.

Grodzins also offers a subtle analysis of the role of a decentralized party system in ensuring decentralized governmental decision making. Grodzins argues that the "multiple cracks" in the government system, where parties and groups can influence decisions, ensure the "decentralization of mild chaos"—decentralization that comes from multiple sources of influence. The decentralization is to be contrasted with decentralization by order. "It exists because of the existence of dispersed power centers. This form of decentralization is less visible and less neat. It rests on no discretion of central authorities. . . . To those who find value in the dispersion of power, decentralization by mild chaos is infinitely more desirable than decentralization by order" (Grodzins, 1967, p. 271). Ironically, Grodzins argues that it would take a strong centralized party system to implement decentralization by order. Grodzins (1967, p. 275) concludes that

there is scant evidence for the fear of the federal octopus, the fear that expansion of central programs and influence threatens to reduce the states and localities to compliant administrative arms of the central government. In fact, state and local governments are touching a larger proportion of the people in more ways than ever before; and they are spending a higher fraction of the total national product than ever before. Federal programs have increased, rather than diminished, the importance of the governors; stimulated professionalism in state agencies; increased citizen interest and participation in government; and, generally, enlarged and made more effective the scope of state action.

Grodzins's prognosis is echoed in Reagan's (1981) recent analysis of the "New Federalism." Fiscal centralization and the growth of federal programs are counterbalanced by the autonomy of state boundaries and officials from federal jurisdiction. The New Federalism, Reagan concludes after a detailed examination of the various sharing arrangements between federal and state governments, is a multifaceted positive relationship of shared action. In the process of joint action, states have the right to share in the design and implementation of programs, as well as to select the program they will administer.

This brief review extends across much transition in the content and scope of governmental activity, from the era of land grants in the nineteenth century to the present day grants-in-aid. Yet, despite these changes, it is possible to discern a common organizational feature across these periods: Federal and state relations have been shaped by their interdependence in fulfilling shared functions. This interdependence between formally autonomous units has produced a relationship in which, when functioning ideally, nonauthoritative means are used and control is diffuse. At the operative relational level, federalism does not appear to have changed much since the nineteenth century. The "Cooperative" and "New" Federalism have more an intellectual than historical significance (Hull, 1982). They mark a change in the way we think about intergovernmental relations.

Current thought about federalism, however, leaves us very uneasy. The ideal type of dual federalism still has too much centrality, no longer as a belief about how the system works but as a standard against which to assess deviations. Deviations are treated as discoveries, and are subject to extensive description. Yet if dual federalism was always a misleading model for the core features of intergovernmental relations, as we and others have argued, why is it used as a standard? There should be another ideal type—against which the actual may still fall short, but that is relevant for the core features of intergovernmental relations. This ideal type must be built from a logical working out of "administrative and political realism" (i.e., skill) in a setting of interdependent units.

The need for this ideal type can nowhere better be seen than in four commission reports on governmental reorganization in the first fifteen years following World War II (surveyed by Grodzins, 1967). Each of these reports called for reforms that would bring intergovernmental relations closer to the standard set by dual federalism—the standard of nonrelations between governmental levels. Such reforms, so out of touch with past, present, or future administrative and political reality, were motivated by the wrong ideal type. One gets the impression that if another ideal type existed that could compete on equal grounds with dual federalism, the commission's recommendations would have been much different.

Decentralization in Large-Scale Business Organization

Decentralization is a central concern in large-scale business, where a single corporation may be involved in scores of product markets. The "Multidivisional" ideal type organizational structure has received much attention in the last two decades, as a panacea for the decentralization needs of multiproduct organizations (Chandler, 1962; Williamson, 1970). The multidivisional bears some remarkable similarities to dual federalism, as an ideal type, and hence shares with dual federalism similar defects as a viable model for large-scale business organizations. Below we take a glimpse at instances of corporate-division function sharing to further develop an ideal type for relations of interdependence.

The multidivisional is an ideal type model of the relations between corporate headquarters (top management) and product divisions (division managers). It seeks to put full responsibility for product performance on a division manager, and does so by giving him or her authority over the functions relevant to product performance. In short, the multidivisional attempts to equate authority with responsibility by giving division managers authority over operational decisions affecting product performance. This contrasts with making divisions functional departments, with managers responsible for only one functional aspect of product performance. The bottom line for the division manager is, in theory, profit performance of his or her product(s). Top management assumes responsibility for capital decisions, investing or disinvesting in its divisions on the basis of their performance and prospects. The theoretical advantage of a multidivisional lies in its separation of strategic from operational concerns, giving the latter to division managers whose "local" knowledge of product nuances would, in total, only blur the strategic vision of top management. The relation between top and division management is not direct and interactive, but mediated through the interface of profits.

Like dual federalism, deviations from the ideal type of multidivisional abound in practice. Vancil (1979) has discussed at length the theoretical tensions created by separating capital from operational decisions, in terms of its consequences for imposing more responsibility on division managers than they have authority to handle. Capital decisions definitely have consequences for profit performance. Vancil (1979) also conducted a survey of 439 "multidivisionals," and found extensive function sharing. The mean percentage of a function performed in the typical profit center (division) was only 54% of administration, 64% of research and development, 70% of manufacturing, 79% of distribution, and 82% of sales. In the other direction, accounts such as Bower's (1972) suggest that divisions have a significant role in defining the frame and influencing capital decisions of top management. Function sharing thus appears to be core, and not frictional, between corporate and division management. The relation between these levels must be more intricate and more crucial than the ideal type multidivisional implies.

The first instance of function sharing we examine concerns the issue of who regulates the internal transfer of goods between divisions. Corporations vary widely on the volume of internal transfers and on their policies regarding them. In the ideal type multidivisional, divisions should have full autonomy regarding the source from which they buy and the price they agree to pay. Hence the division should have the option of going outside the corporation for needed supplies, even when these supplies are produced by another division in the same corporation. In a corporation where one division is heavily dependent on another for goods, as in a "vertically integrated" corporation, going "outside" may prevent the selling division from realizing economies of scale and hence may be detrimental to the corporation as a whole. Any corporate transfer regulation, however, limits the extent to which top management can hold division managers responsible for profit performance, and hence threatens the basic principle on which a multidivisional is conceived.

In practice, Eccles (1985) finds corporate policies varying from mandated internal sourcing and formula-determined price (usually cost-based and sometimes market-based where a market price exists) to a policy of no policy at all. These extremes were usually associated with the extremes of high and low transfer interdependencies between divisions. In the case of high interdependency, the culture of independent and competitive (on profit performance) divisions is downplayed, with emphasis and rewards based on overall corporate performance. In the case of low interdependency, the ideal type multidivisional comes closest to being realized. The case we are most interested in is where interdependence exists, yet there is effort to maintain the autonomy of unit divisions. This "collaborative" situation, in Eccle's terms, is the case that most resembles the situation of federalism.

In the collaborative situation, Eccles found that the task of regulating internal transfers was commonly shared between levels. This occurred when top management mandated internal sourcing, but left the price at which the transfer is made up to the trading divisions to determine. The economist might wince at this situation, as it removes the favored mechanism of "exit" from market exchange. Eccles argues, however, that the logic of this transfer policy is not to be found in purely economic terms (and indeed, economists have failed to provide a usable solution to the transfer pricing problems, as they call it), but rather in widely organizational terms. Division managers have information about market conditions that may be of value to top management, as well as ambitions to be top management one day. The conflict generated in price agreements, and there often is considerable conflict, has relevance for both these organizational concerns.

Eccles has argued that conflict often functions to convey important information to top management, as division managers make arguments for their positions before top management and, more generally, display their styles and concerns that may or may not make them appear as top management material. This argument is supported by the general unwillingness top management displayed before Eccles in moving to resolve the conflict, instead stating they preferred to let it work itself out. Intervention would threaten the role division managers play in regulating transfers, and with it the responsibility they are assigned for the results. In the process of division managers wheeling and dealing amongst themselves and in front of top management, the transfer problem comes to be resolved in a way that diffuses control over the details across all affected parties. For such a sensitive issue, this may be an ideal resolution process from an organizational standpoint.

As a final instance of function sharing, we look at the process of corporate entrepreneurship. The transfer problem is an instance of an operational problem filtering up to involve top management, and hence assuming strategic significance (see Eccles, 1985, for a discussion of transfer policy as a strategic tool for top management). The process of corporate entrepreneurship, whereby corporations come to develop new business activities, is often thought of as an exclusive concern of top management in their capacity as planners. Not surprising to us, this picture is far from accurate in most innovative corporations. The entrepreneurship function is shared with middle-level management in a way that neatly diffuses control over the basic definition of the corporation's "direction"—a joint construct that enlists the efforts of both top and middle management.

Burgelman (1983a, 1983b) gives an insightful description of the process of corporate entrepreneurship, tying together the work of Miles and Snow (1978) and Mintzberg (1978). Corporate entrepreneurship, for Burgelman (1983b, p. 1349), is "the result of the interlocking entrepreneurial activities of multiple participants." Middle-level managers initiate new ventures and support autonomous initiatives by those under them, combining them with various capabilities dispersed throughout the corporation's operating system. These activities produce a diversity of ventures that come before top management's attention for support. Top management's critical contribution, states Burgelman (1983b, p. 1349), "consists in strategic recognition rather than planning. By allowing middle level managers to redefine the strategic context, and by being fast learners, top management can make sure that entrepreneurial activities will correspond to their strategic vision, retroactively."

Burgelman may be going a little too far with this last passage. It is his intent to use the biological selection metaphor, insisting that the strategic choices involved in corporate entrepreneurship in large, complex firms do not reflect top management's strategic vision ex ante, but only ex post (Burgelman, 1983b, p. 1360). Management's strategy pronouncements function as more than ex post interpretations, however, as they undoubtedly influence "autonomous" strategic initiatives from middle level management. The ideal for top management, we hypothesize, is that there be ambiguity over the ex post or ex ante nature of their strategic vision. As Burgelman recognized, to sustain this ambiguity, top management must be very fast learners so as not to appear as mere interpreters. This state of ambiguity over ex post and ex ante, we suggest, creates optimal conditions for the diffusion of control in the corporate entrepreneurship process.[1]

Thus in the diverse areas of transfer policy and corporate entrepreneurship we have found instances of function sharing between top and middle management. The sharing is enacted in such a way that diffuses control over these areas between levels, and this diffusion has significance beyond the details of policy and strategy that emerge. The significance extends to the organization, where motivation is sustained and the flow of information and persons across positions is facilitated. Nowhere is there a place for authority in the portrait we have been painting. Control is the issue. And where skillfully exercised, it is diffused across multiple participants. In the next section, we begin to zero in on the nature of control.

Wheeling and Annealing

In a frequently cited footnote, Parsons pointed out a tension between authority and expertise, both components of Weber's ideal type bureaucracy. How experts are subject to authority, and why there is a need for authority, has been the subject of much research. One mainstream answer, summarized by Perrow (1979) and well illustrated by Goss (1967), is that the expertise of a boss does not conflict with the expertise of a subordinate when their domains of expertise do not overlap. The subordinate might be a technical expert, the boss an administrative expert. In Goss's medical case, doctors accepted the authority of administrators on matters of scheduling, but not on the handling of cases. Authority works here because the functions of each level can be neatly separated, and the tasks of each well defined.

We have been looking at situations in which the task or "expertise" of each level is not well defined, and the functions of each are not separated. Here we respond to Parsons's problem by claiming that authority is not the relevant mechanism in the relations between levels. Control is the central concern across and between position holders, who all share an interest in the same issue. Unlike authority, control among often highly energetic and ambitious position holders is a subtle matter. Rather than involving the ex ante direction of others, control often enlists others to make one's own ideas definite, with those enlisted depending conversely on you for the same purpose. With effective control, direction is jointly determined as is, perhaps more important, the sense of having achieved something. Learning from others and giving guidance, or the ex post and ex ante in social action, become hopelessly intertangled.

We have in mind a kind of acephalous control that is associated with loosely structured arenas of highly skillful wheelers and dealers, or "garbage cans" in now popular terminology (March and Olsen, 1976). It is control in the sense that the fluidly combining and dispersing position holders steer their organization toward outcomes, but there is no ex ante intentionality behind the outcomes. There are no center-periphery directives, but only peripheries looking for a center. The cases we opened the chapter with provide examples of such loosely structured arenas, though from a very narrow viewpoint.

This form of acephalous control is intrinsically incomplete, however. It is not mere coincidence that the opening accounts involved mainly high-level assistants, with the limited presence of their superiors. Arenas of wheelers and dealers require inducements for the individual energies, and stimuli for interlocking to form around. In short, the "garbage can" must be managed (see Cohen and March, 1974; Padgett, 1980, for detailed views on this topic). A second-order form of control is needed, consonant with the first-order, acephalous kind.

We propose a process of annealing occurs, as second-order control. Simulated annealing is a process that has found widespread application in the physical sciences, and, we argue, is well suited for the messy "multibody" problems facing the highest level of large-scale organization. It is applicable where no global solution is known, and where incremental improvement techniques stand the risk of getting stuck in a local optimum. In crystal formation, for example, a system of particles at high temperature can be cooled very slowly, allowing equilibrium configurations to form at each temperature change. At the temperature zone where crystals begin to form, the cooling process can be repeatedly reversed until a satisfactory initial configuration is obtained (which shapes the progressive refinements formed through further cooling). Reversal is key to the annealing process, as it allows one to avoid "bad" local optimums. Simulated annealing has also been used in such diverse areas as the placement of circuits on a computer chip (and chips on a board) and for reasonable solutions to the "traveling salesman" problem, where the salesperson seeks minimal travel costs on a trip through a given set of cities, passing through each only once (see Kirkpatrick et al., 1983).

Annealing can be found in our federal and multidivisional cases. The federal government "heats" up the system by suggesting the need for and offering to support new programs or press for reorganizations, with a crisis atmosphere. The range of funding mechanisms, from revenue sharing to categorical grants, varies in the degree of discretion federal administrative officials have in distributing funds and the restrictions imposed on their use. Revenue sharing with few use restrictions has been part of an effort to "heat up" the system. If it produces innovative programs, the system can be "cooled down" by perpetuating them through categorical grants. Proposals and alignments crystallize from the wheelers and dealers in state and local governments through intermittent periods of "heating" and "cooling," until reasonable alternatives surface. Howitt (1984) offers some excellent cases that illustrate the complex relations between funding mechanisms and levels of activity within state and local government.

Franklin Roosevelt illustrates a more self-conscious form of annealing. Roosevelt was a master of the annealing process, hovering over an arena of coalitions of cartelists, central planners, and anti-trusters that formed and dissolved as the Depression lingered on (see Hawley, 1966). Working within the very flexible framework of the New Deal, Roosevelt's "true" leanings toward these completely inconsistent groups were prudently almost impossible to discern. Roosevelt was annealing, not directing.

Despite Bower's (1983) insistence on a fundamental difference between political and technocratic management systems (though he concedes that there is much politics in business organization), annealing can also be found in our business cases. Transfer policy is a form of "temperature," combined with other incentive systems, which can be used to induce more or less interaction between divisions. Mandated sourcing with no centralized pricing policy is a way to heat up the system, whereas formula pricing cools it down. In the case of corporate entrepreneurship, top management can control the volume of overall entrepreneurial activity, which is the corollary to temperature. Ventures are induced, supported, and dissolved at a high rate until a satisfactory array of business activities crystallize.

Annealing has the right imagery for our purposes. It is tailored for "multibody" problems with process indeterminacies and an irregular terrain of local optimums without known global properties (knowing where to encourage system "crystallization" may be the paramount skill of the very top). It involves no ex ante directives, which would interfere with the perceived autonomy of the wheeling and dealing "bodies" on which it operates. Annealing is thus fully consonant with a decentralized system, where effectively exercised control is diffuse in nature. Annealing is a form of contextual control of the wheeling and dealing arena, enacted without destroying the control properties of the arena itself.

Annealing should not be equated with the biological selection metaphor now popular in the organization literature (see Hannan and Freeman, 1977; Aldrich, 1979). Its reversal mechanism makes "selection" neither blind nor passive. As Weick (1979) and others have observed, selection alone can produce peculiar results, such as superstitions. "Bad" local optimums are always a potential hazard in overly organized systems. Annealing involves actively making a system worse off in an effort to let it right itself. The management philosophy of "putting out fires," or attending to only the most pressing problems and ignoring longer-range concerns, is also not what annealing is. Annealing involves starting an occasional fire so that extant patterns of interlocking will dissolve and form anew as things begin to cool down. If the situation does not improve, the process must be repeated.

Conclusion

The wheeling and dealing, and annealing, we have focused on have no place in the widely transmitted ideal types of organization in sociology. Neat divisions of authority and functional responsibilities characterize these ideal types. Yet our survey leads us to believe there may be little reality to these neat divisions, and that, furthermore, they may not constitute the "best" way of dealing with complex and unsolvable problems. Function sharing between autonomous levels is widespread, and most likely an effective way to get things done, we argue. This sharing is accomplished not through careful adherence to job definitions but through highly skillful maneuvering. Control is the central issue in this sharing arena, not authority, where people are not directing others but struggling with problems and situations with which they need help from others who need help from them.

More description of organizational, *realpolitics* is not, however, the answer to the inadequacy of our ideal types. Inadequate ideal types must be replaced by adequate ones, and not abandoned altogether. We must recognize that much of what we observe falls short of the ideal we build our types around. The ideal we propose is one that is salient to the wheelers and dealers in large-scale organization. This is the ideal of exercising effective control in a setting where control must be shared among others seeking it. It is a matter of skill, not position definition, but one that admits room for skill among multiple others. Hence the ideal we are seeking is not one that will devolve into a laundry list of advice for the "effective manager," but one that will lead us toward the properties of a system in which control can be shared.

Note

1. For another application of this idea, see Leifer (1985).

References

Aldrich, H. 1979. *Organizations and Environments.* Englewood Cliffs, NJ: Prentice-Hall.

Ashford, D. 1982. *British Dogmatism and French Pragmatism.* London: G. Allen & Unwin.

Bower, J. L. 1972. *Managing the Resource Allocation Process.* Homewood, IL: Irwin.

Bower, J. L. 1983. *The Two Faces of Management: An American Approach to Leadership in Business and Politics.* Boston: Houghton Mifflin.

Burgelman, R. A. 1983a. "A Process Model of Internal Corporate Venturing in the Diversified Major Firm." *Administrative Science Quarterly* 28: 223-244.

Burgelman, R. A. 1983b. "Corporate Entrepreneurship and Strategic Management: Insights from a Process Study." *Management Science* 29: 1349-1364.

Chandler, A. D., Jr. 1962. *Strategy and Structure: Chapters in the History of the American Industrial Enterprise.* Cambridge, MA: MIT.

Cohen, M. and J. G. March. 1974. *Leadership and Ambiguity: The American College President.* New York: McGraw-Hill.

Crozier, M. 1964. *The Bureaucratic Phenomenon.* Chicago: University of Chicago Press.

Eccles, R. G. 1985. *The transfer pricing problem: A theory for practice.* Lexington, MA: Lexington Books.

Edwards, R. 1979. *Contested Terrain: The Transformation of the Workplace in the Twentieth Century.* New York: Basic Books.

Elazer, D. J. 1967. "Federal-State Collaboration in the Nineteenth-Century United States." Pp. 190-222 in *American Federalism in Perspective.* Edited by A. Wildavsky. Boston: Little, Brown.

Endurud, H. 1976. "The Perception of Power." In *Ambiguity and Choice in Organization.* Edited by J. G. March and J. Olsen. Bergen, Norway: Universitetsforlaget.

Goss, M. E. 1967. "Influence and Authority Among Physicians in an Outpatient Clinic." Pp. 275-292 in *A Sociological Reader on Complex Organizations.* Edited by A. Etzioni. New York: Holt Rinehart & Winston.

Grodzins, M. 1967. "The Federal System." Pp. 256-277 in *American Federalism in Perspective.* Edited by A. Wildavsky. Boston: Little, Brown.

Hannan, M. and J. Freeman. 1977. "The Population Ecology of Organizations." *American Journal of Sociology* 82: 929-964.

Hawley, E. 1966. *The New Deal and the Problem of Monopoly: A Study in Economic Ambivalence.* Princeton, NJ: Princeton University Press.

Howitt, A. 1984. *Managing Federalism: Studies in Intergovernmental Relations.* Washington, DC: Congressional Quarterly Press.

Hull, N.E.H. 1982. *New Federalism: A Historical Perspective.* Institute of Government, University of Georgia, Athens.

Kirkpatrick, S., C. D. Gelatt, Jr., and M. P. Vecchi. 1983. "Optimization by Simulated Annealing." *Science* 220: 671-679.

Leifer, E. M. 1985. *Skill in Relationship Context: A Salient Dimension in Social Settings.* Manuscript, Department of Sociology, University of North Carolina—Chapel Hill.

March, J. G. and J. Olsen. 1976. *Ambiguity and Choice in Organizations,* Bergen, Norway: Universitetsforlaget.

Meisel, A. (Ed.) 1973. *The New Federalism: Possibilities and Problems in Restructuring American Government.* A Conference of the Woodrow Wilson International Center for Scholars.

Miles, R. E. and C. C. Snow. 1978. *Organizational Strategy, Structure and Process.* New York: McGraw-Hill.

Mintzberg, H. 1978. "Patterns in Strategy Formation." *Management Science* 24: 934-948.

Padgett, J. F. 1980. "Managing Garbage Can Hierarchies." *Administrative Science Quarterly* 25, 583-604.

Perrow, C. 1979. *Complex Organizations: A Critical Essay.* New York: Random House.

Radner, R. 1976. "A Behavioral Model of Cost Reduction." *Bell Journal of Economics.*

Reagan, M. D. and J. G. Sanzone. 1981. *The New Federalism.* New York: Oxford University Press.

Schultz, R. J. 1980. *Federalism, Bureaucracy, and Public Policy: The Politics of Highway Transport Regulation.* Montreal: McGill-Queen's University Press.

Vancil, R. F. 1979. *Decentralization: Managerial Ambiguity by Design.* Homewood, IL: Dow Jones-Irwin.

Weidner, E. W. 1967. "Decision-Making in a Federal System." Pp. 229-256 in *American Federalism in Perspective.* Edited by A. Wildavsky. Boston: Little, Brown.

Weick, K. 1979. *The Social Psychology of Organizing.* Reading, MA: Addison-Wesley.

Williamson, O. E. 1970. *Corporate Control and Business Behavior.* Englewood Cliffs, NJ: Prentice-Hall.

14

Citizen Soldier Versus Economic Man

Charles C. Moskos

IN MILITARY MANPOWER THOUGHT, two contrasting philosophies compete. The citizen soldier concept draws upon the tradition of short-time and part-time military servers who are compensated for at less than the market wage. The economic man viewpoint treats military manpower as part of the labor force with recruitment and retention geared to competitive remuneration with the marketplace.

The citizen soldier has deep roots in American history.[1] The citizen soldier model initially derives from the militia concept of the colonial era when locally based military units could, at least in theory, draw upon every able-bodied man in time of need. The militias played a major role in the American War of Independence and the early decades of the new republic, but declined over the course of most of the nineteenth century. Around the turn of this century the citizen soldier concept revived when state militias were reconstituted in the form of the National Guard. Conscription, another form of the citizen soldier, first appeared in this country during the Civil War and was reintroduced on a massive basis in World War I. From the eve of World War II to the end of the Vietnam War, the citizen soldier concept was based on conscription during peacetime as well as during war along with an expanded reserve force (now including a federal component as well as the state-based guard units).

The "citizen army" was initially raised as the preferred alternative to a large professional military establishment. In point of fact, the American colonies' opposition to a standing army was one of the main points of contention in the events leading to the break with England. In time, proponents of the citizen soldier introduced additional arguments. Every (male) citizen owed an obligation to his country's national security. Citizen soldiers introduced an element of initiative, aptitude, and attitude into the military that would otherwise be absent. Social equity required that all sectors of the population be included in military service.

The economic man model of military service came into formal ascendancy with the end of conscription in 1973. A marketplace philosophy clearly underpinned the rationale of the 1970 Report of the President's Commission on All-Volunteer Force (AVF), better known as the "Gates Commission Report" (see also Military Manpower Task Force, 1982). This dovetailed with the systems analysts who had become increasingly influential within the Department of Defense under both Democratic and Republican administrations starting with that of John F. Kennedy.

Although the political unpopularity of the draft caused by the Vietnam War was the immediate cause of the end of the draft, proponents of the AVF advanced other reasons as well. Conscription is a tax-in-kind that falls unfairly on young men. Coercion, of which military conscription is a particularly onerous kind, is to be avoided when at all possible. A volunteer force will have lower turnover rates than one consisting of short-term draftees, thereby improving military effectiveness. A draft distorts the labor market, the higher educational system, and even the family (if it defers husbands or fathers).[2]

The politics of the AVF are contradictory. Support and opposition to the AVF are found on most points of the ideological spectrum. But, generally speaking, leading opponents of conscription come from the libertarian right and the radical left (albeit for different reasons). Some black spokespersons have been supportive of the AVF, not only because it creates job opportunities for black youth but also because criticisms of the manpower quality of the AVF are seen as aspersions on the high black content of the AVF. Yet other black spokespersons have shown alarm at the disproportionate number of blacks in combat units and advocate a return to the draft. Most feminist groups, who otherwise tend to adopt an antimilitary stance, see the AVF in a favorable light because the increased numbers of women in the military advances female opportunity. At the same time, anti-ERA arguments have been buttressed by those who see an equal rights amendment foreshadowing the conscription of women into the military and the eventual assignment of women into combat arms. The 1980 congressional decision to exclude females from the reinstituted draft registration indicates that the contemporary role of females in any citizen soldier model remains ambiguous.

Survey data show that women and blacks are less likely to support conscription than whites or men (see Davis et al., 1983). Support for conscription is strongly correlated with age—older males, especially military veterans, are the most supportive of a return to draft. Support for conscription generally comes from the political center, especially the right of center. It must be stressed, however, that liberal Democratic administrations have introduced peacetime conscription (1940 and 1949) and peacetime draft registration (1980), whereas conservative Republican leadership has been mainly responsible for ending conscription (in 1947 and 1973).

From an intellectual standpoint, proponents of the citizen soldier have been more likely to be influenced by the institutional and contextual complexities exemplified in the academic disciplines of history and sociology, whereas those supporting the all-volunteer force have typically been influenced by the "rational actor" concepts deriving from economics and the "fixed attribute" model of psychology.[3]

Although the significant fact of the past decade has been the almost complete triumph of economic man over citizen soldier in military manpower policy, there have been two developments that are beginning to reshape the contemporary formulation of the citizen soldier and counter the prevailing econometric understanding of military manpower. The first is an expansion of the concept of the citizen soldier concept beyond the military framework; the second is an effort to reconstruct the citizen soldier concept in an all-volunteer military framework.

The citizen soldier in the American context has historically referred to draftees, draft-motivated volunteers, and those who serve in reserve components. Morris Janowitz (1979) has proposed an expansion of the citizen-soldier concept to include nonmilitary service as well, an outcome that would also result in a major increase in female participation. From this perspective, the citizen soldier becomes the national server who is defined by performance of public duties that can be effectively met in both military and civilian pursuits by young people who do not define these tasks as life careers and who perform these tasks at less than marketplace remuneration. The central thrust is to restore the balance between citizen rights and citizen duties.

Proposals to introduce a citizen soldier concept within the all-volunteer framework have been mainly associated with my own research and writings (Moskos, 1980; Moskos and Faris, 1981). These proposals can be summarized as follows: Set up a new, two-track personnel and compensation system within the military that distinguishes between a citizen soldier—a short-term volunteer in the active force with a follow-on in the reserves—and a career service member who makes a long-term military commitment. Postservice educational benefits similar to the old "GI Bill" would be limited to citizen soldiers serving at a compensation level below that of the career soldier. Establish a comprehensive, but voluntary, civilian service program for youth linked to federal educational benefits. In time, only those who performed some form of national service would be eligible for federal educational or job training aid.

Models of Military Manpower

The contrast between citizen soldier and economic man can, of course, be overdrawn. To characterize the armed forces as consisting either of citizen soldiers or economic men does an injustice to historical and contemporary realities. Both elements have been and always will be present in the military system. But our concern is to grasp the whole, to place the salient fact. Even though terms such as "citizen soldier" and "economic man" have descriptive limitations, they do contain core connotations that serve to distinguish each from the other. These basic contrasts are shown in Table 14.1.

Organizational Principle

The citizen soldier and economic man models of military service correspond to alternative conceptions of the military organization.[4] The basic hypothesis is that as the American military increasingly relies on an economic man approach, the social organization of the armed forces moves from an institutional format to one more and more resembling that of an occupation.

TABLE 14.1: Military Manpower: Citizen Soldier Versus Economic Man

Variable	Citizen Soldier	Economic Man
Organizational principle	institution	occupation
Social composition	cross-section of youth population	economically marginal youth
Basis of compensation	rank and seniority	skill level and military shortages
Mode of compensation	much "in kind" and deferred	salary and bonuses
Level of compensation	decompressed; low recruit pay	compressed; high recruit pay
Personnel mix	larger share in first-term force	larger share in career force
Force mix	larger share in reserve force	larger share in active force
Postservice status	veterans' benefits and preferences	same as civilian

An *institution* is legitimated in terms of values and norms, that is, a purpose transcending individual self-interest in favor of a presumed higher good. Members of an institution are often seen as following a calling, captured in words such as "duty," "honor," and "country." The selective service system was premised on the notion of citizen obligation—a "calling" in the almost literal sense of being summoned by a local draft board. An *occupation* is legitimated in terms of the marketplace, that is, prevailing monetary rewards for equivalent competencies. Supply and demand rather than normative considerations are paramount. The cash-work nexus emphasizes a calculation on the part of the individual of what best serves his or her self-interest, the epitome of the economic man model.

The Gates Commission was strongly influenced by laissez-faire economic thought and argued that primary reliances in recruiting an armed force should be on monetary inducements guided by marketplace standards. Whether under the rubric of econometrics or systems analyses, such a redefinition of military service is based on a set of key assumptions. First, there is no analytical distinction between military systems and other systems, especially no difference between cost-effectiveness analysis of civilian enterprises and military services. Second, social cohesion and goal commitment are essentially unmeasurable (thereby an inappropriate object of analysis). Third, if end-strength targets are met in the AVF, notions of citizenship obligations are incidental concerns. This mind-set has contributed to moving the

American military toward an explicitly occupational model, an organizational format congruent with economic man. It is noteworthy that in 1983 a symbolic threshold was crossed when the Department of Labor counted military personnel, for the first time, as part of the nation's "labor force."

Social Composition

About three out of four eligible men who came of age in the 1940s, 1950s, and 1960s had military experience. The corresponding figure in the 1970s and 1980s has been about one in four. During times of relative economic prosperity and low youth unemployment, the military services, especially the Army, face severe difficulties in recruiting. During the late 1970s, close to half of Army male recruits did not possess a high school diploma. Whereas the number of recruits with some college was close to one in five during the draft period, the corresponding figure was one in thirty during the 1970s. Even more striking, blacks, who made up about one-third of Army entrants in the 1970s, have had higher educational levels than white entrants over the course of the AVF. With the rise in youth unemployment and raises in military compensation during the 1980s, military recruitment has become somewhat more representative of the male youth population. By the early 1980s, Army entrants had high school diploma completion rates and test scores that compared favorably (except for the top levels) with the general youth population. Recruiters reported, however, increasing difficulties during the mid-1980s. It is generally acknowledged that, without a draft, military recruiting basically reflects economic pushes and pulls.

Another major change in the social composition of the all-volunteer force has been the dramatic increase in the number of female service members. Women made up slightly over 1% of military personnel in the draft era; by the mid-1980s females constituted about 10% of the armed forces. Accompanying the rise in female participation has been an expansion of female roles. Although other factors operated, there can be little question that without the eclipse of the male citizen soldier, the expansion of female roles would not have occurred at such a rate.

Basis and Mode of Compensation

The conventional compensation system in the military has been to peg compensation to rank and seniority. Thus the citizen soldier was paid a subsistence wage with much of compensation "in kind" (e.g., food, shelter, uniforms) or deferred (e.g., postservice benefits as in the G.I. Bill). Under the pure marketplace model military members are to be paid no more or no less than what is necessary to meet recruitment and retention goals. This, in turn, means a movement to replace the "pay by rank" system with one based on "pay by skill" (a euphemism for pay by shortage). Moreover, pay should, as much as possible, be given in immediate cash form, thereby allowing for a more efficient operation of the marketplace. In practice, bonuses and off-scale pay are given to attract recruits into the combat arms members and to retain highly skilled technicians in the career force.

The logic of econometric analysis is relentless.[5] Taking economic man considerations on their own terms, it follows that anyone who joins or stays in the service when he or she could earn a better salary outside the military is stupid (or at least unaware of alternatives). It also follows that the most cost-effective enlistment practice would be to recruit from Third World nationals.

Level of Compensation

The "front-loading" of compensation toward the junior enlisted levels in the AVF has compressed enlisted pay grades. A first sergeant in the draft era made five times the income of a private first class; in today's military the ratio is two to one. In fact, a private first class in 1985 earned the equivalent of over $15,000 (or about three times in constant dollars the earnings of a draftee). Once upon a time sergeants measured their incomes and perquisites against those of the soldiers they led and felt rewarded; now they see a relative decline of status within the service and compare their earnings against civilians and feel deprived.

Personnel Mix

A core assumption in the Gates Commission was that military costs would be reduced and military effectiveness enhanced by shifting away from a predominantly first-term force (read citizen soldier) to more of a career force. Retention rather than recruitment would become the operative manpower mechanism. In point of fact, the career share (defined as over ten years of service) of the active-duty Army enlisted force has increased from approximately 15% in 1964 (the last peacetime year before the Vietnam War) to about 20% in 1984 to a projected 30% in 1990 (see Hosek et al., 1984).

A related consequence of the shift to an all-volunteer format was an increase in the average length of initial enlistment terms. In 1964, 58% of Army entrants signed on for two years (mainly as draftees), with most of the remainder joining for three years. During the AVF period, quite a different pattern has emerged: Few Army entrants are two-year volunteers, the largest number are three-year volunteers, and a growing number are four-year enlistments. Put in another way, the average length of initial enlistment has increased from 29 months to 40 months. Because of higher attrition rates (i.e., premature discharges during the first enlistment) occurring in the AVF period, however, turnover rates have been about the same as those during the peacetime draft period. Actually, turnover rates are higher in the AVF period if a "total force" perspective (i.e., inclusion of reserve as well as active force components) is taken. Whereas virtually all two-year draftees upon the expiration of their term of service were obligated for two years of additional service in reserve units, only about one-third of first-term Army separations enter the reserves in the all-volunteer era. The paradox is that the American military has high turnover rates despite the jettisoning of the citizen soldier.

Veteran Status

Precisely because the citizen soldier served at low wages under spartan conditions, a special status developed that gave the veteran important postservice entitlements and benefits. Notable among these were G.I. Bill educational and housing loan benefits, veterans hospital care for (under certain conditions) nonservice-connected disabilities, and priority in public employment. These veterans' perquisites have come under increasing question. With the end of the draft and the concomitant rise in competitive wages and enlistment bonuses for military personnel, the G.I. Bill came to an end in 1976. A new G.I. Bill was enacted in 1985, however, over the objections of the manpower analysts in the Department of Defense.[6] The system of veterans' priorities in public employment confronts the requirements of affirmative action, especially those geared toward women. Inasmuch as the vast majority of veterans are men, it was inevitable that these two modes of preferential hiring would come into conflict. The argument for veterans' benefits becomes less tenable to the degree that military members are recruited and retained on marketplace standards rather than on citizen soldier imperatives.

Conclusion

One crucial question must be addressed, even if we are unable to offer a definitive answer, when assessing the social consequences of the citizen soldier versus economic man models. Which is more likely to preserve peace? Proponents of economic man argue that a highly trained volunteer force would serve as an effective deterrent against a super-power adversary whereas a citizen soldier force is inappropriate for strategic and nuclear weaponry. On the other side, advocates of the citizen soldier hold that reliance on economic man moves the military toward a capital-intensive rather than a labor-intensive operation, which, in turn, more easily leads toward the use of sophisticated, expensive, and possibly uncontrolled nuclear (and conventional) weaponry. It is also likely that in the post-Vietnam era, the use of citizen soldiers in intervention wars would be more seriously questioned than the use volunteer forces.

That a significant part of the American intellectual and media establishments opposes the basic outlines of American foreign policy is also a fact of immense importance. It is not that they disagree on technical details, but that they believe that the United States is on the wrong side of history. That this is the same segment whose children are least likely to serve in the military is equally important. We thus have a correspondence between those hostile toward America's international role and those who prefer an economic man model of military manpower, a curious coming together of left and right. Also, research findings on elite attitudes toward domestic and international affairs present a picture of a divided and somewhat confused national leadership (see Holsti and Roseneau, 1979). The articulation of an overarching consensus on military, strategic, and international issues on the part of the national elite would certainly facilitate a resolution of the citizen soldier versus economic man concepts of military manpower.

From this overview of the contrasting philosophies of military manpower, two truths emerge. One is that the military service has moved much more toward an economic man model than most people are aware. The other is that citizen soldier traits persist, or are reconstituted, much more than econometric approaches can explain. Both truths operate in such a way that the future of national service is best understood as the interplay between citizen-soldier and marketplace trends.

Notes

1. The literature on the citizen soldier is voluminous. Works written from a sociological perspective are rare. See, however, Janowitz (1983, pp. 26-72) and Goldich (1980, pp. 88-112). For the more analytical historical literature, see Weigley (1967), Holley (1982), and Clifford (1972).

2. Good selections on the issues of conscription are found in Tax (1967), Anderson (1982), and Fullinwider (1983).

3. For further elucidation of these points see Segal and Segal (1983, pp. 151-170) and Faris (1984, pp. 251-275).

4. See Moskos (1977) and Moskos (1982, pp. 129-150). Broader reformulations of the institution/occupation thesis are found in Pinch (1982, pp. 575-600), Blair and Phillips (1983, pp. 555-568), and Cotton (1983, pp. 34-49).

5. It is informative to compare the civilian spies of the post-World War II era with the spies uncovered in the military of the mid-1980s. Whereas the former were ideologically motivated, the latter appear to be economically driven. It would seem that even spies are occupational these days.

6. I was instrumental in the conception of the new G.I. Bill. Early indications in 1985 were that over half of entering soldiers were choosing a reduction in immediate pay to be eligible for postservice educational benefits.

References

Anderson, M. (Ed.) 1982. *The Military Draft.* Stanford, CA: Hoover Institution Press.

Blair, J. D. and R. L. Phillips. 1983. "Job Satisfaction among Youth in Military and Civilian Work Settings." *Armed Forces and Society* 9: 555-568.

Clifford, J. G. 1972. *The Citizen Soldiers.* Lexington: University Press of Kentucky.

Cotton, C. A. 1983. "Institution Building in the All-Volunteer Force." *Air University Review* 34: 34-49.

Davis, J. A., J. Lauby, and P. B. Shearsley. 1983. *Americans View the Military.* NORC Report No. 131. Chicago: National Opinion Research Center, University of Chicago, April.

Faris, J. H. 1984. "Economic and Noneconomic Factors of Personnel Recruitment and Retention in the AVF." *Armed Forces and Society* 10: 251-275.

Fullinwider, R. K. (Ed.) 1983. *Conscripts and Volunteers.* Totoawa, NJ: Rowman and Allanheld.

Goldich, R. L. 1980. "Historical Continuity in the U.S. Military Reserve System." *Armed Forces and Society* 7: 88-112.

Holley, I. B., Jr. 1982. *General John M. Palmer, Citizen Soldiers, and the Army of a Democracy.* Westport, CT: Greenwood.

Holsti, O. R. and J. N. Roseneau. 1979. "Vietnam, Consensus and the Belief Systems of American Leaders." *World Politics* 37: 1-56.

Hosek, J. R., R. L. Fernandez, and D. W. Grissmer. 1984. *Active Enlisted Supply: Prospects and Policy Options.* Santa Monica, CA: Rand.

Janowitz, M. 1979. "The Citizen Soldier and National Service." *Air University Review* 31: 3-16.

Janowitz, M. 1983. *The Reconstruction of Patriotism.* Chicago: University of Chicago Press.

Military Manpower Task Force. 1982. Washington, DC: Government Printing Office.

Moskos, C. C. 1977. "From Institution to Occupation." *Armed Forces and Society* 4: 41-50.

Moskos, C. C. 1980. "Making the All-Volunteer Force Work." *Foreign Affairs* 60: 17-34.

Moskos, C. C. 1982. "Social Considerations of the All-Volunteer Force." Pp. 129-150 in *Military Service in the United States.* Edited by B. Scowcroft. Englewood Cliffs, NJ: Prentice-Hall.

Moskos, C. C. and J. H. Faris. 1981. "Beyond the Marketplace." Pp. 131-151 in *Toward a Consensus on Military Service.* Edited by A. J. Goodpaster et al. New York: Pergamon.

Pinch, F. C. 1981. "Military Manpower and Social Change." *Armed Forces and Society* 8: 575-600.

Report of the President's Commission on the All-Volunteer Force. 1970. Washington, DC: Government Printing Office.

Segal, D. R. and M. W. Segal. 1983. "Change in Military Organization." *Annual Review of Sociology* 9: 151-170.

Tax, S. (Ed.) 1967. *The Draft.* Chicago: University of Chicago Press.

Weigley, R. F. 1967. *History of the United States Army.* New York: Macmillan.

15

Social History and the Life-Course Perspective on the Family: A View from the Bridge

Irving Tallman

IN THE TWENTY YEARS since Peter Laslett's *The World We Have Lost* sociologists have become increasingly aware of the contribution made by social and demographic historical analysis to our understanding of the processes of social development and change. A long-standing but dormant interest in the use of history as social explanation has been rekindled and a new breed of social historian (or historical sociologist) has come to prominence. Using methodologies that meld the historian's concern for process and multidimensional detail with the sociologist's concern for reliable data capable of supporting and/or generating universal principles, social historians have produced a body of research that challenges long-standing assumptions about the nature of past social structures and specifies the processes through which key social transitions take place. The conceptual frameworks developed and employed by these scholars, identified by such phrases as "life course" or "life span," have become major forces guiding sociological thinking. In fact, judged by the frequency with which "life course" and "life span" appear in the titles of books, articles, and research proposals over the last decade, they clearly are the "in" perspectives of our discipline at this time.

Nowhere is this influence more apparent than in the study of the family. Indeed the scholars, sociologists, and historians alike, whose names are most closely associated with social-historical analysis— Peter Laslett, John Demos, Glen Elder, Tamara Hareven, John Modell, to name just a few—have all focused their research on aspects of family development, structure, and/or relationships. It should be noted, however, that, in the work of these scholars, the study of the family is integral to the study of social structure and social change. In fact, it is not always clear whether the social historical study of the family is intended to shed light on family development and change or on changes in key aspects of the social structure. What is clear is that, within this general perspective, the study of the family is inseparable from the study of social structure and social change.

The most influential conceptual framework employed by social historians is the "life course" perspective. This perspective examines family development as it covaries and intersects with social historical and individual development. It is the convergence of these forces, each operating within its own time frame, that establishes the conditions for subsequent individual, family, and social maturation and change. Thus, at any given point in time, the behaviors of the collectivity, the family, and individuals within the family are explained, not only as reactions to an extant set of environmental conditions but as the consequence of past experiences, the actor's current place in his or her life cycle, the stage of the family life cycle, and estimates of an anticipated future. Time, that quintessential variable of science, seems at long last to have found a place in sociological analysis.

The life-course perspective casts a large net. It seeks to account for the development and changes in populations, social organizations, and individuals within one conceptual framework. It seeks to combine social, psychological, evolutionary, and biological theories into an approach that explores the " 'coevolution' of human social organization and psychological development" (Featherman, 1984). Of particular interest is the potential for integrating various uses of the term "family" so that it is possible to examine the inter-relationship of the family as an institution, changing over historical time; as a social organization whose personnel and division of labor vary in relation to its developmental cycle; and as a small group of interacting and continuously aging personalities. The life-course framework also offers the potential for linking the family or individual decision maker to large-scale events that mark the course of history (Hareven, 1982; Modell and Hareven, 1978). Inherent in this approach is still another attempt to bridge the macro-micro abyss that has frustrated the development of sociological theory over the past 100 years. In brief, this group of social historians promises much, and, because of their prominence, much is expected of them.

For these reasons, conclusions about the merits of this body of research and theory are unavoidable, though I will avoid cosmic assessments that are best left to history. This essay has the advantages and drawbacks of an outsider's perspective. I make no claim to expertise in the intricacies of social-historical analyses. Nor have my particular experiences in the study of society and the family left me free of biases concerning the direction such study should take. These limitations, however, can also be seen as advantages—they provide the opportunity to examine directions and potential modes of inquiry that those who are closely involved may not have considered or—and this too is possible—may not even view as desirable.

For example, I believe that the new breed of social historians are making significant contributions to the scientific study of human behavior. By this I mean that their research offers the potential for building formal theories pertaining to human development within the context of explaining family development and change. Without elaboration, however, this statement would surely make traditional historians and some philosophers of science cringe. Historians, says John Demos (1970, p. xii) have "a fundamental commitment to the study of individual facts, rather than the discovery of broad conceptual constructs." Their orientation is to "recount" rather than to "compare" (Laslett, 1971/1965, p. 244). It is this commitment to the gathering and reporting of facts relevant to unique events located in a specific time and place that has led to the oft-quoted aphorism that "you can't write history as if." It has also led Popper (1964) and others (Freese, 1980; Cohen, 1980a) to assert that historical analyses cannot lead to a cumulative body of scientific knowledge—primarily because it does not contribute to the development or testing of deductive theory.

The point I hope to develop in this chapter is that, because of the methodologies they employ and in their reliance on a rather clearly articulated conceptual framework, the new breed of social historians have, wittingly or not, deviated from traditional historicism in the direction of building scientific theory. Even more significantly, such theory is being built on principles pertaining to the coordination of different dimensions of time, including historical time.

Many sociologists engaged in social historical research would not agree with or approve of interpreting their work in this way. In fact, some have interpreted the growing reliance on social history in the behavioral sciences as evidence that these sciences have shifted away from "modeling themselves after the physical sciences" and toward identifying themselves with the "historical disciplines" (Rossi, 1985, p. xiv; Campbell et al., 1985). It is not within the scope of this chapter to address the debate over what mode of inquiry is best suited for the social sciences. For good or ill our discipline is multiparadigmatic and it will have to suffice to note that my perspective, or bias, is that the canons of science are the same whether the focus of investigation is physical matter or human behavior (Cohen, 1980b), and that the scientific mode of inquiry is entirely appropriate for building a usable body of knowledge about human behavior. Accordingly, I shall examine the work of some prominent social historians, particularly those using the life-course framework, in terms of its potential for providing scientific explanations for the interplay between social and family development. By "scientific explanation" I mean a set of deductively derived and, therefore, internally consistent general principles.

In the remainder of this chapter I will try to demonstrate that social historians have contributed to this end by: (a) establishing a clearer conceptual and empirical basis for linking family structure with social structure; (b) providing data relevant to lacunae concerning processes through which families accommodate and facilitate changes in social scale and modes of production; (c) providing "error correcting" data that eliminate long-standing assumptions, partial theories, and modes of explanation, thereby clearing the way for the development of a more comprehensive theory; and (d) providing a conceptual framework that contributes to a more precise understanding of how various dimensions of time (historical, family, and individual) are coordinated. Implicit in this conceptual framework are principles that suggest a potential theory linking family, social change, and norm formation. This linkage is illustrated by three papers presented at the thematic session on "Social History and the Family" during the 1984 meetings of the American Sociological Association, by John Modell, Viviana Zelizar, and Ira Reiss.

Social History, the Family, and the Social Structure

The Family as Mirror to the Social Structure

Peter Laslett's (1971/1965) pioneering work demonstrated how the study of the family can provide a basis for drawing inferences about social structure. The ubiquity of the family makes it feasible to study its form, shape, and functioning with consistency and comparability over time in relation to a changing social environment. Laslett also made use of detailed records, carefully maintained over centuries, pertaining to such family-related phenomena as births, marriages, and deaths. But the most compelling reason for using the family as a source of inferences about social structure is that the variables that make up social structure—stratification and normative systems, authority patterns, modes of production, systems of distributing goods and services, and changing population and migration—are all manifest in family behaviors.

In virtually all societies, past and present, kinship represents one of the major criteria for determining where people reside, work, eat, and sleep. Kinship is also the basis for identifying the specific groups and/or individuals who are obligated to provide affection, physical care, economic support, and social support for one another. How and where these activities are performed, and the division of responsibility within the family for carrying them out, has much to do with how the society is structured.

The question of where people work, what they do, who takes care of them when they are infants, ill, aged, or unemployed can be approached historically by asking "if not the family, who?" The answer to that question tells us much about the nature of the social structure. Because the institution of the family tends to be organized around households, it follows that the composition of households, as well as the activities that go on within them, are key indicators of social structure.

Laslett (1971/1965), Hareven (1978), and others have shown, for example, that a principal factor distinguishing preindustrial from industrial Western societies is the shift in the production and exchanges of economic goods from the household to the factory and office. This change had profound implications for both the scale and types of social organizations that evolved in industrial societies. The organization of work increased in size and complexity. Coincidental with the growing dependency of family members on salaries and wages, the family's ability to provide other services to its members declined. (See Demos, 1970, pp. 183-184, for a discussion of the range of economic, social, and personal services provided by the family in colonial America.) The gradual transition of responsibility for individual welfare and protection from families to industries and corporations and, eventually, to governments seems to have fostered egalitarian norms of resource distribution. Laslett (1971/1965, p. 220) argues that, at least in England, it was only after industrialization and the decline in the hegemony of the family that large-scale efforts to tackle issues of poverty and inequality took place.

Hareven's study of the Amoskeag Textile Company documents a process in which worker's dependence on the family for support, protection, and welfare is gradually shared, and at times transferred to the company. The company not only provided jobs; it maintained housing, was concerned with and supervised the morality of its female unmarried employees, and paid for churches, parks and recreation areas, a medical clinic, visiting nurses, a number of recreational clubs, and eventually a pension plan (Hareven, 1982, pp. 36-68). In fact, the process involved making the company an essential part of the worker's identity: "Even those employees who had worked for the Amoskeag for only a limited time considered themselves 'Amoskeag men' and 'Amoskeag women' " (Hareven, 1982, p. 69). The process depicted in the Hareven (1982, p. 365) study is one of mutual accommodation between family and company:

> Mutuality characterized the relationship between workers' families and the corporation. The corporation drew on workers' relatives as a source of labor and used them as training and disciplining agents. Reaching beyond the factory gates, the corporation used the family as a means of socializing workers and fostering loyalty and corporate identification. The workers, in turn, used the corporation as a source of employment and economic stability and as an initial training ground for their children as workers.

Thus the family not only mirrors the social structure, it is an active agent involved in the process of change.

The Family as an Agent of Structural Change

Hareven's research, as well as that of Anderson (1971) and Schwartzweller et al. (1971), suggests that the rural-urban migration into industrial life did not produce the sudden or cataclysmic social and cultural dislocations suggested by Wirth (1938), Frazier (1939),

Thomas and Znaniecki (1958/1918-1920), and others. Hareven (1982, p. 369) describes a process that is neither sudden nor necessarily disruptive: "At home children were taught traditional family ways as well as industrial work habits. Thus in both the family and the work place premigration culture was a major resource rather than a handicap."

Hareven also describes a sometimes cyclical pattern of working in a factory for a period of time and returning to one's rural community, making the adjustment to urban life seem less absolute or definitive than the "Chicago school" sociologists implied. It is likely that a sizable proportion of people who initially sought jobs in city industries considered them as temporary. The emerging picture is of a migration process that maintains large elements of family traditions and structure with minimal social disorganization (see Lomnitz, 1977, p. 37, for a similar description of urban migration in Latin America). These findings suggest the need to reassess some of our most cherished conceptions about the course of social change. For example, Redfield's notion of "folk-urban" communities, Toennie's "gemeinschaft-gesellschaft," Maine's, "status and contract," and Durkheim's depiction of "mechanical and organic" solidarity all share a common conception of the nature and direction of social change. Each of these ideal-type dichotomies implies a continuum that at one end is characterized by the village with its "close, intense, and emotionally gratifying familiar and communal interpersonal relationships" and at the other end by "the city as the community of destination . . . [displaying the] opposite characteristics of distant, cold, and impersonal social relationships" (Balan et al., 1973, p. 149; reprinted in Lomnitz, 1977).

At the very least the data pertaining to the role of kin in migration suggest the need to explicate the processes through which the normative patterns governing interpersonal relations change with the increasing scale of social organization. Such an explication requires a careful specification of the family's role in implementing the changing norms as they evolve probably over several generations. It also requires attention to the power relations between the socioeconomic forces and the family.

If the image of the family as isolated and disorganized under the impact of migration, industrialization, and urbanization is overdrawn, so too is the image that the family is capable of maintaining its traditions and organization regardless of the impact of social forces.

Hareven (1982, p. 364) reports that "Although the balance in the relationship between the family and the corporation constantly shifted, power was always on the corporation's side." As the corporation grew in size and efficiency, "Speedups and stretch-outs made it increasingly difficult for families to manipulate work processes." Prude (1976, p. 424) depicts some of the complexity in this interplay by recognizing that the "family could be both affected by and affective in its milieu, . . . it could be simultaneously unsuccessful in resisting changes in its own traditions and successful in aiding its members to cope with the world in which they found themselves" (quoted in Elder, 1983a).

Elder's (1974, 1981) research demonstrates the complex interplay between environmental conditions and family goals. In particular his work illustrates the role of family history in affecting subsequent behavior. Elder and Rockwell (1978) have shown how male children who suffered economic deprivation during the great depression tended to attain a higher status than would be expected given their class of origin. Elder (1981) also found that women who grew up under deprived conditions during the depression were more likely to marry upward and to value the homemaker role in which they worked to advance the careers of their husbands and children. Such values may be in reaction to the detrimental effects on marital relations produced by income loss during the depression—effects that were manifest particularly in the social and psychological breakdown of husbands (Liker and Elder, 1983). Thus it is conceivable that children of the depression were especially concerned about maintaining and enhancing the role of the father. This was, of course, possible in the 1950s when these children married and became parents. Their decisions had an effect on a social structure characterized by dramatic upward mobility and the growth of the "new middle class."

Elder's data suggest that although the family was not able to control or, at times, even effectively respond to economic crises, its patterns of adaptation nevertheless influence the course of social change. Even more significantly, the decisions that families and family members make to get married, to seek certain types of education or occupations, to move, to reside in certain areas or types of homes, to have children, to get divorced are descriptive of the social structure at one point in time and of changes in the structure over time. It is the special contribution of the life-course social historians to identify the historical, family, and individual conditions within which these decisions are made (Modell and Hareven, 1978).

Social History as Myth Slayer
and Explicator of Loose Concepts

As we have seen, the new breed of social historians has been able to challenge the common assumption that the transition from country to city and from farm to factory resulted in the isolation and disorganization of the family. Their research has also put into question a number of prevalent beliefs: that the sexual mores of the Victorian era inhibited women from the open expression of their sexuality (Degler, 1980); that women were without power in pre-industrial society (Demos, 1970); that the industrial revolution increased opportunities and marital equality for middle-class women (Hareven, 1976); and that the industrial revolution produced a less humane, depersonalized conception of the individual (Laslett, 1971/1965). It is this capacity to destroy myths and to fill in conceptual gaps that is probably the most visible contribution of social history to the literature of family structure and development.

Of equal importance, however, this work helps to clarify ambiguous concepts and to eliminate explanatory systems that are not fruitful. For example, data from many cultures demonstrate that the nuclear family household, far from being a product of industrial society, was the primary type of household organization in pre-industrial England, Europe, and America (Laslett, 1971/1965; Demos, 1970; Laslett and Wall, 1972; Hareven, 1982). Thus the frequently employed generalization that there is a curvilinear relationship between societal complexity and the complexity of the family household (Winch and Blumberg, 1972) does not hold, at least for the Western world. Similarly, extension of this principle to claim that the nuclear family provides the best "fit" for industrial societies because it is isolated and, therefore, dependent upon and vulnerable to the demands of industry (Goode, 1963) has been challenged. Hareven's (1982) research supports earlier studies by Litwak (1960) and Sussman and Burchinal (1962) indicating that although families lived in nuclear residences, kin nevertheless play a critical role in assisting family members in attaining life goals. Hareven's work further demonstrated that kin played a vital role in influencing recruitment and hiring practices, job placement, and even work practices. Thus, although not completely in control of these outcomes, the family was not a passive actor at the mercy of industry without influence or power. The picture that emerges is one of negotiation and interdependence. The family and kin network controlled mechanisms for recruiting new workers and played a key role in maintaining worker morale, training, and production norms; in this sense it was a force with which industry had to contend.

Explaining the family's role in mediating between the social structure and the individual requires that patterns of interaction between families and the social structure be examined. This involves a shift of focus from a conception of the family as an institution among other social institutions to a conception of "families" as separate social units interacting with other social units within a given social collectivity. From this perspective families are viewed as a type of social organization that varies over time in size, composition, division of labor, role expectations, hierarchical structure, and control over key resources. In brief, families can be conceived as having life cycles during which their organization grows and declines in complexity.

Families, however, are also small groups of people, interacting with one another, who are going through individual maturational and aging processes and who seek to meet personal needs and individual goals. Thus individuals within families pursue personal careers as well as facilitating collective goals and the careers of other family members. How the family functions in relation to the social structure depends, in part, on the life experiences of its individual members. Elder (1983b) makes the point as follows:

> The full scope of the (family) cyclical model requires a multidimensional concept of the life course for adult offspring; a moving set of interlocking career lines, such as work, marriage, parenting, etc. Misfortune and opportunity across these pathways may become intergenerational as well as life problems. Failed marriages and careers frequently lead adult sons and daughters back to the parental household, and have profound implications for the parents' life plans regarding the later years, especially when young children are involved. Early misfortune, such as pregnancy in adolescents, may postpone home leaving, higher education or employment, and marriage. Each generation is bound to fateful decisions and events in the other's life course.

Thus the special characteristics or unique events in individual life careers, combined with the interdependency of family members and their joint commitment to mutual aid and support, can fundamentally alter the course of the family life cycle. Such alterations affect how the family qua family deals with the social structure.

The relevance of individual life experiences to the family's mediating role suggests the need to incorporate a third conception of family, best depicted in Burgess's (1926) description of the family as a small group of "interacting personalities." It is with this conception of the family that we are able to deal with such relevant issues as family decision making and problem solving.

We find ourselves now with the three distinct conceptions of the family—as institution, organization, and small group of interacting personalities. Each of these conceptions has received considerable attention from family scholars, but I know of no effort to link or integrate them within a single framework. In my view, the life-course perspective can provide such a framework.

The Life Course Perspective: An Interpretation

Before proceeding further, I must note that although the following presentation has been greatly influenced by the work of Elder, Hareven, and Modell, and the central ideas and concepts I employ are theirs, the dimensions proposed as underlying these concepts are mine and may not be shared by these scholars. Moreover, I have selected only those concepts that I believe meet the purpose of contributing toward a theoretical explanation of the family contribution to norm formation. To my knowledge, building such a theory has never been a concern of these authors. In short, the discussion that follows is both selective and interpretive. It is intended neither to be comprehensive nor authoritative, but rather an exploration of the heuristic implications of some life-course concepts.

The life-course perspective as it applies to the family is concerned with the coordination of three temporal processes: historical time, family time, and individual or lifetime. Historical time pertains primarily to the institutional aspects of the family. The analysis of the family over historical time, therefore, is concerned with its social functions, its residential patterns, the size and character of its viable kin structure, its power in relation to other key institutions, and so forth. At this level social historical research focuses on questions of how family structure and functions change in relation to changes in other social institutions, and the reciprocal influences of such changes. Kin, and the intergenerational kinship structure, provide the basis for continuity across time as well as providing the family members with a collective memory that is manifest primarily in cultural traditions.

Like other institutions such as the polity or the economy, the family neither ages nor deteriorates; it simply changes. If the family should disappear at some future time, its demise could not be attributed to age but rather to malfunctioning or loss of necessary functions. We have no means for assessing the aging process of institutions across historical time. Historical time, as it is currently conceptualized, is linear and infinite. As might be expected, however, its calibration varies with the problem the investigator is seeking to understand. For example, social historians interested in the changing structure and function of the family in relation to major social changes consider time in terms of "eras" that vary considerably in length. Thus the "preindustrial" era lasted for centuries whereas many consider the "industrial" era to have lasted only about 100 years before being supplanted by the "postindustrial" or electronic-information era (Bell, 1976). On the other hand, social historians who have adopted the birth cohort mode of analysis (Ryder, 1965) tend to use smaller time periods ranging from 1 to 20 years. They assume that persons born at a given point in historical time share a set of experiences that are unique to the cohort and that they adapt to subsequent life events in a manner that reflects these experiences.

In general, whether considered in terms of eras or cohorts, whether calculated in centuries or the lifetimes of individuals, historical time provides family members with a set of traditions and experiences that constrain available alternative courses of action. At any given point in time the family's normative system establishes boundaries for appropriate activities and criteria for just rewards for given investments of time, skill, and effort. This normative system, operationalized through the kin network, is not static but is modified on the basis of constant interaction with the environment. Thus Hareven (1982) demonstrates how the family orientation toward factory work and its relation to industry was gradually modified as conditions changed and power/dependency relationships between family and company were altered.

Family time refers to the development of, and changes in, the family unit over the life cycle of that unit. Family time is generally calibrated in terms of the sequence of critical events or transitions, such as marriage, establishing households, births, childrearing, the launching of children, retirement, widowhood, and so forth. This ordering is often described in terms of stages; each stage involving alterations in the organization of positions and roles within the family (Aldous, 1978). The stages also tend to be normatively established (Modell et al., 1976; Elder, 1983a). Time-oriented role expectations form a basis for conceptualizing the family as a changing social organization with a definable life cycle.

Thus students of family development link family time to the family of procreation and shared household residency. This perspective depicts a normatively determined and chronologically changing social organization that begins with two people in marriage and gradually increases in complexity as children are born. Each additional child fosters an exponential increase in roles and organizational complexity. As children begin leaving the household the number and types of roles to be played within the family gradually decline until the family organization during the stages of retirement and widowhood involve fewer roles than were needed at its inception. There are many variations of this conception of the family life cycle. Most stipulate more precisely the various stages the family traverses in terms of the specific role complexes, role sequences, and skills (developmental tasks) required at each stage and to make the transition from one stage to another.

Regardless of the variations, however, the model that I have depicted can serve as a generic example of Reuben Hill's (1964) and his colleagues' (Hill and Mattessich, 1979; Rogers, 1964; Aldous, 1978) conception of family development over the family life cycle. Hill's version of the family life cycle has the merit of examining the family as a collective unit, capable of acting as a cohesive single entity. The Hill model also recognizes the high level of interdependency that characterizes the family and provides the necessary conditions for forming a group in which the goals of the collectivity can take precedence over the goals of individuals. Clearly the family is among the social groups most likely to be tightly bonded, and to have high levels of cohesiveness and shared perceptions of the external world (Kuhn, 1974, p. 415; Reiss, 1981).

Elder (1983a, 1983b) has criticized the family life cycle model on two counts. First, he believes that the life-cycle does not adequately consider the development processes of individual family members. For example, it makes a difference whether parents are in their early twenties or their late thirties during the child-bearing stage of the cycle. Similarly, individual differences in parents or children will make a difference in how the various stages of the family life cycle evolve. A retarded or handicapped child may stay with the family long after the normatively established "launching" period. Conversely, gifted children who excel in the arts may leave the home early in life for special training, and children who are delinquent may be removed from the home at nonnormative stages in the life cycle. The number of possible deviations from the norm are myriad.

Elder's second criticism is that the family life cycle concept does not adequately consider intergenerational relationships. In particular, it fails to integrate into its schema the role of grandparents. "Some couples enter the 'establishment' phase with living parents and grandparents, while others may have only one set of living parents and no surviving grandparents . . . the two types of couples occupy very different positions relative to self-definition and support" (Elder, 1983b, p. 14). The difficulties that may arise at different stages in the life cycle are played out very differently depending on sources of kin support and/or kin demands. For example, childbirth and child rearing is a time when, for many families, costs tend to exceed income. This situation can be eased if the grandparents are able to assist the parents during this stage, just as it can be exacerbated if the grandparents are also dependent. There is, then, an interdependence between generations that is strongly affected by the "vulnerabilities and strengths" of the generations (Elder, 1983a, p. 50). Intergenerational strengths or weaknesses have a cumulative effect that either facilitates or inhibits the family's ability to deal with its developmental problems. Intergenerational relations become both more complex and more significant in view of the lengthening individual life span. Increasingly, the possible effects of four living generations within families must be considered.

The life-course scholar's solutions to the problems they see is to conceptualize the family as a set of mutually contingent individual careers. Thus the perspective changes from the family as a single unit to that of a small collectivity of interdependent individuals moving across individual lifetimes with a consciousness of shared identities and some sense of solidarity. This framework is able to incorporate individual differences in development and nonnormative or atypical career patterns; it can also take into account intergenerational relationships. In fact, given the essential focus on the individual life course, there do not seem to be any natural limits to the number of interrelationships the investigator wishes to analyze. Thus we have the familiar conundrum of a solution the strengths of which carry the seeds of its weaknesses.

The difficulty with the life-course approach as it relates to family time is that the focus on the family as a developing social organization becomes blurred. Blurring occurs in part because of the life-course emphasis on individual development and individual relationships.

Exploring the family in terms of mutually contingent careers, though it may highlight the convergence of those careers within the family setting, does not provide a conceptual mechanism for understanding how the family functions and changes as an organizational unit. Whatever its failings, the life-cycle model provides a clear picture of family change and development in organizational terms. Moreover, because of the system of kin-linked obligations, families are better able than other groups to maintain membership loyalty and dependence. Its boundaries, therefore, are relatively impermeable and it serves as a major source of an individual's identity. As a result the collective and individual decisions made within families are frequently focused on benefiting the family unit even at the immediate cost of the individual member (Tallman, forthcoming). This is apparent in the kinds of self-sacrifice family members are willing to undertake when the family unit is faced with a disaster (Drabek and Boggs, 1968).

In my view, the family life cycle model, as depicted by Hill and his colleagues, has the dual advantage of conceptualizing the family as an organizational unit with a designated and measureable life sequence. It has a zero point, a beginning and an ending. Thus family time, unlike historical time, is bounded within finite limits. It can be seen as an organization that changes in broadly predictable ways within temporal boundaries.

The a priori stages in the family life cycle are normative and arbitrary; and, as Elder and others have noted, they are not likely to fit the empirical realities. They nevertheless serve a valuable conceptual purpose. If they are taken to represent the normative standards extant in a particular historical time, they may serve as an ideal typology for that time. As such they provide a standard against which to measure the forms and variations in family development. The model can also be used to assess changes in the normative stage pattern over historical time. For example, comparing the stages designated in current life-cycle models with the nineteenth century demonstrates rather clearly that a postparental period was much less likely in that day than it is today (Uhlenberg, 1978).

However, Elder's criticism of the life-cycle model for failing to include kin relations and ignoring variations in the individual development of children, parents, and grandparents cannot be gainsaid. The importance of kin in assisting and influencing the course of family development has been demonstrated repeatedly. Yet, as we have seen, inclusion of generational time with family time presents a confusing and muddled picture. One possible solution is to introduce generational time as a fourth dimension that interacts with family and lifetime within a given historical era.

If we use the family life cycle model as the basis for assessing family time, how do we take account of variations in the individual development of children, parents, and grandparents as they relate to each other in terms of their own life histories and conceptions of personal and collective futures? In my view, using the family life cycle notion as an indicator of family time does not negate the simultaneous analysis of individual development for children, parents, and grandparents. The following discussion of the life-course notion of "individual time" is intended to illustrate this point.

Individual time or lifetime is measured in terms of chronological age, but the meanings attached to given ages are multidimensional. The aging process may be seen as incorporating at least three dimensions—the changing statuses associated with age, the changing roles that are associated with the social and occupational development of the individual, and the specific set of developing memories and experiences that are associated with being born at a given time and place in history. Thus, at a given point in time, the individual's lifetime position incorporates his or her past, present, and future in terms of the social meaning attached to the chronological age already attained, the social roles that have been achieved and are yet to be achieved, and the set of beliefs, values, interpretations of events, and expectations that evolve from growing up and living in a particular social era under given social and economic conditions. These three dimensions provide much of the content that makes up the individual's identity (Tallman et al., 1983, pp. 24, 27-28; Tallman, 1976, pp. 87-116). Consequently the dimensions influence the individuals' presentation of self and modes of interaction over time.

The three dimensions of age status, social role development, and historical cohort represent different lifetime curves that also vary over historical time. For example, in the current era of "youth culture" age status may rise rapidly after birth and reach its apex in the early or middle twenties and gradually decline until it reaches its lowest point at old age. Role status, on the other hand, builds more slowly, probably reaching its highest point in the middle forties to early fifties and then rapidly declines in old age. The cohort curve is less predictable because it is more directly influenced by such external events as wars, depressions, the opportunity structure, and the sociopolitical climate at sensitive points in the individual's aging process. It should be noted that each of the dimensions is concerned to some large extent with normative expectations. As demographic changes continue to affect the age structure of the society, we can expect changes in the normative expectations in each of the three dimensions.

These dimensions of the individual's life course or career are interdependent with the careers of other significant persons in the individual's environment; among these are the individual's family. Elder (1983a, p. 34) describes the process as follows:

> The general picture is one of *interdependent* career lines that vary in timetables, synchronization, and resource management. Each career line represents a patterned sequence of activities or roles. In applying the life-course perspective to marriage and the family unit, we begin with the interlocking career lines of individuals. Analysis of the young couple centers on the social patterns formed by the joining of life courses through mate selection and their implications for marital relations, child rearing, and kin ties [emphasis in original].

With this conception of family, individuals represent the basic units of analysis and family characteristics develop out of the interactions of these basic units. In brief, the individual-time perspective views the family as a small group of interacting personalities.

Thus far I have attempted to show how the life-course scholar's ideas of historical time, family time, and individual time can be identified with the conceptions of the family as a social institution, a social organization, and a small group of interacting personalities. Each of these conceptions of family have been used, independent of one another, as a basis for defining the family. The life-course perspective suggests that the three conceptions can be integrated into a more comprehensive view of the family that incorporates the elements of all three definitions and, in the process, highlights the function of the family as an agency for mediating between the social structure and individual family members. This function becomes clearer as we examine the interplay between historical, family, and individual time.

Toward a Theory of Family Mediation and Norm Formation

Time is a continuous process. Consequently, historical, family, and individual time are in constant interaction. Moreover, given our previous discussion, we can infer that the family members, as institution, social organization, and small group of interacting personalities, are also in constant interaction. Finally, at each of these levels of analysis the family is in interaction with elements of the social structure.

We can assume that the nature of these interactions involves exchanges in which the actors are seeking to meet their own individual or collective goals. These exchanges are generally regulated by social norms that establish notions of what constitutes a "fair" or "just" basis for exchanges and the appropriate rules for engaging in interactions. The normative structure holds not only for exchanges between families and other segments of the social structure but also within families. The development of scientifically useful explanations for the formation of such structures has been slow and limited in scope (Berger et al., 1972; Tallman and Ihinger-Tallman, 1979; Jasso, 1980). This may be because we are all born into normative systems that, for the most part, change rather slowly. The life-course perspective is of value precisely because it provides a sufficient time span for analysis while, at the same time, the integration of family and individual time brings into play specific decision-making units operating within finite lifetimes.

Because normative systems are generally interpreted by people as the natural state of affairs, changes in such systems are likely to develop only under conditions that disrupt a given state of affairs. Within the life-course framework this should occur when the various levels of family interaction are out of synchronization. Asynchrony may result from changing economic conditions, changes in the society's demographic composition, or in the distribution of status and/or political power. For the family these changes result in aborted or discontinuous relations with elements of the social structure. Solutions to such problems generally require some accommodation to changing social forces—accommodations that are justified and regulated by altering or modifying relevant social norms.

This accommodation process involves an interplay between individual family members, the family unit, and the relevant agents of the social structure. The various parties in this interplay are seldom mere pawns who are helplessly buffeted about by superior forces; each has something the other needs and therefore some adjustment to meet their respective needs is necessary. Nevertheless, the resources controlled by the contending forces are rarely equal, and therefore their relative power/dependency is also not equal. Some groups have to do more accommodating than others. Hareven's (1982) research demonstrated that as long as the Amoskeag plant needed workers and the family-kin system was able to recruit workers, the family could play a role in establishing norms for hiring, job allocation, and production. In addition, families tended to maintain a strong identification with the company. When economic conditions changed, families' power diminished and they were forced to submit to lower wages, increased work loads, and speedups. The relationship with the company also tended to be more alienative. Despite these changes, families continued to be dependent for income and status. Consequently, there was no diminishing of the work ethic. Throughout this period people needed jobs and parents continued to rear their children to be steady, reliable workers.

These findings suggest that power relations play a significant role in determining the kinds of norms that evolve within the family. Consider, for example, the potential conflict between individual benefits and the benefits to the family as a unit. Strodtbeck's (1958) classic comparison of Italian and Jewish parent-child relationships in New Haven illustrates different resolutions of this conflict. Italians were much more likely to demand, and obtain, family loyalty, including a readiness to forego opportunities for personal economic advancement. Jewish families made no such demands on their children; instead they tended to foster independence and encourage autonomous actions.

Such differences are institutionalized and transmitted across generations. But how did these norms evolve? One possible answer lies in the power/dependency relationship between the family and the individual. For centuries the Italian family and kin network has tended to rely on its collective resources for support and sustenance; its individual members were never as strong as the collective unit. Jews, on the other hand, despite an ideologial and emotional commitment to family, tended to have structurally weak families. Dispersed across the world, the Jewish family has not proved able during years of the Diaspora to protect or provide sustenance for its members. Individuals could and often did fare better alone than in the collectivity.

This discussion can be summarized in two propositions: (1) During periods when historical time, family time, and individual time are not synchronized, the prevailing family normative system will be challenged and new norms governing the relevant relationships will evolve. (2) The nature of these norms can be partially predicted on the basis of the power/dependency relationships of the various parties. More dependent parties will be more likely to acquiesce to less dependant parties.

Extending the second principle leads to the prediction that the more successful the institutional or organizational family's history of carrying out its functions and meeting its members' needs, the more likely its norms will prevail during periods of discontinuity. The migration research discussed earlier suggests that kin networks that are able to assist their members during the processes of change by providing information, housing, and finding jobs seem able to maintain family traditions and loyalties. Hareven (1982, p. 360) reports data that illustrate the ability of the family organization to maintain family-based norms at the expense of individual benefits:

> To implement their plan to achieve a middle-class life-style, first-generation immigrants were prepared to make the necessary trade-offs: children were sent to work to help families purchase homes; daughters dropped out of school early and went to work to allow sons to search for better jobs outside of the mills.

Why did children go to work? Why did daughters agree to limit their future opportunities to benefit the family? A likely reason is that the prevailing normative system said they should. But one reason for the prevailing normative system is that daughters could perceive no alternative course of action. This lack of perceived alternatives increased their dependence on the family. Dependency was also maintained by the family's ability to take care of its members. If the family did not have this ability, its members would be forced by circumstances to consider other alternatives.

Thomas and Znaniecki's (1958/1918-1920) study of the Polish peasant describes a more conflictual situation. It would appear from their research that Polish immigrant families in Chicago were unable to maintain their traditions for their children because they were unable to meet their offsprings' social and economic needs. The children did better for themselves by incorporating the norms of the larger society (see also Thomas, 1967/1923). Thus a possible explanation for the differences between the findings reported by Hareven and Thomas and Znaniecki lies in the differences in the power/dependence relationships with the families studied.

The above discussion suggests that the power of the family as an institution or an organization will vary inversely with the availability of alternative institutions capable of meeting the needs of individual family members. If this hypothesis holds, then the family should be more influential in countries with few social services. The family should be more important as a norm sender in the United States, for example, than in the Scandinavian countries.

In sum, life-course social historians focus on the synchronization of various time dimensions, and their emphasis on the forces that converge to affect a given event at a given time provides both a description and a basis for explaining an existing normative structure. If the timing of historical, social, and individual development in a given era are out of synchronization, the existing normative system is challenged and will probably be altered. The new breed of social historians have shown how such conditions produce strains in the social structure and constraints on choices available to individual actors. The essential mechanism for legitimating these constraints is the normative system. Indeed the works of these scholars suggest that the primary outcomes of interest to them are the transformations of norms that occur at specific periods of historical time. By way of illustrating this focus, I shall briefly review the three papers noted earlier by Modell, Zelizar, and Reiss. These papers, and discussion by Tamara Hareven, provided the source of inspiration for this chapter.

Engagement, Allowances, and Sexual Jealousy: A Tale of Three Norms

Modell's paper, "Social Change and Family Change since 1920," sought to illustrate the rapid changes in a variety of institutionalized patterns that influence the formations of families. He argued that American youth are constantly under pressure to adopt roles that are not necessarily of their own choosing. These pressures are primarily the result of structural variables, "demographic and economic in particular and such external phenomena as wars and decisions of authorities (like school authorities and the legislatures that empower them)." The specific example used was the institution of engagement. Engagement as a social institution is traced back to the early Victorian period. As weddings became more pretentious, engagements took on special meaning and became increasingly important. In the 1920s and 1930s engagement was described as a period of "heightened expectation and intimacy." This was to be a period of anticipation, and couples who engaged in coitus knew enough to be discreet.

The depression and World War II, however, altered the situation by affecting the timing of marriage. Thus a historical event threw the normatively expected match between family time and lifetime out of synchronization. The resulting longer engagements produced growing social pressure and debate about the utility of the normative sanction against premarital coitus during engagement. The debate took many forms. It was carried on from the pulpit, in the media, and in college textbooks. Modell presents one example from a story in *True Confessions*. In this story the writer complains that after two years of "waiting" in the engaged state his "disposition" is being ruined and he thinks about having recourse to "an easy . . . cheap little girl." He worries, too, as to whether his fiancée will wait the necessary time for him to afford marriage. His fiancée, on the other hand, advocates waiting for sentimental and moral reasons. The story ends without resolving the debate. Modell suggests that the debate was ended in the writer's favor and the cohort described in the story set in motion fundamental changes in norms regarding the propriety of coitus during engagement.

Zelizar, in her paper "From Wages to a Weekly Allowance: The Transformation of Children's Money, 1870's to 1930's," explores changes in the norms governing financial relations between parents and children. Child labor laws and compulsory education fundamentally altered the meaning and utility of children's roles within the family organization. "The 19th-century economically useful child" Zelizar states, "was . . . displaced by the 20th-century economically useless but emotionally priceless child." The change in the meanings of the roles and expectations fundamentally affected child-rearing norms, which were clearly manifest in the patterned transfer of money between parent and child. Interpreting these changes within the life-course framework suggests that a key historical event produced a fundamental discontinuity in the synchronization of family time with individual time. If children could no longer be an economic asset, the prevailing norms governing the time to be allocated to children's training and development would no longer be applicable and the nature of children and parents' responsibilities for one another would have to be restructured.

Using a variety of sources ranging from survey materials through professional child care advice and stories in the media, Zelizar shows that, at the turn of the century, children not only were put to work in factories but they were expected to turn over their paychecks to the family. A 1914 study noted that a "broken envelope violates the social standard." Children's money was considered family money in the same way that the money earned by fathers and mothers was to contribute to the family coffers. As children ceased to make economic contributions to the family, the economic resources they used could no longer be interpreted as a reasonable return on their contribution. Because children's needs did not change, a new economic contract had to be developed. Thus the concept of "allowance" was introduced. Child specialists advocated that such money was not to be considered as recompence for work but as an educational device. Money was to be used to teach children how to plan and how to use it effectively. Although allowance was sometimes given for chores carried out in the household, experts warned parents against "commercializing the home."

As children ceased to be regular economic contributors to the home, their allowances were increasingly interpreted as their share of the family income. Thus children's income, even if earned, was gradually differentiated from parents' income. Whereas children had a right to family income, the money they earned through work was their own. Zelizar suggests that the pendulum may be swinging again. In the 1980s there is growing criticism of the "useless child" and suggestions are made that the child be helped to be more accountable and responsible within the home.

Zelizar's paper is illustrative of the weakening influence of the family as an organization as other agencies and institutions take over its regulatory and educational functions. The result is the development of separate interest groups within the family. Thus the family as a small group of interacting personalities takes precedence over the family as a single social organization.

Ira Reiss is not a social historian and does not present himself as such. Nevertheless, his paper "Sexuality and the Social Fabric" is relevant for our purposes because Reiss addresses the issue of norm formation and norm development. Unlike most social historians, Reiss adopts a nomothetic approach to explanation. He seeks to uncover universal laws governing sexual customs.

Human sexuality is viewed in terms of cultural interactional models designed to promote erotic arousal that is likely to lead to genital response. Sexuality is important in all societies because it is a pleasurable and intimate activity. All human beings, Reiss claims, desire pleasure and revelation and these are intrinsic to sexual activity. Revelation occurs in sexuality because "there is a significant difference in the presentation of self when erotically aroused."

Reiss suggests that jealousy is a normative response the function of which is to reinforce the importance of sexuality in marriage. This does not imply that all sexual behavior must be limited to the marriage partner, but does imply that marital sexuality has priority over sexual behavior with nonmates. Thus jealously confronts the issue of marital sexual stability by reassuring the partners as to the priority given to the relationship.

Reiss also develops propositions pertaining to power relations, ideology, and kinship relations as they affect sexual behavior. Essentially he argues that the normative structure pertaining to sexual rights will vary directly with the gender distribution of power. That is, the more powerful gender will have greater access and greater sexual freedom. His propositions pertaining to ideology hold that societies will stress either the rational or emotional aspects of human beings. He then links these types of ideology to egalitarian or nonegalitarian norms. Egalitarian norms are associated with greater sexual permissiveness. His final set of propositions pertains to kinship structure. Here he maintains that male-dominant normative systems will be stressed in patrilineal and patrilocal systems. These systems, of course, are also linked to a male-dominated power structure.

Finally, Reiss suggests that all societies have sanctions against force and fraud in sexual activity. Thus all societies, no matter how much their tendency to link sex with aggression, still have the notion of rape and sanctions against engaging in this activity. Similarly, all societies have sanctions against child abuse although there is great variation between them on the criteria to be used in identifying such abuse.

Reiss's analysis does not consider the three time dimensions used by life-course scholars. I think utilizing these dimensions could contribute to specifying the development of the normative systems that interest him. Modell's paper suggests how the asynchronization of historical, family, and individual time produced by the depression leads to the liberalization of sexual norms. Reiss's analysis, on the other hand, suggests that Modell's interpretation could be generalized to the development of egalitarian norms in social spheres other than sexuality.

Conclusion

I have attempted to identify some of the major contributions of the social historians to understanding the integral and intricate role the family plays as one of the principal weavers of the social fabric. These scholars are justly proud of their role in correcting long-standing errors and myths concerning the family and social structure in earlier eras, thereby altering conceptions of the family's role in social change. The contribution of the social historians, however, extends beyond demystification and clarification.

I have tried to show that the work of social historians with a life-course perspective provides the rudiments of a theory that can account for the family's role in norm formation. In brief, such a theory would be based on the following principles. New norms evolve out of discontinuities in the social structure that result in altering the opportunities for families and their members to attain their personal, social, economic, or political goals. These discontinuities, in turn, develop as the life-course framework suggests, when historical time, social or family time, and individual time are not in synchronization. This condition raises questions about the viability of the prevailing normative structure and puts in motion efforts on the part of relevant parties to alter existing social relationships. Whether this is done through collective action, political activity, educational programs, individual negotiations, or simply by changing lifestyles varies on the basis of a number of conditions including the level of power and dependency of the key actors. If these changes are aggregated over a sufficiently large portion of a population, and if accommodations are reached between key parties, these altered relationships will be legitimated and sanctioned through the establishment of new cultural norms.

References

Aldous, J. 1978. *Family Careers.* New York: John Wiley.

Anderson, M. 1971. *Family Structure in Nineteenth-Century Lancashire.* Cambridge: Cambridge University Press.

Balan, J., H. L. Browning, and E. Jelin. 1973. Men in a Developing Society. Austin: University of Texas Press.

Bell, D. 1976. *The Coming of Post-Industrial Society.* New York: Basic Books.

Berger, J., M. Zelditch, B. Anderson, and B. Cohen. 1972. "Structural Aspects of Distributive Justice: A Status Value Formulation." Pp. 119-146 in *Sociological Theories in Process.* By B. Berger, M. Zelditch, and B. Anderson. Boston: Houghton Mifflin.

Blumberg, R. and Winch, R. 1972. Social Complexity and Familial Complexity: Evidence for the Curvilinear Hypotheses. *American Journal of Sociology* 77: 898-920.

Burgess, E. W. 1926. "The Family as a Unity of Interacting Personalities." *Family* 7: 3-9.

Campbell, R. T., J. Abolafia, and G. L. Maddox. 1985. "Life Course Analysis in Social Gerontology: Using Replicated Social Surveys to Study Cohort Differences." Pp. 301-318 in *Gender and the Life Course.* Edited by A. S. Rossi. New York: Aldine.

Cohen, B. P. 1980a. "The Conditional Nature of Scientific Knowledge." Pp. 71-110 in *Theoretical Methods in Sociology*. Edited by L. Freese. Pittsburgh: Univ. of Pittsburgh Press.

Cohen, B. P. 1980b. *Developing Sociological Knowledge: Theory and Method*. Englewood Cliffs, NJ: Prentice-Hall.

Degler, C. N. 1980. *At Odds: Women and The Family in America from the Revolution to the Present*. New York: Oxford University Press.

Demos, J. 1970. *A Little Commonwealth: Family Life in Plymouth Colony*. New York: Oxford University Press.

Drabek, T. and K. Boggs. 1968. "Families in Disaster: Reactions and Relatives." *Journal of Marriage and Family* 16: 336-347.

Elder, G. 1974. *Children of the Great Depression*. Chicago: University of Chicago Press.

Elder, G. 1981. "Social History and Life Experience." Pp. 3-31 in *Present and Past in Middle Life*. Edited by D. Eichorn et al. New York: Academic Press.

Elder, G. 1983a. "Families, Kin, and the Life Course: A Sociological Perspective." Draft prepared for *The Family*. Edited by R. Parke. Chicago: University of Chicago Press.

Elder, G. 1983b. "Household, Kinship, and the Life Course: Three Perspectives on Black Families and Children." Draft prepared for *Black Children: Affective and Social Development*. Edited by M. Spencer, G. Brookins, and W. Allen. Hillsdale, NJ: Lawrence Erlbaum.

Elder, G. and R. C. Rockwell. 1978. "Economic Depression and Postwar Opportunity: A Study of Life Patterns and Health." Pp. 249-304 in *Research on Community and Mental Health*. Edited by R. A. Simmons. Greenwich, CT: JAI.

Featherman, D. 1984. *Biography, Society, and History: Individual Development as a Population Process*. Working Paper 83-29, Center for Demography and Ecology, University of Wisconsin.

Frazier, E. 1939. *The Negro Family in the United States*. Chicago: University of Chicago Press.

Freese, L. 1980. "The Problem of Cumulative Knowledge." Pp. 13-69 in *Theoretical Methods in Sociology*. Edited by L. Freese. Pittsburgh: University of Pittsburgh Press.

Goode, W. 1963. *World Revolution and Family Patterns*. New York: Macmillan.

Harveven, T. 1976. "The Family and Gender Roles in Historical Perspective." Pp. 97-118 in *Women and Men: Changing Roles, Relationships and Perceptions*. Edited by L. Carter, A. Scott, and W. Matqua. Aspen, CO: Aspen Institute for Humanistic Studies.

Hareven, T. 1978. "Introduction: The Historical Study of the Life Course." Pp. 1-16 in *Transitions: The Family and the Life Course in Historical Perspective*. Edited by T. Hareven. New York: Academic Press.

Hareven, T. 1982. *Family Time and Industrial Time*. Cambridge: Cambridge University Press.

Hill, R. 1964. "Methodological Issues in Family Development Research." *Family Process* 3: 186-205.

Hill, R. and P. Mattessich. 1979. "Family Development Theory and Life Span Development." Pp. 161-204 in *Life Span Development and Behavior*. Edited by P. Balts and O. Brim. New York: Academic Press.

Jasso, G. 1980. "A New Theory of Distributive Justice." *American Review of Sociology* 45: 3-31.

Kuhn, A. 1974. *The Logic of Social Systems*. San Francisco: Jossey-Bass.

Laslett, P. 1971. *The World We Have Lost*. New York: Charles Scribner's Sons. (pub. orig. 1965)

Laslett, P. and R. Wall. 1972. *Household and Family in Past Time*. Cambridge: Cambridge University Press.

Liker, J. and G. Elder. 1983. "Economic Hardship and Marital Relations in the 1930's." *American Sociological Review* 48: 343-359.

Litwak, E. 1960. "Geographical Mobility and Extended Family Cohesion." *American Sociological Review* 25: 385-394.

Lomnitz, L. 1977. *Networks and Marginality*. New York: Academic Press.

Modell, J., F. Furstenberg, and T. Hershberg. 1976. "Social Change and Transition to Adulthood in Historical Perspective." *Journal of Family History* 1: 7-32.

Modell, J. and T. Hareven. 1978. "Transitions: Patterns of Timing." Pp. 245-269 in *Transitions: The Family and the Life Course in Historical Perspective*. Edited by T. Hareven. New York: Academic Press.

Popper, K. 1964. *The Poverty of Historicism*. New York: Harper & Row.

Prude, J. 1976. "The Family in Context." *Labor History* 17: 422-435.

Reiss, D. 1981. *The Family's Construction of Reality*. Cambridge, MA: Harvard University Press.

Rogers, R. 1964. "Toward a Theory of Family Development." *Journal of Marriage and Family* 26: 262-270.

Rossi, A. 1985. "Introduction." In *Gender and the Life Course*. Edited by A. Rossi. New York: Aldine.

Ryder, N. 1965. "The Cohort as a Conception in the Study of Social Change." *American Sociological Review* 30: 843-861.

Schwartzweller, H., J. Brown, and J. Mangalam. 1971. *Mountain Families in Transition: A Case Study of Appalachian Migration*. University Park: Pennsylvania State University Press.

Strodtbeck, F. L. 1958. "Family Interaction, Values and Achievement." Pp. 135-194 in *Talent and Society*. Edited by D. C. McClelland, A. Baldwin, U. Bronfenbrenner, and F. L. Strodtbeck. New York: Van Nostrand Reinhold.

Sussman, M. and L. Burchinal. 1962. "Kin Family Network: Unheralded Structure in Current Conceptualizations of Family Functioning." *Marriage and Family Living* 24: 231-240.

Tallman, I. 1976. *Passion, Action and Politics*, San Francisco: W. H. Freeman.

Tallman, I. forthcoming. "Problem Solving in Families: A Revisionist View." In *Social Stress and Family Development*. Edited by J. Aldous and D. Klein. New York: Guilford.

Tallman, I. and M. Ihinger-Tallman. 1979. "Values, Distributive Justice and Social Change." *American Sociological Review* 44: 216-235.

Tallman, I., R. Marotz-Baden, and P. Pindas. 1983. *Adolescent Socialization in Cross-Cultural Comparison*. New York: Academic Press.

Thomas, W. I. 1967. *The Unadjusted Girl*. New York: Harper & Row. (pub orig. 1923)

Thomas, W. I. and F. Znaniecki. 1958. *The Polish Peasant in Europe and America*. New York: Dover. (pub orig. 1918-1920)

Uhlenberg, P. 1978. "Changing Configurations of the Life Course." Chapter 2 in *Transitions: The Family and the Life Course in Historial Perspective*. Edited by T. Hareven. New York: Academic Press.

Wirth, L. 1938. "Urbanism as a Way of Life." *American Journal of Sociology* 44: 1-24.

16

Religion and the Social Fabric

Robert Wuthnow

HOW DO WE ASSESS the changes that have taken place in religion during the decades since World War II? Can broader comparative frameworks provide a clearer perspective on these changes?

Some of the most exciting contributions to the study of modern religion have in fact attempted to specify theoretical models that place modern religion in a comparative perspective. The most general of these models portray modern religion against the backdrop of a broader evolutionary scheme that traces religious development from earliest times to the present. Although such schemes are admittedly speculative, they nevertheless provide a useful starting point from which to identify some of the salient characteristics of recent religious events. Placing these events in the context of broader evolutionary models provides an opportunity to reflect on the adequacy of the models.

This chapter briefly summarizes the perspective on modern religion found in the evolutionary theories of three prominent contemporary sociologists—Robert N. Bellah, Jurgen Habermas, and Niklas Luhmann—giving special emphasis to their predictions of how the modern social fabric may be affecting the character of religion. These perspectives are then applied to the American case to determine the degree of fit between theoretical predictions and actual developments over the past several decades. The adequacy of the theories is assessed and suggestions are made regarding additional research needed to further understanding of the relation between social change and religion.

Perspectives on Religious Evolution

The strength of evolutionary theories (apart from opinions about the idea of evolution) is that they provide general frameworks that highlight certain aspects of the modern situation and permit comparisons with previous cultural patterns. By tracing broad processes of change, evolutionary theories also suggest the direction of future developments. Theories inevitably are influenced by the times in which one lives, resulting often in biases of the kind that portray the most recent period as a high point compared with all that has gone on previously. These kinds of value judgments need to be clearly recognized, although they may be impossible to avoid entirely. But many of the assumptions implicit in evolutionary theories need not be accepted fully in order to find much of value. As a vantage point, an Archimedes point from which to view the major contours of an entire, complex period of religious change (such as that which American society has witnessed over the past several decades), they are of unique value.

There have been many efforts to describe modern religion in broad, comparative, evolutionary terms. Indeed, the sociological study of religion was largely brought into being by such attempts. Marx, Weber, and Durkheim, not to mention Comte, Toennies, and Spencer, each directed attention to the role of religion in social evolution. Theorists of more recent vintage—Talcott Parsons, Marion Levy, Jr., E. O. Wilson, Peter L. Berger, Thomas Luckmann, Bryan Wilson, to name a few—have also produced treatises in which the evolution of religion was considered, often from widely different perspectives. The perspectives to be considered here, therefore, are not exhaustive of work in this field. They do, however, constitute an important and recent corpus of work in their own right. All three manifest subtlety of argument and appreciation of the modern period that is without parallel. There is, moreover, evidence of progression and refinement as one moves from the earliest of the three to the most recent. Building from certain common premises, each adds a unique perspective on modern religion that is complementary to the other two. At the same time, none of the three has been fully understood or appreciated, perhaps because each has presented his work in a truncated and provisional fashion.

A 1964 article published in the *American Sociological Review* by sociologist of religion Robert N. Bellah outlined a broad comparative theory of religious change (reprinted in Bellah, 1970). Cast in an evolutionary framework, Bellah's description distinguished five ideal-typical patterns of religion, each of which represented a distinct stage or "relatively stable crystallization" in the evolution of religion from early societies to the present: "primitive," "archaic," "historic," "early modern," and "modern." Underlying the progression of each stage to the next was a process, in Bellah's terms, "of increasing differentiation and complexity of organization that endows the organism, social system, or whatever the unit in question may be with greater capacity to adapt to its environment than were its less complex ancestors." Archaic religions were thus depicted as more internally complex and differentiated than primitive religions in terms of their view of the world and the kind of religious action and organization they embodied; historic religions as more complex than archaic religions, and so on. For present purposes, only the modern stage requires special consideration as Bellah traces its origins well back into the nineteenth century and asserts its prevalence, even at the popular level, in the contemporary West.

Modern religious symbol systems are distinguished from all previous religions, Bellah (1970) asserts, by "the collapse of the dualism that was so crucial to all the historic religions." Rather than positing a sharp distinction between "this world" and some "other world"—between the natural and the supernatural—modern religion tends to mix the sacred and the profane. Religious claims are grounded in considerations of the human condition instead of being legitimated in terms of supernaturally revealed wisdom. God becomes more approachable, more imminent.

Seemingly a return to a more undifferentiated condition, as in primitive religion, modern religion's blurring of the distinction between natural and supernatural actually represents an increase in symbolic differentiation. Where reality was once perceived in dualistic terms, it now takes on a "multiplex" character. The allusion here is to Alfred Schutz (1962), whose discussion of "multiple realities" has influenced nearly all contemporary social science definitional treatments of religion. Reality is multiple because it is filtered through symbols: Some orient us to the here-and-now, pragmatic concerns of everyday life; some create alternative realities that we experience as fantasy, daydreaming, and insanity; still others evoke a sense of the "felt-whole" of life, providing a "sacred canopy" (to use Peter Berger's phrase) that shelters us ultimately from chaos, meaning-lessness, and existential despair.

Religious symbol systems in the modern period are uniquely self-conscious about the role of symbolism. Rather than "looking through" symbols to the truths they convey, modern religion "looks at" symbols with greater appreciation of their capacity to shape reality. In Bellah's view this capacity to differentiate symbols from the truths they convey constitutes a prime example of the more complex, more highly differentiated character of modern religion. There is, in a sense, a heightened capacity to work with symbols, to manipulate them to our advantage; an ability to subject sacred symbols to textual criticism and yet to recognize them as truth, to distinguish myth from literal fact and at the same time to gain meaning from both. In other essays Bellah elaborates, both descriptively and normatively, by suggesting that modern culture develops an attitude of "symbolic realism" toward religion that recognizes the humanly constructed nature of religious symbolism and affirms the importance of such symbolism as a source of ultimate meaning and personal integration.

It is no accident that Bellah perceives a close connection between religious symbolism and personal integration. The "self" occupies a role in modern culture that is not only prominent but problematic. Gradually emancipated from all sustaining collectivities, the self is free to determine its own destiny—even to choose its own identity. But the self is also shaped by myriad experiences that in a complex society render it fragile, multifaceted, and in need of integration. In religious matters the frightening responsibility that grew out of the Reformation and, in Weber's terms, left the believer face to face with God, has been greatly extended in the modern era. Now the individual must accept responsibility not only for the duties that God, according to the scriptures, prescribes, but also for the very choice of gods to worship. In other words, creeds must not only be lived up to, but interpreted and selectively combined, modified, and person-alized in a way that the individual finds meaningful. Moreover, because the self tends to be multidimensional and capable of transformation, the process of choosing and adapting religious symbols may acquire the character of a life-long "journey" rather than an ascriptive or once-for-all determined condition.

Religious action, and perforce religious organization, become as a result more open, flexible, and differentiated. No longer can churches or other religious organizations maintain their monopoly over the individual's relation to the ultimate. Membership standards become looser as emphasis shifts away from uniform codes of belief and moral conduct toward individual choice and freedom of conscience. At the same time, the definition of what it means to be "religious" or to have ultimate meaning expands, becoming in the process more the product of individual interpretation, such that ethical conduct in the secular world replaces narrow definitions of salvation, and a larger number of people pursue their salvation through specialized, short-term commitments outside of the church entirely. Bonhoeffer's "religionless Christianity" provides a theoretical image of the potential outcome; at the organizational level Bellah perceives the emergence of "an increasingly fluid type of organization in which many special purpose subgroups form and disband."

The process by which a thoroughly modernized form of religion makes headway is in Bellah's view not accomplished strictly at the expense of more traditional variants of religious expression. Fundamentalist religions and authoritarian religious cults that seek to impose uniform orthodox beliefs and standards of membership in believers will continue and perhaps even experience periodic revivals as reactions against the ambiguities inherent in modern society (Bellah, 1976). There will also be those for whom religious symbols become so thoroughly unsatisfactory that a purely secular world view that denies ultimate meaning is sought as a replacement. Over the long haul, however, Bellah is doubtful that either the fundamentalist or the purely secular mode of accommodation is as viable as an open, multiplex version of the sacred that provides transcendent meaning at the same time that it adapts individuals and organizations to the demands of a complex, changing society.

Although Bellah's description of modern religion is grounded in considerations of long-term social evolution, these considerations remain largely implicit. Since publication of the original essay—which compacted whole theories into a few sentences—Bellah has written many essays that expand on his statements about modern religion, but he has not spelled out in greater detail the dynamics of the underlying evolutionary model. Indeed, he has at times abandoned the more severe premises of progress and linear development on which evolutionary models are based. It is, therefore, of some importance that the idea of religious evolution has been taken up in some of the more recent essays of Jurgen Habermas (1979a, 1979b; see also McCarthy, 1978; Wuthnow et al., 1984).

Trained as a German social philosopher with intellectual debts to the Marxist and neo-Marxist "critical theory" traditions, Habermas departs from Bellah in significant ways with regard to social and religious evolution. For example, Habermas pays more explicit attention to economic development and to the state, credits the social sciences with a more prominent role in cultural evolution, and stresses secular procedures as elements of legitimation rather than emphasizing sacred or religious values. Yet Habermas, like Bellah, is deeply indebted to Weber, Heidegger, and Parsons; he ultimately rejects the Marxist emphasis on historical materialism; and he seeks an evolutionary framework that provides not only a description but also a normative guide for the discussion of modern culture. Indeed, Habermas's treatment of religion draws directly from Bellah, contributing to it mainly by recasting Bellah's efforts into his own somewhat more explicitly elaborated view of cultural evolution.

Habermas distinguishes four stages of cultural evolution: "neolithic," "archaic," "developed," and "modern." The first three correspond roughly to Bellah's "primitive," "archaic," and "historic" stages; Habermas's "modern" period subsumes Bellah's "early modern" and "modern" stages (Bellah also suggests that these two may be treated together). In principle, Habermas's stages are distinguished from one another on the basis of different principles of institutional organization, different levels of productive capacity, and different capacities for societal adaptation to complex circumstances. In practice, the stages are distinguished mainly, as with Bellah, by ever-increasing levels of cultural complexity and differentiation.

Neolithic cultures manifest relatively low levels of cultural differentiation: Motives and behavioral consequences remain undifferentiated, as do actions and world views, human and divine events, natural and social phenomena, and tradition and myth. Archaic cultures make greater degrees of differentiation possible among all of these categories, thus permitting greater clarity about the linearity of history, greater opportunities for calculated action with respect to the control of nature, and expanded opportunities for the development of rational law and the state. Developed cultures contribute additional layers of differentiation, replacing myth and tradition with unified cosmologies and higher religions, articulating well-codified moral precepts, and positing universalistic principles as modes of legal and political legitimation.

Modern culture, which coincides roughly with the period since the Reformation, is typified chiefly by an erosion of confidence in the validity of higher-order principles. Reason, as a process of systematic reflection, replaces absolute, taken-for-granted laws as the basis on which cultural meaning and coherence rests. As a result faith is no longer taken for granted but becomes objectified as a focus for the application of reason. With reason also comes a greater degree of self-consciousness about the procedures used to arrive at and test the validity of statements concerning religion, morality, and nature.

Habermas is here alluding to more than simply the proverbial "warfare" between reason and faith that scholars since the Enlightenment have tended to emphasize. He is also asserting that faith itself increasingly becomes subject to tests of reason, logic, and even empirical procedure. As Bellah also observes, this process leads to greater self-awareness about "statements," in distinction to the meanings conveyed by these statements. Where Bellah sees a somewhat ready solution to the inherent tension between reason and faith, each maintaining its own validity within separate realms, Habermas sees greater evidence of continuing tension. His view suggests considerable, but by no means total, retreat on the part of religion against the onslaught of rationality.

Where religion has a continuing role to play, according to Habermas (here in agreement with Bellah), is in providing personal integration, unity, subjective meaning, and a unified self-identity. Like Peter Berger, whom he quotes, Habermas perceives a requirement for some form of symbolic universe—a sheltering canopy—to integrate the various systems of action in which an individual engages. Religious world views played a prominent role in fulfilling this requirement in "developed" cultures: Greater differentiation of human action from nature allowed a greater sense of individual identity to develop; a unified picture of the forces governing the universe contributed to the internalization of a coherent set of moral principles that in turn facilitated greater unity of the self; and, as Weber observed, religious explanations for the misfortunes of nature helped individuals and collectivities to function more effectively in the face of risk, grief, and ultimate doubt. In the modern period religion continues to perform many of these traditional functions.

However, the role of religion in the modern period has, in Habermas's view, become progressively restricted. With modernization has come greater control over the exigencies of nature, thus diminishing the need for religious explanations for these exigencies and increasing the importance of specialized knowledge devoted strictly to the empirical understanding of nature. Religion has accordingly come to focus less on metaphysical assertions about the world and more on exclusively subjective concerns about individual meaning and integration. In short, religion has been pushed increasingly into the realm of what Habermas calls "civil privatism."

The "privatization" of religion is an emphasis that Habermas shares, in some respects, with Bellah, and indeed with many other observers of contemporary religion. But Habermas remains too concerned with social processes to perceive much value in a religion that merely gives interior solace to the individual. Like Bellah, he recognizes that much of the traditional importance of religion lay in its capacity to instill a sense of community and perform socially integrative functions. For Bellah this function continues to be performed largely through the application of religious values, not through the institutionalized church but through the culturally differentiated set of religious symbols that he, following Rousseau, calls the "civil religion." For Habermas, however, the notion of civil religion seems to be an unworkable throwback to a less modernized set of values.

Perhaps because of his own roots in the more thoroughly secularized setting of western Europe, Habermas sees little continuing significance in the role of traditional religious values as a means of social legitimation and integration. The social sciences, in his view, have seriously undermined the plausibility of such values, rendering them relativistic and secondary to a kind of technical reason devoted to the solution of social problems through the application of technical knowledge. Habermas admits that the social sciences have been relatively ineffective in actually resolving social problems, let alone providing substitutes for religious answers about death, grief, illness, and tragedy. Nevertheless, he maintains that the social sciences, by creating awareness of the social constructedness of religious symbols, have made it impossible to rely on absolute religious claims for social integration. Instead, social integration will, for better or worse, depend chiefly on the rational-legal procedures that have been developed in modern societies for the conduct of business and government and for the resolution of disputes.

Still, Habermas does hold out one function that religious symbols may be able to perform—the function of facilitating communication.

This is at first glance an anomalous position to find Habermas taking because he generally appears to be skeptical of religion, treating it as a form of ideology that systematically distorts communication by virtue of the fact that religious people generally seem to be unable to abandon their own suppositions long enough to truly consider the interests and values of others. Yet in a few scattered passages that remain largely undeveloped, he makes reference to the possibility that some understandings of modern religion seem to promote rather than inhibit communication. Noting the theological work of Metz and Pannenberg in particular, he argues that a new concept of God is evident in this work, which recognizes the socially constructed character of all conceptions of the divine, yet asserts the utility of such symbols because of their emphasis on community and reconciliation.

Habermas then, like Bellah, perceives a serious degree of erosion associated with institutionalized religion—so much so in fact that he seldom bothers to discuss organized religion. In his evolutionary perspective the growing differentiation of modern culture has placed religion in competition with reason, the natural sciences, and most recently the social sciences, all of which have taken over many of the topics on which religion traditionally spoke with authority. In addition, modern religion has become more internally differentiated such that religious knowledge has become more distinct from religious experience and meaning, religious techniques have become more distinct from religious values, and religious statements have become objectified over against the largely privatized meanings and interpretations they are given. Finally, growing self-awareness about the situational relativity of religious symbols, though reducing their absolute plausibility, has perhaps enhanced their role as objects and facilitators of communication about social values.

In criticizing Habermas's work Niklas Luhmann (1982, 1984) has extended the discussion of religious evolution in much the same way that Habermas did for Bellah. A professor of sociology at the University of Bielefeld in West Germany, Luhmann has emerged as one of the leading theorists in contemporary sociology. Known until recently only through his debates with Habermas, he has begun to attract considerable attention among American scholars in his own right. Like the classical theorists, he treats religion as a basic feature of modern society.

Luhmann is a systems theorist, somewhat in the same genre as Talcott Parsons, who understands social evolution chiefly in terms of social differentiation. Thus modern societies differ from traditional societies mainly in terms of having a greater number of clearly differentiated social spheres or subsystems. The basic institutional pattern of modern societies was laid down between the sixteenth and eighteenth centuries with the emergence of a relatively autonomous political system that was accompanied by increasingly autonomous systems in other realms as well, such as science, law, education, and art. In the process religion gradually came to be viewed as just one sphere among many. Like Habermas, Luhmann believes that modern religion has largely lost its capacity to legitimate and unify the society as a whole. Religion is not likely to die out; it may even flourish among reactionary groups critical of political and economic processes. But it must function increasingly without significant connections to other spheres of social action.

This, at least, was Luhmann's position until recently—a fairly pessimistic view of modern religion that did not differ substantially from that of many social theorists in the nineteenth century. But Luhmann's broader framework has been in flux, and so have his views on religion. Like Habermas he has immersed himself in the growing literature on language, discourse, and communication, coming increasingly to conceive of society itself as a vast system of communicative action, and this perspective has given him a number of novel ideas about the nature of religion.

In "Society, Meaning, Religion—Based on Self-Reference," presented at the 1984 meetings of the American Sociological Association, Luhmann outlines the core of his ideas about modern religion. Building on his previous work, he continues to think of modern society as a product of evolutionary development. But he also suggests that a fundamental characteristic of modern society is its inevitable and enduring confrontation with paradox. At one level, the basic paradox confronting modern society can be seen in the fact that there must be closure for communication to occur, yet there must also be openness in order to cope with the high degree of complexity and change in modern society. At another level, paradox is seen in the fact that all statements about the world imply that other possibilities are also available and thus are contingent. In short, we live in a world where, paradoxically, contingency is necessary. It is from this simple recognition of paradox that Luhmann develops his views of the functions of religion.

He writes, "The plentitude and void of a paradoxical world is the ultimate reality of religion. The meaning of meaning is both richness of references and tautological circularity." Because modern society is both a closed system and yet inevitably constrained to remain open to unanticipated contingencies, it must cope with the paradoxical nature of its situation; Luhmann defines religion as the set of forms that society develops to "deparadoxize the world." Religious forms "absorb" paradox, resolving it by revealing that seeming opposites are really one and the same.

The essential insight here is seen most vividly by contrasting it with Weber's description of the function of traditional religion. In his view this function was to "make sense" of the universe by demonstrating that everything could be related to everything else, could be "unified" into a single whole. Thus good and evil, suffering and joy, life and death all became reconciled in a single overarching framework. But Luhmann's argument is that even this framework cannot be accepted as final. It is a system that necessarily recognizes possibilities for meaning beyond itself. This is the paradoxical tension with which modern religion must always deal.

Any concrete religious symbol system or organization is thus inevitably precarious. It exists as a form that resolves ambiguity, but this form must always grant the reality of ambiguity. Religious systems therefore undergo nearly continuous transformations, both altering their social contexts and being altered by them. They become endangered by their own successes, resolving paradox to their long-term detriment, and necessitating new conceptions of paradox itself. Luhmann thus conceives of religion undergoing an evolutionary process but disagrees with Bellah and Habermas in denying that this process can be reduced to a model of discrete stages.

Nevertheless, some significant landmarks in the evolution of religion can be identified. Because the paradoxes religion deals with pertain, in Luhmann's view, to the nature of communication, these landmarks have mostly to do with developments in the nature of communication. One was the invention of the alphabet. This invention led to the capacity to produce written religious texts, which then, along with the gods and their utterances, became objects of religious reflection. No longer could priests and prophets simply offer their own renditions of the supernatural; they were now constrained by what the scriptures said. Luhmann suggests, not entirely facetiously, that the development of Christianity itself may be seen as a desperate attempt by religious specialists to survive the invention of the written word.

This of course happened centuries ago. It continues to affect the course of modern religion insofar as scripture and "the word" have remained to a high degree objects of self-conscious reflection in the Christian religion. As Luhmann notes, the New Testament canon itself seems to reflect a pattern of faith that is more closely circumscribed by religious texts than is the Old Testament. But none of this gets at the distinctive developments that have characterized religion in the twentieth century.

Luhmann's depiction of contemporary religion includes many of the themes already in Bellah and Habermas: privatization, differentiation of beliefs from organizations, special purpose organizations, declining capacity to legitimate political and economic action. He also specifies Bellah's notion of greater differentiation between the supernatural and natural realms by observing again the importance of communication: God remains an object with whom we can communicate; in contrast, we do not normally talk with nature. Most of these are, however, developments that Luhmann traces as far back as the origins of Christianity or even to the Greek city-states.

For the contemporary period the main problem facing religion is, in Luhmann's judgment, that of communicating with a god who has withdrawn into silence. Can we, given our own increasing awareness of the nature of symbols, realize the functions of our beliefs and yet hold firmly to them? Can paradox be resolved if we are aware that the role of our beliefs is to resolve paradox? His answer is that we probably cannot. Yet he also admits that this degree of self-reflectivity is probably limited mainly to the better educated segments of the population.

There is, however, a curious paradox within Luhmann's own discussion of the paradoxical nature of religion. Recognizing both the value of deparadoxization and the manner in which communication functions, it may be possible to reconsecrate the churches for this very purpose. That is, the function that the churches may be best able to fulfill, even in modern society, is that of promoting communication with God. Within the insulated sphere that the churches provide it may be possible to evoke a form of reality in which communication with an otherwise invisible deity makes sense. It may not be possible for such a reality to be constructed for everyone or on a broad scale, for communication with an invisible deity clearly runs counter to the norms of modern culture. Yet this contrast may be important in itself. As Luhmann argues, "Churches seem to cultivate countermores, depending for their success on being different. Religion may have become counter-adaptive, and this may be the very reason for its survival and for its recurrent revival as well. The church itself, by now, may have become a carnival, i.e., the reversal of normal order."

This vision of "church as carnival" contrasts sharply with the ideas of either Bellah or Habermas. Starting from the same premises concerning social complexity and cultural differentiation, Luhmann nevertheless is led along a different route by his emphasis on the paradoxical nature of social relations. Although silent in this perspective, God has by no means collapsed into a monistic world view or been replaced by secular-rational norms of discourse. Religion fails to provide a clear sense of broader societal integration in all three of the models, but in Luhmann's the emphasis on communication tends to preserve the idea of religious community, if only as counterculture. For him, the churches have a lasting, albeit restricted, social function to fulfill.

These of course are broad theoretical visions not to be used, as Bellah reminds us, "as a procrustean bed into which the facts of history are to be forced but a theoretical construction against which historical facts may be illuminated." How well, then, do these theoretical constructions illuminate the historical facts of American religion in the period since World War II?

The Religious Fabric

In varying ways Bellah, Habermas, and Luhmann all stress the importance of greater self-awareness with respect to symbolism as a feature of modern religion. There is, in fact, much evidence that religious symbolism has become increasingly objectified for self-reflection at least at some levels. Theological reflection has, for example, converged to a remarkable degree with some aspects of the social sciences in its concern for the symbolically constructed character of reality. Munich professor of theology Wolfhart Pannenberg (1983, p. 35), in a passage strikingly social scientific in tenor, observes, "It is only by symbols and symbolic language that the larger community to which we belong is present in our experiences and activities." And he goes on to argue that the church not only uses symbols but is itself symbolic. In a similar manner, Yale theologian George A. Lindbeck (1984, p. 33) writes, "A religion can be viewed as a kind of cultural and/or linguistic framework or medium that shapes the entirety of life and thought." Both writers develop their arguments, as Bellah might have predicted, not from metaphysical first principles but from anthropological considerations of the nature of symbolism. In applications of discourse analysis and deconstructionism other theologians have taken the investigation of religious symbols even further (e.g., Brummer, 1982; Taylor, 1984).

At the popular level evidence of greater self-consciousness about the nature of religious symbolism is naturally less apparent. To broach the subject of mythology or textual criticism remains a mark of extreme heresy among the 38% of the public who believes that the Bible is not only divinely inspired but to be taken literally. Yet there are also indications that a substantial number of believers have achieved some degree of mental differentiation between their faith and the symbols with which it is expressed. For example, among those who believe the Bible to be divinely inspired, only half regard it as absolutely free of errors (Gallup, 1984). Or for another example, a study of Lutheran church members showed that only one member in three felt it possible to prove the existence of God, and of these only about half felt this could be done from evidence in the Bible (Wuthnow, 1983).

Studies of new religious movements are particularly replete with evidence of the self-conscious application and manipulation of symbols. Because many of these movements grew from small groups in which symbols were either invented or synthesized from other sources, members tended to be keenly aware of the power of symbols. Being in a position to remake their own rituals and ideologies, and seeing the immediate effect of these symbols on group life, they quickly developed a heightened sense of "symbolic consciousness." Movements that sought to block out the effects of taken-for-granted constructions of reality through meditation, drugs, or religious experiences also sharpened their members' sensitivities to the nature of symbolism (e.g., Stone, 1976; Bainbridge, 1978).

Bellah's argument that greater self-consciousness about religious symbolism tends to be accompanied by a greater emphasis on personal interpretation and a decline in tacit acceptance of official creeds also finds support in a variety of evidence. In the Lutheran study mentioned previously only half of the respondents felt God had given clear, detailed rules for living that apply to everyone; most of the remainder felt that individuals have to figure out how to apply God's rules to their own situations. The study also included members' views of the official theological positions of the church, first by interviewing theologians to determine what the official positions were, then by surveying pastors to see if these positions were taught, and finally by surveying members about their own beliefs. The core theological tenets of the church, as described by its theologians, consisted chiefly of three simple propositions: that Christ was fully God and fully man, that Christ was crucified to forgive our sins, and that men and women are sinners whom God loves and is giving new life. These tenets were uniformly accepted by the clergy and, partly because of the prescribed schedule of sermon topics, emphasized from the pulpit. Yet the laity survey found that only one member in three affirmed all three of these propositions. On other teachings, such as the church's views of baptism and communion, agreement was equally low.

The evidence is less clear with respect to Bellah's claim that modern religion is principally characterized by a collapse of the dualistic world view that distinguishes God from man, the supernatural from the natural, this world from a world beyond life. As Bellah himself observes, upwards of 90% of the American population affirms some belief in the existence of God. Such affirmation scarcely answers the question of whether there has been, as he puts it, "a massive reinterpretation" of the nature of God. But more refined questions suggest that a sizable number of Americans still express their faith in dualistic terms. For instance, nine persons in ten believe Jesus Christ actually lived, seven in ten believe he was truly God, and six in ten think one must believe in the divinity of Christ to be a Christian (Gallup, 1983). The results of studies documenting consistently high levels of belief in life after death, heaven, and Christ's presence in heaven also point to the survival of a strong element of religious dualism in American culture.

But if dualism continues, evidence also suggests that God has, in a sense, become "subjectivized" rather than existing as a metaphysical, transcendent, or omnipotent being. A study conducted in the San Francisco Bay Area found, among persons who said they definitely believed in God, that eight out of ten believed in God's influence on their personal lives, but only about half felt that God influenced social events (Piazza and Glock, 1979, p. 72). In the Lutheran study only three in ten believed that God "shapes events directly through nations and social affairs."

A good deal of speculation—and some research—has also suggested that God is relevant to contemporary Americans mainly because the sense of God's presence is subjectively comforting; that is, religion solves personal problems rather than addressing broader questions. This is true, perhaps particularly so, among evangelicals who in the past at least tended to emphasize God's sovereignty in all things. Now, however, the bulk of evangelical literature focuses mainly on emotional and psychological concerns (Hunter, 1983, pp. 91-99).

Although it may be, then, that a high degree of supernaturalism remains in American religion as a formal tenet, the operational relevance of the supernatural may have largely collapsed into the interior concerns of the self. This conclusion also tends to be supported by the high degree of interest surveys document in questions of personal meaning and purpose, and in the number of quasi-religious self-help movements that have developed since the 1960s (Wuthnow, 1976, 1985).

At the level of religious organization there is also much to support Bellah's contention that religious expression has become increasingly differentiated from traditional religious institutions. High rates of denominational switching and interdenominational marriage, reduced levels of denominational identity and cross-denominational tensions, as well as pervasive amounts of contact across denominational lines all point toward a declining monopoly of specific religious traditions over the enactment of religious convictions. Evidence on the numbers of individuals who consider themselves religious, or who hold certain tenets of faith, and yet do not belong to religious organizations or attend regularly point in a similar direction. The idea of "special purpose groups" also gains confirmation from the evidence on rising numbers of such groups and extent of participation in these groups.

At the most general levels of societal integration and legitimation the evidence, though subject to alternative interpretations, suggests the continuing relevance of religiously inspired ethical concerns, but also reveals the diminishing weight of religious arguments as such, relative to the weight these arguments carry at the individual level. The most obvious religious development with respect to societal integration has been the rise of the New Christian Right (Liebman and Wuthnow, 1983). On the surface this movement—and the countermovements it has elicited—suggests a continuing tendency for religious values to find their way into the public domain as a part of debates over societal goals. Liberals and conservatives alike have resorted to religious arguments in defense of claims about public morality and the role of the state in defending public morality. Yet the very dissension that has been produced by the religious right points up the difficulties of gaining any kind of broad consensus around traditional religious values. Where tacit agreement has been achieved is mostly in relation to the underlying rational-legal procedures to which political action must pay head.

Habermas's assertions overlap considerably with those of Bellah, especially with regard to the privatization of religious expression, the decline of religious orthodoxy, and the erosion of religious institutions. Thus his claims illuminate many of the same bits of evidence as those just considered. His general emphasis, however, tends to suggest an even more pervasive effect on religion due to rationality, natural science, and the social sciences. The evidence suggests that all of these influences have indeed exercised a largely negative effect on traditional religious beliefs and practices. Not only do scientists—and especially social scientists—demonstrate radically low levels of religious commitment, but scientific and social scientific meaning systems appear to operate as functional alternatives to traditional theistic ideas for a number of people, and technical rationality plays an increasingly important legitimating function in the wider society.

At the same time, a clear case cannot be made in support of Habermas's claim that the sciences have so reduced the physical and social contingencies of modern life as to make religious world views largely irrelevant. To the contrary, the sciences seem only to have contributed to a greater degree of sensitivity about the contingencies of life. Indeed, Luhmann's suggestion that modern society is inevitably confronted with the paradoxes of its own contingency seems to be more applicable. Thus the concerns that continue to inspire deep religious discussion, such as the prospect of nuclear annihilation, rights of the unborn, euthanasia, world hunger, Third World dependence, and so on, are clearly the evidence of lingering contingencies in a technologized world.

At a more theological or philosophical level there is, however, a very significant development that Habermas's discussion helps to illuminate; namely, the manner in which religion itself has been redefined in the face of advances in the realm of natural reason. Modern definitions of religion, as Bellah suggests, have come to focus increasingly on symbolism and meaning. Writers such as Clifford Geertz, Peter Berger, and Bellah conceive of religion as a special kind of symbol system that evokes a sense of ultimate, transcendent, encompassing meaning. But what this conception does, in addition to drawing on the social sciences, is to save religion from the onslaught of post-Enlightenment positivism. Specifically, this feat is accomplished by positing religion as a type of symbolism concerned with the meaning of the whole of life. The meanings of anything less—of selected aspects of the world—can be identified by the contexts or frameworks in which those aspects are located. But the meaning of the whole lies beyond any specific context; as Wittgenstein (1974) observed, "The meaning of the world lies outside of the world." Thus the "world of facts" with which the empirical sciences deal must be seen ultimately in another context—a context given meaning by religious symbols—which is beyond the scope of the empirical sciences.

It is, therefore, not irrelevant to Habermas's argument that modern religion tends to be defined the way it is. Not only has there been a greater degree of differentiation between symbols and truth, but there has also been an increasing degree of differentiation among kinds of symbols. As a result religious symbols have been put beyond the reach of rational and empirical criticism by identifying them with a different type of reality construction. Habermas, it should be noted, has himself contributed to this development by identifying different types of validity claims that may be embodied in ordinary discourse— some of which can be subjected to empirical criticism, others of which remain matters of nonempirical metaphysical or philosophical reflection.

Luhmann's discussion, lastly, raises distinct questions mostly in relation to his ideas about communication with God and the role of church as carnival. Although his argument recognizes the precariousness of efforts to communicate with an invisible, silent God, the abiding paradox of living in a world that recognizes its own contingency forces him to concede that such communication will likely continue as a feature of modern life. Much evidence in fact suggests that, despite considerable erosion of religious practices in other areas, manifestations of attempts to communicate with the divine remain strikingly prominent. Prayer in particular seems to have remained a strong feature of contemporary life in comparison with other kinds of religious behavior. For example, a 1984 Gallup survey showed that 60% of the American public personally considered prayer to be very important and another 22% regarded it as fairly important; by comparison, only 39% thought reading the Bible was very important, and 38% thought the same about being part of a close religious fellowship group (Gallup, 1984). Other surveys have documented high levels of interest and involvement in prayer, a high degree of belief in the efficacy of prayer, and a strong tendency to regard prayer as actual communication with God (e.g., Gallup, 1983; Wuthnow, 1983).

Apart from prayer, evidence also suggests that sensing a relationship with God continues to be highly valued and that many people in fact feel they are close to God. The 1984 Gallup survey showed that "growing into a deeper relationship with God" was considered very important by 56% of the public and fairly important by an additional 26%. In a 1983 Gallup survey, 64% of the public felt their relationship to God was very important to their own sense of self-worth and nine out of ten expressed satisfaction with this relationship.

Luhmann observes with some interest that modern religion seems to depict God chiefly as an all-loving being, thus reducing much of the motivation for salvation from damnation that was present in historic Christianity. This depiction may in fact serve a positive role in sustaining the plausibility of communication with an invisible God in the modern era; that is, communication may be easier to sustain when God is envisioned not as distant judge but as lover and friend— as an intimate "God within." At any rate, indications are clear that contemporary imagery regards God in such terms. Of every nine persons, eight say they feel that God loves them; 80% say they feel close to God; and, negatively, only 16% say they have ever felt afraid of God (Gallup, 1983, 1984). In the Lutheran study cited earlier nine in ten said God loved them and was giving them new life; only a quarter felt that they were sinners under the wrath and judgment of God. And evidence from a 1984 NORC survey indicates that, although images of God as judge and king persist, substantial numbers of Americans lean toward more intimate images such as lover and spouse (Greeley, 1984).

Luhmann's idea of the church as a kind of counterculture devoted to maintaining the plausibility of communication with God also appears consistent with a variety of evidence. Although this is by no means a new role for the church to fulfill, it is a role that the church seems to have carried on with surprising success as the culture has become increasingly secularized. To be sure, the religionless Christianity of humanistic ethicalism that Bellah speaks of is evident in many mainline churches. But the importance of the religious community gathered for worship and fellowship with God is also strikingly evident. Protestants and Catholics alike have shown increasing interest in liturgy as the heart of such communal activity. Pannenberg

(1983, p. 31) writes, "The rediscovery of the Eucharist may prove to be the most important event in Christian spirituality of our time, of more revolutionary importance than even the liturgical renewal of our time."

As the sense of guilt and sin that became prominent in the teachings of the Protestant reformers erodes, Pannenberg suggests, the church will increasingly find its reason for existing that of serving as a symbol of wholeness in a broken world. This is the purpose of the Eucharist: to dramatize communion with God and to evoke the healing presence of God in the world. Moreover, in an argument with which both Habermas and Luhmann have shown familiarity, he suggests that the Eucharist can be interpreted in distinctly modern terms as a symbol that dramatizes freedom by casting ossified structures in doubt and that enhances adaptiveness and communication by emphasizing openness and provisionality: "The human predicament of social life is not ultimately realized in the present political order of society, but is celebrated in the worship of the church, if only in the form of the symbolic presence of the kingdom to come" (Pannenberg, 1983, p. 47).

The typical congregant may well not participate in "the worship of the church" with the sense of sophistication that Pannenberg suggests. Yet in some form the church does continue to attract largely as a place in which to experience the closeness of God and the communion of fellow worshippers. Among the gratifications from church mentioned most often in a national survey of regular church attenders (Annenberg/Gallup, 1984), for example, were the following: feeling close to God (77%), the experience of worshipping God (60%), and a sense of companionship or fellowship (54%).

Theoretical Considerations

If the foregoing is any indication, American religion demonstrates many of the characteristics that theorists have identified with modern culture. Many religious beliefs and practices remain much in evidence, contrary to simpler predictions that have envisioned a sheer decline in religious vitality. These beliefs and practices may have retained their vitality in fact by accommodating to the contemporary cultural situation. In becoming more oriented to the self, in paying more explicit attention to symbolism, in developing a more flexible organizational style, and in nurturing specialized worship experiences, American religion has become more complex, more internally differentiated, and thus more adaptable to a complex, differentiated society.

For several reasons this is a fairly speculative conclusion, however. In the first place it has to be defended largely without comparable evidence from other times or places. Some of the characteristics of American religion that bear directly on the theories of Bellah, Habermas, and Luhmann can be shown to have intensified even in the short period since World War II. But many of these characteristics can legitimately be questioned as to whether they are truly distinct to the recent period, whether they are intensifying, or whether they might also have characterized Western religion a century or even a millennium ago.

Another difficulty is that evolutionary theories tend to be cast in such broad terms that data can be readily manipulated to support them when the same data might also be viewed from a less sympathetic angle. It often seems less than clear what counts as evidence of increasing differentiation and what might be regarded as counterevidence. Habermas has indeed argued specifically against trying to make such connections with concrete historical examples, suggesting that evolutionary theories are better viewed as normative guides toward the future than as testable theories. Thus it may be that American religion only seems to have accommodated itself to modernity because of a selective interpretation of the facts.

This criticism, however, should not overshadow the positive role that evolutionary perspectives can play. If we admit that their purpose is not to provide us with testable hypotheses, then we can make use of them, as suggested earlier, to illuminate what might otherwise seem to be disparate or insignificant developments. We are led to think about the possibility that some seeming signs of decay in American religion may actually have beneficial consequences for its survival over a longer period. For example, the decline of orthodoxy may be associated with a rise in personalized religious interpretations that make religion more adaptable to changing circumstances. We are also led to think about the relations among certain developments and the significance of these developments in a wider context. If it is true that religion is becoming more highly differentiated, then greater effectiveness in dealing with new distinctions, with new understandings of symbolism, and with new kinds of religious organizations may be especially important.

The more serious limitation of existing evolutionary approaches to religion is that they fail to illuminate much about the relations between religion and the broader social environment. Bellah, Habermas, and Luhmann all relate religious evolution to the growth of complexity and subsystem differentiation in the larger society. But none of the three draws explicit connections between these two levels of development; that is, of the kind that would indicate how a particular form of religious differentiation might be related to a specific example of societal complexity. And because all three leave open possibilities for maladaptive reactions, it becomes exceedingly difficult to pin down what constitutes complexity and what the effects of complexity may be.

Beyond this general problem, mechanisms of cultural change are seldom identified either. At times it appears that each theorist regards religious evolution, like other dimensions of cultural evolution, as resulting from its own internal dynamics. Previous symbolic structures set the constraints and provided the opportunities for new cultural developments. Thus one is forced to look mainly at the internal logic of Christianity, the legacy of Reformation Protestantism, and theological debates of the eighteenth and nineteenth centuries to understand what has shaped the character of American religion. Implicit in this approach is the view that institutional differentiation has progressed to such a high degree that religion is no longer significantly affected by anything other than developments within the religious institution itself.

Habermas has openly challenged this view in some of his more recent work. Although he holds the view that the general patterns of cultural evolution are internally determined, he observes that other aspects of social structure are likely to be particularly influential during the transition from one general phase to another. He specifically mentions protest groups and religious movements as examples of mechanisms that may play a critical role in times of transition.

In the American case evolutionary theories are most deficient in interpreting religious characteristics in relation to elements of the broader social fabric. Most of the empirical characteristics that fit in one way or another with these theories do not apply uniformly to the entire population. Many of them pertain most clearly to the young and to the better educated—factors that suggest the growing prominence of these characteristics. But the theories provide little help in answering questions such as, why education, and why now?

What is obviously needed, as a complement to highly abstract evolutionary theories, are comparisons with other times and places. The recent period in American history has been fraught with rapid changes in education, technology, and in the character of the state. To understand how these developments have affected religion in the past, and how they may shape American religion in the foreseeable future, comparisons are needed that draw on concrete historical material.

References

Annenberg/Gallup Study Team. 1984. *Religious Television in America*. Philadelphia: University of Pennsylvania.

Bainbridge, W. S. 1978. *Satan's Power*. Berkeley: University of California Press.

Bellah, R. N. 1970. *Beyond Belief*. New York: Harper & Row.

Bellah, R. N. 1976. "New Religious Consciousness and the Crisis of Modernity." Pp. 333-352 in *The New Religious Consciousness*. Edited by C. Y. Glock and R. N. Bellah. Berkeley: University of California Press.

Brummer, V. 1982. *Theology and Philosophical Inquiry*. Philadelphia: Westminster.

Gallup Organization. 1982. *Self Esteem Study*. Princeton, NJ: Author.

Gallup Organization. 1983. *Jesus Christ in the Lives of Americans Today*. Princeton, NJ: Author.

Gallup Organization. 1984. *How Can Christian Liberals and Conservatives be Brought Together?* Princeton, NJ: Author.

Greeley, A. M. 1984. *Religious Imagery as a Predictor Variable in the General Social Survey*. Presented at a Plenary Session of the Society for the Scientific Study of Religion.

Habermas, J. 1979a. *Communication and the Evolution of Society*. Boston: Beacon.

Habermas, J. 1979b. "History and Evolution." *Telos* 39: 5-44.

Hunter, J. D. 1983. *American Evangelicalism*. New Brunswick, NJ: Rutgers University Press.

Liebman, R. and R. Wuthnow. (Eds.) 1983. *The New Christian Right*. New York: Aldine.

Lindbeck, G. A. 1984. *The Nature of Doctrine: Religion and Theology in a Postliberal Age*. Philadelphia: Westminster.

Luhmann, N. 1982. *The Differentiation of Society*. New York: Columbia University Press.

Luhmann, N. 1984. *Society, Meaning, Religion—Based on Self-Reference*. Paper presented at the annual meetings of the American Sociological Association.

McCarthy, T. 1978. *The Critical Theory of Jurgen Habermas*. Cambridge, MA: MIT Press.

Pannenberg, W. 1983. *Christian Spirituality*. Philadelphia: Westminster.

Piazza, T. and C. Y. Glock. 1979. "Images of God and Their Social Meanings." Pp. 69-92 in *The Religious Dimension*. Edited by R. Wuthnow. New York: Academic Press.

Schutz, A. 1962. *Collected Papers*, Vol. 1. The Hague: Nijhoff.

Stone, D. 1976. "The Human Potential Movement." In *The New Religious Consciousness*. Edited by C. Y. Glock and R. N. Bellah. Berkeley: University of California Press.

Taylor, M. C. 1984. *Erring: A Postmodern A/theology*. Chicago: University of Chicago Press.

Wittgenstein, L. 1974. *Tractatus Logico-Philosophicus*. Atlantic Highlands, NJ: Humanities Press.

Wuthnow, R. 1976. *The Consciousness Reformation*. Berkeley: University of California Press.

Wuthnow, R. 1983. "Religious Beliefs and Experiences: Basic Patterns." Pp. 10-32 in *Views from the Pews: Christian Beliefs and Attitudes*. Edited by R. A. Johnson. Philadelphia: Fortress.

Wuthnow, R. 1985. "Religion as Sacred Canopy." In *Making Sense of Modern Times: Peter L. Berger and the Vision of Interpretive Sociology*. Edited by J. D. Hunter and S. Ainlay. London: Routledge & Kegan Paul.

Wuthnow, R., J. D. Hunter, A. Bergesen, and E. Kurzweil. 1984. *Cultural Analysis: The Work of Peter L. Berger, Mary Douglas, Michel Foucault, and Jurgen Habermas*. London: Routledge & Kegan Paul.

17

Media Linkages of the Social Fabric

S. J. Ball-Rokeach

THE 1984 ASA THEMATIC SESSION on "media linkages of the social fabric" occurred a quarter of a century after Bernard Berelson's (1959) assessment that "the state of communication research" was dismal and a dozen years after Gans (1972) declared a "famine" in American media studies. More recently, Holz and Wright (1979) noted how little sociologists know about the media's role in socialization and social change—central processes constituting, and changing, the social fabric. This chapter begins with a brief analysis of the possible causes of the lack of vitality of sociological inquiry in this vital area. A representative set of the more than 25 papers devoted to media analysis that were presented at the 1984 ASA Meetings is then reviewed. This is followed by an assessment of the present state of the art, with respect to quantity and quality, and a possible resurgence of media studies within American sociology.

Accounting for the Decline

At least four major factors might explain the lack of sociologically informed programmatic theory and research into the mass media from the mid-1950s to early 1980s. The first three are internal to the discipline, the last external. Discussion of these factors in this chapter is limited to American sociology because the historical and structural conditions in English and European sociology have been more conducive to systematic media inquiry.

Premature Closure Concerning the "Power" of the Media System

The 1940s and early 1950s are generally viewed as the heyday of media studies in general, and of sociological media analysis in particular (e.g., Berelson, 1959). This period was spearheaded in American sociology by the conceptually and methodologically innovative work of Lazarsfeld and his many colleagues and students—for example, Berelson, Katz, and Merton. It came to a close with a set of broad theoretical and empirical conclusions best articulated in Klapper's (1960) work, *The Effects of Mass Communication*. In capsule form, those conclusions were as follows: (a) Mills (1939) and other left-wing or mass society theorists were wrong in their attribution of enormous sociopolitical power to the mass media; (b) the evidence from the classic research reported, especially in *The People's Choice* (Lazarsfeld et al., 1944) and in *Personal Influence* (Katz and Lazarsfeld, 1955), demonstrated that the media have only weak sociopolitical effects, because (c) the processes of selective exposure, selective perception, and interpersonal influence equip the audience and its interpersonal networks with the "power" to determine both short-term and long-term media effects. This conclusion, valid as it may have been for its time and for its analysis of voting behavior, was interpreted and generalized by Klapper (1960) to mean that in analyses of all social phenomena, the media system can be expected to be a relatively impotent force when compared to family, peer, or other social influences. This "weak media-powerful audience" position was widely accepted, and is known today in its elaborated form as the "uses and gratifications" approach (Katz, 1980).

From a commonsense point of view, young and talented sociologists are not likely to study what are judged by their peers and mentors to be "weak" or unimportant social forces. We can, however, identify two of the more important reasons why a reexamination of the "weak media" dictum as it is applied to political phenomena or, more generally, to all social phenomena, should be undertaken. One is that the structure of the American political system and political action in the mid-1980s has changed markedly from that of the 1940s. Changes, such as the rise of primaries and the decline of political parties, may reasonably be expected to empower the media system not only with respect to individuals' political behavior, but, probably more important, with respect to political decision making. As Jeffery Alexander (1981) has pointed out, we can expect the power of the media system in matters of politics to rise when traditional political structures, such as the party system, are weak.

A second reason for reexamining the "weak media" position is the rise of the "information society." Such fundamental societal change prompts reconceptualization, away from prior conceptions of the media system as a weak agent of persuasion or as an omnipresent agent of "low" culture. The information/communication resources that the media system controls—gathering, creating, processing, and disseminating—warrant reconceptualization of the media system as one of the most centrally located information/communication systems in modern Western societies (Ball-Rokeach and DeFleur, 1976; Ball-Rokeach, 1985). Conceptualized in this way, the media system may be seen to have effects that go well beyond individuals and well beyond voting or escapist behavior, effects that are more sociologically interesting (e.g., effects pertaining to social control, integration, conflict, and change).

The Ubiquity of the Media

The media system is so embedded in the everyday life of American society that it is difficult to articulate and to research. The ubiquitous nature of media phenomena thus places heavy demands on the dedication of personal and professional resources necessary to create theory and to develop creative methodologies required to give the theory convincing test. Sociologists are more likely to incur such costs if they are sufficiently convinced of the media system's importance. Many excellent sociologists who were active in the development of media theory and research early in their careers (in the 1940s and 1950s) later left this area of inquiry (e.g., Merton, Coleman, and Janowitz).

Structural Considerations

The peripheral nature of the structural position of media studies within American sociology can be demonstrated with the following observations: (a) In 1983, only twelve Ph.D.-granting sociology departments offered a media speciality; (b) there is no media/mass communication section in the ASA, (c) there are no sociological journals that include media studies as part of their scholarly mission and, thus, many "media" sociologists publish in the journals of other disciplines, (d) many of the best-known "media" sociologists hold their faculty positions wholly or largely outside sociology departments and are thus marginal to graduate training in sociology—for example, Gladys Engel Lang, Elihu Katz, Charles Wright, George Gerbner, Kurt Lang, James Beniger, Eleanor Singer, Paul Hirsch, David Altheide, Harold Mendelsohn, and Michael Shudson; and (e) media studies are typically classified as a subarea of social psychology, thus leaving media studies largely outside training and discourse in macrosociology (social organization, social control, social change, social institutions, and political economy).

External Constraints

Probably all research-oriented subdisciplines of sociology are affected by the ebbs and flows of resources and funding priorities of public and private agencies. Media sociology has been no exception, as evidenced both by the spasmodic nature of funding available for media research and by governmental and industry-defined research priorities. Historically, the most common priorities have been audience research and the effects of media violence and pornography on individuals—priorities that are not well-suited to the sociological level of analysis. Even related sociological research questions have not received government or industry support. For example, a proposal to study the effect of media coverage (or lack thereof) of social conflict, and its effects on the social control beliefs of the audience and the social control behaviors of powerholders, is far less likely to be funded than study of the effects of TV violence on individuals (Ball-Rokeach, 1971).

In addition to these more typical external constraints, a unique constraint exists: the "power" of the media to affect the resources of a discipline and the careers of media sociologists. Most sociological research is conducted out of the public eye, but sociological research on certain types of media effects attracts media, and, therefore, public attention. Media coverage of such research usually is in the interests of the media rather than in "science" or "scientists." It is common practice, for example, for media organizations to hire consultants to "shoot down" research findings publicly that are inconsistent with media interests. In one well-publicized case, researchers were blackballed by the TV networks from working on a

Surgeon General's Scientific Advisory Committee exploring the effects of television violence. Publicity and controversy of this sort are generally avoided by social scientists, who may thereby be discouraged from devoting research attention to the media.

In summary, a sociology of media sociology of the last quarter century reveals several factors that have contributed to a decline in the vitality and the once-strong leadership position of sociology in the study of media systems, mass communications, and media effects. At the base of the decline is the questionable assumption that the media system is an impotent social force. This assumption, when coupled with the inherent difficulty of theory and research on ubiquitous media, may account for the peripheral structural position of media studies within American sociology. External constraints on the conduct of sociological media research have reinforced this peripheral structural position. In the course of this brief discussion, however, hints may be found of developments that may be stimulating a resurgence of sociological inquiry and a reopening of the question of the importance of the media system to integration and change in the social fabric.

Review of Selected Papers

Approximately eight sessions at the 1984 ASA sessions were devoted, in whole or in part, to media studies. The papers reviewed here constitute a fair representation of the range of concerns and orientations of contemporary American "media" sociologists.

The Information Society

The previously discussed tendency to treat the mass media system as a vehicle of persuasion has given way to a view that it is an information system that controls scarce information-gathering, creating, processing, and disseminating resources essential to the social organization of modern societies. In a sense, this shift in focus represents a move back to the perspective of sociologists of the 1900-1940 era, such as Small, Ross, Park, and the Lynds (Wright, forthcoming). In the paper, "The Control Revolution," for example, James Beniger treats the mass media as part and parcel of that revolution. Beniger examines "the technological and economic origins of the information society." In contrast to most heralds of the information

society, Beniger locates the contemporary expansion of the infor-
mation/communication service economy in the historical roots of the
industrial revolution. He argues that we are witnessing the rapid
expansion of control systems brought on by technological innovation
and societal requirements for organic solidarity, requirements that go
beyond the control capacities of bureaucracy or the control technology of rationalization. The incorporation of new information/
communication technologies into production, distribution, and consumption sectors of the economy is thus both cause and consequence
of a social transformation. "The computer revolution," with its
telecommunications and mass media, is not treated as a new era in
and of itself but as a basic tool of this larger control revolution.
Beniger provides a well-articulated analysis of media systems and
technologies in terms of classical social control theory.

W. Russell Neuman and the late Ithiel de Sola Pool directed their
attention to the question of the natural limits imposed upon the
growth of information consumption, limits imposed by audiences'
avoidance of "information overload." Their paper, "The Flow of
Information Into the Home," notes that, from 1960 to 1980 in the
United States, "The supply of mass communications per capita grew
at an average annual rate of 6.7 percent. . . . But media use grew at just
2.1 percent per year." A result of the gap between information-
supplied and information-consumed is heightened competition for
audience attention, competition that might be expected to produce
information bombardment. On the basis of their findings, however,
Neuman and de Sola Pool conclude "that the central equilibrium of
media exposure is a decline in attentiveness to each medium as the
number of media to which one is exposed goes up."

The Organization and Structure
of Media Production

With the intellectual leadership of Muriel Cantor, Herbert Gans,
Gaye Tuchman, and Todd Gitlin, analysis of the economic, political,
and audience constraints on the media production process has
become one of the most lively areas of contemporary media theory
and research. Many of the papers presented at the 1984 ASA meetings
reflect the influence of one or more of these scholars.

James Parker ("The Organizational Environment of the Motion
Picture") focuses on constraints affecting movie production, using as
his vehicle of historical analysis the documented shift in the criminal
character of the "businessman racketeer/gangster of the 1930s to the

psychopathic, fringe criminal of the 1940's." He identifies as crucial a change from the Catholic Church as the chief censoring body up through the 1930s to the agencies of the federal government in the early 1940s. Parker identifies the impetus for this change as the American government's concern, during and after World War II for defending capitalism around the world. Because movies were widely seen abroad, the government's concern was that criminal characters not be portrayed in a manner that would tend to undermine the legitimacy of established American ideologies and institutions. Parker concludes that "the suggested association of gangsters with ordinary businessmen weakened the legitimacy of American capitalism." The psychopathic criminal became suitable because "he was properly distanced from the group life of America."

Discussing "Culture by the Millions," Victoria Billings directs attention to another influence upon media content, namely, the audience. In her analysis of the theater and the development of movies, she departs from the dominant view of the audience as "a mass of powerless individuals" having, at best, a limited and indirect role in the production of popular culture. She notes that in eighteenth- and nineteenth-century theater, the audience's role was normatively set as "loud" and direct, not only inside the theater through controlling expressions of approval and disapproval, but also outside the theater in the form of class-conscious protest activities (e.g., about ticket prices and elite seating areas). She argues, also, that early motion picture audiences consisted largely of working- and middle-class patrons. These audiences shaped the length and content of movies, and the "star system." The intense protest led by the NAACP against "The Birth of a Nation" set the stage for audience participation in setting the limits of movie content, a role that was buttressed by the formation of codes and censoring bodies.

Herman Gray includes the audience as one of many factors constraining "The Production of Alternative Media." Using community radio as his case in point, Gray concludes that "legal, economic, organizational, and ideological variables . . . collectively shape the programming, content, and work of community broadcasters." Most important of these are regulation (FCC and Corporation for Public Broadcasting), market structure (competition for small local audience marked by historically based structural inequalities), funding (reliance on the audience, federal and state government, and corporations), organization (nonprofit, budget size and base, target audience, size of paid/volunteer staff, range, nature of governing board), and ideology (ranging from alternative culture, liberal politics, to participatory organization). Gray identifies the satellite as the most significant of the new technologies for the organization and operation of community radio. Satellites provide a vehicle for cooperation between stations to create joint programming materials without having to rely on a centralized sponsoring agency. Despite very real pressures to take on the bureaucratized form of commercial media, Gray holds out promise that community radio, being located in the unique environs of the local community, will be able to maintain its alternative media structure and content.

The Structure of Media Content

A clear influence of European media scholars is found in semiotic and hermeneutic analyses of media content. Daniel Dayan, Elihu Katz, and Paul Kerns provide a hermeneutic analysis of "Armchair Pilgrimages: The Trips of Pope John Paul II and Their Television Public." This analysis of a religious celebratory experience is part of a larger inquiry into "televised ceremonies or 'media-events.'" They ask whether the "pilgrimage" may reasonably be said to include the viewing television audience, and they base their affirmative conclusion heavily on the concept of "liminality." Liminality is a "borderline, . . . a specialized state involving the entire life of the deeply devoted" in which the subjective mode of culture dominates; "it encompasses *communitas* as a moral fiction and as chimaeras of carnival." These are ceremonial occasions not to be understood as pseudoevents because the media's role is to integrate the media audience into the event itself. Such incorporation requires live media of radio or television. The suspension of "normal" journalistic practice of assessing and evaluating the event gives way in a parallel fashion to the suspension of "normal" life for the participants who enter the subjunctive mode of moral fiction. The audience is thus transformed into a long-distance "communitas."

Jeffery Alexander examines one of the most important media events in recent American history: Watergate ("The Form of Substance: The Watergate Hearings As Ritual"). He asks, What are the social conditions under which television does and does not achieve its potential as the portrayer of "ontological reality"? He argues that "the degree to which factual television is believed . . . depends on the degree to which it is viewed as a differentiated/unattached/unbiased medium of information." Television coverage of Watergate was not accepted as truth as long as the Nixon-Agnew characterizations of the television industry as nonindependent "rad lib" proponents of McGovern and left-wing Democrats were accepted. The postelection acceptance by other institutions (e.g., the Senate) of previously reported "facts" as "truth" was required before Watergate could emerge as televised "reality." Alexander goes on to note the substance as well as the form of the television truth of Watergate: "The form was realism/truth/ritual; the content was 'listen, America, fundamental values are at stake . . . it's not just politics.' "

The Message in the Messages

In addition to semiotic and hermeneutic analysis of media content, the more traditional quantitative content analysis strategy continues to be used and developed. One relevant question addressed in this manner by Eleanor Singer and Phyllis Endreny is the following: If sociology is ignoring the media, are the media ignoring sociology or, more generally, social science? With few exceptions, the literature on media coverage of the "sciences" ignores social science. The Singer-Endreny paper, "The Reporting of Social Science Research In The Mass Media," comes from a larger ground-breaking effort launched by Singer and Carol Weiss that was designed to fill this vacuum. Singer and Endreny compare the quantity and quality of media coverage of the social sciences from 1970 to 1982 by content analyzing systematically sampled materials from major print and electronic media (e.g., *The New York Times, Wall Street Journal*, and the nightly network news). They conclude that the major increase in the quantity of coverage is due to "ancillary" use of social science findings, often poll results, in stories focused on a related topic and not focused on social science research per se.

Qualitative characteristics of such coverage include a common failure to cite sources, decontextualization, an emphasis upon conflicting views, frequent attribution of "social science research" that most social scientists would reject as pseudo-research, and use of the research to validate a story conclusion. These authors pessimistically conclude that media coverage of social science will most likely continue to conform to media needs and, in so doing, convey a picture of social science to the consuming public that is likely to "erode whatever confidence social science has managed to accrue."

Social and Political Effects

The virtual hiatus of media effects research in American sociology that followed the earlier productive era would seem to be over. Sociologists are again exploring media effects, but the contemporary emphasis is upon the media as an "information" system with resources that bear upon the audience's social and political life. Ralph Turner and Denise Paz, for example, reported on "The Media in Earthquake Warning: Research in Southern California." Many Southern Californians have experienced, or have associates who have experienced, earthquakes. Yet Turner and Paz find that the media are trusted more than interpersonal associates as sources of earthquake information. This finding points to one of the many ways in which the media system has become structurally located as an informational link between citizens and institutional authorities; in this case, with the emergency and scientific earthquake prediction agencies. Among the mass media, magazines and books were found to be the most credible sources, but television was employed by a majority of the respondents (55%) as the primary source of information about earthquake warnings. It would thus appear that the media are regarded as information systems superior even to "experienced interpersonal associates" for most Southern Californians as they attempt to anticipate and respond to earthquakes. Moreover, it is when the media system is inattentive to earthquake concerns that interpersonal communication in the form of rumor formation takes over. This finding is fully consistent with prior research on the role of the media in disaster situations; the Turner-Paz research points to the ongoing centrality of the media system in a community that chronically faces the prospect of a natural disaster.

In collaboration with Milton Rokeach and Joel Grube, I reported on a quasi-experimental field experiment designed to affect egalitarian and environmental beliefs and behaviors ("The Great American Values Test: Influencing Behavior and Belief Through Television"). Cognizant of the criticisms of prior research that failed to deal adequately with threats to external validity, we created a separate-sample pretest-posttest control group design that allowed assessment of long-term effects on persons who voluntarily watched a 30-minute television program created for the research. The program—*The Great American Values Test*—was viewed in the most natural setting for TV viewing, in the privacy (and under natural media exposure conditions) of viewers' homes. Also cognizant of the failure of prior research to demonstrate long-term effects on socially important behavior, we obtained behavioral measures based on viewers' donations of money in response to solicitations from real organizations. The solicitations occurred some 8-13 weeks after the program had aired. The goals of these organizations were related logically to the egalitarian and environmental treatments embedded in the TV program.

The research design was dictated by two theoretical orientations—Ball-Rokeach's media system dependency theory and Rokeach's belief system theory with its "self-confrontation" strategy of belief and behavior change and stabilization. The findings provide strong evidence that the TV program had long-term effects upon egalitarian and environmental values, attitudes, and behavior. Both TV dependency and exposure to the self-confrontation treatments showed significant effects (Ball-Rokeach et al., 1984). These findings thus take us full circle back to the question of the conditions under which the mass media may affect the political process by affecting individuals' political beliefs and behaviors—the initial impetus to the research of the Lazarsfeld group some four decades ago. Contrary to the earlier research, however, the findings strongly suggest that there are indeed certain conditions under which the media may powerfully affect political values and related attitudes and behaviors.

Media Linkages of
Culture and Structure

One of the least researched classical sociological issues is the role of the media system in the structure and culture of a society, and how these macrolevel relationships affect microlevel social relationships. George Gerbner and other critical theorists have focused on the media system as the dominant creator of "culture" in modern societies, the culture that includes the symbolic rationale for a capitalist social structure.

Karl Eric Rosengren, a prolific and influential Swedish sociologist, has tackled the problem of media linkage of culture and structure in a large-scale theoretical and empirical research effort in Sweden. His report of this effort ("Vertical and Horizontal Links of Culture and Social Structure") begins with a distinction between horizontal linkages of culture and structure—macrorelations between social systems distinguished by their degree of interdependency—and vertical links—the macro-to-micro relations wherein culture takes form through processes of socialization at the level of the individual. He views the media's major roles in these linkages in terms of the maintenance, change, and dissemination of the culture of society. This view places the media system as a unique culture apparatus that, unlike other culture-creating systems, crosses over the boundaries of all social systems within a society.

Rosengren identifies two ways in which the media link culture to other societal systems: by "transforming abstract patterns of ideas, values and beliefs into patterns of actions and artifacts ('vertical linkages')" and by "acting as a generalized (cultural) mediator between different systems of society, relating them to one another— say politics to art, science to literature and religion ('horizontal linkages')." Rosengren is developing empirical measures of such linkages by examining relations between economic, social, and cultural indicators: "Economic indicators tap societal characteristics pertaining to the production and accumulation of goods in society. Social indicators tap societal characteristics pertaining to the distribution and consumption of goods (and ills) in society. Cultural indicators tap societal characteristics pertaining to continuity and change: the structure of ideas, beliefs and values serving to maintain and reproduce society as a whole and its various sub-systems, but also serving change and innovation in society." The results of this ambitious research effort are not yet in, but should be of interest to persons working in many subdisciplines of sociology.

Conclusion

There is great diversity in the theoretical orientations and the specific foci of these papers. I had the pleasure of chairing the thematic session on media linkages of the social fabric, in which papers by Dayan et al., Alexander, and Rosengren were presented. The section on social psychology devoted its entire session to the media, chaired by Charles Wright. The Turner and Paz and Ball-Rokeach et al. papers were presented at this session, as well as a paper by Lang and Lang not here reviewed. Regular sessions were chaired by Muriel Cantor, Eleanor Singer, James Wright, and others as participants.[1] There would seem to be a unifying search for a better understanding of the organizational and cultural forces that determine the structure and process of the media system's production of cultural products, and the macro- and microeffects of the consumption of these products. The dual emphasis on production and consumption stands in contrast to earlier eras of sociological inquiry in which the emphasis was primarily on consumption and on audiences of consumers. The dual emphasis is a clear advance in the sense that it lays a more solid foundation for integrated explorations of media linkages of the social fabric at societal, group, and individual levels of analysis.

Note

1. These sessions and their organizers are as follows:

Mass Media Primary Focus

- S. J. Ball-Rokeach: Media Linkages of the Social Fabric
- Muriel G. Cantor: The Production of Popular Culture
- Muriel G. Cantor: The Sociology of Popular Culture
- Eleanor Singer: Mass Media
- Charles R. Wright: Do the Media Matter? New Contributions from Social Psychology

Mass Media Papers Included as
Relevant Part of a Larger Inquiry

- J. Michael Armer: Social Change/Technology
- Gerald Marwell: Collective Behavior and Social Movements
- James Wright: Public Opinion

Many of these papers will be included in Ball-Rokeach and Cantor (forthcoming).

References

Alexander, J. 1981. "The Mass News Media in Systemic, Historical, and Comparative Perspective." Pp. 17-51 in *Mass Media and Social Change.* Edited by E. Katz and T. Szecsko. Beverly Hills, CA: Sage.

Ball-Rokeach, S. J. 1971. "The Legitimation of Violence." Pp. 100-111 in *Collective Violence.* Edited by J. F. Short, Jr., and M. E. Wolfgang. Chicago: Aldine.

Ball-Rokeach, S. J. 1985. "The Origins of Individual Media System Dependency: A Sociological Framework." *Communication Research* 12 (October): 485-510.

Ball-Rokeach, S. J. and M. G. Cantor. forthcoming. *Media, Audience and Social Structure.* Beverly Hills, CA: Sage.

Ball-Rokeach, S. J. and M. L. De Fleur. 1976. "A Dependency Model of Mass Media Effects. *Communication Research* 3: 3-21.

Ball-Rokeach, S. J., M. Rokeach, and J. W. Grube. 1984. *The Great American Values Test: Influencing Behavior and Belief Through Television.* New York: Free Press.

Berelson, B. 1959. "The State of Communication Research." *Public Opinion Quarterly* 23: 1-6.

Gans, H. 1972. "A Comment: Famine in Mass Media Research." *American Journal of Sociology* 77: 697-705.

Holz, J. R. and C. W. Wright. 1979. "Sociology of Mass Communications." Pp. 193-217 in *Annual Review of Sociology*, 5. Edited by A. Inkeles, J. Coleman, and R. Turner. Palo Alto, CA: Annual Reviews.

Katz, E. 1980. "On Conceptualizing Media Effects." In *Studies in Communication*, Vol. 1. Edited by T. McCormack. Greenwich, CT: JAI.

Katz, E. and P. F. Lazarsfeld. 1955. *Personal Influence*. New York: Free Press.

Klapper, J. 1960. *The Effects of Mass Communication*. New York: Free Press.

Lazarsfeld, P. F., B. Berelson, and H. Gaudet. *The People's Choice*. New York: Columbia.

Mills, C. W. 1939. *Power, Politics, and People*. New York: Ballantine.

Wright, C. R. forthcoming. "Mass Communication Rediscovered: Its Past and Future in American Sociology." In *Media Audience and Social Structure*. Edited by S. J. Ball-Rokeach and M. G. Cantor. Beverly Hills, CA: Sage.

Part V

Science, Scientists, and the Social Fabric

18

Sociology and the Nuclear Debate

Theodore Caplow

THE PAPERS PREPARED for the thematic session, "The Role of Sociologists in the Nuclear Debate," at San Antonio, were diverse in style and emphasis, but they tell a coherent story and converge to a common recommendation.[1] This is the first time that the history of sociological involvement with nuclear issues has been systematically reviewed and interpreted. The findings are not very creditable to the discipline. All of the participants agreed that nuclear issues are an appropriate topic for sociological research, and that the work done on them so far has been conspicuously insufficient.

The main points of this consensus are as follows:

(1) Nuclear weapons are social products and they have momentous social consequences, which are fully amenable to study by social scientists. There is an implicit canon of science that calls for some proportionality between the attention given to a phenomenon and its importance. The societal importance of the topic can hardly be exaggerated as all future social development appears to be contingent upon the discovery of means to control the destructive potential of nuclear technology.

(2) As Boulding showed in her masterful narrative, physical scientists were the first to respond to the issues raised by the invention and use of atomic weapons. Social scientists lagged behind, and when they did develop an interdisciplinary dialogue on nuclear issues, the sociologists among them remained on the periphery.

(3) The avoidance of nuclear issues by social scientists in general, and by sociologists in particular, is so striking that it calls for explanation as an independent problem. Examining 40 volumes of the *American Sociological Review*, the *American Journal of Sociology*, and *Social Forces* from 1945 to 1984, Finsterbusch found that 11 papers out of about 6500 dealt with nuclear issues, and only 4 of these had anything to say about nuclear weapons—.0006 of the total!

(4) This astounding neglect is not attributable, in the opinion of the panelists, to any unsuitability in the subject matter. Among the aspects particularly amenable to sociological investigation are attempts to predict the social consequences of various levels of nuclear warfare, the application of conflict theory to the nuclear arms race, the development of new models of world order, the analysis of public opinion on nuclear issues, and the assessment of alternative strategies for dealing with nuclear terrorism. If the social sciences are taken collectively, and the possibility of interdisciplinary work is included, a much wider range of problems becomes accessible, including the novel problem of how historically temporary human institutions can manage the historically permanent dangers associated with nuclear technology.

(5) The sense of the panel was that sociologists ought to become much more closely engaged with nuclear issues, as sociologists, than we have been so far. The reasons range from the nearly trivial—to protect the intellectual claims of the discipline—to the nearly sublime —sociological work on nuclear issues might help to diminish the nuclear danger that hangs over contemporary society.

The four papers presented at San Antonio interlocked in several ways. The papers by Elise Boulding ("The Participation of Sociologists in the Nuclear Debate") and Finsterbusch ("The Sociological Literature on Nuclear Issues") reviewed what has been accomplished since 1945, from slightly different perspectives. Boulding summarized the intellectual reaction to the appearance of atomic weaponry in the world and to the subsequent evolution of the nuclear arms race, with special attention to the small, but significant, sociological contribution. Finsterbush proceeded by identifying a series of major nuclear issues, measuring the amount of attention they have received in the sociological literature, and summarizing the results of that rather limited research effort.

Louis Kriesberg ("Where Are We and Where We Could Go in Peace Research") and Theodore Caplow ("The Feasibility of World Government: A Research Assignment for the World Sciences") attempted to explain why sociologists have been so reluctant to enter this research arena. Each of them proposed research strategies calculated to overcome that reluctance and to bring about a more adequate application of sociological and other social-scientific resources to the nuclear situation.

The proposed research strategies are quite different, however. Kriesberg would expand, refine, and sociologize the tension-reduction approach to the cold war and other international conflicts. Caplow calls on social scientists to recognize that nuclear weapons have made the modern state obsolete by reducing its capacity for self-defense. That position suggests a research strategy of exploring alternatives to the existing international system, such as a world federation composed of nations with diverse political and economic systems. A third, more eclectic research strategy was outlined by Boulding, who would have us study a wide range of topics from the pervasiveness of military symbolism in our culture to sociological implications of nuclear winter. Boulding's research agenda is more closely related to the peace movement than either of the others. It views war as pathological, and military influence as baneful in any context. Finsterbusch succinctly presents still another research agenda.

This summary will first discuss the sociological neglect of nuclear issues, then specify what we know or think we know about the contemporary nuclear situation, then examine as critically as possible the proposed research strategies.

The Neglect of Nuclear Issues
by Sociologists

Finsterbusch quotes Lauer (1976) and Sofios (1983), who inspected most of the social problems textbooks published between 1940 and 1983. Only a few of these books had a chapter on war and peace, although during the same period the American public rated war or the threat of war as a major social problem more often than any other. Introductory sociology textbooks gave the topic even shorter shrift.

The almost complete omission of nuclear issues from the major sociological journals has already been noted. Finsterbusch also inspected the leading journals of public opinion, social problems, military sociology, and the popular magazines that deal with sociological issues. The number of nuclear references is very small in each case. Boulding's independent analysis of the *American Sociological Review* confirms Finsterbusch, and also shows that nuclear weapons and related issues were very lightly represented in her (1979) *Bibliography on World Conflict and Peace*. She concludes that "sociologists scarcely deal with these issues at all."

The refusal of sociologists to confront nuclear questions is not for want of scholarly leadership. Numerous clarion calls have failed to move the rank and file of the discipline since Angell's 1951 presidential address on Sociology and the World Crisis. Boulding mentions Horowitz (1973/1957), Mills (1957), Aron (1958, 1965), Etzioni (1961, 1962), Dentler and Cutright (1963), Moore (1966a, 1966b), Gamson and Modigliani (1971), and Kriesberg (1973), among others, who launched intellectual initiatives in this field and saw them encapsulated by scholarly indifference.

Each of the four papers presented in San Antonio proposed at least a partial explanation for the extraordinary neglect of nuclear issues by sociologists. These range from an aversion to interdisciplinary research to "adaptive amnesia." Without attempting to decide among these explanations, I should like to call attention to certain additional peculiarities of the nuclear topic that sociologists confront when they enter this field.

(1) The underlying paradigm for the study of social problems is that a system of unwanted behavior (classified as deviant, anomic, maladaptive, exploitative, abnormal, or whatever) is identified, together with an ascription of causality that implies courses of action that would reduce the incidence of the unwanted behavior. More often than not, the proposed remedial actions consist of some application of governmental powers. This appears to be the standard pattern in all contemporary societies, whether the unwanted behavior is too many pregnancies in China, drunk driving in the United States, famine in Africa, racism in Britain, or piracy along the coasts of Indo-China. But the nuclear threat is created by the unwanted behavior of *governments*, and all of the world's more powerful

governments are directly implicated. With government as the source of the problem, the usual sequence of social problem solving is unworkable.

(2) Sociologists, like other citizens, locate themselves somewhere on a political spectrum from left to right, and that identification involves compulsory loyalties and antagonisms. Conservative sociologists are inclined to fear and distrust the Soviet Union. Liberal sociologists are inclined to disapprove of the foreign policies of the United States under a Republican administration. But a dispassionate analysis of nuclear issue may require the analyst to view the two superpowers symmetrically and to reject the moral pretensions of both. This is an uncomfortable position; it does not fit anywhere on the political spectrum and invites disapproval from all sides.

(3) The unimaginability of large-scale nuclear war constitutes a technical obstacle to the study of nuclear issues. In recent years, with the development of phenomenology, semiotics, and symbolic-structural analysis, sociologists have become more aware of the mixed nature of social reality—tangible organisms and artifacts bound together by powerful, imprecise symbols. The scenarios of nuclear danger fall outside of our inherited symbolic repertory; they induce a kind of metaphysical panic. We have had many millenia to come to symbolic terms with the death of persons, but the death of the human species is not readily imaginable.

And there are other features of the situation that are nearly as difficult to grasp intellectually. The existence of 50,000 nuclear warheads when the use of even one of them involves unacceptable human costs is an obstacle to rational modeling, and it is not easy to assimilate the fact that forces under human control are now more destructive than earthquakes, hurricanes, tidal waves, and volcanos. What becomes of the delicate balance between nature and man, or for that matter, between time and eternity? Nuclear arsenals have been constructed to defend political systems that will probably change unrecognizably within 100 years and will almost certainly not endure for a hundredth of the half-life of some of the waste products produced in manufacturing those nuclear arsenals. Metaphysical panic may be the only reasonable response to the thought that the need to prevent nuclear destruction is henceforth a permanent feature of human society, in view of the fact that the collective response to this overwhelming necessity in the first forty years of the nuclear age has been to arrange for thousands of nuclear explosions.

Opportunities for Sociological Research

The foregoing peculiarities of the nuclear topic—and some others not mentioned—may help us to understand the reluctance social scientists have shown to work on nuclear issues, or even to acknowledge their existence. The question remains whether it would be useful for us to overcome that reluctance and to devote a substantial share of our scholarly resources to this social problem. Are the intellectual tools of sociology likely to be of any practical use? Will they enable us to analyze the nuclear predicament, or to devise means of escape from it? The answer to those questions is necessarily hesitant. It seems improbable that the sociological study of nuclear issues will save the world. But it is not altogether impossible. Social science has not developed as fast and as far as physical science; we have no reliable tricks to neutralize the demonic achievements of our colleagues in physics and engineering. But we do have more experience with social problems than they do, and a fairly good sense of what is possible in the realm of social engineering. We are not likely to do any worse than the diplomats, generals, and arms control experts who have been responsible for nuclear solutions so far, and there is always a chance that ideas developed in the scholar's study will ignite a new social movement, as has happened so many times in Europe and the United States since the sixteenth century.

Meanwhile, where to begin? What are the salient nuclear issues? Finsterbusch lists eight of them: "institutional collapse" versus "human resilience," the rationale of the arms race, nuclear deployment, deterrence, proliferation, accidental war and its prevention, arms control, and nuclear terrorism. Not all of these are equally amenable to sociological study, as Finsterbusch notes. Sociologists ought to have much more to say about nuclear terrorism than about the deployment of missiles.

Boulding presents a list of researchable topics that is somewhat different from the foregoing and reflects the preoccupations of the organized peace movement rather than those of official policymakers. She would study the world military system as a single interdependent system, expand the concept of the military-industrial complex to take in other institutional sectors supportive of military development, and examine the alleged shift of decision making on national security issues from the civilian to the military sector.

Under the general rubric of war symbolism, she would study military symbolism throughout contemporary culture, uncover the deep imagery that underlies defense policy debates, analyze bellism as analogous to sexism and racism, and expand the concept of human rights to include a measure of safety from nuclear threats. She proposes also to analyze trends with respect to civilian-military resource allocations, security policy planning, and diplomatic capability; to develop improved social-psychological models of deterrence; to explore decision making under stress in several different ways; and to join in the nuclear winter discussion by trying to estimate the destruction of social networks and infrastructures that would accompany nuclear war—a rich varied menu of research assignments.

My own paper takes a different tack by proposing to focus the attention of sociologists—and of other social scientists—on the problems and possibilities of world government. I argue that there is no conceivable way to prevent nuclear war in the existing international system, and that the most useful contribution we can make by social research is to transform world government from a nearly vacuous concept to a set of thoroughly researched alternatives and practicalities. The reason the project of world government is out of favor may well be that it carries so little substantive content.

But although I believe that we ought to give our first attention to the intellectual problem of how to design a world government, I do not question the value of the other sorts of studies proposed by my colleagues. It seems doubtful that the existing international order can survive for many years, but it exists now, and that is an irrefutable claim to be taken seriously. Then, too, macrosociological prediction is such an uncertain art that even the most plausible prophecies may go awry. Nuclear war seems to be inevitable in the existing international system unless that system is drastically transformed. But there is always the possibility that some unexpected turn of events will cancel today's inevitability and substitute a new set of parameters tomorrow.

Kriesberg, if I interpret his paper correctly, starts from the assumption that conflict, not nuclear technology, is the phenomenon that sociologists are equipped to handle. His approach to the problem of war and peace in the nuclear age is less messianic and more professional than those of the rest of us. Regardless of its scale, the cold war is a conflict like any other, subject to the same principles of escalation and reduction. Nuclear weapons, despite their awesome power, are dangerous not in themselves but as instruments of conflict. The cold war should be viewed not as a unique but as a typical international conflict.

Within that framework, Kriesberg shows that a great deal is already known about the reduction of tensions and about how to avoid escalation. For example, he proposes to study the relationship between national leaders and their constituencies, particularly the way leaders' behavior toward external adversaries is conditioned by the expectations of their internal constituencies. Kriesberg would also examine the various types of collective identification that contribute to nationalism, the ways in which constituency support for nonviolent alternatives can be mobilized, the general problem of escalation in international conflicts, and the various ways escalation can be interrupted. Kriesberg would pay particular attention to negotiated international settlements, again pushing out the boundaries of an established field of sociological investigation to meet the requirements of this special case. He is particularly interested in the development of enduring agreements and the strengthening of transnational bonds that might follow an increasing traffic of people, goods, and ideas across national boundaries.

The Ongoing Nuclear Debate

The panelists in San Antonio were in complete agreement that sociologists ought to take a more active role in the nuclear debate than they have done heretofore. They did not agree about all of the details of that participation—as we saw in the previous section—but they all envisaged the same style of work, that is, the conduct of empirical research on nuclear issues according to the usual canons of sociological method, followed by the dissemination of the findings that might eventually influence official decisions, the public opinion that influences official decisions, or the social movements that form public opinion. That is the usual, and appropriate, way for modern scholars to involve themselves in debates on public policy.

Needless to say, the nuclear debate has not been quiescent pending the arrival of sociologists. With protagonists drawn from many fields—statesmen, physicists, journalists, physicians, soldiers, activists, philosophers, and theologians, among others—the debate has raged for forty years, orienting itself, as all great controversies do, to certain fixed polarities of perception and preference. If sociologists are at last to participate in the nuclear debate, they must recognize it as an existent social system with its own history. It may be instructive to review that history briefly in order to get a better idea of what contributions might be made by sociologists entering the arena at this late but critical hour.

The two most fundamental positions in the nuclear debate were articulated almost before the echoes of the Hiroshima bomb had died away. One view of that event was that nuclear weapons had made national sovereignty obsolete and that the safety of humankind could only be secured by the immediate development of a global political order to place international relations under the rule of law. Albert Einstein was the best known protagonist of this view, which he put forward on every possible occasion between 1945 and his death in 1955 (Michelmore, 1962, pp. 222-224). The opposing opinion, which provided the intellectual foundation for the governmental policies adopted in the name of deterrence, was first set forth in 1946 by Bernard Brodie, a political scientist. Starting from the premise that it would be impossible to limit national sovereignty in the near term, Brodie (1946) argued that force would continue to be used by nations because that is what sovereign nations do, and that the atomic bomb, being the most forceful of all weapons, would certainly find widespread military use. But Brodie did not think that atomic bombs would be used for aggressive purposes if there were any possibility of retaliation in kind. On this slender pedestal the vast literature of deterrence, and vast nuclear arsenals, were built in subsequent years.

In 1985, this is still the most basic issue in the nuclear debate. But the massive adoption of the Brodian position by the superpowers and the installation of nuclear weapons and delivery systems in unimaginable profusion all over the planet have reduced the popularity of the Einsteinian position without invalidating its logic. Even Jonathan Schell, who advocates the total abolition of nuclear weapons with exceptional eloquence, does not refrain from disparaging the project of world government. Indeed, in one place he goes beyond mere disparagement:

> The requirement for world government as the inevitable price for nuclear disarmament is at the heart of the impasse that the world has been unable to break through in almost four decades of the nuclear age. . . . Until it is removed—until we find some way of ridding ourselves of nuclear weapons without having to establish world government, or something like it—major relief from the nuclear peril seems unlikely [Schell, 1984, p. 88].

Schell's (1984, p. 85) impression of world government as an obstacle to nuclear solutions can be traced to his mistaken belief in "an unbreakable linkage between full nuclear (or total) disarmament and world government." Once that linkage is accepted—unbreakable or not—the project of world government becomes chimerical indeed. Any government at all must be armed, and a world government in the nuclear age will have to be formidably armed, as I have tried to show elsewhere (Caplow, 1979). The impracticality of installing a world government in this century has not been established either by close reflection or by the examination of relevant evidence, which is why research on the feasibility of the project is so inviting.

Meanwhile, it is incontrovertible that the proponents of world government have less voice than ever before in the current phase of the nuclear debate. We are a long way from 1944, when the U.S. Senate called on the United States to join an international organization "having the power to prevent aggression and preserve the peace of the world" with only five dissenting votes.

Additionally, the nuclear debate now places those who regard the arms race as leading us inevitably toward nuclear war (Kennan, 1982) in opposition to those who regard arms reduction, or even negotiated arms control, as riskier than unrestrained nuclear competition (Ehrlich, 1985).

Disagreements about nuclear strategy build upon certain more fundamental differences of opinion that divide intellectuals in the United States and Western Europe sharply and arouse intense passions. It is difficult for people who regard the Soviet Union as engaged in the unrelenting pursuit of world domination (for example, George Will) to acknowledge the good faith of their fellow citizens, who see the Soviet leaders as ineffective and frightened (Kennan), or of other observers, who see the superpowers as having nearly indistinguishable nuclear policies.

Those who invoke moral principles derived from religion or philosophy against preparations for nuclear war make a powerful case. But it goes unanswered. Few rise to answer the charge that nuclear strategy is wicked in principle[2] because it risks the destruction of the human species, and wicked in practice because any use of nuclear weapons implies the infliction of untold pain and suffering on innocent persons. As the nuclear debate is now organized in the United States and Western Europe, and to some extent in Eastern Europe as well (Washington Post, 1985) it involves a multifaceted confrontation between "hawks" and "doves," who differ about everything connected with nuclear weaponry except the proposition that fundamental changes in the existing international system are too impractical to consider.

The major facets of this confrontation[3] are as follows:

HAWKS	DOVES
(1) A nuclear war can be fought and won.	Nuclear war will exterminate the human species.
(2) A nuclear war can be limited.	A nuclear war is almost certain to spiral out of control.
(3) Nuclear weapons differ only quantitatively from other weapons.	Nuclear weapons are intrinsically immoral.
(4) Deterrence is an obsolete strategy.	Deterrence is the only safe nuclear strategy.
(5) The real goal of the Soviet leadership is world domination.	The real goal of the Soviet leadership is peaceful coexistence.
(6) Arms control is essential to prevent nuclear escalation.	Arms control institutionalizes nuclear escalation.
(7) Nuclear disarmament is inconceivable.	Nuclear disarmament is essential.

Neither of the two main positions is fully integrated across all the issues.[4] Some hawks regard arms control as a subterfuge designed by the Soviets to lull the United States into slackening its defense effort, and many doves prefer any form of arms control to unregulated nuclear competition. Not all hawks believe that nuclear wars can be won or that they can be limited; that is why they want the United States to develop nuclear superiority. But, in general, the left-hand column accurately represents the official U.S. viewpoint (Secretary of Defense, 1984) for the time being.

The general problem of nuclear proliferation includes a variety of diverse situations, from the acquisition of a few weapons by "irresponsible" states such as Libya and Iraq to the role played by British and French nuclear forces in the intricate scenario of European defense. What these situations have in common is that all of them seem to have a destabilizing influence on the U.S.-Soviet relationship.

Nuclear blackmail is a grave social problem waiting to appear. Nearly everyone who has thought about the matter expects cities to be held for ransom by criminal gangs within the next few years. Appropriate reaction to these future crimes have yet to be proposed, and only token efforts are being made to prevent their occurrence.

Threaded through all of the hawkish and dovish positions on nuclear issues are unexamined assumptions about individual collective behavior in situations that are unprecedented in some

respects but nevertheless fall into familiar sociological categories—
negotiations, conflicts, disasters, rituals—and contain only familiar
types of social action—stereotyping, reification, mythologizing,
exchange behavior. Sociologists are better equipped than any one
else to study the nuclear predicament as a sociological phenomenon,
to test the assumptions about social action that underlie various
positions in the nuclear debate, and to assess the plausibility of the
various scenarios on which governments have staked their existences
and our lives.

As a company of scholars, we may not be able to do as much with
these problems as we would like, but there is little to be lost by trying,
and possibly a great deal to be gained.

Notes

1. Papers prepared for the thematic session on "The Role of Sociologists in the Nuclear
Debate," American Sociological Association Meetings, San Antonio, Texas, August 1984 are as
follows:

- Boulding, Elise, "The Participation of Sociologists in the Nuclear Debate."
- Caplow, Theodore, "The Feasibility of World Government: A Research Assignment for the
  Social Sciences"
- Finsterbusch, Kurt, "The Sociological Literature on Nuclear Issues"
- Kriesberg, Louis, "Where We Are and Where We Could Go in Peace Research"

2. Among the rare exceptions see James Woolsey (1984), especially Chapters 2 and 3.
3. For a different profile of the hawk-dove confrontation, see Ehrlich (1985, Table 1.1). For
additional details of the confrontation, see Kennan (1982), Bracken (1983), Wieseltier (1983),
Schell (1982, 1984), Lifton and Falk (1982), and Trudeau (1985).
4. Two very important issues fall outside the nuclear debate as presently structured: nuclear
proliferation and nuclear terrorism.

References

Aron, R. 1958. On War: Atomic Weapons and Global Diplomacy. London: Secker and Warburg.
Aron, R. 1965. The Great Debate: Theories of Nuclear Strategy. New York: Doubleday.
Boulding, E., R. Passmore, and R. S. Gassler. 1979. Bibliography on World Conflict and Peace.
    Boulder, CO: Westview.
Bracken, P. 1983. The Command and Control of Nuclear Forces. New Haven, CT: Yale University
    Press.
Brodie, B. 1946. "War in the Atomic Age and Implications for Military Policy." Pp. 21-107 in The
    Absolute Weapon: Atomic Power and World Order. Edited by B. Brodie. New York: Harcourt
    Brace Jovanovich.
Brucan, S. 1982. "The Establishment of a World Authority: Working Hypotheses." Alternatives 8:
    209-223.
Caplow, T. 1977. A Feasibility Study of World Government. Occasional Paper #13, Des Moines,
    Iowa: The Stanley Foundation.
Caplow, T. 1979. "The Contradiction Between World Order and Disarmament." Washington
    Quarterly.

Castel de St. Pierre, C. I. (1613). *Projet de Paix Perpetuelle*. Utrecht.

Dentler, R. and P. Cutright. 1963. *Hostage America: Human Aspects of a Nuclear Attack and a Program of Prevention*. Boston: Beacon.

Ehrlich, R. 1985. *Waging Nuclear Peace*. Albany, NY: Suny Press.

Etzioni, A. 1961. "Our First Manual of Nuclear War." *Columbia Forum* 4, 4.

Etzioni, A. 1962. *The Hard Way to Peace*. New York: Collier.

Gamson, W. A. and A. Modigliani. 1971. *Untangling the Cold War, A Strategy for Testing Rival Theories*. Boston: Little, Brown.

Horowitz, I. L. 1973. *War and Peace in Contemporary Social and Philosophical Theory*. London: Sovreign Press. (pub. orig. 1957)

Kennan, G. F. 1982. *The Nuclear Delusion: Soviet-American Relations in the Nuclear Age*. New York: Pantheon.

Kidron, M. and D. Smith. 1983. *The War Atlas: Armed Conflict—Armed Peace*. London and Sydney: Pan.

Kriesberg, L. 1973. *Sociology of Social Conflicts*. Englewood Cliffs, NJ: Prentice-Hall.

Kriesberg, L. 1984. "Social Theory and the Deescalation of International Conflict." *Sociological Review* (August).

Lauer, R. H. 1976. "Defining Social Problems: Public and Professional Perspectives." *Social Problems* 24: 122-130.

Lifton, R. J. and R. Falk. 1982. *Indefensible Weapons: The Political and Psychological Case Against Nuclearism*. New York: Basic Books.

Mandelbaum, M. 1981. *The Nuclear Revolution: International Politics Before and After Hiroshima*. New York: Cambridge University Press.

Michelmore, P. 1962. *Einstein: Profile of the Man*. New York: Dodd, Mead.

Mills, C. W. 1957. *The Causes of World War III*. New York: Simon & Schuster.

Moore, W. 1966a. "Global Sociology: The World as a Singular System." *American Journal of Sociology* 61: 475-482.

Moore, W. 1966. "The Utility of Utopias." *American Sociological Review* 31: 765-772.

Schell, J. 1982. *The Fate of the Earth*. New York: Alfred A. Knopf.

Schell, J. 1984. *The Abolition*. New York: Alfred A. Knopf.

Secretary of Defense. 1984. *Annual Report of the Secretary of Defense*. Washington, DC: Government Printing Office.

Sofios, N. 1983. *The Threat of Nuclear War as a Social Problem: Denial, Disregard, or Despair?* (unpublished)

Stanley Foundation. 1984. *Strategy for Peace 1984*. Muscatine, IA: Author.

Trudeau, P. E. 1985. "The Nuclear Imperative." *World Press Review* (January): 25-30.

Washington Post. 1985. "A-Arms Issues Enter Soviet Public Debate." January 5, pp. A1, A11.

Wieseltier, L. 1983. *Nuclear War, Nuclear Peace*. New York: Holt, Rinehart & Winston.

Woolsey, J. R. (Ed.) 1984. *Nuclear Arms: Ethics, Strategy Politics*. San Francisco: ICS.

19

Uses and Control of Knowledge: Implications for the Social Fabric

Harriet Zuckerman

THE FOUNDERS OF SOCIOLOGY—Marx, Durkheim, Weber, and Pareto—each in his own way, put an imprimatur on the uses and control of knowledge as subjects worthy of serious inquiry. But for a long while, sociologists did not, with notable exceptions such as Mannheim, follow their lead and devote sustained and cumulative research attention to them.

In the last two decades or so, this condition has begun to change in sociology as in several related disciplines, but a new specialty is yet to coalesce. Interest has, however, converged on two subsets of the larger problem domain: first, on the ways in which scientific and social scientific knowledge is used in individual and collective decision making, and, second, on social factors affecting the production and dissemination of knowledge. This is becoming evident in a new journal, *Knowledge,* which reports research in this sphere. A review of the disciplinary affiliations of its contributors finds them coming from about 25 disciplines and specialties. Nor has there been any slackening in the tendency to multidisciplinarity since the first issue of *Knowledge* appeared in 1979.[1]

Researchers as diverse as economists, political scientists and policy analysts, information scientists, industrial engineers, students of public opinion and of risk and technology assessment, cognitive psychologists, systems analysts, historians, peace researchers and conflict researchers, philosophers, and sociologists of science and of knowledge have all been addressing themselves to one or another aspect of these general subjects. Moreover, the pace of research activity appears to be quickening. Again, content analysis of the sorts of articles published in *Knowledge* shows both an increase in the proportion of papers reporting empirical investigations (and especially those drawing on quantitative data) and a decrease in the incidence of programmatic papers, those that lay out territories of research but report none themselves. Such changes may of course represent editorial decisions as well as actual changes in the kinds of research in progress and submitted for publication, but they are much like those observed in the emergence and development of other research specialties.[2]

Other signs of a developing area of research specialization are also beginning to appear: An infrastructure is being assembled to facilitate research and communication, which is, in addition to newly established specialized journals, comprising new scientific and scholarly societies such as the European Association for the study of Science and Technology founded in 1981 and the slightly older group, the Society for the Social Studies of Science founded in 1974, and more or less frequent meetings of those at work on related problems. At the same time, there is not yet a consolidated and agreed-upon set of ideas to guide research, let alone a solid theoretical base for it.[3]

The reason for the social infrastructure preceding the development of a coherent cognitive structure in studies of the uses and control of knowledge is itself a question in the sociology of scientific knowledge. Various conditions may account for it, some structural and some cognitive. Among the structural reasons are, I think, the marked multidisciplinarity of research and the structure of academic careers. The multidisciplinary character of research in this area means that there are multiple audiences to whom research is addressed, each having distinct theoretical orientations and each having an interest in particular empirical phenomena. Although this may lead scholars to establish arrangements to improve the sharing of ideas, it also militates against the emergence of a single theoretical perspective. A second related structural reason is that researchers' careers here, as in other multidisciplinary areas, depend much more on the evaluation of their work within the parent discipline than in the newly evolving hybrid research area. This weakens incentives for developing transdisciplinary theoretical ideas.

There are cognitive reasons as well for a theoretical orientation not having developed in this area. For one thing, the uses of knowledge, its production, and its dissemination are comparatively peripheral to ongoing research in the various sciences and social sciences from which most researchers are drawn. By way of example, economists' studies of returns to investment in research are considered interesting but are not regarded as strategic to developments at the center of the discipline. Similarly, political scientists' inquiries focusing on the uses of knowledge in the policy process are not at the center of work in that discipline. So also in sociology where studies in what might be thought of as the applied sociology of knowledge are not closely tied to core specializations such as social stratification or formal organizations. Ongoing inquiry in the parent disciplines therefore does not depend on advances made by examining the uses of knowledge and its production.

This is prelude then to noting that current research is far from easy to describe and summarize. It is more a congeries than a well-organized, theoretically oriented program of inquiry. Thus the papers presented in the Thematic Session on the Uses and Control of Knowledge do not neatly sum up research progress on this or that well-defined set of questions. Rather, they provide analytic case studies by knowledgeable participant-observers—Otto N. Larsen, William D. Carey, and David A. Goslin, with commentary by Irving Louis Horowitz—on their own experience in thinking about and setting policy for the production of knowledge, its uses, and control. As such, they amount to testimony by expert witnesses rather than reports of research.[4] These I review briefly and then follow with a limited agenda for further inquiry.

Case Studies in the Uses and Control of Knowledge

I begin with Larsen's analysis of contending forces affecting the allocation of resources for the production of social science knowledge in the National Science Foundation. Larsen is of course something more than an expert witness on the politics of the production, uses, and control of knowledge, having played diverse

roles in each of these domains, as researcher, social science administrator, and public policy maker. He has been disinterested observer
and interested advocate, sometimes simultaneously. Most recently,
as the highest ranking social scientist in the NSF bureaucracy, he has
occupied a position that provides especially good opportunities to
observe the internal operations of the system. His account of the
precarious history of funding for the social sciences at the National
Science Foundation suggests that it is not only the uses to which social
science knowledge has actually been put that have affected subsequent support for research, but a complex mix of actual uses,
expectations of future uses, and the assessed validity of research in
these disciplines that have led to ups and downs in the fortunes of
American social science research over the last three decades.

The social sciences appear to have suffered, at different times, from
the twin excesses of over- and undervaluation. Many social scientists
(and their supporters) have been overly optimistic about the powers
of social science, whereas detractors have been overly pessimistic
about the capacity of the social sciences to produce any valid
knowledge about social life. Although the National Science Foundation has not been the only source of research support for basic social
science research in the United States, it has for some time been the
principal one. Thus, although the "uses and control of social science
cannot be captured from one site . . . the case at hand is not a trivial
one" (Larsen, 1985, p. 12). It matters a great deal, as Larsen puts it, that
"social science today is held in the same disesteem [at the National
Science Foundation] that marked its beginning." Indeed, he is
persuaded that the support base for social science research is
"precarious," that "little progress" has been made in "legitimating its
scientific status," and that it "confronts a serious, collective intellectual challenge bearing on the uses and control of knowledge. Over
a thirty-year history there have been gains, but some are illusory and
others have been offset by losses." (Larsen, 1985, p. 12).

Whatever the real gains in knowledge that have occurred—and in
Larsen's view there have been some—many of the physicists, engineers, chemists, and mathematicians at the Foundation and outside it
continue to question the scientific standing of the social sciences.
These attitudes are, Larsen (1985, p. 15) observes, "real data." They
affect the extent of support the social sciences receive and their
relative share of NSF funds. Scientists are skeptical about the social
sciences and they are also well aware of their "political trouble-
making capacity" (Larsen, 1985, p. 12). Such "trouble making" by

social science, it is believed, can jeopardize basic science support in all fields.

All of this underlies the small increases, as compared to other sciences, in the Foundation's total proposed expenditures on social science research from 1956, when the first budget was $55,258, to the peak reached in 1982, of $65.1 million.[5] That same year the Reagan-Stockman cuts reduced the opening bid for the social sciences in the NSF budget deliberations by two-thirds. Perhaps more revealing is that the social sciences have garnered no more than 2%-4% of the overall Foundation support in these years, at a time when these sciences have accounted for 25%-30% of all Ph.D.s conferred in science and engineering.

Trends in financial support tell one part of the story. The changing organizational and legal status of the social sciences at the National Science Foundation tells another. Larsen (1985, p. 13) recounts the gradual organizational evolution of the social sciences and their finally achieving full legitimacy in 1968 when the original Act of 1950 was amended to include social science in the NSF mandate. A year later, the social sciences finally reached divisional status within the Foundation. In the years that followed, when indicators of financial support suggested that the social sciences were not sharing in absolute increases in the Foundation's budget, indicators of organizational status such as the absence of institutionalized representation of social scientists at the highest policy levels were no more encouraging.

These developments scarcely occurred in a political and social vacuum. Growing public concern with domestic social problems in the early 1970s "coincided with" the establishment of the RANN Program (Research Applied to National Needs) in which the social sciences were expected to "contribute to . . . the solution of the Nation's social problems" (Larsen, 1985, p. 14). During its lifetime, RANN had a larger budget each year than the entire Division of Social Science put together. This mandate set the groundwork for political resistance to the social sciences among those whose definitions of the nation's social problems and solutions for them differed sharply from those responsible for establishing the program and for disappointment among others who really had expected applied social science to solve compelling social problems.

This history underscores Larsen's (1985, p. 14) observation that "the expected uses of social science knowledge have in a variety of ways" and all apart from their actualities "led to effective control of opportunities to extend that knowledge." Larsen's diagnosis of what is needed for the survival of the social sciences is in point for purposes of understanding how the production of knowledge, its uses, and control interact in a political context. The social science research community must continue concerted political action to defend its interests and it must also reorganize procedures for setting the collective research agenda. In particular, it must be recognized that multidisciplinary inquiry is in order, not only to develop new lines of research, which is the primary objective, but also to enlarge support for the social sciences "in this era of heightened competition for research resources" (Larsen, 1985, p. 15). In short, the character of controls exerted on knowledge production, its directions, and scale has much to do with the political climate and much to do with the ability of the relevant scientific community to respond effectively to opportunities and assaults without making undue claims about what it can do if only "enough" support were available.

William D. Carey was asked specifically to examine recent developments in efforts to control the free flow of scientific information, for the control of scientific knowledge and its uses are of course connected. Executive officer of the American Association for the Advancement of Science, the largest and most influential independent association of scientists in the United States, Carey has served in the Bureau of the Budget as overseer of various domestic programs including research and development policy. In that role, and at the AAAS, he has confronted efforts to restrict the flow of scientific and technological knowledge. Although he begins his piece by noting that he has been a "science watcher for some forty years," he has been considerably more than just an observant bystander.

Carey sets his discussion of current pressures to restrict free communication of scientific and technological information in three contexts: the unprecedented growth and significance of scientific knowledge as a resource for government and business, the enormous rise of its cost in the last decade, and the long-evolving compact between government and science in the United States in which it was understood that the former invested in science and the latter set standards and directions for research.

The emergence of the sciences' "strategic centrality" has, Carey proposes, altered long-lived presuppositions about the relations between science and government. Science, long "pictured" as nonaligned, had developed a series of arrangements—free publication, peer review, and open controversy—that sociologists of science readily identify as the institutional outcroppings of the ethos of science (see Merton, 1973/1942, chap. 13). Moreover, scientists were given to asserting that these were not only conducive to scientific excellence but necessary for it. Carey (1985, p.5), careful as he is to separate imagery from reality, nevertheless, concludes that "the evidence argues powerfully that it is [so]" and that the compact "in the main . . . has worked."

Although the symptoms were not readily visible, the relationship began to become unbalanced as early as the 1950s as science developed what Carey diagnoses as a "dependency syndrome," in large measure the outcome of the escalating costs of research. The irony that its success "has undermined both the autonomy of science and its negotiating strength" has been noted in another context (see Cournand and Zuckerman, 1970, pp. 941-962). The key point is that the growing significance of science provided incentives for government to pay the tab and to exercise control. In Carey's view, this has led to a "crisis of trust" in the relationship between the scientific community and government. Mutual suspicions have become greatly heightened.

Along with enlarged fears about national security and about the competitiveness of the United States in the world market, all this has led to growing and varied governmental intrusion of a variety of sorts into scientific activities. Most recently, for example, the Commerce Department has begun to consider a policy that would impose export controls on scientific exchanges—applications for export licenses would be required for submission of papers to foreign journals, for teaching foreign nationals, and for doing research in a foreign country. Such developments focus attention on the consequences that flow from such controls for the development of knowledge and for national security. Will the sealing off of information interfere with the evaluation of new scientific information, with its confirmation, with scientists' choice of problems in the first place, and the willingness of government institutions to support potentially "troublesome" lines of research?[6] And will the imposition of such controls really enhance "national security"?[7]

These questions about the effects of controls being imposed on the communication of scientific knowledge bring us to David Goslin's paper. Goslin, now executive director of the Commission on Behavioral and Social Sciences and Education at the National Research Council, has considered the potential uses and misuses of social science knowledge in both his administrative and research roles.

Goslin (1985, p. 7) begins by recounting an episode in which he was asked by a researcher at the BBC if there was a repository where " 'the core of accumulated knowledge of Western civilization might be found.' The idea behind this remarkable question was that there might be something like a vault, protected from nuclear destruction containing all of the knowledge necessary to enable the survivors of a nuclear holocaust to rebuild society." The request led Goslin to speculate about the possibilities of such a repository, which, in turn, set the stage for considering the consequences of three significant developments in the United States, Europe, and Japan since World War II.

- The accelerating pace of scientific and technological innovation, which has brought increased uncertainty, greater dependence on technology, and recently much more knowledge about the costs of using various technologies. Knowing more about risk has led to increased concern and has reduced rather than increased a prevailing sense of power.

- The growing understanding of decision-making processes involving estimates of risk that suggest that individuals and organizations are uncertain about when to seek further knowledge, especially when what is known is consistent with previously established plans for action.

- The enormous increase in the availability of information that has "immersed [policymakers and citizens] in a tumultuous sea of communication, constantly, changing, often conflicting—designed to inform us or persuade us, or both" (Goslin, 1985, p. 9). This vast increase has accentuated the practice of seeking knowledge before making decisions; it is clear, however, that not all those who participate in decision making have equal access to relevant knowledge.

These three sets of developments have affected the social fabric as well as the production of knowledge in the social sciences. To cope with the need for devising ways to manage, assess, and use information in an increasingly "noisy environment," the social sciences have contributed to developing what Bell (1968, pp. 145-246)[8] has aptly labeled "intellectual technologies," such as systems analysis, linear programming, and decision theory—in short the various science-based technologies for the processing of information. All well and good. Still, Goslin returns to his initial theme in recalling the paradoxical paper, written some 35 years ago, by Wilbert Moore and Melvin Tumin (1949, pp. 787-795) on the functions of ignorance. They noted then that ignorance has "specifiable social functions in social structure and action" and, more important, for immediate purposes here, that "there is *no* exception to the rule that each time a culture works out an empirically valid answer to a problem, it thereby creates a host of derivative problems . . . [thus] the acquisition of new knowledge makes continuous the introduction of new problems" (Moore and Tumin, 1949, pp. 788, 794-795). Goslin is himself skeptical about the assumption that knowledge is an unalloyed good. In effect, he implies that neither of the two ancient justifications for the pursuit of scientific knowledge may hold any longer—neither that it is good for its own sake nor that it yields endless social benefits. If so, much more thinking is needed about what knowledge is desirable to have and how much of it we need.

Characteristically, Irving Louis Horowitz, professor, publisher, and, on this occasion, commentator, draws vividly on practical politics, social and political theory, and sociological psychology in assessing the mood and substance of the preceding three papers. None of the three, Horowitz suggests, suffers from an excess of optimism concerning the likely outcomes of the uses of scientific knowledge or its control. Goslin's disappointment—that enlarged knowledge has not made for human progress—adopts, Horowitz maintains, an unfounded eighteenth-century conviction. Moreover, science cannot be judged according to its applications because the same scientific contributions can be used for both good and ill. Larsen's more specific disappointment, arising from his judgment that the social sciences have made meager progress, that they are not fully legitimatized, and that they seem inchoate and disorganized also appears to Horowitz as an excessively gloomy reading. Especially when viewed from the long term, "we may be in an era of middle-range discoveries with congruences that are still in the incubation stage" (Horowitz, 1985, p. 19). As for Carey's paper, conflict between advocates of the view that science is a partisan enterprise dedicated to the nation's glory and advocates of the view that science is nonpartisan and "organized for the greater benefit of knowledge to society" largely exemplifies the competing views of Weber and Schmoller on the proper role of science in society (Horowitz, 1985, p. 16). This observation may not make those who must fend off encroachments on the autonomy of science comfortable but it does put the current conflict in perspective and suggests that it is a recurrent phenomenon, one that has appeared before and will appear again. In taking this position, Horowitz has not become a Pollyanna; consider only his hard-headed observations on the impossibility of avoiding, in a democratic society, the "tensions which are built into a system in which the political process and the policy process are separated" and thus that "disenchantment [on the part of policymakers] is almost built into the administrative structure, into the architechtonic of appointive positions" (1985, p. 16).

At least four themes appear and reappear in these pieces. First, the uses and control of knowledge have a variety of unintended and sometimes unwanted consequences that sometimes accompany and sometimes displace those that were intended.[9] Carey draws our attention, for example, to disruptive outcomes for science of efforts to control the transfer of scientific and technological knowledge, efforts designed to reduce the "hemorrhage" of sensitive information and thus to augment national security and competitive economic position. Similarly, Larsen points to the unanticipated effects of large infusions of money for applied research on social problems (the RANN Program) on the later credibility and support of the social sciences in changed political circumstances. Because these applications appeared to serve particular political ideologies and because they were, in some measure, premature, heavy funding for applied research was no blessing for basic social science.

A second, related theme apparent principally but not only in Goslin's paper holds that increasing knowledge is not necessarily beneficial, especially when it cannot be processed effectively. Third, this expert testimony supports the view that a simple model of knowledge-application in which policy decisions are made after the pertinent knowledge is weighed is far removed from the way things actually work. Rather, policymakers' definitions of useful knowledge depend on their purposes and interests, and these also determine the amount of resources they are willing to commit to find out what they want to know and then how hard they will work to apply and control that knowledge. Larsen suggests that this is so in the case of policymaking for science within the National Science Foundation, as does Carey, in his discussion of policymaking on national defense and economic development. Last, all three suggest that the scientific and scholarly community is not a passive actor in the political process that determines the way scientific knowledge is used and the controls imposed on its production and distribution. Carey, for example, asks why the scientific community has been so weak in resisting governmental incursions into free communication and concludes that some have decided that outright conflict with those in power would be far too costly. Larsen enjoins the social science community to do the hard work of setting research priorities for the next decade. If it does not, these will be set by others and support will be meager indeed.

A Limited Research Agenda

The diversity of unanswered questions in these papers makes it clear that much remains to be learned about the uses and control of knowledge. Because sustained work on the subject is still in its beginnings and because there is little agreement on the sorts and ordering of problems that need to be taken up, judgments about the research agenda must be based on personal estimates of what is feasible and interesting.

It seems to me that a half dozen questions about the uses and control of knowledge are especially worth further investigation.

On the Uses of Knowledge

Headway is being made in identifying the characteristics of knowledge, particularly social science knowledge, variously used in policymaking.[10] Carol Weiss's (1980) empirical investigations of the kinds of research attended to by policymakers in the field of mental health argue that a not unexpected array of attributes actually affect the choice of knowledge-claims by policymakers: relevance to practical problems, scientific merit, plausibility, the extent to which the research seems to provide guidance for direct implementation, and occasionally challenges to received wisdom.[11] It is not yet known, however, whether the same criteria are used by policymakers responsible for applying other kinds of knowledge, for example, from physics, biology, geology, and chemistry. Are such policymakers more expert or less than those Weiss studied? Do their conceptions of received wisdom operate in the same ways? Plainly, comparative analysis of the uses of different kinds of knowledge, possibly along the lines of the Weiss study, is essential for a more general understanding of the uses of knowledge.

More attention needs to be paid to the modes and tempo of knowledge transmission in different social and cultural contexts, more specifically to the intervals between publication of research and its use. Social science knowledge seems to inform policymaking in a more diffuse fashion than the physical and biological sciences. Longer intervals and more complex chains of influence may therefore be involved in the uses of social science than a simple model of research, dissemination, and immediate use implies. At any rate, this is so in the medical sciences. Comroe and Dripps's (1976, pp. 105-111, 1977) pioneering study of the antecedents, basic and applied, of major innovations in cardiopulmonary medicine and surgery suggests that it can take a very long time (in some instances, a quarter century or more) for basic research to be applied in clinical medicine. What are the comparable patterns in organizational decision making and policy formation? Comroe and Dripps's investigation shows that careful study by experts in the particular field of research is needed to track down the original sources of particular innovations and uses. This may be particularly so if research findings are transformed into commonsense knowledge, that is, if their scientific sources are obliterated. Under these conditions, policymakers may not know that their decisions are based on research knowledge and therefore cannot be relied on exclusively to report on such influences on policymaking.

Along quite different lines, further inquiry is required on the patterns of choice by policymakers among competing knowledge claims. Are such choices made primarily on grounds that accord with political interests and values? Studies now under way on how lay people assess competing knowledge claims pertinent to decision making in, for example, choosing dietary regimens (see Cole, 1985), may be relevant here for understanding generic processes involved in assessing and choosing between competing knowledge claims. Further inquiry into the politics of the use of knowledge is also in order. Although it will certainly be difficult to identify the diverse and subtle effects of policymakers' political ideologies on the knowledge they deem useful and that they actually use, these would seem to be central. In particular, policymakers' uses of evaluation studies, that is, studies that assess the effects of policy, may be one strategic site for inquiry because policymakers are obligated to pay attention to such research as part of their status obligations—unlike other kinds of research that they may or may not notice given their individual proclivities.

On the Control of Knowledge

For a time, there has been a small but lively literature on the effects of government financial support on the research agenda of the social sciences. Michael Useem (1976a, 1976b) for example, has examined claims that funding requirements have shaped both the questions social scientists study and the methods they use (see also Cole et al., 1981; Zuiches, 1984). Similar claims have been made about the effects of patterns of government support on the research agenda of the physical and biological sciences, but little analysis has yet been done of these questions or on the impact of the peer review process on what gets studied and how. Jonathan Cole, Stephen Cole, and James Zuiches, among others, have made a start here and it would seem to be time for more inquiry into these matters. But it is no easy task because it requires research on such questions as what investigators would have done or what they would have done differently if they had not been required to seek support for their research.

Finally, this list should include studies of a question touched on in William Carey's paper and one that has deep roots in the literature of the sociology of science; namely, whether the character and intellectual quality of scientific inquiry are affected by the varying extent of autonomy of scientific communities. Many scientists believe that they are, but I know of no systematic, cross-national analysis of how different sciences fare under varying conditions of external control and the effects of restraints on autonomy for varying periods of time. [12]

All this suggests that when James Short proposed a thematic session on the uses and control of knowledge and the implications for the social fabric, he was following an instinct for sociological challenge. Plainly, there is much work to be done.

Notes

1. Disciplinary affiliations of authors, subject matter of articles, and procedures of research were classified and counted for the first and fourth issues of each volume, 1979-1984.

2. For analysis of the development of new specialties and a bibliography of pertinent studies, see Cole and Zuckerman (1975, pp. 139-174); for more recent work, see Small (1977, pp. 139-66) and de May (1982, Chap. 9).

3. Efforts along these lines are being made. See, for example, Holzner and Marx (1979) for one of the more comprehensive of these.

4. These papers and the commentary have been published; see Carey (1985, pp. 5-7), Goslin (1985, pp. 7-11), Larsen (1985, pp. 11-15), and Horowitz (1985, pp. 16-19).

5. This figure is in unadjusted dollars; the real peak was reached four years earlier.

6. See Wallerstein (1984, pp. 460-466) for an account of controls and their implied effects.

7. On September 28, 1985, it was reported in the New York Times (page 7) that federal government efforts to control publication of unclassified research would cease but that parallel efforts to stop the flow of sensitive findings and of technological information would not.

8. Goslin draws on the work of Bell (1968, pp. 145-246) here.

9. This diagnosis draws on Merton (1936, pp. 894-904).

10. See the massive compendium edited by Lazarsfeld et al. (1967), which examines the use of sociological knowledge in thirty different domains and considers the ethical problems of applied sociology. See also Lazarsfeld's later effort, written with Reitz, to systematize the subject (1975). For studies analyzing the reasons why social science knowledge fails to be used, see Lindblom and Cohen (1979). See also Scott and Shore (1979).

11. See Weiss with Bucuvalas (1980, p. 250) and Weiss (1977). See also Lynn (1978). The Weiss-Bucuvalas findings are consistent with Yaron Ezrahi's theoretical analysis of the criteria such knowledge must satisfy in order to enter the policy process. See Ezrahi (1977, pp. 285-327).

12. Students of Soviet science such as Graham (1974) and Solomon (1975, pp. 554-582) have treated this question in the case of particular fields and their development in the Soviet Union.

References

Bell, D. 1968. "The Measurement of Knowledge and Technology." Pp. 145-246 in *Indicators of Social Change.* Edited by E. Sheldon and W. Moore. New York: Russell Sage Foundation.

Carey, W. D. 1985. "Force, Foresight and Science." *Society* 22: 5-7.

Cole, J. R. 1985. *Distortions of Health Risks in the Media.* Paper presented to the American Association of Public Opinion Research, Annual Meetings, McAfee, NJ, May 17.

Cole, J. R. and H. Zuckerman. 1975. "The Emergence of a Scientific Speciality." Pp. 139-174 in *The Idea of Social Structure.* New York: Harcourt Brace Jovanovich.

Cole, S., L. Rubin, and J. R. Cole. 1981. *Peer Review in the National Science Foundation: Phase One of a Study.* Washington, DC: National Academy of Sciences.

Comroe, J. H. and R. P. Dripps. 1976. "Scientific Basis for Support for Bio-Medical Science." *Science* 192: 105-111.

Comroe, J. H. and R. P. Dripps. 1977. *The Ten Top Clinical Advances in Cardio Vascular Pulmonary Medicine and Surgery between 1945 and 1957: How They Came About* (2 Vols.). Springfield, VA: U.S. Dept. of Commerce, National Technical Information Service.

Cournand, A. F. and H. Zuckerman. 1970. "The Code of Science." *Studium Generale* 23: 941-962.

de May, M. 1982. *The Cognitive Paradigm.* Dordrecht: Reidel.

Ezrahi, Y. 1977. "Political Contexts of Science Indicators." Pp. 285-327 in *Toward a Metric of Science.* Edited by R. K. Merton et al. New York: Wiley-Interscience.

Goslin, D. A. 1985. "Decision Making and the Social Fabric." *Society* 22: 7-11.

Graham, L. 1974. *Science and Philosophy in the Soviet Union.* New York: Vintage. (pub. orig. 1971)

Graham, L. 1981. *Between Science and Values.* New York: Columbia University Press.

Holzner, B. and J. H. Marx. 1979. *Knowledge Application: The Knowledge System in Society.* Boston: Allyn & Bacon.

Horowitz, I. L. 1985. "Elite Roles and Democratic Sentiments." *Society* 22: 16-19.

Larsen, O. N. 1985. "Social Science out of the Closet." *Society* 22: 11-15.

Lazarsfeld, P. F., W. H. Sewell, and H. L. Wilensky. (Eds.) 1967. *The Uses of Sociology.* New York: Basic Books.

Lindblom, C. E. and D. K. Cohen. 1979. *Usable Knowledge: Social Science and Social Problem Solving.* New Haven, CT: Yale University Press.

Lynn, L. (Ed.) 1978. *Knowledge and Policy: The Uncertain Connection.* Washington, DC: National Academy Press.

Merton, R. K. 1936. "The Unanticipated Consequences of Purposive Social Action." *American Sociological Review* 1: 894-904.

Merton, R. K. 1973. *The Sociology of Science.* Chicago: University of Chicago Press. (pub. orig. 1942)

Moore, W. and M. Tumin. 1949. "Some Social Functions of Ignorance." *American Sociological Review* 14: 787-795.

Reitz, J. 1975. *An Introduction to Applied Sociology.* New York: Elsevier.

Scott, R. A. and A. R. Shore. 1979. *Why Sociology Does Not Apply: A Study of the Use of Sociology in Public Policy.* New York: Elsevier.

Small, H. G. 1977. "A Co-Citation Model of a Scientific Specialty: A Longitudinal Study of Collagen Research." *Social Studies of Science* 7: 139-166.

Solomon, S. 1975. "Controversy in Social Science: Soviet Rural Studies in the 1920's. *Minerva* 13: 554-582.

Useem, M. 1976a. "Government Patronage of Science and Art in America." *American Behavioral Scientist* 19: 785-804.

Useem, M. 1976b. "State Production of Social Knowledge: Patterns in Government Financing of Academic Social Research." *American Sociological Review* 41: 613-629.

Wallerstein, M. 1984. "Scientific Communication and National Security in 1984." *Science* 224: 460-466.

Weiss, C. (Ed.) 1977. *Using Social Research in Public Policy-Making*. Lexington, MA: Lexington Books.

Weiss, C. with M. Bucuvalas. 1980. *Social Science Research and Decision-Making*. New York: Columbia University Press.

Zuiches, J. J. 1984. "The Organization and Funding of Social Science in the NSF. *Sociological Inquiry* 54.

Index

About the Authors

S. J. BALL-ROKEACH received her Ph.D. from the University of Washington and is now Professor of Sociology at Washington State University. She is author of *Theories of Mass Communication* (Longman, 1982; with M. L. DeFleur), *The Great American Values Test: Influencing Behavior and Belief Through Television* (Free Press, 1984; with M. Rokeach and J. W. Grube), and coeditor of *Violence and The Media* (GPO, 1969; with R. K. Baker) and *Media, Audience and Social Structure* (Sage, 1986; with M. G. Cantor).

RICHARD A. BERK is a Professor of Sociology at the University of California, Santa Barbara. He is also affiliated with UCSB's Program in Applied Statistics and is Director of the UCSB Social Process Research Institute. He specializes in applied social research and has recently been engaged in research on violence within families. Other ongoing work includes an evaluation of a program in literacy training for unemployed single parents, and an evaluation in California of the switch from indeterminate to determinate sentencing. His methodological interests of late have centered on combining econometric and experimental traditions. He has published widely in major social science journals.

FREDERICK H. BUTTEL is Associate Professor of Rural Sociology at Cornell University. His research interests include environmental sociology, technology and social change, and agrarian structure and development. He is coauthor of *Environment, Energy, and Society* (1982) and *Los Movimientos Ecologistas* (1983) and coeditor of *The Rural Sociology of the Advanced Societies* (1980) and *Labor and the Environment* (1984). He currently serves as chair-elect of the ASA Section on Environmental Sociology.

THEODORE CAPLOW, author of *The Sociology of Work, Principles of Organization, Two Against One, Toward Social Hope, Managing an Organization,* and other studies of large-scale organizations, is Commonwealth Professor of Sociology at the University of Virginia and Secretary of the American Sociological Association.

WILLIAM R. CATTON, Jr., Professor of Sociology at Washington State University since 1973, held similar positions at the University of Canterbury (New Zealand) and the University of Washington (Seattle). A past President of the Pacific Sociological Association, his publications include *Overshoot: The Ecological Basis of Revolutionary Change* and numerous articles on environmental topics.

MARY DOUGLAS is a Visiting Professor at Princeton University. Educated at Oxford, she spend 26 years reading in the Anthropology Department at the University College of London, 4 years as Program Director at the Russell Sage Foundation, and 4 years as Avalon Foundation Professor in the Humanities at Northwestern University. Her recent publications include *Edward Evans-Pritchard* (1980, Viking, Fontana) and *Risk and Culture* (with A. Wildavsky; 1982, California University Press).

KAI ERIKSON is Professor of Sociology and American Studies at Yale University as well as Editor of *The Yale Review.* He is the author of *Wayward Puritans and Everything in Its Path,* among other works, and he is the immediate Past-President of the American Sociological Association.

WILLIAM J. GOODE'S work has focused on three great institutions: work, family, and religion; and on processes of social control. His most recent work has dealt with prestige-esteem as a social control process, and on power. He has been a Guggenheim Fellow; he also received the MacIver Prize and the Burgess Awards. He was President of the Eastern and the American Sociological Associations. He is a Professor of Sociology at Stanford University.

MORRIS JANOWITZ is a Professor of Sociology at the University of Chicago, where he earned his Ph.D. in 1948. He is founding editor of *Armed Forces and Society: An Interdisciplinary Journal,* and has served as the editor or on the editorial board of several other journals. He was elected a Fellow of the American Philosophical Society in 1983.

ERIC M. LEIFER is currently Assistant Professor of Sociology (Ph.D. Harvard 1983) at University of North Carolina, Chapel Hill. He is interested in the subtleties of control in interactive settings, and has investigated these subtleties in relationship, organization, and market settings. He is currently writing articles on "Equality through Ambiguity," showing that the experience of equality is tied to modes of decision and action distinct from rational choice expectations, and "Sustaining Inequality Amongst Equals," showing that inequality can be induced through partisan social contexts.

GERHARD LENSKI is Alumni Distinguished Professor of Sociology at the University of North Carolina at Chapel Hill. He is author or coauthor of *The Religious Factor, Power and Privilege,* and *Human Societies,* and editor of *Current Issues in Research in Macrosociology.* He is currently working on a volume tentatively titled, *Ecological-Evolutionary Theory: Principles and Applications.*

GARY T. MARX teaches sociology and political science at MIT. He received his Ph.D. from the University of California at Berkeley. He is the author of *Protest and Prejudice* and *Undercover Police: Paradoxes and Problems.*

S. M. MILLER, Professor of Sociology and Economics at Boston University, is the coauthor of the recently published *Recapitalizing America* (with Donald Tomaskovic-Devey) and coeditor of *Dynamics of Deprivation* (with Szusza Ferge). His interests center on poverty and stratification, economic and social analysis and policy, and political mobilization in the United States and Europe. He is developing a theory of American society with the special perspective of one engaged in trying to change it.

THOMAS S. MOORE is an Assistant Professor of Sociology at the University of Wisconsin—Parkside, where he has taught since receiving his doctorate from Boston University. His current research is on the effect of manufacturing job loss upon community employment and wage structures.

CHARLES C. MOSKOS is Professor of Sociology at Northwestern University. The author of numerous articles and books on military sociology, he serves as president of the Research Committee on Armed Forces and Conflict Resolution of the

International Sociological Association. He has been a Fellow at the Woodrow Wilson International Center for Scholars and a Rockefeller Humanities Fellow.

PETER H. ROSSI is currently Stuart A. Rice Professor of Sociology and Director of the Social and Demographic Research Institute at the University of Massachusetts at Amherst, and coeditor of *Social Science Research*. He has been on the faculties of Harvard University, Johns Hopkins University, and the University of Chicago, where he also served as Director of the National Opinion Research Center. He has been a consultant on research methods and evaluation to (among others) the National Science Foundation, the National Institute of Mental Health, the Federal Trade Commission, and the Russell Sage Foundation. His research has been largely concerned with the application of social research methods to social issues, and he is currently engaged in research on natural disasters and criminal justice. His works include *Prison Reform and State Elites* (with R. A. Berk, 1977), *Money, Work and Crime* (with R. A. Berk and K. J. Lenihan, 1980), and *Handbook of Survey Research* (with J. D. Wright and A. Anderson, 1983). In 1979-1980 Professor Rossi was president of the American Sociological Association, and in 1981 he received the Evaluation Research Society's Myrdal Award for contributions to evaluation research methods. He was the 1985 recipient of the Commonwealth Award for Career Contributions to Sociology. He was also awarded the 1985 Donald Campbell Award for outstanding methodological innovation in public policy studies.

RICHARD D. SCHWARTZ is the Ernest I. White Professor at the College of Law and Professor of Sociology in the Maxwell School, Syracuse University. He has written on a number of subjects in sociology of law, including legal evolution, labor relations, legal stigma, and tax compliance. His current research concerns public participation in environmental protection proceedings. He taught sociology and law at Yale and Northwestern, before becoming dean of the Law School at Buffalo. He is the founding editor of the *Law & Society Review* and is a past president of the Law and Society Association.

JAMES F. SHORT, Jr., is Professor of Sociology at Washington State University. He currently serves as Associate Editor of the Annual

Review of Sociology, and he was editor of the *American Sociological Review* from 1972-1974. He has also served in editorial capacities for several other journals and books. He was President of the American Sociological Association in 1984, having previously been elected as a Council-at-Large member (1968-1970), and as Secretary of that Association (1977-1980). Short was Codirector of Research for the National Commission on the Causes and Prevention of Violence (1968-1969). His books include *Suicide and Homicide: Some Economic, Sociological and Psychological Aspects of Aggression* (with A. F. Henry), *Group Process and Gang Delinquency* (with F. L. Strodtbeck), *Delinquency, Crime, and Society,* and *State of Sociology: Problems and Prospects.* Short is a Fellow of the American Association for the Advancement of Science and the American Society of Criminology. He has been a Guggenheim Fellow, a Fellow at the Center for Advanced Study in the Behavioral Sciences, the National Institute of Mental Health, the Institute of Criminology at Cambridge University, and the Centre for Socio-Legal Studies at Oxford University. He has held a number of Visiting Professorships. In 1975 he received an honorary doctorate from his alma mater, Dension University. His M.A. and his Ph.D. degrees are from the University of Chicago. In 1977 he received the Paul W. Tappan Award of the Western Society of Criminology and, in 1979, the Edwin H. Sutherland Award of the American Society of Criminology. He was elected a member of the Board of Trustees of the Law and Society Association (1980-1982) and appointed to the Committee on the Executive Office of that association in 1983. He has held elective offices also in the Sociological Research Association, The Society for the Study of Social Problems, and the Pacific Sociological Association.

NEIL J. SMELSER is University Professor of Sociology at the University of California, Berkeley. He is author of many books and articles on social change, social theory, social movements, and economic sociology. He has served as editor of the *American Sociological Review.* He has also served many years on the Council of the American Sociological Association, as its Vice-President in 1973-1974.

IRVING TALLMAN is Professor of Sociology at Washington State University. He has also held positions at the University of

366 • The Social Fabric

Minnesota and the University of California, Riverside. He received his Ph.D. in 1963 from Stanford University. He is the author of *Passion, Action and Politics* (1976, W. H. Freeman) and coauthor with Ramona Marotz-Baden and Pablo Pindas of *Adolescent Socialization in Cross-Cultural Perspective* (1983, Academic Press). He is currently doing research on testing a decision-making model developed with Louis Gray, and is writing a monograph with Louis Gray on a theory of problem solving as it pertains to families.

HARRISON C. WHITE is Head of the Department of Sociology and Eller Professor of Management in the School of Business and Public Administration at the University of Arizona, Tucson. He was previously Professor and Chair at Harvard University. His areas of work include mobility, networks, role structures, markets, and, most recently, processes of control among elites and in business.

ROBERT WUTHNOW is Professor of Sociology at Princeton University. His books include *The Consciousness Reformation* (1976); *Experimentation in American Religion* (1978); as editor, *The Religious Dimension* (1979), and *The New Christian Right* (1983); and as coauthor, *Cultural Analysis* (1984). His *Meaning and Moral Order: Explorations in Cultural Analysis* is forthcoming.

MORRIS ZELDITCH, Jr., is Professor of Sociology at Stanford University. He received his Ph.D. from Harvard University and taught at Columbia University before going to Stanford. He was chair of the Department of Sociology at Stanford from 1964 to 1968 and editor of the *American Sociological Review* from 1975 to 1978. He is coauthor or coeditor of *Status, Rewards, and Influence* (1985), *Status Characteristics and Expectation States* (1977), *Sociological Theories in Progress*, vols. 1 (1966) and 2 (1972), and *Types of Formalization in Small Groups Research* (1962).

HARRIET ZUCKERMAN is Professor of Sociology at Columbia University, the author of *Scientific Elite: Nobel Laureates in the United States*, and coeditor of two volumes on science indicators. In collaboration with Jonathan Cole, she is now studying the research careers of American men and women scientists. She has been a Visiting Scholar at the Russell Sage Foundation, a Fellow at the Center for Advanced Study in the Behavioral Sciences, and is a Fellow of the American Academy of Arts and Sciences.